EMPTY NAMES, FICTION AND THE PUZZLES OF NON-EXISTENCE

EMPTY NAMES, FICTION AND THE PUZZLES OF NON-EXISTENCE

edited by
Anthony Everett & Thomas Hofweber

CSLI
PUBLICATIONS
Center for the Study of
Language and Information
Stanford, California

Copyright © 2000
CSLI Publications
Center for the Study of Language and Information
Leland Stanford Junior University
Printed in the United States
15 14 13 12 11   2 3 4 5

Library of Congress Cataloging-in-Publication Data

Empty Names, fiction and the puzzles of non-existence / [edited by]
Anthony J. Everett, Thomas Hofweber.
    p. cm. – (CSLI lecture notes ; no. 108)
Includes bibliographical references.
ISBN 1-57586-253-0 (hardback : alk. paper) –
ISBN 1-57586-254-9 (pbk. : alk. paper)
1. Ontology.   I. Everett, Anthony J., 1968–   II. Hofweber, Thomas,
1969–   III. Series.

B311.E48 2000
111–dc21

CIP

00-056413

ISBN 13: 978-1-57586-253-8 (hardback : alk. paper)
ISBN 13: 978-1-57586-254-5 (pbk. : alk. paper)

∞ The acid-free paper used in this book meets the minimum requirements
of the American National Standard for Information Sciences—Permanence
of Paper for Printed Library Materials, ANSI Z39.48-1984.

CSLI was founded in 1983 by researchers from Stanford University, SRI
International, and Xerox PARC to further the research and development of
integrated theories of language, information, and computation. CSLI headquarters
and CSLI Publications are located on the campus of Stanford University.

CSLI Publications reports new developments in the study of language,
information, and computation. Please visit our web site at
http://cslipublications.stanford.edu/
for comments on this and other titles, as well as for changes
and corrections by the author and publisher.
SRDP

Contents

Contributors

HARRY DEUTSCH: Department of Philosophy, Illinois State University, Normal, IL 61790, USA.
hdeutsch@ilstu.edu

ANTHONY EVERETT: Department of Philosopshy, Stanford University, Stanford, CA 94305, USA.
heverett@turing.stanford.edu

AVROM FADERMAN: Oracle Corporation, 500 Oracle Parkway, Redwood Shores, CA 94065, USA.
faderman@pacbell.net

STACIE FRIEND: Department of Philosophy, Stanford University, Stanford, CA 94305, USA.
sfriend@turing.Stanford.edu

THOMAS HOFWEBER: Department of Philosophy, University of Michigan, Ann Arbor, MI 48109, USA.
hofweber@umich.edu

FRED KROON: Department of Philosophy, University of Auckland, Auckland, New Zealand.
f.kroon@auckland.ac.nz

MARK RICHARD: Department of Philosophy, Tufts University, Medford, MA 02155, USA.
mrichar2@emerald.tufts.edu

STEPHEN SCHIFFER: Department of Philosopshy, New York University, New York, NY 10003, USA.
ss72@is4.nyu.edu

Kenneth Taylor: Department of Philosopshy, Stanford University, Stanford, CA 94305, USA.
taylor@turing.stanford.edu

Peter van Inwagen: Philosophy Department, University of Notre Dame, Notre Dame, IN 46556, USA.
vaninwagen.1@nd.edu

Kendall Walton: Department of Philosophy, University of Michigan, Ann Arbor, MI 48109, USA.
klwalton@umich.edu

Stephen Yablo: Department of Linguistics and Philosophy, Massachusetts Institute of Technology, Cambridge, MA 02139, USA.
yablo@mit.edu

Edward Zalta: CSLI, Stanford University, Stanford, CA 94305, USA.
zalta@mally.Stanford.edu

Much Ado About Nothing

A Short Introduction to the Debate and the Essays

ANTHONY EVERETT AND THOMAS HOFWEBER

0.1 Speaking of what there is not

We often speak of things that do not exist. This can happen without
our knowing, as when we talk about things that we think exist but that
in fact do not. Or it can happen intentionally, as for example, when we
make up stories. This way of speaking constitutes a large part of our
discourse. It occurs when we talk about Santa Claus, Austin Powers,
aliens, and maybe Homer or God. But even though this talk constitutes
a substantial part of our discourse, it isn't one that the study of language has spent a lot of time trying to understand. This is unfortunate.
For on the one hand speaking of what there isn't gives rise to a number of difficult philosophical problems. And on the other hand a proper
understanding of this topic has the potential to give rise to a better understanding of a number of other topics related to the study of language
and to philosophy. This book collects together new essays dealing with
these issues.

The issues that arise from our talk about what there isn't can be
split up into three interconnected subgroups, and this book will generally follow this tripartite division. Firstly, there are a number of questions concerning how we can talk *about* something that doesn't exist.
This problem is closely related to a number of well know debates in the
philosophy of language, and it provides a problem case for several theories of reference. The first part of this book is devoted to this issue.
Secondly, there is the general question of how we should understand
fictional discourse. What are we doing when we make up or retell stories? What is it for something to be true in a fiction? How is the real

Empty Names, Fiction, and the Puzzles of Non-Existence.
Anthony Everett and Thomas Hofweber (eds.).
Copyright © 2000, CSLI Publications.

world related to truth in fiction? The essays in the second part of this book deal with the nature of fiction in general, and how it relates to specific philosophical problems, such as the problem of how we are to understand so-called negative existential claims, claims that something does not exist. Thirdly, there are more metaphysical questions about the non-existent. In what sense, if any, are there non-existent objects? Are fictional characters real constituents of the world? Have the issues of ontology and ontological commitment been misunderstood because we have not payed sufficient attention to the question of how nonliteral discourse functions? The essays in the third part of this collection deal with these questions.

Of course, these three groups of questions are not independent. We will see this once we look more closely at each one of them, and at the associated philosophical debates.

0.2 Empty names

It has been a longstanding puzzle for philosophers and theorists of language, how we can meaningfully talk about what doesn't exist.[1] Since antiquity it has been pointed out that if one says of a that it is F, and a does not exist, then one has said something that is neither true nor false. It would only be true if a was F, and false if a was not F. But if there is no a then neither of these two options obtains. And so it appears that any statement about what doesn't exist must be devoid of truth value. But this seems to be clearly erroneous, since it appears that one can say a number of true or false things about things that don't exist. Classic examples of this are negative existential statements, statements that say that a certain thing does not exist. For example, in cases where a is a non-referring expression such as "Santa" or "The present King of France," then:

(1) a doesn't exist.

clearly seems to be true. Conversely, existential claims about the non-existent, such as:

(2) a exists

seem to be false.

An important contribution towards solving these problems was Russell's Theory of Descriptions. Russell understood sentences of the form "the F is G" as really making a kind of complicated existential state-

---

[1] The puzzle goes back, at least, to ancient Greece. See Denyer (Denyer 1991) for an excellent discussion of the Ancient Greek's preoccupation with the question of how it is possible to talk of what is not and to speak falsely.

ment, namely "there is a unique thing which is F and G." Given this, one can see how definite descriptions that stand for nothing can occur in true or false sentences. If there is no golden mountain then "the golden mountain" stands for nothing, but the sentence "the golden mountain is large" will have a truth value. According to Russell this sentence will really be a quantified statement, claiming the existence of a unique large golden mountain. Since there is no such thing the statement will be false, not truth-valueless.

This seems to be a promising strategy to understand talk about what doesn't exist, but it has a number of limitations and problems. There are at least the following:

- It seems unlikely that all terms can be understood along the lines of descriptions. It has been extensively argued for, and is now widely accepted, that proper names, indexicals, demonstratives, and natural kind terms, cannot be understood as descriptions.[2] If this is right then Russell's theory would at most provide an account of how descriptive terms may be used to talk about what doesn't exist. But the same problems would remain for names, and other non-descriptive terms.

- The truth of Russell's Theory of Descriptions is not itself universally accepted. For one thing, there is some controversy over whether all occurrences of descriptions should be analyzed along the lines of the Russellian model or whether some occurrences of descriptions should be understood as behaving semantically like proper names.[3] For another, there are a number of subtle issues about the relationship that definite descriptions have to presuppositions. It has been argued that definite descriptions presuppose, but don't assert, the existence of what they denote.[4] On such a view, in cases of presupposition failure we would again not have a truth evaluable statement.

We shall not, in this book, be concerned with the second set of issues concerning descriptions. Rather we will be primarily concerned with the

---

[2]The classic proponents of this position include Donnellan (Donnellan 1974), Kaplan (Kaplan 1989), Kripke (Kripke 1980), Perry (Perry 1993) and Salmon (Salmon 1981).

[3]See Donnellan (Donnellan 1966) and Recanati (Recanati 1993) for the view that sometimes descriptions function like names semantically. See Kripke (Kripke 1977) and Neale (Neale 1990) for the view that the semantic behavior of all descriptions is Russellian.

[4]See for example Strawson (Strawson 1950). But see Russell (Russell 1959a) and Dummett (Dummett 1978) for defenses of Russell on this issue, or Neale (Neale 1990) for a more recent discussion.

issues that arise from our use of names to talk about what doesn't exist.

Names that do not stand for anything are called *empty names*. Classic examples of such names include "Santa Claus," "Sherlock Holmes," and "Pegasus." (It is controversial, as we will see below, whether or not these names, or any names, really are empty.) Empty names give rise to special problems for any theory of names in which names are distinguished from descriptions: and in particular for the Theory of Direct Reference. The Theory of Direct Reference holds that the contribution of a name to the truth conditions of utterances in which that name occurs is the referent of that name and nothing else. In case of an empty name, however, there is no referent that can be contributed to the truth conditions. Thus utterances of sentences with empty names will not have complete truth conditions. In more theory-laden terms: according to the Theory of Direct Reference a name contributes only its referent to the proposition expressed by an utterance of a sentence in which it occurs. In the case of an empty name the name makes no such contribution. And so utterances of sentences containing empty names will not express complete propositions. Consequently it appears that such utterances can be neither true nor false. But, of course, this seems to be in direct contradiction with the apparent truth of such claims as:

(3) Santa Claus doesn't exist.

There are several possible ways out of this dilemma, and all of them are taken by some contributor or other in this collection. These ways are:

1. Deny the Theory of Direct Reference, and treat empty names as one would treat non-denoting descriptions.

2. Deny that utterances of sentences containing empty names express complete propositions, and accept that they do not have a determinate truth value.

3. Deny that empty names do not stand for anything, but rather claim that they stand either for abstract objects, or for Meinongian non-existent objects.

4. Affirm that there are names that stand for nothing, accept the thesis of direct reference, and grant that utterances of sentences with empty names in them have truth values, but deny that there is a conflict between these claims.

For some, empty names can be seen as showing that the thesis of Direct Reference is mistaken, or at least they can be taken as lending support for a more descriptivist account of reference, one that in some way or other correlates the semantic value of a name with that of a description. In his contribution to this volume Avrom Faderman takes this line. Faderman considers in particular the baptismal/causal account of reference-fixing, an account which is generally accepted by advocates of Direct Reference. He considers cases where once full names come to be empty, being co-opted into a practice of story-telling or myth making, and he argues that these pose a problem for the baptismal/causal theory. On the basis of these considerations, Faderman argues for a descriptivist account of reference-fixing and of the semantic content of names.

Others, however, take the Theory of Direct Reference to be beyond question and rather try to deal with empty names within the framework of that theory. In his contribution to this volume Kenneth Taylor takes this second option. For Taylor an empty name like "Santa Claus" does not stand for anything and can make no contribution to the proposition expressed by an utterance of a sentence in which it occurs. Consequently such utterances will not express complete propositions and will be devoid of truth values. They will, rather, express truthvalueless incomplete propositions, or propositional schemas, propositions with "gaps" corresponding to where empty names fail to make semantic contributions. However Taylor attempts to account for our intuitions that certain sentences containing empty names are true, and others false, by suggesting that certain *descriptive* propositions are *pragmatically* expressed by the utterances of such sentences. Each such descriptive proposition will have a truth value. And we mistakenly confuse this with the literal truth value of the corresponding, literally truth-valueless, utterance. Taylor provides an account of what the descriptive content of such propositions might be, and of the pragmatic mechanism by means of which they get expressed.

The third option, basically claiming that there are no truly empty names, is endorsed or at least seriously considered by a number of contributors to this volume. Most of them, however, do not take this to be a claim about reference in particular but about fiction more generally. For example, van Inwagen argues that "Santa Claus" does stand for something which exists, and he brings evidence from quantification in support of this claim. Deutsch offers a theory of fiction according to which fiction is descriptive of some part of a what he calls a "fictional plentitude," and in particular, fictional names refer to entities in that plenitude and thus are not truly empty. Zalta offers a formal theory of a plentitude of abstract objects, and takes the objects talked about in fiction to be among them. All of these authors would disagree with the suggestion that "Santa Claus" does not stand for anything in reality. According to them, so-called "empty names" in fact are not *really* empty.

The fourth option noted above is to maintain that empty names are genuinely empty, that at least some utterances containing them have truth values and express propositions, but that Direct Reference is broadly correct.[5] Clearly such an approach will have to advocate some sort of reformulation of the thesis of Direct Reference which, while retaining the spirit of Direct Reference, allows that empty names can make some sort of non-descriptive semantic contribution to the utterances in which they occur. In his contribution Anthony Everett suggests we might take empty names to make some sort of *degenerate* semantic contribution to utterances in which they occur in virtue of their contributing the fact that they lack referents. He suggests that this sort of *degenerate* semantic contribution may suffice to bestow truth values upon certain sorts of utterances containing empty names, in particular negative existential utterances. Everett then goes on to offer an account of the sense in which utterances of "Santa" and "Father Xmas" can be taken to be about the same thing, even though there is nothing in reality to which they refer.

Stephen Schiffer, in his contribution, offers a solution to these problems taking recourse to a form of minimalism about propositions and concepts he calls *Pleonastic Fregeanism*. In his paper he mainly deals with empty names in belief ascriptions, but his account is supposed to extend to unembedded sentences with empty names, too. According to Schiffer names in belief ascriptions stand for contextually determined concepts which can either be object dependent or object independent. Using this Schiffer accounts for why we sometimes judge that-clauses to fail to refer if a name in them fails to refer, but sometimes judge them to express complete propositions even if an empty name occurs in them. Schiffer's Pleonastic Fregeanism is supposed to preserve the elements of truth in Direct Reference theories while avoiding their problems with empty names.

We have seen that empty names give rise to a number of semantic problems due to their apparent lack of reference. However, the problems concerning how we should understand talk about what doesn't exist are not simply limited to issues concerning reference. In fact, it seems likely that the debate about reference can't be dealt with satisfactorily without also examining the issue of what we do when we engage in fictional discourse. Many of the examples of empty names cited by those interested in questions of reference are of names taken from fiction. And how we should understand such names in these examples will be related to the question of how we should understand fictional discourse in general.

---

[5]Something like this view was advocated, at least for existential and negative existential claims, by Donnellan in his (Donnellan 1974). Fitch (Fitch 1993) also tries to develop a sense in which empty names may make contributions to the truth conditions of (certain sorts of) utterances containing them.

0.3 Fiction

To interpret and evaluate fiction is, of course, not primarily the domain of philosophy, but of literary criticism and related disciplines. However, there are a number of issues concerning the nature of fiction that can be seen as properly philosophical issues. One of them is the debate about whether or not fictional discourse is descriptive of some domain of fictional entities, or is rather of a quite different nature. On the one hand there are object-theorists like Parsons, van Inwagen, Zalta, Deutsch, and others, who in some form or other believe that fictional discourse is about some domain of entities, and that truth in fiction is truth of what is said about these entities.[6] On the other hand there are pretense theorists like Walton and Currie who take fictional discourse to be a complicated form of imagining, pretense or make believe.[7]

Object theories come in a number of flavors. Following Meinong purportedly empty names may be taken to refer to non-existent concrete objects. Alternatively, following Meinong's student Mally, they might be taken to refer to existent abstract objects. Usually these objects, whatever their status, will be individuated by certain of the properties which they bear. However there is further scope here for a variety of different approaches, depending upon what sort of properties are taken to be relevant to individuation, upon how we understand what it is for an object to bear a property in the sense relevant to that object's individuation, and so on.[8] Object-theories are nevertheless united in taking the truth or falsity of statements containing empty names to turn upon facts concerning the status and nature of some sort of object.

In contrast pretense-theories try to dispense with such objects. Walton suggests that when we engage with a representational artwork we engage in the pretense that what it represents is really the case. We make believe that it is true. Thus, for example, when we read Anna Karenina we make believe that what the story claims to be true is in fact

---

[6] For various positions along these general lines, see Deutsch (Deutsch 1985), Kripke (Kripke 1973), Lamarque and Olsen (Lamarque and Olsen 1994), Lewis (Lewis 1983), Mally (Mally 1912), Meinong (Meinong 1904), Parsons (Parsons 1980), Routley (Routley 1980), Salmon (Salmon 1999), Thomasson (Thomasson 1998b), van Inwagen (van Inwagen 1977), Wolterstorff (Wolterstorff 1980), and Zalta (Zalta 1983) and (Zalta 1988).

[7] See Walton (Walton 1990) and Currie (Currie 1990).

[8] A nice discussion of the different options available to the object-theorist, and of how various sorts of object theories result from adopting different approaches, see Fine (Fine 1984). Although Fine is himself sympathetic to the object-theoretic approach, his (Fine 1984) also contains an excellent discussion of the philosophical and technical problems which face each type of object-theory. Wettstein (Wettstein 1984) and Friend (Friend 2000) also raise some important questions concerning object-theoretic approaches.

true. We do not believe that Anna left her home and husband. But we make believe that she did. Where the object theorist sees there as being a non-standard object, Walton sees us as pretending that the relevant object exists. Where the object theorist wants us to understand *Anna Karenina* in terms of Anna's being an abstract or non-existent object, Walton wants to explain it in terms of our entering into a pretense that Anna exists. What, for the object theorist, is true in virtue of the status, nature, or qualities of an object, is not literally true for the pretense theorist. Rather it will only be true within the scope of a game of make believe.

While there is much that is attractive in pretense-theoretic accounts of fiction, such accounts are not without their difficulties. One important criticism which is often made of pretense-theoretic accounts of fiction is this. Such theories understand our engagement with representational artworks as our making believe that their representational content is real, as our pretending that what they describe is the case. However, it has been noted, we often have emotional responses to artworks, very often extremely visceral ones. For example, when watching a horror film I might feel genuine terror at what I see. Yet, it might seem that if pretense theorists such as Walton are correct, if I am simply pretending that what I see is real, I should experience not real terror but rather pretend terror. I should make believe that I am frightened when in fact I am not.[9] And since this does not seem to be what happens in such cases, the argument continues, pretense accounts must be flawed.[10]

In her contribution Stacie Friend takes issue with this argument. She argues that make believe emotions do not involve us pretending that we feel emotions. Rather they are responses we have in the course of a game of make believe. The difference between a belief state and a state of make belief is not their content but rather the function these states play in our mental economies. Likewise the difference between real fear and make-belief-fear is not a difference in representational content or in qualitative nature, but rather a difference in the role these states play in our mental economies. Friend illustrates and argues for these points in the course of defending Walton from a technical criticism made by Fred Kroon.

In his contribution to this volume Harry Deutsch articulates a different challenge to Walton's view of fiction. According to Deutsch, Walton gives the notion of make believe too central a role. And in doing so he puts too much emphasis upon the role of the reader in generating and

---

[9] See Walton (Walton 1978).
[10] See for example, Carroll (Carroll 1990), pp. 73–74.

responding to fiction. Deutsch proposes his own account of fiction in which he gives the notion of the author's making up a story the central role.

Edward Zalta, in his contribution, challenges the dichotomy between object theories of fiction and pretense theories. He argues that pretense theories can be embedded into object theories, and that object theories can be understood in a way that is compatible with pretense theories. He proceeds to outline in some detail how such an embedding might go and to outline his own favored version of object theory. Both Zalta's and Deutsch's discussions deal not only with the nature of fiction but also with issues of ontology as well.

The debate concerning the nature of fiction spills over into the issue of how we should understand existential and negative existential claims, claims that a certain thing does, or does not, exist. For object theorists such claims are made true or false by the nature of the object in question. For example, on one interpretation of Zalta's theory, the claim that an object a doesn't exist is true if a is a certain abstract object and false if a is concrete. For other object-theories such a negative existential claim might be counted true just in case a is a fictional object, or a subsistent object, or a non-actual possibilia, and so on. The precise truth-conditions for such claims will depend upon the details of the theory in question.

Pretense theorists have also sought to extend their account to cover existential and negative existential claims.[11] In his contribution Kendall Walton himself suggests an account of existential and negative existential claims which invokes his pretense theory, and he defends this account against various criticisms. And Fred Kroon offers a related, though different, account in his contribution. Both accounts regard negative existentials such as

(4) Santa does not exist.

as involving a pretend-reference to Santa together with a certain sort of disavowal of that particular reference attempt. As Kroon would put it, when we assert (4) we make a reference attempt of the Santa kind, followed by the claim that reference attempts of that kind fail. In other words, we provide a little demonstration of a certain kind of reference attempt, and then we assert that reference attempts of the demonstrated kind fail.

Walton's theory and Kroon's theory differ primarily in the means by which this disavowal is taken to be achieved. For Walton, existential

---

[11]Perhaps the most well known attempt is by Gareth Evans in chapter 10 of his (Evans 1982). However as it stands the account offered there by Evans does not appear to work. Dummett (Dummett 1993) makes this point very nicely.

and negative existential claims are idiomatic. Existence is not a genuine property. However when we make an existential or negative existential claim we make believe that there is a property of existence which applies only to those things which there really are. That is to say, we make believe that there is a property of existence which applies, within the scope of our game of make believe, to those things there really are outside our game of make believe. Thus, when we claim that Santa doesn't exist we are making believe that existence is a property and that Santa lacks it. In so doing we idiomatically express the claim that our attempt to refer to Santa failed.

In contrast Kroon takes existence to be a genuine property possessed by all real actual things. When we make an existential or negative existential claim we make believe that what we are talking about exists, but we make a metaphorical claim about the real nature of certain reference attempts outside the make believe. Kroon and Walton discuss the merits and demerits of their two approaches in their papers.

The Walton-Kroon approach presupposes some notion of what it is for something to be a "reference attempt" of a given kind, something neither Walton nor Kroon spell out. However, although they are not concerned with developing or defending pretense based accounts of negative existentials, both Taylor and Everett provide material in their contributions which might be used to flesh out this notion. Taylor's notion of two names being *marked as co-referential* might be seen as corresponding to the notion of utterances of the two names being reference attempts of the same kind. Or alternatively, Everett's notion of two name-utterances *sharing a common source* might be seen as corresponding to their being reference attempts of the same kind.

Mark Richard, in his contribution, offers a broad criticism of the pretense based approach to fiction and negative existentials advanced by Walton, and a pretense based approach to negative existentials and propositional attitude ascriptions which has recently been proposed by Mark Crimmins.[12] Richard argues that Crimmins approach, as well as Walton's approach to talk about fiction, are mistaken. If Richard is right his conclusion would also have broad implications for the view Stephen Yablo defends in his contribution to this volume, which will be discussed shortly.

---

[12]Crimmins, in his recent paper (Crimmins 1998), uses ideas from Walton to propose a solution to some puzzles about belief ascriptions negative existentials and identity statements.

0.4 Ontology

Closely related to these issues concerning the reference of empty names and the nature of fiction are a number of classic metaphysical questions. For, of course, there is a longstanding metaphysical debate about the nature of ontology and ontological commitment. How can we decide whether or not Santa Claus and Sherlock should be considered to be part of reality? And if they are in some sense real, what is their ontological status? These questions bear directly upon the questions we have discussed above. If it turns out that we should accept Santa Claus as part of reality, a real thing in some way or other, then presumably the name "Santa Claus" will refer to that thing. And the puzzles about empty names would disappear since names such as "Santa" wouldn't be empty in the first place. Moreover if we have to accept that Santa is in some way real then presumably the truth of what we say about Santa would in some way depend on the properties that this thing has. Clearly if considerations of ontological commitment drive us to accept the reality or existence of fictional entities then a object-theoretic view of fiction would seem to suggest itself quite strongly.

The standard way to look at ontological commitment is the one generally attributed to Quine, and spelled out in (Quine 1980). According to Quine, we are ontologically committed to the things that the quantifiers in our best theories of everything have to range over. Thus to see whether or not we should accept an ontology of fictional entities we should look, according to Quine, at whether or not we have to accept quantified statements that have to be considered as ranging over fictional entities.

This is precisely what Peter van Inwagen does in his contribution to this volume. He accepts a Quinean view of ontological commitment and argues that the best account we can give of the validity of certain inferences involving quantified statements is to endorse a ontology of fictional objects. According to van Inwagen, fictional objects exist, even though they exist nowhere in space and time. He explains how in accordance with this view we can say that Sherlock Holmes doesn't exist. And he distinguishes between a fictional object having a property and holding a property in order to to account for the fact that even though Sherlock Holmes is a detective living in Baker Street, there is no object in space and time which is a detective living in Baker Street.

Thomas Hofweber, in his contribution, disagrees with van Inwagen's and Quine's approach to ontological commitment. Hofweber looks at the standard debate about non-existent objects and argues that both sides of the debate make a mistake about what role context can play in different uses of quantifiers. He outlines a different way to understand the role of context in the use of quantifiers, gives an account of some of the different uses that quantifiers have in communication, and proposes an account of what we do when we quantify over non-existent objects on ordinary occasions. If Hofweber is right then Quine's approach to ontological commitment seems to be based on a mistaken view of the function of natural language quantifiers.

Van Inwagen and Hofweber are concerned with the ontological presuppositions of our talk about fictional and non-existent things. In contrast, Yablo turns the tables around by arguing that a pretense-theoretic account of fiction has far wider applications than merely to our talk of obviously fictional beings, such as Sherlock Holmes and Santa Claus. According to Yablo, many things which we think of as real are better understood as having a fictional status. More precisely, Yablo notes that several domains of discourse, in particular ones that are philosophically and ontologically problematic, don't seem to have the ontological presuppositions they might be expected to have. He accounts for this by arguing that much of such talk is not to be taken literally but that rather should be understood metaphorically. Yablo develops an account of how this might come about and how such metaphorical talk might serve various purposes for us. Yablo adopts Walton's theory of make believe to give an account of such discourse. According to Yablo, a number of very important philosophical issues need to be understood in such terms. If Yablo is right then Walton's theory of make believe does not simply provide an attractive account of fiction. It, and the study of fiction in general, will have the broadest philosophical relevance.

Acknowledgments

Many of the papers in this collection, and indeed the idea for this collection itself, grew out of the *CSLI Conference on Empty Names, Fiction and the Puzzles of Non-Existence*, organized by the editors, and held at CSLI, Stanford University, on March 22–24, 1998. Some of the papers included here were not presented at this conference. Others are revised versions of the papers presented. All of the papers are published here for the first time.

The editors would like to express their thanks to CSLI and the Stanford Philosophy department for making the conference possible, and to all the speakers and contributors who participated. Special thanks go to John Perry for his constant support, and to Ed Zalta, for his hands on help, his expert advise on the issues, and his encouragement.

Part I

Empty Names

1

Pleonastic Fregeanism and Empty Names

STEPHEN SCHIFFER

There is a certain version of Frege's theory of intentionality which has some plausibility and is worth exploring. Among other virtues, it has interesting consequences for the semantics of empty names. For reasons that will emerge, I call the theory *Pleonastic Fregeanism*.

1.1 Fregeanism

1.1.1 The Fregean theory baldly stated

I'll begin with a brief refresher course of what it is, at least for present purposes, to be a Fregean of any stripe. The Fregean theory, baldly stated, begins with the claim that believing is a *two-place relation to propositions*; that is, a relation that holds between believers and the propositions they believe (for simplicity, I'm ignoring the temporal position in the belief relation). Thus, the fact that Lester believes that eating liver enhances sex appeal is a fact which enjoys the form-revealing representation

> B(Lester, the proposition that eating liver enhances sex appeal).

The invoked notion of a proposition is the familiar generic one: propositions are abstract, mind- and language-independent entities that have truth conditions. This generic characterization leaves plenty of room for propositionalists to disagree among themselves about the further nature of propositions. What defines the Fregean is that she holds that believing is a two-place relation to propositions that satisfy the following further characterization:

Empty Names, Fiction, and the Puzzles of Non-Existence.
Anthony Everett and Thomas Hofweber (eds.).
Copyright © 2000, CSLI Publications.

(1) Fregean propositions are *compositionally determined* in that there's a finitely specifiable function that maps sequences of "propositional building blocks" onto all the propositions to which our that-clauses refer. These propositional building blocks are the references words have in that-clauses.

(2) Fregean propositions have *truth-values that are compositionally determined* in that the truth-value of a proposition is a finitely specifiable function of features of its propositional building blocks.

(3) Fregean propositions are *structured entities whose basic constituents are the already mentioned propositional building blocks.* The claim that propositions are structured entities composed of propositional building blocks is best construed as the claim that propositions are individuated by those entities in the following sense. Let f be the unique finitely specifiable function that maps sequences of propositional building blocks onto the propositions they build. Then propositions may be regarded as composed of propositional building blocks that determine them just in case

$$[f(< x_1, \ldots, x_n >) = p \,\&\, f(< y_1, \ldots, y_n >) = p]$$
$$\rightarrow [< x_1, \ldots, x_n >=< y_1, \ldots, y_n >].$$

(Note that by this criterion propositions construed as sets of possible worlds are not structured entities with constituents.)

(4) In contrast with the extreme direct-reference theorist's "singular propositions," Fregean propositions satisfy what we may call *Frege's constraint*: at no given time can one rationally both believe and disbelieve a proposition.

(5) The final defining feature of Fregean propositions is a virtual corollary of the foregoing features. The propositional building blocks that compose Fregean propositions are not the objects and properties our beliefs are about, but rather things we may call *concepts*, or *modes of presentation*, of those objects and properties. Given this, the truth-value of a proposition will be a function of "semantic values" of its constituent concepts. These semantic values will be the objects and properties our beliefs are about. A major task for the Fregean is to say how concepts determine their semantic values, i.e., to define the relations *x is a concept of y* or, equivalently, *x is a mode of presentation of y*. This is the task of defining the reference relation for concepts.

1.1.2 Motivation

The Fregean theory enjoys a simple yet powerful motivation, as we can appreciate by pretending that the Superman fiction is fact and ruminating on the following pair of sentences:

> Lois Lane believes that Superman eats groundhogs.
> Lois believes that Clark Kent eats woodchucks.

(I borrow the groundhog/woodchuck example from Ed Zalta.)

It's easy to motivate the view that these that-clauses are referring expressions which refer to things Lois is being said to believe. I'll skip the exercise.

It's easy to motivate the view that the referents of these that-clauses are propositions—abstract, mind- and language-independent entities that have truth conditions and have their truth conditions both essentially and absolutely. I'll skip the exercise.

It's easy to motivate the view that these propositions are compositionally determined in the sense already glossed. For it's entailed by the assumption that the reference of a that-clause is determined by its syntax and the references of its component words.

It's patently easy to motivate the view that the displayed belief sentences may differ in truth-value—Lois may believe that Superman eats groundhogs without believing that Kent eats woodchucks.

Consequently, it's also easy to motivate the view that the propositions we believe satisfy Frege's constraint.

Consequently, it's also easy to motivate the view that propositional building blocks aren't the objects and properties our beliefs are about, but rather concepts, or modes of presentation, of those objects and properties.

It's easy to motivate the view that the objects and properties our beliefs are about are the "semantic values" of the conceptual building blocks of the propositions we believe.

It's easy to motivate the view that belief sentences of the form "A believes that S" have the logical form they appear to have—two argument terms flanking a two-place relational predicate. In the first place, that's all that's revealed by the surface structure of such sentences. And in the second place, attempts to treat "believes" as a three-place relation holding among a believer, a proposition, and mode of presentation under which the believer believes the proposition end up confusing singular terms in adverbial phrases with terms of a relation. In the sentence

1 Lois believes, under such-and-such mode of presentation, that Superman flies, "under such-and-such mode of presentation" is on all fours with "under the boardwalk" in

2 Lois kissed Superman under the boardwalk.

Kissing isn't a three-place relation holding among a kisser, a kissee, and boardwalk; rather, "under the boardwalk" occurs in (2) as an adverbial phrase (what linguists call an adjunct). Likewise, "under such-and-such mode of presentation" is an adverbial phrase in (1), but it wouldn't be if "such-and-such mode of presentation" were referring to the third term in an instance of the three-place belief relation.

Finally, it's easy to motivate the view that the propositions we believe are structured entities, in the sense already glossed, whose basic components are concepts. For it's difficult to see how Frege's constraint could be satisfied if different concepts could determine the same proposition.

From all this the Fregean position follows.

1.1.3 The Individuation of Fregean theories

So much for what defines being a Fregean; it's at this point that Fregeans may disagree among themselves. The most significant respect in which they may differ *qua* Fregeans is on what they take concepts, or modes of presentation, to be. Concepts, for the Fregean, must satisfy two constraints. First, they must determine the things of which they're modes of presentation; they must, that is, determine semantic values of which the truth-value of a proposition is a function. Thus, a complete account of Fregean concepts must explain the reference relation for them, that relation that must obtain between a concept and a thing in order for the latter to be the former's semantic value, or, equivalently, the thing of which the concept is a "mode of presentation." Second, they must yield propositions that satisfy Frege's constraint. Beyond these two constraints, Fregeans are free to go their separate ways.

Well, how should one complete the Fregean theory? What, that is to ask, is the best account of concepts that a Fregean can offer? What, in still other words, are Fregean modes of presentation? Since the notion of a mode of presentation, or concept, has been in effect functionally defined by the foregoing characterization of them, we're taking them to be whatever things play such-and-such theoretical role. The question we're now asking is *what things*, if any, play that role. One strategy for answering this question would be to try to give an account of modes of presentation which satisfies what I've elsewhere called the *intrinsic-description constraint*.[13] According to this constraint, if a thing is a mode of presentation—if, that is, it plays the mode-of-presentation role—then it must be intrinsically identifiable in a way that does not describe it as a mode of presentation or as a possible mode of presentation. If a thing is

---

[13] See, e.g., my (Schiffer 1990).

a mode of presentation, then it must be intrinsically identifiable as some other kind of thing. Denying this constraint is apt to seem tantamount to introducing the notion of a gene as whatever plays such-and-such role in the transmission of inheritable characteristics and then insisting that the things which play that role enjoy no more intrinsic characterization than "things that play such-and-such role in the transmission of inheritable characteristics." To deny the intrinsic-description constraint is to insist that propositional building blocks enjoy no more intrinsic characterization than that they are propositional building blocks. So the intrinsic-description constraint is hardly unmotivated. At the same time, it's apt to seem doubtful that the Fregean can satisfy the constraint, for it's apt to seem that when you go through the list of things that would satisfy the constraint, there are good reasons for crossing each of them off the list.

As we are about to see, however, there may be a Pickwickian sense in which the Fregean may have concepts that satisfy the intrinsic-description constraint. The Fregean, I'll propose, needs to identify modes of presentation, her propositional constituents, with what I'm about to call *pleonastic concepts*. Let me explain.

1.2 Pleonastic propositions + pleonastic concepts = Pleonastic Fregeanism

1.2.1 Relieving the itch of conceptualism

Conceptualism about Xs is the view that Xs are, somehow, mind or language created. *Somehow*, Xs are mere "linguistic posits," hypostatizations of certain linguistic or conceptual practices. *Propositions* are among the things for which philosophers have been tempted to go conceptualist.

But there is problem with the attempt to take conceptualism about propositions seriously. The fact that there are rocks would have existed no matter what linguistic or conceptual practices did or did not obtain, and facts are simply true propositions. What, consequently, can it mean to say that propositions are mind or language created in any sense that hopes to be true? Certainly they're not created by anything we do in anything like the way we create computers and running shoes

In some recent work—and most recently in (Schiffer 1996)—I've argued that there is a view that should at least relieve the itch to be a conceptualist, a view which the erstwhile conceptualist would have adopted had she thought of it, a view which gives the cash-value of the metaphor that propositions are shadows of sentences but doesn't imply the absurdity attached to a strictly literal reading of conceptualism.

My conceptualist *manqué* theory is about the ontological and conceptual status of things I call *pleonastic entities*. The part of the theory most relevant to the present occasion may be conveyed by the following inter-related statements. Although I claim that many sorts of entities—including, incidentally, fictional entities—are pleonastic entities, I'll state the theory now only as it applies to propositions, the only pleonastic entities immediately relevant.

(a) *Pleonastic propositions* get their epithet from what may be called the *something-from-nothing transformation* associated with their introduction into our conceptual scheme. This is the trivial transformation that take one from a sentence which doesn't contain any singular term that refers to a proposition to a pleonastically equivalent sentence that does contain such a singular term. Thus, from

> Fido is a dog,

whose only singular term is "Fido," we can infer its pleonastic equivalent

> That Fido is a dog is true,

or, more colloquially,

> It's true that Fido is a dog,

which contains the singular term "that Fido is a dog" whose referent is the proposition that Fido is a dog. It's because of our ability to move back and forth between any sentence "S" and its pleonastic equivalent "That S is true" that we have the well-known truth schema for propositions:

> (The proposition) that S is true iff S.

(b) The existence of the something-from-nothing transformation does not imply that all references to propositions can be paraphrased away. There's no paraphrasing away the that-clause in "Ralph believes that dogs are reptiles." But the use of that-clauses in such cases is parasitic on their use in the hypostatizing something-from-nothing transformation. For example, the practice of characterizing belief states in terms of that-clauses is contingent on our being able to say that a belief that S is true iff S, and this feature is in turn dependent on the truth schema for propositions—that S is true iff S—which is entailed by the something-from-nothing transformation.

(c) We have knowledge of propositions. We know that they exist and we know a lot about them. How do we obtain such knowledge? Clearly, this isn't to be answered by appeal to any causal interaction between us and these immaterial entities. What's required for our knowledge of propositions, and all that's required, is that we be party to our that-clause involving linguistic and conceptual practices. Nothing comparable can be said of rocks, islands, electrons, trees, and other nonpleonastic objects. The point can be made vivid in the following way. Imagine a possible world exactly like ours except that the people in that world have no concept of propositions; they lack our that-clause-involving practices. At the same time, it's a consequence of *our* proposition-hypostatizing practices that the propositions to which we, in the actual world, refer exist in this other world. So, the possible world we're imagining is populated by propositions and people very much like us, but those people have no knowledge of those propositions. What would it take to bring them up to epistemological snuff with us, to put them suitably *en rapport* with the propositions of which they're currently ignorant? The pleonastic claim is that what it would take, and all that it would take, is for those people simply to adopt a certain manner of speaking—namely, our that-clause-involving practices.

(d) There's nothing more to the *nature* of propositions than can be read off our that-clause-involving linguistic practices. What we can learn about them is what our linguistic practices license us to learn about them. Unlike electrons, trees, rocks and other things that enjoy the highest degree of ontological and conceptual independence from our linguistic and conceptual practices, pleonastic entities like propositions have, as Mark Johnston would put it, "no hidden and substantial nature for a theory to uncover. All we know and all we need to know about [them] in general" is determined by our hypostatizing linguistic practices.[14]

(e) For present purposes, the most important aspect of the "nature-determination" point concerns the *individuation* of propositions: Belief reports don't presuppose a prior individuating conception of the propositions referred to in them; rather, propositions are individuated in terms of our criteria for evaluating belief reports. Typically statements of the form aRb (e.g. the statement that John kissed Mary) require for their understanding a prior individuating conception of b in at least the following sense: in order to know that $(aRb \& \neg aRc)$, one must have conceptually prior knowledge that $b \neq c$ (e.g. you can't directly discover that John kissed Mary but not Betty unless you already know that Mary $\neq$ Betty). With

---

[14]See (Johnston 1988).

propositions, however, the situation is the opposite. One has criteria for the assessment of belief reports that are conceptually prior to criteria for the individuation of propositions, and it's in terms of these conceptually prior criteria that we individuate propositions. For example, we know that the proposition that Superman flies $\neq$ the proposition that Clark Kent flies because we know that "Lois believes that Superman flies" can be true while "Lois believes that Clark Kent flies" is false. A neat corollary of this is that our demand for an explanation of how Lois Lane can rationally believe that Superman adores groundhogs but that Clark Kent loathes woodchucks is trivially satisfied in that the that-clauses in a sentence of the form "A believes that S and that not-S'" count as referring to distinct propositions just by virtue of the fact that the belief ascription can be true of the rational agent A. This is why the truism that $p \neq q$ if a person can believe p without believing q can serve as a *criterion* for the individuation of propositions. How is it that we know that the proposition that whoever believes that all opthamologists are opthamologists believes that all opthamologists are opthamologists $\neq$ the proposition that whoever believes that all opthamologists are opthamologists believes that all opthamologists are eye doctors? Precisely because we appreciate that the following two sentences can differ in truth-value:

> Nobody doubts that whoever believes that all opthamologists are opthamologists believes that all opthamologists are opthamologists.
> Nobody doubts that whoever believes that all opthamologists are opthamologists believes that all opthamologists are eye doctors.

We couldn't establish that Betty $\neq$ Carla in any comparable way. We should also notice that what was just said about the individuation of propositions applies even when the same that-clauses are involved. Kripke's Paderewski examples provide one illustration, but so do that-clauses containing demonstratives. Thus, it may be that an utterance of "Algernon believes that she is a philosopher" makes a true statement in one context and a false statement in another, even though both utterances of "she" refer to the same woman. This tells us that the two utterances of "that she is a philosopher" refer to distinct propositions.

1.2.2 Pleonastic concepts

Just as we have pleonastic propositions, so, too, do we have pleonastic concepts. For concepts in effect enjoy a something-from-nothing transformation in that the premise in the valid inference

Floyd believes that Satan lurks everywhere.

So, Floyd has a belief involving his concept of Satan.

contains no explicit reference to a concept. I say "in effect" a something-from-nothing transformation, because once we see how the existence of a concept can be inferred in this way, we're able to construe expressions in that-clauses as referring to concepts. Now, what holds for pleonastic propositions holds as well, *mutatis mutandis*, for pleonastic concepts, but it's worth making explicit some of the important consequences of the way concept talk devolves from out that-clause ascribing practices.

As I just remarked, concepts may be construed as the references expressions have in that-clauses. This is so even when a word in a that-clause also refers to something other than a concept. Thus, although an utterance of "you" in an utterance of "Ralph believes that you are coming to the party" refers to a certain person B, we may nevertheless say that the reference of "you" is Ralph's contextually-relevant concept of B—albeit an *object-dependent* concept, a concept whose existence depends on the existence of B. Consequently, the propositions to which that-clauses refer may be construed as structured entities made up of concepts.

Concepts are individuated by the propositions that contain them: the concept of X counts as distinct from the concept of Y (even when $X = Y$) if it's possible for someone to believe that ...X... while disbelieving ...Y... Criteria for ascribing beliefs come first, and from them we cull our ways of individuating propositions, and from them we cull our ways of individuating concepts.

Do concepts satisfy the intrinsic-description constraint? Yes and no. For there are two senses of "concept" in play. The first is the term of art (equivalent in meaning to the term of art "mode of presentation") functionally introduced as whatever acquits the rationality of Harold when he believes that George Eliot adored groundhogs but that Mary Ann Evans loathed woodchucks. Let's call the property of being a concept in this sense the property of being a concept$_1$. The other sense of "concept" is the pleonastic sense directly derived from the occurrence of words in that-clauses. Let's call the property of being a concept in this sense the property of being a concept$_2$. Every concept$_1$ is a concept$_2$, and vice versa; but "concept$_2$" is an intrinsic characterization of those things that are concepts$_1$ which doesn't characterize them as concepts$_1$. At the same time, pleonastic concepts—i.e. concepts$_2$—fail to satisfy the intrinsic-description constraint, for the only intrinsic characterization of Floyd's concept of Satan is "Floyd's concept of Satan."

We noticed that for the Fregean propositional building blocks must determine semantic values that can be used to determine the truth-values of the propositions those building blocks help to build. A major task for the Fregean is to give a theory of this determination, a theory that tells us how the constituents of propositions determine their semantic values. Such a theory would be a theory of the reference relation for concepts, an account of that relation that must obtain between a concept and a thing in order for the concept to be a concept, or mode of presentation, *of* the thing, or in order for the thing to fall under the concept. With pleonastic concepts, however, we don't need a *substantial* theory of this relation; the pleonastic conception of concepts affords us an easy way of characterizing the determination relation. Since the position of "X" in "the concept of X" is intentional, we can't say that a particular object or property falls under the concept of X just in case that object or property $= X$. However, we *can* adequately explain the reference relation for concepts by pointing out that every instance of the schema

If X exists, then X falls under the concept of X,

is analytic in just the way that every instance of the schema

The proposition that S is true iff S,

is analytic. These schemas are trivial consequences of our ways of introducing talk of concepts and propositions respectively.

1.2.3   Pleonastic Fregeanism

As already noted, the way pleonastic concepts are obtained from that-clauses suggests we can construe them as the references words have in that-clauses, for each word in a that-clause determines a concept involved in the proposition to which the whole that-clause refers. In this way we arrive at a version of Frege's theory of propositions which, since I'm already speaking of pleonastic propositions and concepts, we might as well call *Pleonastic Fregeanism*. It's the view that the propositions we believe and assert are pleonastic propositions composed of pleonastic concepts.

1.3   The Pleonastic Fregean's account of empty names

1.3.1   Pleonastic Fregeanism and names in that-clauses

I'll begin by recounting some of the vagaries of belief reports whose that-clauses contain names.

Very often, a particular occurrence of

A believes that n is F,

is such that we deem each of the following three things to be entailed by the utterance:

(a) From the utterance of

> A believes that n is F,

we may infer

> There is something—to wit, n—such that A believes that it is F.

(b) We deem the proposition to which the that-clause refers—the proposition that n is F—to be true in any given possible world only if n (i.e., the thing that is *actually* n) is F in that possible world.

(c) If the belief reporter were to learn that she was mistaken in presupposing that "n" referred, then she'd deem her utterance of "that n is F" to have failed to refer to a complete proposition. Similarly, if you say "I believe that that dog has fleas" and you learn that you were hallucinating a dog, you're apt to deem your that-clause to have failed of reference.

When such facts obtain, there's a clear sense in which the occurrence of "n" in the that-clause refers to n. Yet, at the same time, even when an occurrence of a name in a that-clause refers to its bearer, we still can't say—at least in the normal case—that *the reference* of the name is its bearer. For even in such cases, we still typically can't substitute co-referential names *salva veritate*. For example, an utterance of "Algernon believed that George Eliot wrote *Middlemarch*" may have been true, whereas an utterance of "Algernon believed that Mary Ann Evans wrote *Middlemarch*," in the same context, may have been false, notwithstanding that both name occurrences referred to the one person who bore both names. But if the reference of a name token in a that-clause were its bearer, then one could substitute co-referential names *salva veritate*.

Yet the occurrence of a name in a that-clause needn't refer at *all* to its bearer; the that-clause containing the name *may* refer to a complete proposition whether or not the name even has a bearer. This is pretty clearly true of the that-clauses in the following examples:

> Giorgio believes that Satan lurks everywhere.

> Emily believes that Santa Clause lives at the North Pole.

> Lester believes that God doesn't exist.

And it's evidently also true of such examples as:

> Bob believes that Saddam Hussein is a dangerous dictator—he doesn't realize that such a person has never existed; it's all been a smoke-and-mirror hoax perpetrated by the CIA.

> I *believe* that Shakespeare had the career that Professor Jones attributes to him, but I'm also aware that some scholars think Shakespeare never existed, and for all I *know*, they may be right.

To be sure, another utterance of "Bob believes that Saddam Hussein is a dangerous dictator" may require a reference to Hussein, thus showing that even though a sentence may be both indexical-free (in the sense of not containing any explicit or hidden indexicals) and unambiguous (in the sense that it contains no ambiguous words or structures), an utterance of it may or may not require its that-clause to refer to a proposition whose *existence* depends on the name in the that-clause having a bearer.

These features of our use of that-clauses containing names are well accounted for by Pleonastic Fregeanism. According to this theory, the propositions referred to by that-clauses are individuated by conceptually prior criteria for determining the truth conditions of particular utterances of belief sentences. These criteria are highly context dependent, where the contextually-relevant factors are related to the communicative interests of the speaker and her audience in ways that are neither easily codified nor an obvious function of the sentence's meaning. Sometimes these contextual factors require a name in a that-clause to have a bearer; sometimes they don't. Thus, sometimes that-clauses containing names refer to *object-dependent propositions*, where the objects on which they depend are the bearers of the names in the that-clauses that refer to them, and sometimes they don't. But in either case Pleonastic Fregeanism holds that the reference of the token "n" in a token of "A believes that n is F" is A's (*contextually-relevant*) concept of n. This is reflected in the fact that even when "Fido" in a particular utterance of "Ralph believes that Fido is a dog" refers to Fido, we can still validly infer

> Ralph has a belief involving his (contextually relevant) concept of Fido.

Similarly, when "that man" refers to a contextually demonstrated man in an utterance of

> Ralph believes that that man is a philosopher,

a person in the same context may validly infer

> Ralph has a belief involving his (contextually relevant) concept of that man.

Thus, whether or not "n" in an utterance of "A believes that n is F" refers to its bearer, the Pleonastic Fregean holds that *the reference of*

"n," if it has one, is something that may itself be called A's *concept of n*. If it's required that there be a bearer of "n" to which the occurrence of "n" refers and it succeeds in so referring, then the reference of that occurrence of "n" is an object-*dependent* concept of n, a concept that wouldn't exist if "n" didn't refer. In this case, the fact that "n" refers to n, as well as to the concept of n, emerges in the fact that the concept which is the reference of "n" is an object-dependent concept—a concept that wouldn't itself exist if the name didn't have a bearer. But if it's required that there be a bearer of "n" and it fails in so referring, then the that-clause in "A believes that n is F" also fails to refer, since there is no object-dependent concept to which that occurrence of "n" can refer. And even when the names in the that-clause of, say,

> Algernon believes that George Eliot wrote *Middlemarch* but doesn't believe that Mary Ann Evans did.

refer to object-dependent concepts, those concepts can be different, no matter that the objects on which the concepts depend are the same. This is why for the Pleonastic Fregean nothing prevents the displayed sentence from being true even when both embedded names refer to the same person.

1.3.2 The punchline for empty names

So Pleonastic Fregeanism recognizes that very often, if not typically, that-clauses containing names refer to propositions whose existence depends on those names having bearers. At the same time, unlike direct-reference theories, Pleonastic Fregeanism has no trouble with empty names in that-clauses. Names in that-clauses refer to pleonastic concepts, and these can be either object-dependent or object independent; in either case they may be referred to by a description of the form "A's concept of n"—e.g., "Giorgio's concept of Satan," "Ralph's concept of Fido." Thus, Pleonastic Fregeanism accounts for the fact that sometimes we want to accept belief reports as true even though their that-clauses contain empty names. In such cases, those empty names refer to object-independent pleonastic concepts. Sometimes we want to count the that-clause in a belief report as failing to refer to any complete proposition when a name in it turns out not to have a bearer. This, too, is accounted for by Pleonastic Fregeanism, which holds that in such cases there is no pleonastic object-dependent concept to which the empty name can refer.

Nor does Pleonastic Fregeanism have trouble with empty names in unembedded sentences. For the proposition expressed by an utterance of "n is F," if any, is just the one believed by one who believes what the utterance says. If the utterance of "n" requires an object-dependent proposition, then the utterance of "*n* is *F*" expresses no complete proposition if "*n*" fails to refer. And whether or not "*n*" refers, an utterance of "*n* is *F*" may or may not, depending on context, express an object-independent proposition. In utterances of the form "*n* exists/does not exist" a predication is being made of an object-independent concept.

The so-called *problem of empty names*, I conclude, is only a problem for direct-reference theories. Pleonastic Fregeanism has no problem of empty names, but it does accommodate what's right about direct-reference theories.

2

Emptiness without Compromise: A Referentialist Semantics for Empty Names

KENNETH A. TAYLOR

Grant for the sake argument that Referentialism is true. It seems obvious what one should then say about empty names. To put it crudely, the Referentialist believes that names are devices of direct reference which contribute nothing but their referents to propositions expressed by sentences in which they occur. But if that is so, then given the fact that an empty name is devoid of reference, such names must fail to contribute anything at all to propositions expressed by sentences in which they occur. It would seem to follow, by a fairly short argument, that a sentence containing an empty name must fail to express any determinate proposition. Call this the Natural Referentialist thesis about empty names. Unfortunately the Natural Referentialist thesis has a *prima facie* troubling consequence. It implies that sentences containing empty names fail to be either true or false. This conclusion, to put it bluntly, is hard to swallow. For each of the following seems clearly to be true:

(1) Santa Claus doesn't exist.

(2) Santa Claus isn't coming tonight.

(3) Holmes is more clever than any actual detective.

And each of the following seems clearly to be false:

(4) Santa Claus exists.

(5) Santa Claus is coming tonight.

(6) Mark Fuhrman is more clever than Sherlock Holmes.

Empty Names, Fiction, and the Puzzles of Non-Existence.
Anthony Everett and Thomas Hofweber (eds.).
Copyright © 2000, CSLI Publications.

If the Referentialist has to deny the truth-evaluability of statements like (1)–(6), so much the worse, many are bound to conclude, for Referentialism.

So what is a Referentialist to do? Referentialists have often resorted to special pleading when faced with sentences containing empty names. Two poignant examples were Russell, (Russell 1905) and (Russell 1959b), and Meinong (Meinong 1960). Russell went so far as to deny that empty names were really names at all. Meinong infamously introduced special objects—non-existent ones—for empty names to denote. Though few contemporary Referentialists go quite as far as either Russell or Meinong did, it would, I think, be fair to say that special pleading remains a permanently tempting option. In this essay, by contrast, I shall argue that empty names are in no way semantically special. They do not abbreviate definite descriptions and they denote no special realm of fictional, non-existent, or abstract objects. Since I think that empty names are in no way semantically distinguished from non-empty names, I enthusiastically embrace both the natural referentialist thesis about empty names and its *prima facie* troubling consequence, at least when both are rightly understood. At the same time, I acknowledge the deference due to the widely shared intuition that one who utters any of (1)–(3) may speak truly, while one who utters any of (4)–(6) may speak falsely. The obvious key to paying due deference (but no more) to those intuitions, while remaining steadfastly Referentialist about empty names is to distinguish between what we might call compositionally determined propositional contents and what we might call pragmatically determined utterance contents. Sentences containing empty names lack any compositionally determined propositional content. But despite that fact, a speaker may, by an utterance of such a sentence manage to "say"—though not strictly, literally—*something* truth evaluable. One of my goals in this essay is to say something at least a bit informative about how such utterances manage that feat.

I begin by characterizing more precisely what, by my lights, Referentialism amounts to. I follow Francois Recanati (Recanati 1993) in thinking that genuinely or directly referential expressions are characterized by the fact that their lexical meanings include a semantic feature **REF**.[15] The presence of the feature **REF** indicates that the truth conditions of any utterance in which the relevant expression occurs will be singular. That is, the presence of **REF** indicates that the relevant expression contributes just its referent and not any mode of presentation thereof to the proposition expressed by any sentence in which it occurs.

---

[15] For a critical evaluation of Recanati (Recanati 1993) see my (Taylor 1997).

Now Recanati appeals to **REF** mainly as a way of distinguishing *de facto* rigid designators, like "the square root of 9" from *bona fide* expressions of direct reference. The latter are distinguished from the former, he claims, by the fact the rigidity of the latter follows directly from facts about lexical meaning. Directly referential expressions can thus be said to be *semantically rigid designators*.

Recanati is, I think, exactly right about the distinguishing characteristic of genuine referentiality. I add only that an expression can bear that distinguishing characteristic whether or not it actually has a referent. So, by my lights, even empty names include the semantic feature **REF** as an ingredient of their lexical meanings. To that extent, an empty name has a fully determinate lexical meaning, which is not yet a reference and which is insufficient to determine a reference. Moreover, at the level of lexical meaning, there is no fundamental semantic difference between empty and non-empty names. So at the level of lexical meaning, empty and non-empty names are members of a uniform semantic category— the category of expressions which, as we might say, aim to name (and thus to rigidly designate). To be sure, there remains an important difference between empty and non-empty names. Non-empty names succeed in naming; empty names do not succeed. Just because empty names lack reference, it would not be quite right to call such expressions referring expressions full stop. But we can justly call empty names referring-expressions-in-intention. The special status of empty names as referring-expressions-in-intention is a consequence of their being lexically marked with the semantic feature **REF**.

An immediate and welcome consequence of treating **REF** as a lexical semantic feature, shared by empty and non-empty names alike, is that it gives genuinely referential expressions something besides mere reference to mean. And we may therefore hope to avoid some of the unpalatable consequences of the paleo-Russellian equation of meaning with reference. Since names have something to mean even when they fail to refer, we need not be tempted by the bare fact of the meaningfulness of sentences containing empty names to suppose that empty names are disguised definite descriptions in attributive use. Of course, it is fair to wonder whether the semantic property of aiming to name is enough to prevent us from having to take departures as drastic as those taken by Russell and Meinong? The answer to that question is, I think, a definite yes. And part of the point of this paper is to defend that answer. But to that we shall come in due course.

Notice too that our approach gives the competent user of the language something besides mere reference to grasp. Even if a competent user does not know what object a certain referring expression stands for, she may still know of the relevant expression, as a consequence of her semantic competence in the language, that it is a referring expression (in intention) which rigidly designates its bearer. To say this is not to deny that to fully understand an utterance containing a token of a "successful" genuinely referential expression a cognizer must know what object the tokened referring expression stands for. But such knowledge-*wh* of a successfully designated object will be a contextual achievement for which knowledge of lexical meaning does not suffice.

Suppose that it is true that empty names have the lexical semantic property of "aiming" to name, even though they fail to name, then it is clear what we ought to say about sentences containing such names. Such a sentence will express no compositionally determined proposition at all. Nonetheless, such sentences typically will express what we might call a propositional scheme or a proposition-in-waiting.[16] Propositions-in-waiting *are* compositionally determined semantic properties of sentence types containing empty names. To a first approximation, a proposition-in-waiting is like an object dependent or singular proposition, except that where a singular proposition contains an object, a proposition-in-waiting contains an unfilled object slot. Moreover, each such slot is "associated

---

[16] Braun (Braun 1993) very briefly sketches an idea similar in spirit, though not in detail, to the ideas introduced here. For one thing, Braun's understanding of Referentialism requires that empty names be entirely devoid of "semantic value." This seems to me a mistake. An empty name lacks a reference and thus has no contribution to make to any proposition. But empty names have, nonetheless, fully determinate (derived) lexical meanings. And that, surely, is a kind of semantic value. Moreover, Braun thinks that simple atomic propositions-in-waiting are false (because not true), while the negations simple atomic propositions-in-waiting are true. This seems to me a mistake. Finally, Braun claims that there is only one simple atomic proposition in waiting. This again seems to me a mistake.

See also Evans (Evans 1982), especially chapter 10. Though Evans is no Referentialist, (at least not by his own lights), he too endorses a view about empty names similar in spirit, but quite different in detail, from the view expressed here. Evans makes heavy appeal to Walton's pretense theory to explain some of our intuitions about the apparent truth evaluability of sentences containing empty names. While it may be that much of what I say here can be happily endorsed by pretense theorists, I remain steadfastly neutral on that score.

Donnellan (Donnellan 1974) struggles, unsuccessfully by my lights, to distinguish, within a Referentialist framework, between the proposition expressed by a sentence containing an empty name and the truth conditions of such a sentence. He holds that such sentences have metalinguistic truth conditions. And he apparently thinks that there are determinate propositions expressed by such sentences. But he seems to want to deny that the propositions expressed by such sentences are metalinguistic. Donnellan never manages to spell this out in sufficient detail to make his proposals fully evaluable. But I think the way the untangle the thicket into which he gets himself is just to deny that sentences containing empty names express fully determinate propositions, but are associated with determinate propositions-in-waiting. See also Crimmins and Perry (Crimmins and Perry 1989) and Kripke (Kripke 1980).

with" a rule for filling that slot with an object. Were a determinate object provided to complete the relevant propositional scheme, the scheme would yield a complete object-dependent or singular proposition. We might write such a scheme as follows:

A <__ REF(x bears "Santa"), <lives at>, North Pole>

Such scheme are subject to all the usual logical operations. For example, the denial of the foregoing scheme is the following scheme:

B <Not <__ REF(x bears "Santa"), <lives at> North Pole>>

It too is not yet a determinate proposition, but merely a proposition-in-waiting. We might also suppose that cognizers can stand in various cognitive relations to such propositions-in-waiting. One who believes that Santa lives at the North Pole entertains scheme A in the believing mode. But in so doing, she does not thereby believe a determinate proposition. For the belief that Santa lives at the North Pole is strictly speaking not yet a fully determinate thought content. It too stands in need of completion by an object. Similarly, she who wishes that Santa would come down the chimney tonight does not thereby wish for any determinate state of affairs. Her wish is, as it were, merely a wish-in-waiting. But that wish-in-waiting is associated with a determinate scheme, a scheme complete in all respects save one.

We need to say more about the characters of the associated rules for filling the unfilled object slots in a proposition-in-waiting. It will help to begin with indexicals. With each indexical expression type, there is associated, in virtue of its lexical meaning, a certain reference fixing rule. For example, the reference fixing rule for the expression type **I** might be written as follows:

$(\forall \iota)(\forall \mathbf{C})$ (if ι is a token of the expression type **I** produced in a context $\mathbf{C}$, then ι rigidly designates the agent x such that x used ι in $\mathbf{C}$).

Several things are worth noting. First, our rule quantifies over, and does not refer to, particular tokens of the type **I** . Similarly, the rule neither explicitly refers to nor explicitly quantifies over what we might call token-reflexive modes of presentation. It just gives a general reference-fixing rule. However, one who grasps this rule will tacitly know that tokenings of the type **I** "generate," as we might say, token-reflexive modes of presentation. For each token of the type **I**, we can regard the token-reflexive mode generated by its tokening as part of the descriptive content of that very token. So although our rule is explicitly a rule for fixing reference, it is also implicitly a rule for fixing descriptive contents of particular tokens. Moreover, the rule implies that the generated descriptive contents are truth-conditionally irrelevant by explicitly saying that each token of the type **I** is a semantically rigid designator which contributes only its referent to any proposition expressed by any sentence in which it occurs. It is this clause of the rule which, in effects, marks **I** with the semantic feature **REF**.

Names merit largely parallel treatment, except that we can give a completely general meaning rule that applies to all names in virtue of their membership in the category **NAME**. Our general meaning rule for the category **NAME** determines for each name, merely as a consequence of its type identity as name, what we might call a derived lexical representation. The general meaning rule is as follows:

> $(\forall \mathbf{N})(\forall \nu)(\forall \mathbf{C})$ (If ν is name token of the name type **N** produced in context **C**, then ν rigidly designates the individual o such that o bears **N**).

The derived lexical representation of "Cicero," for example, will look like the following:

> $(\forall \nu)(\forall \mathbf{C})$ (If ν is name token of the name type "Cicero" produced in context **C**, then ν rigidly designates the individual o such that o bears "Cicero").

Notice that both the semantic representation of the category **NAME**, and the derived lexical representation for any particular name, mention both the relation *bears* and the *rigidly designates* relation. It is important to distinguish these two relations. The *bears* relation is a this-worldly relation that holds in world between a name and that of which it is actually a name. On the other hand, the *rigidly designates* relations holds across the worlds. That is, a name ν may rigidly designate its bearer o even at worlds in which o fails to bear ν. The lexicon is presumably silent about what in nature the name-bearer relation is. But the lexicon explicitly represents that (tokens of) a name type rigidly designate whatever object bears that name (type), thus explicitly marking names with the semantic feature **REF**. Moreover, just as indexicals have a lexically determined, but truth-conditionally irrelevant, descriptive content, so too, by our lights, do proper names. Names do not have token-reflexive descriptive contents, but they do have what we might call type-reflexive descriptive content. A name token ν presents its referent as the bearer of the very name type of which ν is a token. It follows that every token of a given name type has the same lexical descriptive content. For the lexical descriptive content of a name token is fully determined once its type identity is determined. Moreover, no two name tokens of different name types share lexical descriptive contents, even where the two names denote the same object and thus make identical contributions to the propositions expressed by sentences in which they occur. Hence although "Cicero" and "Tully" denote the same object, nonetheless tokens of "Cicero" differ in lexical descriptive content from tokens of "Tully." Tokens of "Cicero" present Cicero as the bearer of the name (type) "Cicero," while tokens of "Tully" present Cicero as the bearer of the name (type) "Tully."

The question arises just what makes two name tokens to be tokens of the same or different name types. Syntactic and phonological similarities and differences seem intuitively relevant to the type individuation of names. Indeed it seems intuitively plausible that wherever we have the right sort of syntactic and phonological differences we *ipso facto* have distinct name types. The bare fact that "Tully" and "Cicero" are neither spelled nor sounded the same is arguably sufficient to make "Cicero" and "Tully" to be different name types. If distinctness of sound and shape are sufficient for distinctness of name type, should we say that sameness of sound and shape is sufficient for sameness of name type? We should not, I think. In order to have the same name again, we must have not only the same shape/sound pattern again, but also the same reference again, with the tokening of that shape/sound pattern constituting a further episode in a continuing history of such tokenings. The crucial challenge for this approach to the type individuation of names is to say just when two tokenings of the same shape/sound pattern again, with the same reference again, does and does not count as a further episode in the same continuing history of such tokenings. For convenience sake, we may call that which makes two tokenings of the same shape/sound pattern again to be further episodes in the same continuing history of tokenings a mechanism of co-reference. But talking this way requires some caution. We must be careful to distinguish the type level property of co-referring from the token level property of being bound together by a mechanism of co-reference. "Cicero" and "Tully" are co-referring name types, but tokenings of "Cicero" and tokenings of "Tully" are not bound together by a single mechanism of co-reference. Think of tokens which are bound together by a single mechanism of co-reference as being not merely co-referential, but also as being "marked" as co-referential. "Cicero" and "Tully" co-refer without being marked as co-referential. Two tokens of the same name type both co-refer and are marked as co-referential. So I shall say that tokens of the same name type are explicitly co-referential.

We need to say more about how mechanisms of co-reference are constituted. Such mechanism are partly constituted out of the interlocking and interdependent referential intentions of a community of co-linguals.

When I token the sound/shape pattern "Cicero" I do not intend to be tokening a brand new name under the sun. Rather I intend to be tokening again a name that others have tokened before. And I intend to refer via that name to what others have referred to before. Those intentions are at least partly responsible for making my use of the sound/shape pattern "Cicero" a use of the same name again as that which my co-linguals have used before me. Still it is important to see that intentions to conform to the usage of my co-linguals sometimes misfire. Imagine an agent Smith. Suppose that unbeknownst to Smith opinions are divided among his co-linguals about the beauty of London. Some of his co-linguals think that London is a city of outstanding beauty; others think that it is horrendously ugly. Imagine that the name "London" is first introduced into Smith's referential repertoire via interaction with a collection of apparently knowledgeable people, all of whom think that London is one among the more beautiful cities of the world. Smith is inclined to take apparently knowledgeable people at their word. So he acquires the word "London," intending to use it in accordance with the usage of his co-linguals. Subsequently, Smith comes in contact with other apparently knowledgeable people. He is inclined to take them at their word. These apparently knowledgeable people believe that London is one of the more ugly cities in the world. Because Smith mistakenly, but not irrationally, believes that knowledgeable people in a single community of co-linguals are unlikely to hold such divergent opinions about one and the same city, he reasons that the apparently knowledgeable people encountered later and the apparently knowledgeable people encountered earlier are not talking about one and the same city. So he concludes that there must be two cities called "London." And he resolves to use the sound/shape pattern "London" in two different ways, but each time in conformity with the usage of his co-linguals.

Smith would, of course, be surprised to learn that (as he would put it) "London is London" but no more surprised than an average speaker would be to learn that Cicero is Tully or than the average Babylonian would have been to learn that Hesperus is Phosphorus. It seems that Smith must really have two distinct, but co-referential, though not explicitly so, names for London. Where do these two names come from?

Suppose we distinguish two (sub)communities of Smith's co-linguals: the **A** community and the **B** community. The **A** community consists of those who think that London is among the most beautiful cities in the world. The **B** community consists of those who think that London is horrendously ugly. Suppose further that we distinguish two sequences of Smith's tokenings of the sound/shape pattern "London"—an **A**-sequence and a **B**-sequence. A tokening is a member of the **A**-sequence when Smith produces it, intending to conform to the usage of the **A** community. But it is important to state that Smith intends, by conforming to the usage of the **A** community, to be conforming to the usage of the community at large. Similarly, a tokening is a member of the **B** sequence when Smith produces it intending to conform to the usage of the **B** community. Again, Smith intends, by conforming to the usage of the **B** community, to be conforming to the usage of the community at large.

At first blush, it appears reasonable to say that Smith's **A**-sequence is bound to the usage of the **A** community by a mechanism of co-reference which is rooted in Smith's intention to conform to the usage of the **A** community. But if there is such a mechanism of co-reference then Smith's **A**-sequence "London" must be explicitly co-referential with the "London" of the **A** community, without being explicitly co-referential with the Smith's **B**-sequence London. Similarly, if we suppose that Smith's **B**-sequence "London" is bound to the "London" of the **B** community by a mechanism of co-reference, then Smith's **B**-sequence "London" must be explicitly co-referential with the "London" of the **B** community, but not explicitly co-referential with Smith's **A**-sequence "London." But members of the **A** and **B** communities are really joint masters of the one word "London." That means that the **A** community's "London" and the **B** community's "London" are bound together by a mechanism of co-reference and are thus explicitly co-referential. If we assume, as seems reasonable, transitivity of explicit co-reference, then it seems that we must, on pain of contradiction, deny that Smith's **A**-sequence "London" is explicitly co-referential with the "London" of the **A** community and deny that his **B**-sequence "London" is explicitly co-referential with the "London" of the **B** community. But if that is so, then Smith does not succeed in doing what he originally intended. Each time Smith tokens the sound/shape pattern "London," he clearly intends merely to be sustaining an already existing mechanism of co-reference by tokening again what others have tokened before. Contrary to Smith's own intentions, however, he appears to token at least one, and arguably two, brand new names under the sun, initiating at least one, and arguably two, brand new mechanisms of co-reference under the sun.[17]

---

[17]I note in passing that Francois Recanati has defended a different account of the type identity of names which denies that names simultaneously borne by many are ambiguous. Homographic and homophonic names simultaneously borne by many are no more ambiguous, according to Recanati, than is an indexical such as "you" which may be used now in this context to refer to that person and now in that context to refer to a distinct person. Names are, in fact, quite indexical-like, by Recanati's lights.

For all that we have said so far, a mechanism of co-reference may seem to require an actually existing object as its founding cog. But that is not so. Tokenings of empty names must also be bound together by mechanisms of co-reference, if they are to count as tokenings of the same name again. It is just that in the case of empty names, the founding tokens of the relevant mechanism of co-reference will be tokened in the making of fiction or myth or in the course of failed attempts at reference to putatively existent object. And the mechanism of co-reference will be sustained not by interlocking intentions to refer to some actual existent, but, in the case of myth and fiction, by interlocking intentions to carry on a mythical practice or by interlocking patterns of deference to acts of fiction making, performance and interpretation. In the case of failed attempts at genuine reference, by contrast, there will occur shared intentions to fail together, if success is not to be had. Suppose, for example, that there had been no planet causing perturbations in the orbit of Uranus. What then would we say about the name "Neptune?" That it was not a name at all because there was no mechanism of co-reference by which to constitute its tokenings as events in the history of single name type? I think not. For it would still be the case that "Neptune" aimed to name. And by virtue of the existence of a mechanism of co-reference which bound tokenings of "Neptune" into one continuing history of tokenings, the tokens of "Neptune" would be marked, as it were, as standing or falling together.

Similarly, though there is a sense in which all empty names might be said to be co-referential, since they one and all refer to the same object, nonetheless, the tokens of one empty name are not bound together with the tokens of another empty name by a single mechanism of co-reference. "Santa Claus" and "Pegasus" are name types like any other. The tokens of "Santa Claus" are bound together by a mechanism of co-reference which, in effect, explicitly marks them one and all as co-referential. The failure of "Santa Claus" to refer is a failure shared by all of its tokens, a failure they share in virtue of their aiming to name together. "Pegasus" too is constituted as the very name type that it is by a mechanism of co-reference, a mechanism of co-reference initiated in a founding act of myth-making, sustained for an historical period by intentions to continue the relevant mythical practice, and sustained to this day by intentions to co-refer which are no longer moored to ancient mythical practice. That mechanism of co-reference explicitly marks the tokens of "Pegasus" as one and all co-referential, as succeeding or failing together to achieve reference. Now the career of "Pegasus" as a name is sustained by an entirely independent mechanism of co-reference from that which sustains the career of "Santa" as a name. Consequently, the failure of "Pegasus" to refer is a fact entirely independent of the failure of "Santa Claus" to refer. So although "Pegasus" and "Santa" are, in a trivial sense, co-referential, they are not explicitly co-referential. The absence of explicit co-reference between "Santa" and "Pegasus," I claim, is all there is to the feeling that the Santa Claus myth and the Pegasus myth have different subject matters, despite their co-referentiality. It is decidedly not the case, by my lights, that there are two mythical figures such that the Santa Claus myth is about the one and the Pegasus myth is about the other. The making of myth and fiction may indeed make name types to exist; but they do not make mythical or fictional objects to exist.[18]

I have so far argued that empty names are distinguished from non-empty names neither lexically, semantically, nor metaphysically. Empty names, like names generally, are devices of direct reference. They are lexically marked with the semantic feature **REF**. Like non-empty names, empty names have truth conditionally irrelevant, type-reflexive descriptive contents. An empty name, like a non-empty name, presents its would be bearer as the bearer of that very name. Finally, as with names generally, the type-individuation of names depends on the existence of mechanisms of co-reference, mechanisms which mark all the tokens of the same name type as sharing a referential aim and fate. I take up now what

---

[18]It is worth pointing out in passing that it is a quite general phenomenon that wherever singular terms are not explicitly co-referential, there will always be a felt implication that the two terms are have different reference. Consider the following, for example:

(a) John just arrived at the party and he is already drunk,
(b) John just arrived at the party, and the man in the blue hat is already drunk,
(c) John just arrived at the party and that man is already drunk,
(d) John just arrived at the party and John is already drunk,
(e) That man over there just arrived at the party and he is already drunk,
(f) That man over there just arrived at the party and that man over there is already drunk,
(g) That man over there just arrived at the party and John is already drunk,
(h) That man over there just arrived at the party and the man in the blue hat is already drunk,
(i) The man in the blue hat just arrived at the party and he is already drunk,
(j) The man in the blue hat just arrived at the party and John is already drunk,
(k) The man in the blue hat just arrived at the party and the man in the blue hat is already drunk,
(l) The man in the blue hat just arrived at the party and that man over there is already drunk.

Suppose that, in fact, John just is the man over there who just is the man in the blue hat. All though all of the sentences above are surely logically consistent with this possibility, all except those which involve some sort of explicit co-reference actually carry a felt implication that two different people are in question. Any complete theory of singular terms had better explain where this felt implication comes from.

might be called the psychological organization of the referring mind. I will argue that the empty and non-empty names play quite similar roles in the psychological life of the directly referring mind. And once we have shown this, we will finally be in a position to say something informative about how utterances of sentences which contain empty names manage to say something truth evaluable, despite the fact that such sentences express no compositionally determined propositions.

I begin by introducing the notion of a conception. A conception is a kind of mental particular, a labelled, perhaps highly structured, and updatable database of information about the extension of an associated concept. For example, each thinker who can deploy the concept <cat> in thought-episodes is likely to have stored in his head a database of information (and misinformation) about cats. In English speaking deployers of the concept <cat> such a database might be labelled "CAT." Such a database may contain a variety of different kinds of information (and possibly misinformation) about cats. It may contain a list of properties that some, many, most, all or typical cats are taken to satisfy. It may contain information which determines the categorial basis of the concept <cat>—that is, whether <cat> is a natural kind concept, a functional concept, an artifactual concept. It may contain an image of an exemplary cat, a list of atypical cats, and pointers to sources where more can be found out about cats. Each time I learn (or think I learn) more about cats, more goes into my database of information about cats. This ever-developing labelled database of information (and misinformation) about cats may play a decisive role in both my reasoning about cats and my behavior toward cats. Now just as we have conceptions of kinds of things, so too do we have conceptions of individual things. I have, for example, a relatively rich and ever developing conception of my colleague John Perry. That database is actually labelled "John Perry." And the label is quite important. It serves as a kind of access point to all the information in my conception of John Perry. When I hear and process utterances of sentences containing the name "John Perry" I, as it were, activate my conception of John, and thereby make that information available for further processing.

Now I mention in passing that conceptions are closely related to concepts. Indeed, there are many who think concepts just are conceptions, or at least that to have a concept one must have a conception of the right sort. To have the concept <cat>, such thinkers might say, one must have a conception that contains, perhaps, the information that cats are animals. But it is a serious error to conflate concepts and conceptions. This claim deserves a more full scale defense than space permits. But since I have been more fulsome elsewhere, perhaps a brief indication of my reasons for resisting the conflation will suffice. There are two main reasons:

(1) Conceptions don't relate to their extensions in concept-like ways,

(2) Conceptions don't compose in concept-like ways.

That conceptions don't relate to their extensions is concept-like ways has to do with the fact that conceptions may be conceptions of things of which they are not true and may fail to be conceptions of things of which they are true. Concepts are not like that. Nothing falls within the extension of a concept except things of which the concept is true. All and only cats fall within the extension of the concept <cat>, for example. But a cat conception may fail to be true of any actual cat and may be true of many non-cats.[19] That conceptions don't compose in concept-like ways has to do with the fact that there is no systematic connection between a more "complex" conception and the putatively "simpler" conceptions out of which it is composed. So, for example, a cognizer may have a conception of gray cats, a conception of gray things, and a conception of cats. But her conception of gray cats will not be predictable from facts about her conceptions of gray things and her conception of cats. Again concepts are, in the general case, not like that.

I have been stressing the distinctness of concepts and conceptions, But I grant to both concepts and conceptions their well-deserved places in a good theory of our cognitive organization. Conceptions play a quite important role in organizing our knowledge and beliefs and in mediating the deployment of our concepts in thought episodes. Indeed, without conceptions to mediate their deployment in thought episodes, concepts would generally be cognitively inert. For concepts, on their own, are largely powerless to move the mind. Or at a minimum I should say that to determine how a concept will move the mind of one who possess a concept we will often have to determine what conception mediates the deployment of that concept in that cognizer's thought episodes. On the other hand, without concepts, conceptions would be largely powerless to reach out to the world and have determinate extensions. Conceptions

---

[19]For example, suppose that it is part of my conception of cats that they were carriers of a certain disease, so that in my "cat" database there entered a line of information that said, in effect, cats carry disease x. But suppose it turns out that I am wrong. No cat carries the relevant disease. That does not prevent my conception from being a conception of cat. And even if there is an animal—say dogs—of which that information is true, that would not suffice to make my conception a conception of dogs. Indeed, even if most of the things in my conception of cats were in fact true of dogs, that would not suffice to make that conception a conception *of* dogs, rather than cats.

largely inherit their extensions from the concepts whose deployments they mediate. Here is a slogan: *Concepts without conceptions are inert; conceptions without concepts are empty.*

When I first introduced the notion of a conception a few paragraphs back, I wrote as if a cognizer will have a single conception of each thing or kind of thing for which she has any conception at all. But cognizers often have a plurality of conceptions of the self-same extension. Jocasta, for example, had two distinct conceptions of Oedipus—one labelled "Oedipus," the other labelled "Tad." And many ancient Babylonians apparently had at least two distinct conceptions of the one planet Venus— one labelled "Hesperus" and other labelled "Phosphorous." Moreover, when a cognizer has two or more conceptions of a given extension, those conceptions are often dynamically unlinked. In that case, the unlinked conceptions typically will not be updated simultaneously even though they are databases of information about one and the same object and even though they independently mediate the deployment of the same concept again in thought episodes. It takes a special and explicit linkage of numerically distinct conceptions to make them co-evolve. Thus when Lois Lane learns a new bit of information about Clark Kent, aka, Superman, she may, depending on just how that information is delivered, store it in either in a database labelled "Clark Kent" or in a database labelled "Superman." Storing it in the one file does not guarantee that it will also be stored in the other file. And accessing or activating information in the one file does not guarantee that the other file will also be accessed. However, if Lois were to learn of the identity of Clark Kent and Superman, we can presume that her psychological organization would undergo a significant change. Her previously dynamically independent conceptions of Superman, aka Clark Kent might either merge into one more encompassing conception or remain separate but linked.

We have said a fair amount about conceptions and a little about concepts, but what, the reader may impatiently ask, does any of this have to do with empty names? The answer is that it is a fundamental fact about the role of names—empty and non-empty alike—in our psychological organization that they serve as labels for and access points to conceptions of individuals. Cognizers like us are such that she who acquires a name, as it were, opens a file, a file ready for writing in, which is labelled with the relevant name and sometimes accessed via the relevant name. There is, of course, a difference between files associated with empty names and files associated with non-empty names. Files labelled by non-empty names are conceptions of real individuals. And we try to see to it that such conceptions list, for example, only properties actually had by the individuals of which they are conceptions. Moreover, we try, ceteris paribus, to see to it that conceptions which are conceptions of the very same individual are dynamically linked in one of the two ways mentioned above. That is, we try to make our concern for truth govern the evolution of those of our conceptions which are conceptions of actually existent individuals.

But what governs the evolution of our "empty" conceptions? Recall our earlier discussion of mechanisms of co-reference. I argued above that mythic and fictive practices amount to mechanisms of co-reference which have the power to constitute fictive and mythic name types as the very name types that they are. It is a short step to the conclusion that the very practices which constitute the type-identity of a name also condition the contents of the conceptions associated with the relevant name by those who participate in the relevant identity constituting practice. A fictive conception, serves, in the competent practitioner, as storehouse of fictive contents, contents derived from the very practice that constitutes the relevant name as the name that it is.

The contents of fictive and mythical conceptions are conditioned in quite a different way from the way in which the contents of our veridical conceptions, as we might call them, are conditioned. In updating our veridical conceptions on the basis of our experience in the world, we are governed by a concern for truth, for getting things right, as things go in the world. In updating our fictive and mythic conceptions, by contrast, we are concerned merely for getting things right as things go in fictions and/or myths which condition those conceptions. Getting things right as things go in a fiction is not a matter of getting at a certain kind of truth—truth in a fiction, say. We do indeed use expressions like, "It is true in the Santa Claus myth that..." and "It is true in the Holmes Stories that..." but neither truth in a story nor truth in a myth is a species of truth. To be sure, such devices do play what we might call a dialogic role that resembles the dialogic role of genuine truth talk. The predicate "...is true" functions as a device for claiming entitlement to make assertoric moves in dialogic games of inquiry, argument, and deliberation. A player who asserts that p is true, that is, thereby claims an entitlement to assert that p. Similarly, expressions like "true in the story" or "according to the story" function as entitlement claiming devices for moves in a dialogic games played among producers and consumers of myth and/or fiction. But there remains an important difference between moves in fictive dialogic games and moves in dialogic games for inquiry, argument and deliberation. Moves in fictive or mythic dialogic games typically are not fully propositional. Fictive assertions, that is, typically are only assertions-in-waiting and as such are strictly speaking neither true nor false. Though fictive "assertions" typically are merely assertions-in-waiting which fail to be fully propositional, it does not follow that all such assertions either stand or fall together with respect to entitlement and commitment. I hasten to distinguish fictive assertions *qua* moves in fictive dialogic games from what I call metafictional assertions *about* a work fiction. Metafictional assertions typically are fully propositional. Such assertions, like assertions generally, are moves in "veridical" dialogic games of inquiry, deliberation, and argument, dialogic games governed by a concern for truth.

Finally, I show how an utterance of a "mixed" sentence like "Santa Claus isn't coming tonight" can manage to "say"—though not strictly literally—something truth-evaluable. I begin by amending a distinction due to Francois Recanati. Recanati has argued forcefully for the importance of distinguishing between primary and secondary pragmatic processes. Primary pragmatic processes operate, according to Recanati, "below" the level of the completed utterance and antecedently to the determination of a complete propositional content. Such processes play a role in constituting what is strictly literally said by an utterance in context. We may suppose, for example, that there is a primary pragmatic process of "saturation" which fills the unfilled object slots in a proposition-in-waiting. It takes such a process to get us from the context-independent meaning of a sentence like "I am hungry now" or "Cicero was a great Roman orator" to the determinate proposition expressed by an utterance of that sentence in context. Secondary pragmatic processes, on the other hand, presuppose that some determinate proposition has already been yielded by primary pragmatic processes. Such processes take the propositional outputs of primary pragmatic processes as inputs and yield further "implications" as outputs—paradigmatically Gricean conversational implicatures.

With a modest, but crucial amendment, Recanati's two-stage pragmatics can be usefully extended to explain how sentences containing empty names manage to say something truth-evaluable, despite the fact that they strictly literally express no proposition. We need to introduce pragmatic processes which are neither primary nor secondary. I call such processes one and half stage pragmatic processes. One and a half stage pragmatic processes happen where primary pragmatic processes "misfire" or fail to come off. Because such processes happen where primary pragmatic processes fail to come off, such processes presuppose a failed or misfired attempt at constituting a strict, literal propositional content. For that reason, it would be a mistake to think of one and half stage processes as playing a role in constituting strict propositional contents. Nonetheless, one and half stage processes do associate propositional contents with utterances. It is just that such utterance do not strictly literally express the associated propositions. But neither are the associated propositions merely conversationally implicated by those utterances. It takes the application of a secondary pragmatic process to the propositional outputs of primary pragmatic processes to generate a conversational implicature. But where primary pragmatic processes fail to come off, there is no proposition generated to serve as the input to any secondary pragmatic process. The proposition associated by one and half stage processes with an utterance is less tightly connected to the utterance than is the proposition generated by the successful application of a primary pragmatic processes, but more tightly connected than a mere conversational implicature. We need a tag for the distinctive relation between the outputs of one and half stage pragmatic processes and the utterance itself. I will say that an utterance *pseudo-expresses* a proposition if that proposition is associated with that utterance by the application of a one and half stage pragmatic process. And I will say that a sincere speaker who makes an utterance which pseudo-expresses the proposition *p*, *pseudo-asserts p*.

Consider saturation—the primary pragmatic process whereby the empty object slots in a proposition-in-waiting are filled to generate a more nearly complete proposition. Empty names are names for which the process of saturation fails to come off. Because saturation misfires, the relevant proposition-in-waiting remains "unsaturated." Consequently, there is no proposition which is strictly, literally asserted by the relevant utterance of the relevant sentence. Nonetheless, there is what we might call a proposition in the descriptive neighborhood of the relevant proposition-in-waiting. And that proposition is pseudo-asserted by the relevant utterance. That proposition is generated by a one and half stage pragmatic process which I call pseudo-saturation. Pseudo-saturation steps in where saturation falters.[20] Pseudo-saturation "fills" the unfilled object slots in a proposition-in-waiting not with an object, but with descriptive contents drawn from the conception, if there is one, which is labelled and accessed via the relevant name. Thus, for example, a speaker who utters the sentence "Santa Claus isn't coming tonight" does not assert any fully determinate proposition at all. But she does pseudo-assert a proposition in the neighborhood of the following proposition-in-waiting:

---

[20]So I agree with an early insight of Donnellan's (Donnellan 1974). Sentences containing empty names fail to express truths because there occurs a failure of reference. I also agree—though Donnellan is not entirely clear on this point—that such sentences do not, for that reason, express metalinguistic propositions about such reference failures. Nonetheless, the fact of reference failure plays a crucial role in, as it were, the dynamics of pseudo-assertion.

$$<\text{Not} <\_\_ \text{REF}(x \text{ bears "Santa"}), <\text{coming tonight}>>$$

In particular, she pseudo-asserts the proposition that no jolly, white-bearded, red-suited fellow, who lives at the North Pole and delivers toys via a reindeer-drawn sleigh is coming tonight. Of course, the proposition pseudo-asserted by an utterance of "Santa Claus isn't coming tonight" is truth-evaluable. So there is, after all, a sense in which one who utters the sentence "Santa Claus isn't coming tonight" manages to "say" something truth-evaluable. She pseudo-asserts a fully determinate proposition which happens, in fact, to be true.

It is important to stress the difference between assertion and pseudo-assertion. One who utters "Santa Claus isn't coming tonight" does not thereby *assert* that no jolly, white-bearded, red-suited fellow, who lives at the North Pole and delivers toys via a reindeer-drawn sleigh is coming tonight. One who utters this sentence *asserts* no proposition at all. Moreover, one who assertorically utters the form of words "No jolly, white-bearded fellow... is coming tonight" does thereby assert that no jolly, white-bearded, red-suited fellow... is coming tonight but does *not* assert that Santa Claus isn't coming—there being, in a sense, no such assertion. Nor does one who assertorically utters the form of words "No jolly, white-bearded, red-suited fellow ... is coming tonight" pseudo-assert that Santa Claus isn't coming. Again, pseudo-assertion happens only where, due to the misfiring of some primary pragmatic process, assertion fails to get off the ground. When one straight-out asserts that no jolly fellow white-bearded, red-suited fellow is coming tonight via the form of words "no jolly, white-bearded, red suited fellow is coming tonight" no primary pragmatic process will have misfired. Hence there is no room for pseudo-assertion to get off the ground.

Now when a speaker utters the sentence "Santa Claus isn't coming tonight" we typically report her speech act by saying that she has said that Santa Claus lives at the North Pole. We do not say of such a speaker that she has said that no jolly red-suited white-bearded fellow is coming tonight. Nor do we say that she has merely pseudo-asserted that Santa isn't coming tonight. Does our ascriptive practice not give the lie to my claim that an utterance of "Santa Claus isn't coming tonight" amounts to a pseudo-assertion rather than an assertion? I think not. The following facts seem beyond dispute. A speaker who utters the form of words "Santa isn't coming tonight" has, in some sense, expressed a determinate proposition. Moreover, when we ascribe a saying to such a speaker we ascribe the determinate proposition that she has managed to express, whatever that proposition is. My view is entirely compatible with these indisputable facts. Pseudo-asserting a proposition is a way of "expressing" a proposition. Moreover, it is clear that the proposition expressed by one who utters the form of words "Santa isn't coming tonight" cannot be a singular proposition, but must be a purely descriptive one. What makes it true that Santa Claus isn't coming tonight is the fact that no one satisfying a certain description is coming tonight. So the remaining challenge is to say just how the utterance of a sentence containing the name "Santa Claus" manages to express such a descriptive proposition.

There are at least the following four options. One can hold that such an utterance strictly, literally expresses a descriptive proposition. One can hold that such an utterance conversationally implicates, via Gricean mechanisms, the relevant proposition. One can adopt some form of Meinongianism, and suppose that putatively empty names aren't really empty at all but denote special non-existent, fictional or mythical objects and that sentences containing such names strictly, literally express propositions about such objects. Finally, one can adopt the approach I have been articulating here of distinguishing assertion from pseudo-assertion and primary and secondary pragmatic processes from one and half stage pragmatic processes. There is, I think, something to be said against each of the other alternatives which counts in favor of my own. Unless one wants to be a descriptivist about all names, the first alternative amounts to *ad hoc* special pleading on behalf of empty-names. I take the arguments against such general purpose descriptivism about names to be decisive. But my approach requires no such special pleading. Names are members of a quite uniform semantic category, the character of which can be specified in one fell swoop. The second alternative requires some account of just how the supposed implicature might be generated. The problem is that Gricean implicatures are always generated with the mediating intervention of something strictly, literally said distinct from what is merely implicated. So the implicature alternative requires that there be a proposition distinct from the putatively merely conversationally implicated descriptive proposition for the utterance to strictly literally express. But there would seem to be no such proposition. That is, the expressed descriptive proposition would seem to be more directly associated with the utterance than a mere conversationally implicature. My approach, in contrast to the Gricean approach, fully reflects the relatively direct association between the utterance and the expressed descriptive proposition. And it does so without making the descriptive relevant proposition the strict literal content of the relevant utterance. Finally, considerations of parsimony seem to weigh decisively in favor of my approach and against Meinongian approaches. There may indeed be some independent grounds to posit non-existent, fictional, and/or mythical objects. But the availability of the approach I have outlined here is surely sufficient to demonstrate that there is nothing about the semantic/pragmatic behavior of putatively empty names which compels us to posit such entities. And it is surely a reasonable principle that in the absence of any compelling reason for positing such entities, we ought to refrain from positing them.

3

Referentialism and Empty Names

ANTHONY EVERETT

3.1 Introduction

In this paper I will be considering empty names and I will be concerned
with two questions in particular. I will be concerned with the question
of how certain utterances of sentences containing empty names, such as
existential and negative existential statements, can have truth values.
And I will be concerned with the question of why utterances of certain
empty names, such as "Santa Claus" and "Father Xmas" seem, in at
least some loose sense, to be about the same thing, even though there
is nothing in reality that they are about.[21]

The structure of this paper is as follows. In section 2 I outline these
two problems in greater detail. In section 3 I examine the bearing these
have upon the semantic doctrine of *Referentialism*, the doctrine that the
sole semantic function of a proper name is to refer to its bearer. I suggest
a view of the semantic function of empty names which, while it is compatible with Referentialism, allows that certain utterances containing
empty names may have truth values. In sections 4 and 5 I develop some
technical apparatus. Then in section 6 I use this to provide an account
of the sense in which two utterances of empty names may be counted as
being about the same thing.

Before proceeding further, however, I want to clarify precisely what
it is that I shall be talking about and what I shall not be talking about.
I want to distinguish three different ways in which empty names might
be employed. For in what follows I will only be concerned with empty

---

[21]This paper is based upon a paper presented at a conference on "Empty Names,
Fiction, and the Puzzles of Non-existence" (sponsored by the Center for the Study of
Language and Information at Stanford University), on March 23, 1998. I would like
to thank John Perry, Ken Taylor, and Stacie Friend, for their help and comments.

Empty Names, Fiction, and the Puzzles of Non-Existence.
Anthony Everett and Thomas Hofweber (eds.).

names which are used in the third of these ways and I think that an
an account of language should handle these cases differently. The three-
fold distinction is as follows. In the first place empty names might be
employed in a *conniving* manner as when we tell a story or relate a
myth. Such statements are not to be taken as literal assertions about
our real world but rather as part of the process of story-telling or myth-
making. They will be claims about the world of the story or myth. And
they will be true or false within that story or myth. Examples of such
uses include my telling a child "Santa has twelve reindeer" and my saying "Holmes lives at Baker Street" while recounting a Sherlock Holmes
story to someone. In the second place empty names may be used in a
metafictional way to talk about stories or myths from the perspective
of our real world. Thus, for example, we might say "Holmes is a character in a Conan Doyle novel," or "In the Conan Doyle stories Holmes
is a detective." Such claims are literally true or literally false. They are
claims about our real world, for they are about our real-world practices
of story-telling and myth-making. But their truth depends in part upon
what is the case in the relevant stories or myths. Finally, there are *non-
fictional* uses of empty names. Claims which involve non-fictional uses of
empty names talk about only the real world and not about fictional or
mythic worlds. The truth values of such claims depend only upon what
is the case in the real world and in no way depend upon what is the
case in any fictional or mythical world. Examples of such claims include
"Santa does not exist," "Santa is not to my immediate left," and "I am
not identical to Vulcan." These claims seem to be literally true, and
whatever it is that makes these claims true it is something about our
real world and not anything about the world of the Vulcan-story or the
Santa-myth.

No doubt a great deal more needs to be said about the different ways
in which empty names might be used. But I am not going to consider
these matters here. My point for the moment is simply to note that I
am going to be concerned only with those uses of empty names which
fall into the *last* of the three categories. I am going to be concerned with
non-fictional uses of empty names.

3.2 The problems

Suppose that, intending them to be literal claims about the world, I
utter the sentences:

(1) Santa Claus does not exist,
(2) Father Xmas does not exist.

And suppose that, intending them to be literal claims about the world, you utter the sentences:

(3) Dr. Jekyll does not exist,
(4) Mr. Hyde does not exist.

Intuitively, I suggest, it is reasonable to suppose that all these utterances are true. Moreover, there is intuitively a sense in which I said the same thing when I made both of my utterances, and in which you said the same thing when you made both of your utterances, but in which what I said was different from what you said. More precisely there is a sense in which both of my utterances were about the same thing (Santa), in which both of your utterances were about the same thing (Dr. Jekyll), and in which my utterances were about something different from your utterances.

Unfortunately it is not immediately obvious how we might account for these two phenomenon. For, of course, there is no Santa Claus and there is no Dr. Jekyll, and so it seems as if there was nothing that you or I were talking about. In the first place, this raises the problem of explaining how you and I can have spoken truly if we were not talking about anything. Whatever it is that underwrites the true of our utterances, it certainly cannot be the fact that the object we were talking about satisfies the properties or conditions we ascribed to it. In the second place it is not easy to explain how, in uttering (1) and (2), I was able to talk about the same thing, and how, in uttering (3) and (4), you were able to talk about the same thing, while you and I were talking about different things, given that in reality neither of us were talking about anything.

The importance of these problems should not be underestimated. For one thing, any adequate account of of Natural Language needs either to provide an explanation of the sense in which utterances of (1) and (2) are true and are about the same thing, or at the very least explain away our intuitions to this effect. An account which fails to provide an adequate account of these phenomena will have failed to account for a very important aspect of our use and understanding of language. One should not suppose that because many empty names such as "Austin Powers" occur in light-hearted works of fiction a serious theory of language need not concern itself with them. On the contrary, at least arguably, most of the occurrences of names in English are occurrences of empty names.[22]

Furthermore, the way in which we account for the sense in which utterances of (1) and (2) make true claims about the same thing will have

---

[22] This seems at least true for printed occurrences of names. Most printed material is fiction. And most of the names which occur in such material are empty.

a considerable bearing upon the way we understand the nature of myth and fiction, and the way in which we understand our engagement with fictional works. Suppose, for example, one believed that the only possible way in which we could explain the sense in which (1) and (2) make true claims about the same thing is by supposing that they both refer to some common object. Then one would be lead to postulate some form of Meinongian, or abstract, objects as the referents of "Santa Claus" and "Father Xmas," and of "Dr. Jekyll" and "Mr. Hyde." And it would then be natural to take fictional works to describe various realms of these objects. This issue is not merely of importance within the metaphysics of fiction. A number of philosophers have recently suggested that certain ontologically problematic areas of discourse, such as mathematical discourse and discourse about modality, might be understood as fictional discourse.[23] What precisely this suggestion amounts to, and whether it would really result in a deflation of our ontology, will, of course, depend upon how we ultimately understand fiction. If fictional discourse is ultimately to be understood as making reference to Meinongian or abstract objects, the suggestion that these ontologically problematic areas of discourse be understood as fictional discourse is unlikely to defuse their ontologically problematic status.

Consequently, the questions of how we should account for the truth of utterances of (1)–(4), and how we should account for the sense in which certain empty names are about the same thing, have wider philosophical repercussions than it might at first appear. It is with these questions that we will be concerned below.

3.3 Referentialism and empty names

In this paper I am going to assume that the sorts of arguments offered by Kripke, Donnellan, and others, against Fregean accounts of proper names are correct.[24] That is to say, I shall assume that the semantic contribution of a proper name is not a Fregean sense, or a description, or a mode of presentation, or anything like that. I shall not argue for this point here.

These arguments are usually not merely taken to establish the falsity of Fregeanism. Rather they are generally taken as establishing, or at least as suggesting, a positive view of the semantics of proper names. They are usually taken as establishing the view commonly called *Referentialism*, which can loosely be stated as the view that the sole semantic function of

---

[23] See for example Field (Field 1980), (Field 1989b), Balaguer (Balaguer 1998), and Rosen (Rosen 1990).

[24] See for example Kripke (Kripke 1980), Donnellan (Donnellan 1972) and (Donnellan 1974), and Salmon (Salmon 1981).

a name is to refer to its bearer. So understood, however, Referentialism faces a particularly acute problem when it comes to empty names. For since such names lack bearers, it is not clear that the Referentialist can ascribe *any* semantic function to them. They cannot refer to their bearers because they have none. And so it is unclear how the Referentialist might explain the truth of (1)–(4), let alone the fact that utterances of "Santa" and "Father Xmas" are in some sense about the same thing. At least *prime facie* these two problems, the problem of accounting for the truth of (1)–(4), and the problem of explaining how utterances of "Santa" and "Father Xmas" can be about the same thing, pose serious difficulties for the Referentialist.

Some have been lead by these difficulties to postulate Meinongian or abstract objects as the referents of empty names.[25] Others have been lead to deny our intuitions that utterances containing empty names genuinely have truth values or are genuinely about things.[26] And yet others have taken the problems generated by empty names to provide a refutation of Referentialism.[27] Now I do not want to argue against such views here. But I do want to suggest that none of these options are particularly happy. They are all somewhat drastic positions of last resort. And they should be avoided if it is at all possible. Fortunately I think that the Referentialist may avoid them.

I think that a better response to these worries can be given. Let us take the two problems discerned above in turn. We will begin by considering how the Referentialist might account for the truth of utterances of (1)–(4). Then in the next three sections we will consider how she might account for the fact that (1) and (2) are, in some sense, about the same thing.

With respect to the first problem, I suggest we should hold that empty names make a form of *degenerate* semantic contribution to the sentences in which they occur in virtue of their referring to nothing. For consider again utterances of (1)–(4). It is reasonable to suppose that these are true *in virtue* of the fact that the names which they contain fail to refer to anything. For it is *precisely* the fact that empty names *fail* to refer that makes negative existential claims containing them true. To

---

[25] See for example Zalta (Zalta 1983) and (Zalta 1988). For further accounts which take empty names to refer to Meinongian or abstract objects see Parsons (Parsons 1974) and (Parsons 1980), van Inwagen (van Inwagen 1977) and (van Inwagen 1983), and Thomasson (Thomasson 1996).

[26] See for example Adams and Stecker (Adams and Stecker 1994) and Taylor (Taylor 2000). Braun (Braun 1993) allows that such claims can have truth values but denies that we can take utterances of "Santa" and "Father Xmas" to be about the same thing.

[27] See for example Devitt (Devitt 1989).

make the same point in a different way, the reason why such negative existential claims are true is because empty names fail to make the normal sort of semantic contribution which full names make. In this way, then, it looks as if empty names can sometimes make some sort of semantic contribution to the utterances containing them in virtue of their failing to make a normal sort of semantic contribution. At least it seems reasonable to suppose that the occurrences of empty names in negative existential utterances, such as utterances of (1)–(4), can make semantic contributions to those utterances in virtue of their failing to refer to anything.

Let me briefly indicate how this idea might be fleshed out. The semantic contribution of a name N might be modeled as the singleton of its referent (if any).[28] For example, if N refers to n then we can model its semantic value as $\{n\}$. If N is empty then we can model its semantic contribution as φ. And so on. Let us for the moment treat "exists" as a first-level predicate.[29] Its semantic value can then be modeled as a function $\chi_\exists$ from sets to truth values which maps the empty set to *FALSE*, singletons to *TRUE*, and is otherwise undefined.[30]

---

[28] The view suggested in Braun (Braun 1993) has some affinities with the view developed above but Braun develops his account rather differently. In particular Braun's view cannot accommodate the fact that utterances (1) and (2) samesay while utterances of (1) and (4) do not.

[29] Here I follow Evans (Evans 1982), chapter 10, and Salmon (Salmon 1987).

[30] I have been concerned with the question of whether we can allow that we can take empty names to make some sort of *degenerate* semantic contribution to certain sorts of *non-fictional* utterances in which they occur, such as utterances of the negative existential claims (1)–(4). However, of course, a question arises concerning precisely *which* utterances containing non-fictional occurrences of empty names we should take to have truth values. For example, the empty name "Santa" occurs in sentences which have a straightforward subject-predicate or relational form, such as the sentence "Santa is happy" and the sentence "Santa is more jolly that Hyde." And while it is plausible to suppose that negative existential claims containing empty names, such as (1)–(4) are true, it is much less clear that we should assign truth values to non-fictional utterances of "Santa is happy" and "Santa is more jolly that Hyde." Understood as literal claims about the world, rather than as claims made in the context of a game of make-believe, it is plausible to suppose that such claims should be regarded as truth valueless. This is no bar to our maintaining that the occurrences of empty names in such claims make degenerate semantic contributions to them. But it *is* to note that such degenerate semantic contributions may not suffice to bestow truth values upon these claims. My point is simply that, in so far as we *do* count non-fictional utterances containing empty names as having truth values, the Referentialist can accept this fact. For the Referentialist is not forced to deny that empty names make any semantic contribution to the claims in which they occur. In some cases this will suffice to establish a determinate truth value for the claim. But in other cases it may not. Obviously it is important to investigate which sorts of non-fictional claims involving empty names have truth values, and why. But I shall not pursue this matter further here.

Unfortunately, of course, this does not help with the second problem which we discerned above. For it does not help us explain the sense in which utterances of "Santa" and "Father Xmas" are about the same thing while utterances of "Dr. Jekyll" are about something else altogether. We need a separate account of this phenomenon. Here is what seems to me to be a reasonable first stab at analyzing what it is for two utterances of proper names to be about the same thing. Put crudely, two utterances of proper names count as being about the same thing just in case they *share a common source*. Obviously, as it stands, the notion of *sharing a common source* is rather vague and imprecise, but I will attempt to clarify and elaborate it below. For the moment note that the common source shared by utterances of co-referential full names will be their common referent. And in virtue of sharing this source such utterances count as being about the same thing in a *thick* sense. It is more complex to say what it is for utterances of empty names to share a common source, to say what it is for two utterances of empty names to be about the same thing in the *thin* sense that utterances of "Santa" and "Father Xmas" are about the same thing. But, as I said, in what follows I will offer a more precise account of this. In order to do this we must first consider how proper names get introduced into our language and how their reference is fixed. This will be the task of the following two sections.

3.4   Notions of objects

For the moment I will assume that something along the lines of the causal-historical picture of reference for proper names is correct. I shall flesh out and expand this sort of account along the sorts of lines which have been suggested by John Perry in a number of places.[31] To this end I want to tell a short story concerning how a name gets introduced into our language and used thereafter. Obviously this story will have to be rather incomplete and brief. But I trust that it will serve to provide a useful model of how this happens in reality.

Our story begins with a rudimentary picture of the human mind, a picture which draws upon some of John Perry's and Mark Crimmins' work in this area.[32] On this picture the mind can be viewed as containing notions of objects and of properties which can be put together in various ways to form thoughts about those objects and properties.[33] These

---

[31] See for example the later papers in Perry (Perry 1993).

[32] See Crimmins (Crimmins 1992), Perry (Perry 1990) and (Perry 2000), and Perry and Crimmins (Crimmins and Perry 1989).

[33] I take thoughts to be structured particulars. Thoughts stand in various logical and causal relationships to other thoughts. And in virtue of their standing in these

notions might be understood as concrete particulars: as expressions of mentalese, or connectionist structures within the brain, or something such. Or they might be understood as something more abstract, as properties or features of the mind. I want to remain neutral here as to their precise nature. For the moment I want to concentrate upon notions of objects. Let us call these notions *o-notions*. Each o-notion is a notion of a particular entity and will have associated with it a store, or a file, of information or misinformation about the object of which it is a notion. We can have more than one o-notion of the same object. However typically each o-notion will only be about a single object.[34]

There are at least three important ways in which we can form new o-notions. We can form new o-notions when we perceive objects.[35] We can formulate descriptions and introduce new o-notions to be about whatever satisfies these descriptions at the time of introduction. Or we can hear or read a name or another referential expression and introduce a new o-notion to be about whatever this referential expression refers to. Associated with a new o-notion will be the (mis)information about the corresponding object which we gain from our perception, from our stipulative description, or from what we have just been told or read.

Let us bring these ideas out by considering an example. Suppose I see Stacie to my immediate left and form an o-notion which is about her. Let us say that I form a *Stacie-notion*. This Stacie-notion will be associated with a file containing the information which comes from my perception of Stacie. It will, for example, contain the information that its object is female, that she is human, that she consequently has or is likely to have many of the properties which humans normally have. As well as this general information about the nature of the object that I am perceiving, the new Stacie-notion will contain information locating her with respect to me. It will contain, for example, the information that she is currently to my immediate left, that I am currently perceiving her, and so on.

Of course, not all our perceptions are veridical. For example, we

---

relations they will interact with other thoughts in various ways and stimulate various forms of behavior. Thoughts may be entertained in various modes (belief, desire, etc.) where each such mode will correspond to a distinct sort of role that thought might play in our mental economies.

[34] I say "typically" because we shall that there are, perhaps, cases where an o-notion can be taken to be about several objects which the thinker fails to distinguish. For the moment let us simply assume that each o-notion is about only one object.

[35] The question of how a perception comes to have the content which it does is, of course, vexed. I shall not, however, attempt to address this question here. Rather, for the purposes of this paper I would merely note that, *somehow* or other, our perceptions are intentional. They are perceptions *of* things.

might perceive there to be an object present when in fact there really is none, as when we hallucinate or when we are fooled by a trick of the light. In such a case, on the basis of our misperception, we will form an *empty* or a *non-referring* o-notion which is not about anything. This notion, though empty, may nevertheless be associated with a file of (mis)information gained from perception which we mistakenly take to apply to the referent of the notion. For example, suppose that I hallucinate that there is a little green man sitting in front of me. Then I will form an empty o-notion on the basis of this misperception, an o-notion which is 'about' the little green man. And the file associated with this o-notion will contain various pieces of (mis)information about that notion's supposed referent. For example it might contain the (mis)information that he is little, green, and male.

Likewise, even if there really is an object which we are perceiving, we might misperceive its qualities and nature, perceiving it as being different from the way it really is. I might, for example, think I am seeing a little green man coming towards me and form an o-notion on the basis of my perception, although in fact I am seeing a large stationary oxidized copper statue. In this case I will form an o-notion of the copper statue but this o-notion will be associated with the misinformation that its referent is a little, green, and male. Thus, in general, an o-notion formed on the basis of misperception will be associated with any misinformation we gain on the basis of that misperception.

Note that in all these cases the referent of my new perceptually formed o-notion will be the object, if any, which I perceived. It will be the object, if any, that was the direct causal source for our new notion and consequently was the source of the new perceptually based (mis)information which the file associated with the new notion contains. It will *not* be whatever object satisfies most of the (mis)information in the file associated with my new notion. The referents of our o-notions are not determined descriptively as being those objects which satisfy the information associated with the o-notion. Thus, even if the world did contain a little green man, he would not be the referent of the empty o-notion which I formed on the basis of my hallucinatory misperception. Nor would he be the referent of the o-notion which I formed on the basis of my misperceiving the oxidized copper statue. The former notion would still be empty. And the latter o-notion would still refer to the statue which I misperceived. In neither case would the referent be an unperceived object which happened to fit the misinformation acquired from my misperception.[36]

---

[36] The fact that the referent of a perceptually introduced o-notion is not determined

This sort of *directly referential* quality holds true, not merely of o-notions which are introduced as the result of perception, but for all o-notions, even those which are introduced by reference-fixing description. For example, suppose I begin by formulating a description such as "the person just around the corner" or "the inventor of the zip." I may then introduce o-notions to refer to whatever object, if any, actually satisfies the associated description at the time at which the o-notion is introduced. But, though the referents of these o-notions are initially fixed by definite descriptions, these o-notions are to be thought of as behaving analogously to proper names which are introduced by reference fixing descriptions. Once their reference is secured they will continue to refer to that same object even if it no longer satisfies the original description.[37] Once the referent of the o-notion has been initially secured, it is not required that its referent subsequently satisfy the body of information associated with the notion. Note that not all notion-introducing descriptions need denote. We may simply be mistaken about the denotational status of the description we employ, believing it to denote an object when in fact it does not. In such cases an o-notion, albeit an *empty* o-notion, will still be introduced. And this notion will remain empty even if some object should *subsequently* come to satisfy the associated information.

The final manner in which o-notions may be introduced is this. Suppose we encounter a name or a demonstrative in discourse, either reading it or hearing it somewhere. We might then introduce an o-notion to correspond to the referent of that name or demonstrative. This o-notion will depend for its reference upon the mechanism which secures reference for the name or demonstrative, and it will not depend upon the referent satisfying the information which is associated with the notion. Thus, for example, I might overhear a conversation in which people use

---

descriptively is particularly important. For not only is it quite possible for much of the (mis)information associated with a notion to be wrong, but, even if it is correct, very often the information associated with a notion may be insufficient to pick out a unique object. For example, Emma's notion of Cicero gained from her elementary Latin class might only be associated with the information that he was a Roman called "Cicero," a description which is insufficient to distinguish between the more famous Cicero who wrote philosophy denounced Catiline and was murdered by his enemies, his cousin who was one of Caesar's commanders in Gaul, and any number of other family members. Nevertheless in such a case Emma's notion would still refer to the famous Cicero (we can suppose) in virtue of that gentleman being the original source of that notion and the information associated with it.

[37] It is an interesting question whether any description whatsoever may be used to introduce an o-notion or to fix the reference of a proper name. I know of no compelling reason for denying that any description may be used to fix the reference of a proper name, though I cannot argue for this here. In a similar way I allow that any description may be used to introduce an o-notion.

the name "Louis." I might then form an o-notion corresponding to that name. This o-notion will refer to whatever the name "Louis" was used by the conversers to refer to, irrespective of whether the information in the file associated with this new o-notion singles out that object. Of course it might turn out that the relevant name or demonstrative fails to refer. In this case the newly introduced notion will also fail to refer.

I have sketched three important ways in which new notions may be introduced into a cognizer's mental economy. At this point I want to make two general observations concerning such notion-introductions.

3.4.1 O-notions and make-believe

My first point is as follows. Although I shall not argue for this here, I shall follow Walton and others in taking us to engage in games of make believe whenever we make up, or engage with, stories, myths, and fictions.[38] So far we have considered cases where an o-notion is introduced in the course of our normal interactions with the world. However we may also introduce o-notions in the context of a game of make-believe. So at this point I want say a little concerning precisely what I take make-believe to consist in and how we might introduce new o-notions in the course of it. Obviously I can only offer a very simple sketch of this phenomenon here. Nevertheless I take this sketch to be essentially correct and to provide a useful way of understanding our practices of make-believe.

Engaging in a game of make-believe involves our entertaining and manipulating thoughts in ways that are analogous to the ways we normally entertain and manipulate them.[39] The intrinsic nature of the thought itself will remain the same whether we entertain it normally or employ it in a game of make believe. However a thought which is employed in a game of make-believe differs from a thought which is not so employed in the *precise role* which it plays in our mental economies and in the behavior which it generates. For example, normally, the thought that a monster is approaching will, if the cognizer believes it, stimulate the cognizer to run away. But if this thought is made-believed rather than believed, it will not generate this response. Thus we may regard a game of make-belief as a context in which certain thoughts are hooked up to

---

[38] See for example Walton (Walton 1990) and Currie (Currie 1990).

[39] Recall that I take thoughts to be structured particulars. Thoughts stand in various logical and causal relationships to other thoughts. And in virtue of their standing in these relations they will interact with other thoughts in various ways and stimulate various forms of behavior. Thoughts may be entertained in various modes (belief, desire, etc.) where each such mode will correspond to a distinct sort of role that thought might play in our mental economies. In all these respects a thought which is being normally entertained does not essentially differ from a thought which is being entertained in the course of a game of make-believe.

our mental economies and our behavior in a different way from normal. If a thought is employed in this game of make-believe it will no longer stand in the all its usual sorts of causal relations to other thoughts and to bodily behavior.[40]

Now just as we may introduce new notions in the normal course of things, so we may introduce new notions when engaging in make-believe. While engaging in make-believe I might perceive a certain object and introduce a notion which is, in the course of my game of make believe, to refer to whatever I make-believe the object which I perceived to be. For example, I might be engaged in a game of make-believe while watching a play. I see a new actor walk on stage and introduce a new notion on the basis of that perception. This new notion will not refer to the actor. Rather, within the context of my game of make-believe, it will refer to whatever character the actor is playing. And outside of the context of my game it will refer to nothing at all, it will be an empty notion.

Again, I might engage in a game of make-believe in which I pretend that there is a sun-god. I introduce a new notion for this deity by means of the descriptive condition "the deity corresponding to the sun." This new notion will, within the context of my game of make believe, refer to the sun-god. Outside of that context, however, it will be empty. It will refer to nothing.

Finally, suppose that you are telling me a story. We both make-believe that what you are telling me is true. I might hear you utter a name and introduce a new notion to refer to whatever you referred to. Suppose you are referring to something which only exists within the story you are telling me. Then my new notion will refer to that thing within the context of our game of make-believe and will refer to nothing outside of that context. If, however, your name-utterance *does* refer to something outside the context of our make-believe then my new notion will refer to that thing.[41]

---

[40]This is not to deny that, depending upon the details of the game, it may still stand in *some* of these relationships. For example, suppose I engage in make-believe when watching an exciting film. In such circumstances my heart might beat faster, just as it would if my make-beliefs were real beliefs. Note moreover, that entertaining a thought during a game of make-believe may also lead that thought give rise to *new* patterns of bodily behavior. I might engage in a game of make-believe in which I make believe that trees are evil aliens. The thought that there is a tree in front of me may then lead me to behave in ways it would not normally, I might run away and hide.

[41]It is important to realize that your name-utterance *might* genuinely refer to something *outside* the scope of the make-believe. It should certainly not be thought that all notions involved in our practice of make-believe need be new empty notions introduced in the course of our engaging in that make-believe. On the contrary we will often *import* pre-existing notions, indeed pre-existing non-empty notions, into

Thus, both in the course of our normal activities and while engaging in games of make-believe, new o-notions may be introduced by perception, description, and on the basis of our encountering name-utterances. Notions which we introduce during a game of make-believe on the basis of perception or description will refer to something within the context of that make-believe. But they will refer to nothing outside that context. Outside of that context they will be empty. Notions introduced during a game of make-believe on the basis of our encountering a name-utterance will refer to whatever that name-utterance refers to.

3.4.2   Mediated notion-introduction

The second point which I want to make is this. When we introduce a new notion our introduction will often be *mediated* by some item or description through which we initially gained access to the referent of our new notion. This is most obvious in cases where a notion is introduced on the basis of a reference-fixing description. Suppose that I introduce a new notion descriptively. Here, the description which I employ to fix my notion's referent, the set of properties and conditions which I invoke, will occupy an intermediate position between the new notion and its referent. For it is *through* this description that I initially pick out the object to which the new notion will subsequently refer. Note that this phenomenon holds both for full names which are introduced on the basis of a reference-fixing description, and for empty names which are introduced on the basis of such a description. Suppose that I introduce a notion and attempt to fix its referent on the basis of the misdescription

---

our game of make believe. These notions will be about whatever it is that they are normally about, whatever it is that they are about outside the context of the game. And such games will involve our making-believe various things about the real-world referents of these imported notions. Some of the information with which these notions are usually associated may be employed in the game. Such importation is an important mechanism whereby fictional works are able to talk about real things, and whereby information about the real world and items therein may be brought into play in our engagement with fiction. For example, when we read a Sherlock Holmes novel we import our London-notion. This is why we take Holmes stories to be talking about London. It is how we are able to bring any knowledge we might have of London, in particular Victorian London, to bear upon the Holmes stories. And it allows us sometimes to learn things about the real Victorian London on the basis of what the Holmes stories say and the information we consequently come to associate with our London-notion when we are engaged in a game of Holmes-make-believe. For example, I may learn geographical facts about London from the Holmes stories, associating that information with my London-notion while engaging in the pretense that the Holmes stories are true, but then retaining the information when I retrieve my London-notion from this pretense and use it to think about London outside my game of Holmes-make-believe. This sort of process is no doubt very complex but I shall not discuss its details here.

"the round square." Here, even though my new notion does not refer to anything, the description "the round square" will still serve to mediate the introduction of my new notion. For it is through being associated with this reference-fixing description that my round-square-notion is introduced, even though it is this association which ultimately determines that my new notion *fails* to refer to anything.

We have been considering one sort of case where the connection between notions and he world is *mediated* by an intermediate description. However this sort of phenomenon may hold true, not merely of notions which are introduced purely on the basis of a reference-fixing descriptions, but also of notions introduced on the basis of perception. Consider, for example, the following scenario in which a new notion is perceptually introduced. Suppose that I hear the door closing and, recognizing that the door is being closed by a person, I form a new notion which is to refer to that person. In this case the event which I directly perceive, the closing of the door, and the description "the person who just shut that door" will serve as an intermediate complex through which reference to the person closing the door is initially secured. What I directly hear is the event of the door closing. But when I hear the door closing I introduce a notion to refer, not to the event of the door's closing, but rather to the person who stands in the given relation to that event. In this way the event of the door's closing and the description "the person who just shut that door" *mediate* the introduction of my new notion. Once again, this sort of phenomenon may also hold true for empty notions introduced on the basis of perception. Perhaps, to modify the example just given, the wind blows the door shut and so the notion I introduce does not refer to anything. This does not prevent the event of the door's closing, and the description "the person who just shut that door," from mediating the introduction of my new empty notion. For I attempted to employ them to secure the reference of my new notion. It was on their basis that I introduced my new notion.

I would point out that this sort of mediation may occur not only in normal cases of notion-introduction, but also in cases where I introduce a notion in the course of a game of make-believe. For example, if I make-believe that there is a sun-god, introducing a new notion on the basis of the description "the deity corresponding to the sun" then the introduction of this notion will be mediated by that description. Again, suppose I make-believe that trees are people and introduce a new person-notion on the basis of seeing a tree. The introduction of my new notion will be mediated by the tree I perceive together with some description such as "the person corresponding to that tree." Thus, mediated notion-introduction can occur both in normal contexts and within contexts of make-belief.

Now I do not mean to claim that we are always explicitly aware of the precise nature, or even the existence, of such mediating elements. I may introduce a notion to refer to a door-shutter without my explicitly formulating the description "the person who just shut that door." Nevertheless, I suggest, in cases where we introduce notions on the basis of some mediating element we *do* have at least some sort of tacit awareness of that element. The mediating element can, with sufficient reflection, be brought to mind. I shall not at the moment attempt to explore the psychological details of how we may use such intermediate descriptions and complexes to secure reference to other entities. I shall simply assume that, somehow or other, such mediation occurs.

3.5 Referential frameworks

I suggested above how new o-notions might be generated when we encounter an unfamiliar name and subsequently introduce a new o-notion to be about whatever that name refers to. However the interrelations between o-notions and names are more complex than this. On the one hand, while engaging in discourse we might encounter a name which we already associate with an o-notion **N**. In this case we might well take the name to refer to whatever that notion **N** is about, and we will augment our relevant file of information with the information we glean from the discourse.[42]

On the other hand we might also use a name to express thoughts which involve one of our notions. It may already be that there is a name which is associated with the notion in question, just as the name "Stacie" is associated with my Stacie-notion. If I wish to express thoughts which involve my Stacie-notion, if I wish to express thoughts about Stacie, I will tend to use this name. Other people will associate this name with their Stacie-notions and form thoughts about Stacie, involving those notions, on the basis of hearing my utterance.

However I might also choose to coin a new name to express a notion, in which case this new name will gain its reference from that notion. It will refer to whatever that notion does. Let us suppose that I introduce the name "S" to express my Stacie-notion. When other people hear my new name they will form notions (let's call them "S-notions") which are to be about its referent. They will in turn associate the name "S"

---

[42] Whether we do indeed take the name to refer to whatever **N** is about will, of course, be complex matter in which we assess the context to determine how likely it is that the utterance is about that object. If we deem it unlikely that our interlocutor is talking about the referent of the o-notion we associate with **N** then we will simply take them to be using **N** to talk about some other object.

with these S-notions and they will use the name "S" to express thoughts involving them. Yet further people will hear these utterances and form S-notions on their basis, they will use the name "S" to express these S-notions, and so on. This whole process will continue with more and more people developing S-notions and using the name "S" to express them. And after a while the use of the name "S" to express S-notions will become well entrenched within our linguistic community. The reference of all these S-notions and utterances of "S" used to express them will be determined by the reference of my original Stacie-notion.

In this way, a complex framework of name utterances, mental notions, and notion-introducing perceptions or acts of description is built up. This framework allows people who never encounter Stacie to form notions of her when they encounter utterances of her name, notions whose reference is fixed by the proceeding framework of name utterances and notions. And it allows them to use the name "S" to express their S-notions, again securing reference to the original Stacie via the pre-existing framework of name utterances and notions. They may even introduce a new name to express their S-notions and pass this new name on to others. Let us call this apparatus of mental notions, linguistic utterances, and notion-introducing acts, a *referential framework*.

Thus each name we use will be associated with a complex referential framework stretching back to a *base* at which a base-notion was introduced through an act of perception or description. In cases where these base-notions have a referent the associated referential framework will have that object as its *referential source*. And the name-utterances which occur within the referential framework will refer to that object. In cases where the base-notions lack a referent, being introduced by misperception or misdescription, the framework will not have a referential source. And the name-utterances which occur within the framework will not refer to anything but will be empty. Consequently what, if anything, the referent of a name-utterance is will be determined by the referential framework within which that name-utterance occurs. Note that referential frameworks may grow up in this way, not merely for notions which are introduced normally, but also for notions introduced in the course of a game of make-believe.

Let us illustrate these ideas by considering some examples. Suppose that I see Stacie and form a notion of her upon this basis. I introduce the name "S" to express thoughts involving my new notion and a referential framework arises for this name in the usual manner. Then Stacie is the *referential source* of this framework. My new notion of Stacie lies at the *base* of the framework. And the utterances of "S" which occur as parts of this referential framework will refer to Stacie in virtue of their being part of a referential framework with Stacie as its referential source. This situation is illustrated in figure 1.

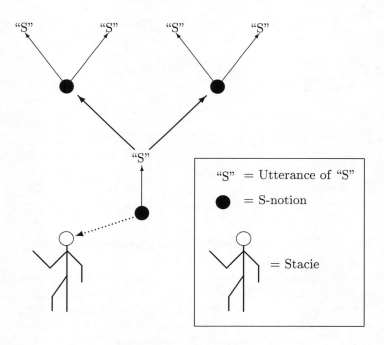

Figure 1: The Referential Framework for "S"

Suppose now that I introduce an o-notion on the basis of misperception. Suppose that I hallucinate that there is a little green man standing before me, form a notion on that basis, and introduce the name "Fred" to express thoughts involving that notion. Finally suppose that a referential framework then grows up for the name "Fred" in the usual way. In this case the referential framework will have my perceptually based notion at its base. However, since that notion is empty, it will not have a referential source. And the utterances of "Fred" which occur as parts of this referential framework will refer to nothing in virtue of their being part of a referential framework which has no referential source. This situation is illustrated in figure 2.

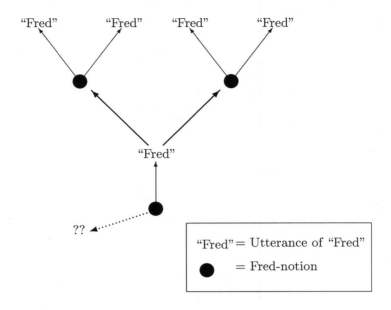

Figure 2: The Referential Framework for "Fred"

In my discussion of notion-introduction above I noted that in many cases the introduction of a notion will be *mediated*. The introduction might be mediated by a set of descriptive conditions which the referent of the introduced notion is taken to satisfy. Or it might be mediated by some object or event which is directly perceived taken together with some description which relates the referent of the new notion to the object of the perception. Let us say that a referential framework which arises from the mediated introduction of a notion has its *reference-fixing source* in the mediators which give rise to that framework. In this way the referential frameworks associated with certain names may have as their reference-fixing sources various reference-fixing descriptions, perceived objects, and so on, items which mediate the introduction of the base notions of those frameworks.

This holds true for both full and empty names. Suppose, for example, that I introduce an empty notion to correspond to the referent of the misdescription "the round square" and subsequently coin the name "P" to express that notion so that a referential framework develops for utterances of the name "P." Since the description "the round square" fails to pick out an object this resulting referential framework will not have a referential source. It will, however, have as its *reference-fixing source* the description "the round square." Again, suppose that I hear the wind blowing the door shut and mistakenly suppose there is some person who shut the door, introducing a notion and name to refer to that person. The referential framework associated with utterances of this new name will not have a referential source. But nevertheless it will have as its *reference-fixing source* the event of the door's shutting and the description "the person who just shut that door."

3.5.1 Three ways to share sources

Now observe that two quite separate referential frameworks might share the same *referential source*. Suppose for example that there were two tribes which lived on different sides of a big mountain but which never met or interacted in any way. Indeed suppose that one of the tribes died out before the other tribe even arrived on the scene. Finally let us suppose that one tribe used the name "Q" to refer to the mountain, while the other tribe used the name "R." Clearly the referential frameworks associated with the names "Q" and "R" are completely disjoint. Nevertheless, given that the two frameworks latch onto the same mountain, they will share their *referential source*.

Likewise, note that two quite separate frameworks might share a common *reference-fixing source*. Suppose that our two tribes both take the mountain to be a god, and they both introduce notions to refer to this deity on the basis of the mediating description "the deity corresponding to this mountain." They go on to introduce the names "S" and "T" to express thoughts involving those notions, and referential frameworks develop for those names in the standard way. The names "S" and "T" will be empty, they will not have any object as their referential source. Moreover, the referential framework associated with utterances of "S" will be completely distinct from that associated with utterances of "T." Nevertheless both frameworks will share a *reference-fixing source*. The big mountain, and the description "the deity corresponding to this mountain," will serve as the reference-fixing source of both frameworks.

Finally, observe that a referential framework might grow up for a name and then grow two branches, each associated with a different name. Consider the following case. The Romans used the names "Cicero" and "Tully" interchangably to express the same thoughts. And a single referential framework for both names grew up with the famous Roman orator as its *referential source*. However, let us suppose, at some time Person-R was talking to Person-S employing both the names "Cicero" and "Tully" in her conversation. Person-S, not recognizing that the two names were supposed to refer to the same individual and were used by Person-R to express the same thoughts, introduced two different notions corresponding to the two different names. She formed a Cicero-notion on the basis of her hearing Person-R's utterances of "Cicero." And she formed a separate Tully-notion on the basis of her hearing Person-R's utterances of "Tully." Person-S then used the name "Cicero" to express thoughts involving her Cicero-notion, and the name "Tully" to express thoughts involving her Tully-notion. In turn others heard her utterances of "Cicero" and formed Cicero-notions, and heard her utterances of "Tully" and formed Tully-notions, without ever recognizing that Cicero was Tully. In this way over time the single referential framework which was initially associated with the names "Cicero" and "Tully" developed two branches, one associated with the name "Cicero" and the other with the name "Tully." These branches stretched back to Person-R and merge in her Cicero-Tully-notion. For it was at the point of her conversation with Person-S that the initial common referential framework for "Cicero" and "Tully" split into two, with a different branch corresponding to each name. Let us say that two branches of a referential framework which share an initial segment share a *framework source*.

Let us recap. Each use of a name will be associated with a referential framework of name utterances, notions, and notion-introducing perceptions, or descriptions. The notion-introducing acts of perception or description, together with the notions they introduce, lie at the *base* of the framework. The *referential source* of the framework will be whatever, if anything, the base notions refer to. In cases where the base notions are not introduced directly but are rather introduced via some mediating description (etc.) these mediating items will form the *reference-fixing source* of the framework. And in cases where two branches of a referential framework share a common initial segment they will share a common *framework source*. Now of course, as I said earlier, this picture is of necessity rather simplistic. It is only a sketch of what is no doubt in reality a terribly complex phenomenon. Nevertheless it does, I think, provide a good model of how names get introduced into a language and how they function subsequently. We are now in a position to provide an account of what it is for two utterances of proper names to be thinly about the same thing.

3.6   Thick aboutness and thin aboutness

I suggested above, you will recall, that two utterances of proper names which are about the same thing have a common source. We can now offer the following more precisely characterization:

Thick aboutness: Two utterances of proper names μ and ν are about the same thing in a *thick* sense just in case the referential framework which includes μ and the referential framework which includes ν share a common *referential source*.

Thin aboutness: Two utterances of proper names μ and ν are about the same thing in a *thin* sense just in case (1) they are not about the same thing in a thick sense (2) the referential framework which includes μ and the referential framework which includes ν share a common *reference-fixing source* or a common *framework source*.

Let us consider some simple examples to illustrate the basic idea. Suppose that two people, Person-A and Person-B, both hear the wind blow my door shut and they both assume that the door was in fact closed by a person. On the basis of this they each introduce an empty notion which they take to refer to that person. And they each introduce a different name with which to express these notions. Person-A introduces the name "Peter" and Person-B introduces the name "Brian." Person-A talks to her friends about the person who closed the door, using the name "Peter" when she attempts to do this. After a while her friends start to use the name "Peter" themselves. They make such claims as "Person-A is still puzzled by Peter's disappearance" and "Peter doesn't really exist, Person-A probably just made a mistake." In this way a referential framework will develop for the name "Peter" amongst the linguistic subcommunity who use that name, a framework leading back to the point at which Person-A introduced her empty notion.

Likewise we can imagine that Person-B also talks to her friends about the person who closed my door, using the name "Brian" when she attempts to do this. After a while her friends start to use the name "Brian" themselves. They make such claims as "Person-B is still puzzled by Brian's disappearance" and "Brain doesn't really exist, Person-B probably just made a mistake." In this way a referential framework will develop for the name "Brain" amongst the linguistic subcommunity who use that name, a framework leading back to the point at which Person-B introduced her empty notion.

In these circumstances it would be reasonable, I suggest, to take Person-A and her friends to be, in some sense, talking about the same thing as Person-B and her friends. It would be reasonable to take utterances of "Peter" to be thinly about the same thing as utterances of "Brian," even though neither name referred to anything. Of course the referential frameworks associated with utterances of the two names "Peter" and "Brian" would not share a referential source. Nevertheless these two referential frameworks would both share the same *reference-fixing source*. For the same event and description would mediate their introduction. The reference-fixing source of both frameworks would be the event of the door's closing and in the description "the person who just shut that door." So the referential framework containing utterances of "Peter" would share its reference-fixing source with the referential framework containing utterances of "Brian." It is our implicit recognition of this fact, I suggest, that explains why we take Person-A's utterances of "Peter" and Person-B's utterances of "Brian" to be thinly about the same thing.

Next, consider "Dr. Jekyll" and "Mr. Hyde." When writing his famous book Stevenson engaged in a game of make-believe in which he made-believe that the story he was writing was true. Let us suppose that, in the course of this game he introduced a new notion on the basis of various descriptions, a notion which would come to serve as his Jekyll-Hyde-notion. That is to say, he made up various stories and descriptions and he introduced his Jekyll-Hyde-notion to be about a person who, he made-believe, satisfied those stories and descriptions. And he employed this single Jekyll-Hyde-notion when he was subsequently engaging in the Jekyll-and-Hyde game of make-believe.

Now of course Stevenson wrote the story of Jekyll and Hyde into a book, told the story to friends, and so on, only revealing the identity of Jekyll and Hyde at the very end. Nevertheless the utterances of "Jekyll" and of "Hyde" which Stevenson made in order to tell his story all served to express thoughts and make-beliefs involving the same Jekyll-Hyde-notion. The sentences he wrote using the name "Jekyll" served to express thoughts and make-beliefs in which he employed his Jekyll-Hyde-notion.

Suppose that I start to read Stevenson's story. I engage in a a game of Jekyll-Hyde make-believe but I do not realize that Jekyll is Hyde. I form two separate notions, a Hyde-notion formed upon my encountering tokens of "Hyde" and a Jekyll-notion formed upon my encountering tokens of "Jekyll." And I use distinct names to express these distinct notions, using the name "Hyde" to express my Hyde-notion and the name "Jekyll" to express my Jekyll notion. Nevertheless, the referential frameworks containing my utterances of "Jekyll" and "Hyde" will share a common reference-fixing source in the descriptions and stories on the basis of which Stevenson introduced his Jekyll-Hyde-notion. Moreover, if we follow these frameworks back towards their origin we will find that they merge in Stevenson's Jekyll-Hyde-notion and so share a common (albeit short) initial segment. Consequently the referential frameworks containing my utterances of "Jekyll" and "Hyde" will share *both* a common reference-fixing source, *and* a common framework source. It is our implicit recognition of this, I suggest, that explains why we take utterances of "Jekyll" and "Hyde" to be thinly about the same thing.

Finally consider utterances of the names "Santa" and "Father Xmas." Now I shall not suggest an account of what the reference-fixing source, if any, of these name-utterances might be. I don't want to delve too deeply into the precise origins of the Santa myth at the moment. For not only are such details both obscure and complex, they are also besides the point. The crucial point is simply this. Eventually, through various no doubt complex, processes, our ancestors came to have Santa-notions. They employed these Santa-notions in various games of make-believe and they associated various descriptions and stories with them. They expressed thoughts involving these notions using an Ur-name which was the ancestor of our names "Santa" and "Father Xmas." And a referential framework grew up for this Ur-name in the usual way. Eventually, at some point, the names "Santa" and "Father Xmas" came to be associated with this framework. However at this point that framework came to split into two branches, with speakers of British English using the name "Father Xmas" to express thoughts involving their Santa-notions, and speakers of American English using the name "Santa" to express thoughts involving *their* Santa-notions.

Now both these branches grew out of a *shared initial segment* of referential framework. If we were to follow the referential frameworks associated with our utterances of "Santa" and "Father Xmas" back towards their origin we would find that they *merge*. Consequently it does not matter *what* the reference-fixing source of the referential framework associated with utterances of "Santa" might be. The fact that this framework shares an initial segment with the framework associated with utterances of "Father Xmas" *guarantees* that both frameworks share a common framework source. And it is our implicit grasp of *this* fact, I suggest, which underwrites our sense that utterances of "Santa" and "Father Xmas" share a common source.

3.7   Concluding remarks

I began this paper by discerning two problems generated by empty names, problems which seemed particularly pressing for a Referentialist. The first of these was the problem of accounting for the truth value of certain claims, such as negative existential claims, which involve empty names. And the second was the problem of explicating the thin sense in which utterances of "Santa" and "Father Xmas" seem to be about the same thing. In the course of the paper I have attempted to answer both these difficulties. I suggested that the Referentialist might view empty names as making some form of *degenerate* semantic contribution to the utterances which contain them. I then offered an account of what it is for two utterances of proper names to be about the same thing in a thin sense. I suggested that in order for two utterances to be thinly about the same thing, the two utterances needed to share a common source. And I sketched an account of what this might amount to. Obviously there remains a great deal more to be said about the sorts of issues which I have been considering. Nevertheless I have tried to sketch the outline of, what seems to me to be, the correct account of this.

4

On Myth

Avrom Faderman

I'm going to talk about what I'll call mythical names empty names that weren't introduced (or turned into empty names) by a deliberate choice to use the name as empty. There are probably a fair number of names like this: "Bigfoot," "Scylla," and the names children or the insane attach to imagined companions. These names pose several problems not posed by fictional names, including the problem I'm going to discuss here, which is a problem for baptismal pictures of reference.

According to baptismal pictures of reference, the descriptions associated with a name (unless such descriptions are explicitly used to introduce the name) are irrelevant to determining the name's referent. Rather, a name refers to the object it does because that object (to borrow a term from Kripke) was baptized with that name; that is, the name or its linguistic ancestor was originally used to refer to that object. As the name is passed down a cultural chain of transmission, its reference goes with it, so that no matter what descriptions we currently associate with a name, the name continues to refer to whatever it originally referred to. There are some usually pretty vaguely specified restrictions on the cultural chain, so that not all cultural chains will preserve reference, but this much is important to a baptismal picture: The picture cannot simply reduce to a form of descriptivism, and any way of specifying restrictions on the cultural chain that make it essentially a form of descriptivism are inadmissible.

The baptismal picture famously has problems with names that change their referents over the course of their history. Kripke himself suggested the first problem cases: He notes, for example, that "Santa Claus" is supposedly a perversion (the linguistic heir) of "St. Nicholas," who was a real historical figure, not a fictional character who delivers toys (See

Empty Names, Fiction, and the Puzzles of Non-Existence.
Anthony Everett and Thomas Hofweber (eds.).
Copyright © 2000, CSLI Publications.

Kripke, (Kripke 1980), p. 93).

Kripke has a simple reply to these cases. It's important, he says (p. 96), that the cultural chain down which the name is passed satisfy the following condition: all receivers of the name must intend to use it with the same reference as their teachers. He points out that if he hears the name "Napoleon" and decides to bestow it on his pet aardvark, he is not referring to the French general when he calls his aardvark—this is by virtue of not satisfying this condition. Similarly, if someone decides to loosely base a fanciful fictional story (like the stories about Santa Claus) on a real-life figure (like St. Nicholas), they do not satisfy the condition and so can be the cause of a reference shift. That one link in the cultural chain is "bad," and the term refers to different things before and after it.

There is a class of reference shifts that is substantially harder for the baptismal picture to accommodate: The class of shifts where someone in the causal chain is mistaken about what their predecessor is talking about. The most famous example of these sorts of shifts is Evans' "Madagascar" story, and it goes like this: "Madagascar," claims Evans, originally referred to a portion of the mainland of Africa. But explorers in the employ of Marco Polo misunderstood the Africans who taught them the term, and applied the name to the great island off the African coast—which is its referent today. The referent of "Madagascar" is not its baptismal source.[43]

Certain sorts of fictionalizations can occur this way as well. The explorers might well have thought that the Africans were telling them a fanciful story, that Madagascar was a purely fictional entity, and it's quite plausible that, if they had and their usage had caught on, "Madagascar" would have been a fictional name today. Note that despite the fact that this reference shift depended on a mistake, it is a fictionalization and not a mythologization: "Madagascar" became empty because some people decided to use it as empty, although they didn't know they were the first to make this decision.

Kripke's aforementioned reply doesn't deal with either of these examples. Nobody in Evans' story intended to make a break with the Africans' usage. Moreover, it might seem at first that no account that makes reference to a single bad link that shifts reference could be the right one since presumably, in both Evans' story and mine, the referent of "Madagascar" shifted gradually. Three days after the explorers made their mistake, "Madagascar" still referred to a portion of the African mainland they were just using it incorrectly. It took quite a while for

---

[43] See Evans (Evans 1973).

the standard referent of the term to actually shift.

But Kripke has a more complex reply to Evans, which he explains in a footnote in later editions of Naming and Necessity. The social character of language, he says, "dictates ordinarily that a speaker intend to use a name the same way as it was transmitted to him; but in the "Madagascar" case this social character dictates that the present intention to refer to an island overrides the distant link to native usage" (Kripke (Kripke 1980), p. 163).

This passage needs some explication. For one thing, the social character of language (even in non-ordinary cases) clearly doesn't dictate that I should follow my own intentions instead of those of the people who transmitted a name to me. What it presumably dictates is that, given that current members of my society (including those who transmitted a name to me) use a name to refer to an island (or to nothing real), I should use it the same way, however it was used hundreds of years ago. I should intend to refer to those objects people around me intend to refer to.

This makes use of a distinction Kripke made in Kripke (Kripke 1977) (p. 17) between "speaker's reference"—what a specific speaker intends to refer to with a use of a term—and "semantic reference"—the official referent of a term in a language and the normative requirements on speaker's reference. The baptismal picture, one might suppose, is only a picture of semantic reference, one that makes essential use of our concept of speaker's reference. This concept is one as of yet not given a solid theoretical grounding—Kripke says it is the "object which the speaker wishes to talk about," but this itself requires an account, and until it is given such an account, the baptismal picture will remain only a picture, and so essentially immune to counterexamples.

The extended picture, then, goes like this. The semantic referent of a name or natural kind term starts out as the term's baptismal object. It stays as such unless and until a fair number of people use the term refer to something else (that is, until enough people use the term who satisfy the conditions of whatever theory we come up with for speaker's-referring to something else). If this occurs, it becomes the case that people should use the term to refer to the new entity (the "social character" of language dictates they must do this if they wish to communicate); that is, the semantic referent of the term drifts over to whatever this something else is.

It is important to realize that this reduces the baptismal component of the "baptismal picture" to at best a description of an epiphenomenon. What's really going on is simply that the semantic reference of a term is whatever most people in the immediate community use it to refer to. Of course, the baptizer (by definition) uses the term to refer to the baptismal source, and so initially, "most" (in fact all) of the community use it to refer to the baptismal source. So of course, initially the term refers semantically to its baptismal source—but this is just a consequence of the more general account, and is subject to change as soon as the community's practices change.

Allowing for this unfortunate consequence, however, this response seems to work against Evans' and my aforementioned modified case. Something happened (the miscommunication) that made Marco Polo's sailors speaker's-refer to the island. At first, this wasn't sufficient to shift semantic reference, since the large majority still used the term differently. But as the sailors' practice spread, the normative requirement to use the term to talk about the island gradually grew and the requirement to use it to talk about the section of the mainland gradually lessened.

Fictionalization of the sudden and deliberate sort (like "Santa Claus") is easy for the baptismal picture to accommodate. Gradual and accidental fictionalization (like my modified "Madagascar" example) is considerably harder, but it's quite possible that it can be done in a way consistent with the general point of the baptismal picture. What of mythologization?

I'm now going to tell a story about the origin of the name "Bigfoot." I don't believe this story is true although there are plausibly true stories about the origins of several mythical kind terms that fall along just these lines (see my (Faderman 1997)); I'm simply considering it as a thought experiment, an epistemic possibility (albeit a remote one), a device to test our intuitions about what would happen if it were true.

Let us imagine that, some time in the late 19th century, a retired prospector named Elwood Fritchey lived in a cabin high in the Sierra Nevada mountains. Elwood was a big man (about seven feet tall, and broadly built), with big feet (size 18 1/2), who had a predilection for bearskin coats. He also had one of the most abominable singing voices ever to go west.

One day, we are imagining, a drunken late 19th-century hiker was wandering along a high Sierra trail when he saw, off in the distance, the silhouette of Elwood, wearing his bearskin coat, big feet resplendent in the late-afternoon sun. And coming from the monstrous silhouette was the most horrible series of roars and howls the hiker had ever heard. He ran (the hiker, not Elwood, who was oblivious to all but the sunset and his song) as fast as his legs could carry him, and he didn't stop running until he had reached town.

Once there, he told a mixture of awed and skeptical townspeople about "Bigfoot," his name for the large-footed creature he had seen.

And this term passed down through the culture to us today and so did the legend that surrounded it, although the latter got gradually embellished over time, which is why those who believe in Bigfoot nowadays generally believe it to be about ten feet tall, with two-foot long feet, and a member of an almost extinct species called "sasquatch" that some Native American tribes had stories about.

Now, Elwood was the baptismal origin of the name "Bigfoot." So according to the simplest version of the baptismal picture for names, the one with no caveats, it seems that we should say that Bigfoot existed, and was in fact Elwood Fritchey. It is, according to the baptismal picture, an epistemic possibility that Bigfoot was an ordinary (if eccentric) human being, who made a small fortune during the gold rush (and was, perhaps, Levi Strauss' first big and tall customer) before retiring to a peaceful mountain life. This discovery would disappoint Bigfoot enthusiasts, as it would turn out that Bigfoot was not really nearly as exciting an individual as they had thought. But it would still be the discovery that Bigfoot really existed.

Now that's just not right. This discovery about the origins of the term "Bigfoot" would not be tantamount to a discovery that Bigfoot really existed. It would rather be a discovery that, while Bigfoot doesn't exist (and never did), there was an individual who was the baptismal source of our term "Bigfoot" and the cause of our "Bigfoot" legends.

What about the extended baptismal picture, the one that worked not only for "Santa Claus" but for "Madagascar?" Can it work against this case too? Not, I shall argue, unless it is allowed to import descriptivism at another level, reducing the picture to really just a novel form of descriptivism (violating the one restriction on restrictions on the cultural chain). The reason is that our example involves gradual shifts of reference in a way very different from Evans'. In Evans' example, the semantic reference of "Madagascar" shifted gradually, but the various referential intents of speakers using the term were always quite discrete. All the Africans used the term to refer to the mainland; all the Europeans used it to refer to the island. The gradual change in the term's semantic reference was caused by the gradual spread of the European usage. Because the shift in speaker's reference between individuals happened at a distinct place in the cultural chain of transmission and surrounding an unusual event (the miscommunication), it seems plausible that a causal or otherwise non-descriptivist account of speaker's reference—one that involved some feature of the event other than the differences in identifying descriptions between the individuals involved—might explain it.

The gradual change in the referent of "Bigfoot," however, was not of this character. It was not that a small population started to use it to refer fictionally and their usage gradually became more popular (this would have been the case if the term was fictional and not mythical, or if the myth had started with a single serious misunderstanding); on the contrary, there was presumably an extended period (when the stories had undergone considerable embellishment, but not to the phenomenal extent they have by now) during which there was no clear answer to what anyone in the culture was referring to with "Bigfoot."

This shift in reference did not happen as a new usage spread gradually, but rather as old usage changed gradually—and it changed as the stories about "Bigfoot" became more and more wildly fanciful. While the Kripkean reduction of semantic reference to speaker's reference might be correct, it seems that a descriptivist account of speaker's reference can best explain the shift in reference of "Bigfoot."

In fact, however Kripke's picture is expanded to accommodate this example, it seems that descriptivist considerations are going to end up being relevant—more relevant, given our notes about the epiphenomenal nature of baptism above, than any aspects of the picture already in place. The relevant causes of the reference shift in the "Bigfoot" case—from Elwood to nothing real—simply seem to be the increasing remoteness of our beliefs about "Bigfoot" (where and when, for example, the original sighting took place) that are true of Elwood and the increasing prominence of our beliefs about "Bigfoot" (its being a sasquatch, for instance) that are true of nothing real.

Kripke could of course allow this, and truthfully claim it was a way of filling out the picture he presented. That's one of the advantages of presenting a picture rather than a theory. But if he does so, his picture will no longer be a "better picture" (as he claims on p. 94) than the descriptivist one—since it will turn into essentially the same picture.

Myth is a well-known problem in the study of empty names, particularly about the study of their content it makes difficulties (though perhaps not fatal ones) for both pretense and different-logic approaches. I hope to have shown here that it can make special difficulties for some theories of reference as well.

Part II

Pretense

5

Existence as Metaphor?

Kendall Walton

A person who asserts:

> Deposed government officials are sent to Siberia and written out of history; they no longer exist.

or

> She has a life; she really exists.

or

> You know what I've come to think, Jake? I think you don't exist at all. There is too many of you ... you're different all the way through, every time. You cancel yourself out... You're nothing... [44]

is likely to be using the predicate "exist(s)" metaphorically. I will *not* be talking about statements like these. I shall be concerned, instead, with garden variety singular existential statements such as:

> Neptune (the planet) exists.

and

> Sir John Falstaff does not exist.

uttered in ordinary garden variety contexts in which they are understood to be (probably true) characterizations of the real world. It would seem bizarre to suggest that *these* are metaphors. Statements "about fiction" such as

> Falstaff is a buffoon.

and

---

[44] See Barth (Barth 1967), page 67.

Empty Names, Fiction, and the Puzzles of Non-Existence.
Anthony Everett and Thomas Hofweber (eds.).
Copyright © 2000, CSLI Publications.

> Narnia is inhabited by rabbits, dogs, and unicorns.

may seem, if not metaphorical, at least less (more?) than literal in some manner. The same can be said of existential statements such as:

> Godot is only a figment of Vladimir's and Estragon's imaginations; he doesn't exist.

understood as a (possibly true) statement about the world of Beckett's *Waiting for Godot*. But how could it even occur to anyone to imagine that ordinary occurrences of "Falstaff does not exist" and "Neptune exists" are metaphorical?

I will argue for the astonishing thesis that indeed they are *not* metaphorical—anyway, my conclusion will be *more or less* this. I hope there will be some interest in the *more or less*, and in my reasons for raising the question in the first place, and for not being entirely confident about the answer.

Here is how the question occurred to me. A few years ago I found myself thinking about metaphor in terms of what I called *prop oriented* make-believe. Prop oriented make-believe was central to my earlier account of existential claims, although I didn't call it that then.[45] This raised the question of what connection there might be between metaphor and ordinary existential statements. More recently, Fred Kroon has argued that some close relatives of ordinary claims of nonexistence are metaphorical.[46]

5.1 Overview of the make-believe approach

I begin by sketching, with blinding speed, the outlines of my make-believe theory and its treatment of existential statements—the best I can do in twenty five words or less, give or take a few.[47] My tempo will be just slow enough to bore readers who are familiar with my views, I am afraid, but sprightly enough to mystify those who aren't. (I wish I could believe in the existence of the *average* reader. It would be nice if there were *someone* who will be neither bored nor mystified. But at least I can pretend.)

The central idea of the make-believe approach is, of course, that what seem to be commitments, by speakers or theories, to nonexistent entities

---

[45] See Walton(Walton 1993), pp. 39–59, and (Walton 1990), Part 4.

[46] See Kroon (Kroon 1996). Yablo (Yablo 2000) proposes regarding talk about various philosophically controversial (purported) entities as metaphorical, although he does not focus on existence claims. Crimmins (Crimmins 1998) proposes a pretense account of existence claims.

[47] In this section I sketch some of the main ideas of Chapter 1 of (Walton 1990). The notion of prop oriented make-believe, which I introduce in the following section, is developed more fully in (Walton 1993).

are to be understood in a spirit of pretense or make-believe. They are, *in one sense*, not meant seriously and not to be taken seriously. When, having exposed our parents' lies about Christmas, we go on to "talk about" Santa Claus anyway, and when we "talk about" Sherlock Holmes, the Fountain of Youth, Vulcan, and ether, while accepting that there aren't really any such things, that they don't exist, we are recognizing and utilizing *fictions* to the effect that they do exist, or better, fictions to the effect that in using names and referring expressions like "Santa Claus," "Sherlock Holmes," "the Fountain of Youth," "Vulcan," and "ether," we successfully pick out (existing) objects.

Pretense and make-believe have a reputation for frivolity, like computer games played while taking a break from serious number crunching or word processing (when the boss isn't looking). But the pretense I speak of is serious business, even if it doesn't involve seriously supposing that we actually refer to what we pretend to refer to. We engage in make-believe in order to think and talk about features of the real world—often ones that matter, and sometimes ones that are not easy to think or talk about in any other way.

The main theoretical resources needed for my account are, first, the notion of a kind of mental activity or mental attitude which I call imagining. (Others speak of pretending or making-believe.) This often goes with pretense behavior, *actions* of pretending, as when children flail around with sticks pretending to have a sword fight, imagining that their sticks are swords and their flailing fencing. Secondly, I need the notion of something being "true in a fiction," or "true within a pretense," or "fictional."

These resources are ones that we must have on hand quite apart from a theory of existence and of "nonexistent entities." We need them to understand the nature of stories, pictures, and theatrical performances, our interest in such things and our emotional responses to them—not to mention children's games. I can't imagine trying to make sense of the institution of fiction or games of dolls without giving a prominent place to some kind of imagining or making believe, and to the notion of propositions being *fictional*—"true in a story" or "true in a fiction." So the make-believe account of existential statements gets the main resources it needs pretty much for free.

There are differences of degree to be attended to. And perhaps some extensions, as well as refinements, of ordinary notions of pretending and of fictions are needed. Imaginings can be more or less vivid, conscious, explicit. We can be caught up emotionally in a fiction or pretense or make-believe activity, or we can stand back and observe it coldly, intellectually, "objectively." A fiction or a game of make-believe may be large or small, recurrent or fleeting, it may be engaged in deliberately, or more or less automatically. I count it an advantage of my theory that it allows us to understand thinking and speaking "about things that don't exist," even in contexts remote from obvious works of fiction, as continuous with the understanding and appreciation of ghost stories, historical novels, and games of dolls or mud pies.

What is true in a fiction, or fictional, depends on real world facts. Children may play a game in which bicycles are horses, and a garage is a corral. The real world fact that a bicycle is in the garage makes it fictional, true in the make-believe, that a horse is in the corral. I call the bicycles and the garage *props*. Facts about them *generate* fictional truths. The colors and shapes on the surface of a painting and events occurring on stage in a theatrical production are props which generate fictional truths, thereby establishing the "world of the picture" or the "world of the play."

Participants in the make-believe *imagine* what they recognize to be fictional, they pretend that it is true. They imagine that there are horses in a corral when they see bicycles in the garage. But it is fictional that there are horses in the corral, if bicycles are in the garage, even if no one knows about the bicycles and so no one imagines horses in the corral. What is fictional is something for participants to discover, something they can be ignorant of or mistaken about. The fictionality of a proposition consists in there being a prescription, in a given cultural context, that participants imagine it to be true, whether or not anyone knows about the prescription or actually imagines the proposition. All that is needed, in the context of the game, for the prescription to imagine horses in a corral to be in force, is the presence of bicycles in the garage.

Participants and their actions are often props themselves, generating fictional truths about themselves. The fact that Jennifer is riding a bike makes it fictional that she is riding a horse. This goes for verbal actions as well. If Jennifer says "Giddyup!," or "The cattle rustlers were here last night," she makes it fictional that she is urging her horse on, or saying that cattle rustlers were around the night before.

5.2   Prop oriented make-believe

Make-believe serves different purposes in different situations. Sometimes we are interested primarily in what is fictional, in the *content* of the fictional or make-believe world. On other occasions our interest is primarily in the *props*, or the real world facts that generate the fictional truths. I speak of *content oriented* and *prop oriented* make-believe.[48] Props can be mere tools or vehicles for establishing fictional worlds which we find

---

[48] See Walton (Walton 1993).

exciting or interesting or poignant or moving. But in some cases it is the props themselves that matter. Their role in generating fictional truths in a game of make-believe may help us to understand them, to think and talk about them, even if the fictional world itself is of no interest at all.

Fictions in the arts are often content oriented, and so are children's games of make-believe. We focus on what happens in the world of a story: on whether the hero will arrive in time to rescue the heroine, why Hamlet was so wishy washy, "who done it," etc. Content orientation is especially evident when appreciators are, as we say, caught up emotionally in the fiction. They may hang on a story teller's every word, but only because of what the words reveal about the characters and their fates.

Here is an extreme example of the opposite kind, an example of prop oriented make-believe. A small fiction can help one learn how to tie a bowline. First you make a loop. Then you say to yourself, "The rabbit comes out of the hole, goes under the log, and back into the hole," as you manipulate the rope accordingly. This is hardly a gripping story. I certainly wasn't caught up in it when I was taught how to tie the knot, as a child might be caught up in the story of Peter Rabbit. And my purpose in manipulating the rope was not to make it fictional that a rabbit scampers around in a certain way, as a child pushes a toy truck around on the floor in order to create a fiction in which a truck tries to outrun a pursuing police car, crashes into a barrier, or whatever. I wasn't interested in the fictional scamperings of a rabbit. I just wanted to know how to tie the knot correctly.

Consider this Not Very Tall Tale:

> Once upon a time an organism was infected by a virus. *The End.*

This is no great shakes as a story. But if your computer tells it, i.e. if your computer is such as to make it fictional that it suffers from a viral infection, this says something important about the computer. Describing the computer in this manner—saying that it has a virus—is a simple and efficient way of conceptualizing and communicating what has happened to your computer. (Of course the metaphor works only for people who already know what viruses are.) We don't examine the computer, as we do the words of a story, to discover the fictional events it establishes; we look at what fictional events it establishes in order to understand the state that *it* is in.

Many metaphors involve prop oriented make-believe. "Computer virus" is one. Here are two others:

The sky is a snotty handkerchief.[49]

We add his letter to the large delta of unanswered mail on his desk. [The letter will be there until] it has been gently silted over by about twenty other pleasantly postponed manuscripts.[50]

A bronze or stone equestrian statue generates fictional truths about the shapes of a horse and its rider, hence about the carriage and demeanor of both and possibly their characters or personalities as well. Our interest, typically, is in these fictional truths. We think of a mountain as a sculpture also, when we speak of the shoulder or a saddle of the mountain, and when we see a head or a face in it. This make-believe might be content oriented, but it is likely to be prop oriented. We may want to know about the saddle of the mountain in order to decide how best to cross over to the next valley, and we may have no interest in the fictional saddle for its own sake.

I do not want to leave the impression that make-believe in the arts and in children's games is exclusively or even mainly content oriented, or that the make-believe associated with metaphors is always exclusively or mainly prop oriented. And of course there are combinations of prop- and content-orientation, and intermediate cases. Also, we may have various different kinds of interest in either content or props. A few examples will illustrate some of the complexities:

When the children are playing their bicycle-horse game, Mom might tell Johnny not to ride the fence even if some of his cattle are wandering away, because she doesn't want him to be playing near a busy street. What for the children is probably a largely content oriented make-believe, is for her a prop oriented one. In this case, she could just as easily talk simply about the props, without invoking any make-believe. She could just tell Johnny not to go near the busy street. But given that the game is up and running, she can play along with it as a way saying what she wants to say.

Even the children may, sometimes, be more concerned with the props than the fiction. A child who challenges a friend, "I'll bet my horse is faster than yours," might be interested in nothing more than whether he can beat the friend in a bicycle race. He may not care at all about fictional truths concerning horses.

Representational works of art are often of interest partly for the manner in which they generate fictional truths as much as, or more than, for the fictional truths they generate. Consider Picasso's *Bull*, constructed

---

[49]Marge Piercy, quoted in (Sommer and Weiss 1996), p. 391.

[50]Christopher Morely, quoted in (Sommer and Weiss 1996), p. 2.

from the seat and handlebars of a bicycle. The fictional bull is no big deal, and neither are the bicycle parts. What is interesting is the relation between them, the generating of a surprisingly "convincing" bull by such simple and unexpected means. The bull is noteworthy only for what it is made of, and the bicycle parts only for what they make.[51]

"The sky is a dirty handkerchief" is not just a way of pointing out certain physical features of the atmosphere. It also expresses an attitude about the weather. It does so by virtue of the content of the make-believe, the content of the make-believe in which the condition of the atmosphere is thought of as a prop. This remark is very different from describing the sky as, for instance, a warm bubble bath.

Even if a metaphor is intended to introduce an almost entirely prop oriented make-believe, the content often has a way of sneaking back in. If I describe a particularly brutal ax murderer as an animal or a beast, you might reply that I am being unfair to the animal kingdom, to the likes of Buddy, Checkers, and everyone's Fido. Maybe *what I asserted* was just about the ax murderer. But there was a Gricean implication about animals, due to the metaphor I chose to use in making my point. On the other hand, if I describe the ax murderer as, say, a vicious rabid dog, and you respond that this is unfair to vicious rabid dogs, you may be, not defending the honor and reputation of vicious rabid dogs, but rather emphasizing, even more, the brutality of the ax murderer.

> [Rex Morgan has] all the personal pizazz of decaffeinated jello.[52]

is a metaphor masquerading as a device to describe Rex Morgan, as though he is the focus of interest. But the content of the make-believe steals the show. Probably we don't really care whether Rex Morgan (the cartoon character) really is boring enough to justify the metaphor. The speaker has in effect created his own intriguing little absurdist fiction, disguised as a metaphorical description of Rex.

5.3   Assertion

Acts of verbal participation can be real assertions. In pretending to say one thing, one may actually be saying, asserting, something else. I will make do with a fuzzy, intuitive notion of assertion.[53] All I want to do now is to outline several different patterns that may obtain, on most any reasonable account of assertion, several ways in which what is asserted

---

[51]See my discussion of *ornamental representation* in (Walton 1990), pp. 274–289.

[52]National Public Radio, 3 March, 1995.

[53]What is asserted is one kind of "speaker's meaning." It might be understood in Gricean terms as an instance of what a speaker means by an utterance.

may be related to what is pretended. (I will say nothing about the related issue of whether, when a speaker utters a sentence in pretense, thereby asserting something other than what it literally means, the *sentence* has a special secondary meaning, e.g., a "metaphorical" meaning.)[54]

When the make-believe is content oriented, the assertion is likely to be about the content of the make-believe. The reader of *Gulliver's Travels* who says, in pretense, "There is an island southwest of Sumatra where the horses are 4.5 inches tall" is likely to be asserting that it is fictional in the novel that there is such an island.

When the make-believe is prop oriented the speaker is (naturally enough) likely to be saying something about the prop, not about the fiction or make-believe. Johnny may say to his mom that his horse is in the corral, as a way of telling her that his bicycle is safely stowed in the garage for the night. He is pointing out the real world circumstance which makes it fictional that his horse is in the corral. There is nothing about make-believe or fiction or pretense in the content of the assertion. Make-believe simply explains how the sentence, "My horse is in the corral" can serve as a way of saying that his bicycle is in the garage. To say that a computer has a virus is probably to assert something about the contents of the computer's hard disk, not anything about a fictional virus, or about fiction or pretense at all. A complex feature of the hard disk makes it fictional that the computer has a virus, and in pretending to assert that the computer has a virus, the speaker simply indicates that the hard disk is in this condition.

In many instances of verbal participation, however, the words uttered, taken literally, do not express a proposition, or at least it is arguable that they do not. The speaker cannot be asserting that the proposition expressed by her words taken literally is fictional, nor that the circumstances which make it fictional obtain, if there is no such proposition. I accept the view that, since there is no such thing as Lilliput, "Lilliput is an island southwest of Sumatra" does not express a proposition. I also subscribe to the view that there is no such property as being a unicorn, or a hobbit, or a snark, and hence that "There once was a family of hobbits" fails to express a proposition.

Many metaphorical statements are not just false when taken literally (some of them are true, of course), but are in one way or another incoherent, often committing egregious category mistakes. Some complex predicates with obvious metaphorical uses are composed of bizarre combinations of adjectives or nouns; the predicate as a whole, taken literally, refers to no property that anything could conceivably possess, and

---

[54]See Davidson (Davidson 1984).

perhaps—depending on what we are willing to count as a property—to no property at all. Here are some examples:

> Hateful thoughts enwrap my soul in gloom,
>
> [*Radio voice*] We have a cello concerto on tap, after this announcement,
>
> I warrant they would whip me with their fine wits till I were as crestfallen as a dried pear,[55]
>
> When it comes to public relations, [Kenneth Starr] is a one-man train wreck.[56]

Some metaphorical statements, or anyway some idiomatic expressions, are not even grammatical.

> I won't have any truck with *that*,
>
> He took a shine to her,
>
> She lost her cool.

We also speak of "burning issues," "food for thought," "mountains of debt," "weighty arguments," "chewing someone out," "wrestling with a problem," and being "saddled with responsibility." It is arguable that attributing these predicates to a subject is not to express, literally, a proposition.

A speaker may pretend that her words express a proposition, however, even if they don't, and she may pretend to be asserting a proposition by means of them. Moreover, it may be fictional, true in the pretense, that she asserts something true, even if there is no proposition which, fictionally, she asserts. Whether this is fictional will depend on real world circumstances. It is fictional that one speaks truly when (in discussing Tolkien's *The Hobbit*) one says "Bagins is a hobbit." Fictionally, that sentence expresses a true proposition, although it doesn't actually express a proposition at all. Features of the text of the novel, together with conventions about how to understand them, make this fictional. (I won't try to spell out the details). The novel is such that to say, "Bagins is a hobbit" is, fictionally, to speak truly, and to say "Bagins is a unicorn" is, fictionally, to speak falsely.

What might speakers actually be asserting, when there is no actual proposition that they are pretending to assert? In place of the proposition that one's words (taken literally) express, we have the proposition that in uttering them, in pretending to assert as one does, one is speaking the truth. When the make-believe is content oriented, the speaker typically asserts that to pretend in this manner is fictionally to speak truly.

---

[55] Falstaff in Shakespeare, *Merry Wives of Windsor,* IV, 5.
[56] *New York Times,* editorial, 5 April 1998.

When the make-believe is prop oriented, the speaker typically asserts that certain circumstances obtain—the circumstances that do or would make it fictional that she speaks truly. In saying "Bagins is a hobbit" one is likely to be asserting that to pretend in the way demonstrated is fictionally to speak truly (in official games using *The Hobbit* as a prop). In describing something as "food for thought," one is probably saying that it is interesting, puzzling, and thought provoking, these properties being what makes it fictional that the speaker is expressing a truth.

We must not suppose that it will always or even usually be possible to specify the relevant circumstances without mentioning the make-believe. We may have epistemological access to the facts of which we speak only by means of their role in make-believe, and we may be able to refer to them only via the fictional truths they generate, only as the circumstances that generate such and such fictional truths. Or it may be difficult, at least, to conceptualize the underlying facts or to think about them perspicuously without engaging in or alluding to make-believe. I and others have discussed several kinds of cases in which make-believe is essential or helpful, in one way or another, in our thinking about various kinds of facts.[57] Here is another example:

There is (I assume) no such thing as absolute motion and rest. One object is in motion or at rest relative to another, but neither is in motion *simpliciter*, or stationary *simpliciter*. Our perceptual experiences seem not to accord with these facts, however. We see one object as fixed, and another as in motion. What we see as fixed can change. When my train pulls out of the station I may at first see it (and myself) as stationary and a train on the next track as in motion; I may then switch to seeing the other train as fixed and mine as moving. Neither perspective is correct; neither train is in motion *simpliciter*, or stationary *simpliciter*. The switch in perspective may be induced by the realization, or the perception, that the other train is not moving relative to the earth, while my train is. The earth is not fixed absolutely or in motion absolutely either, however, but only relative to other things (the sun, the solar system.)

We can think of this familiar phenomenon as one of perceiving in accordance with a fiction, with what we know to be a fiction—the fiction that there is such a thing as absolute motion and rest. The perceptual content of one's visual experience, at a particular moment, includes the fiction that one or another particular object is fixed.

It is not impossible to *describe* events without relying on this fiction;

---

[57]See, for example, Walton (Walton 1993), pp. 43–45, Crimmins (Crimmins 1998), pp. 2–8, and Yablo (Yablo 2000). See also Hills (Hills 1997).

we can say that two objects are at rest, or in motion, relative to one another. Speaking this way may be necessary to avoid ambiguity, when different people are thinking of different things as fixed. But descriptions of relative motion are awkward. When ambiguity is not a danger, it is usually easier and more perspicuous to speak and think as though the fiction is true, pretending that some things are really stationary and others really in motion—even if everyone involved knows that this is not so. We recognize a kind of make-believe in which facts about relative motion and rest generate fictional truths about absolute motion and rest. By speaking in terms of this fiction, pretending to be making claims about absolute motion and rest, we actually describe relations of relative motion and rest, i.e. the circumstances that do or would make it fictional that, in pretending as we do, we speak truly.

Perceiving in terms of the fiction seems not to be optional, even if speaking and thinking in terms of it is. Try as I might, I *cannot* perceive things as I think they really are; I cannot see two objects as moving relative to one another without seeing one of them, or a third thing, as fixed absolutely. (I wonder if it would be possible to train myself to do this.) The make-believe seems to be indispensable as far as perception is concerned; only by means of it do I have perceptual access to the actual facts, facts about relative motion and rest. The convenience and perspicuity of descriptions of things in terms of absolute motion and rest is, no doubt, a result of this feature of perception.

It is arguable that notions of absolute motion and rest are not merely mistaken as applied to events in the real world, but that they don't even make sense. It may be best to say that there are no coherent propositions, perhaps no propositions at all, which we pretend to assert when we say, e.g., that a car came to a complete stop at a stop sign. The difference between perceiving my train to be (absolutely) stationary and another one (absolutely) in motion, and perceiving the reverse to be the case, may not amount to perceiving one or another (coherent?) proposition to be true. It does involve perceiving the trains in a way that makes it natural for English speakers to apply the predicates, "moving" and "stationary" differently. (More needs to be said about what this difference amounts to.)

5.4 Establishing and extending fictions; conniving pretense

No elaborate ceremony is needed to initiate or introduce a new game of make-believe, in many cases, even an unfamiliar one. (This is already obvious, given that metaphors, fresh as well as established ones, involve make-believe.) I might just say, "I bet my horse can run faster than yours," as we are riding our bikes, and you get the idea. If I refer to a person who happens to be an elevator operator as an "indoor aviator," it may be obvious, without my spelling it out, that I am introducing a make-believe practice in which to operate an elevator is, fictionally, to pilot an aircraft. In these and many other instances, the game is introduced by making what is in the context easily construed as a "move" in it, by participating verbally. I pretend to say something about horses, for example, thereby launching a fiction in which bicycles count as horses.

Once a game is begun, there are usually natural ways of extending it, ones that do not have to be explained or made explicit. The make-believe introduced by remarking that "we are all in the same boat" is naturally extended by the suggestion that, since we are all in the same boat, it behooves us to row in the same direction.

Engagement in make-believe tends to be infectious. One speaker may extend another's metaphor, continuing the pretense begun by the first. A storyteller pretending to report on a house break-in by three bears may inspire his listeners to inquire, in pretense, whether the bears meant any harm, or to observe that they didn't. A listener may, in pretense, report to a third person that three bears did break into a house, the residence of a certain Goldilox and her family. What I called work worlds thus spawn larger game worlds in which the work is a prop, and in which appreciators participate.[58]

Stories and other representational works of art are designed to initiate games of make-believe of certain kinds, to introduce pretense with which appreciators play along (implicitly if not explicitly). But sometimes we take liberties, combining or extending or altering fictions in ways that contravene the established or official limits of the original. Many such "unofficial" games (as I call them) are intuitively natural, however, and recognizing them may serve our purposes, purposes which go beyond simply appreciating the work. Manguel and Guadalupi's *The Dictionary of Imaginary Places* is a travel guide describing, in alphabetical order, exotic places like Brobdingnag, Middle-earth, Shangri-la, Oz, and Ruritania, places which share the property of being "imaginary," the blurb on the back cover tells us, and also the property of having been invented by writers like Jonathan Swift, J. R. R. Tolkien, Edgar Allen Poe, L. Frank Baum, and Edgar Rice Burroughs. We can say that Brobdingang is larger than the Blessed Island. Brobdingang (from *Gulliver's Travels*) is a 6000 mile long peninsula on the coast of California north of Monterey, while the Blessed Island (from Lucian of Samosata, *True*

---

[58] See Walton (Walton 1990).

History, 2nd c. A.D.), an island in the Atlantic Ocean whose bodiless inhabitants wear purple spider webs, is a mere 500 miles long. This is a nice example of an "unofficial" game of make-believe—unofficial, that is, with respect to *Gulliver's Travels* and *True History*. It is made official by *The Dictionary of Imaginary Places*.

The make-believe in this case is likely to be prop oriented (with respect to the unofficial game one is participating in). Saying that Brobdingang is larger than the Blessed Island is likely to be a way of pointing out the circumstances that make it fictional in the unofficial game that one speaks truly, namely the fact that there is a size such that it is fictional in *Gulliver's Travels* that Brobdingang is larger than it, and fictional in Samosata's *True History* that the Blessed Island is smaller. The content of the utterance concerns these other fictional worlds, though not the world of the unofficial game the speaker is participating in.[59]

Sometimes we "play along with" discourse or activities that are not themselves pretense. We pretend to be "serious" in a way others really are. And in so pretending we may be reporting on their "serious" discourse or activity. In discussing the findings of the court at the Salem witch trials I might say, "Martha Carrier is a witch," pretending to believe and to assert what the court decided was true. One might declare that the planet Vulcan has such and such mass, as a way of specifying the content of the Vulcan hypothesis.

Quoting someone directly can be understood as pretending to speak in a certain way in order to show how the quoted person spoke—most obviously when there is sarcasm or mimicry in the quoting person's tone of voice. An example from Herb Clark and Richard Gerrig:

> So her mother said "[whinny voice] No, you can't go out before you make your bed."[60]

Moments of pretense often creep into indirect quotation and other predominantly third person descriptions of other people. One might say,

> John is absolutely determined to get to the summit of the mountain, by golly. Life won't be worth living if he doesn't.

In using the words, "by golly," the speaker pretends to express determination, thereby indicating John's determination to achieve the summit. The speaker probably is not saying that her own life won't be worth

---

[59] See my discussion of "Robinson Crusoe was more resourceful that Gulliver," "Napoleon was more pompous that Caesar," and "Sherlock Holmes is more famous than any other detective," in Walton (Walton 1990), p. 406 and pp. 413–414.

[60] See (Clark and Gerrig 1990), p. 776. Apparently this is not an actual case, Clark and Gerrig say, but it is "characteristic of ones we have heard from children six to ten years old" (p. 775). See also Clark and Gerrig (Clark and Gerrig 1984).

living if John doesn't finish the climb; she is again pretending to express what she takes John to feel, what he does or might "seriously" express. The speaker connives with, plays along with, what she takes to be John's attitudes and the ways he might "seriously" express his attitudes.[61]

5.5   Existential statements

To say that Neptune or Falstaff exists, I have suggested, is to say that attempts to refer of a certain kind are successful. (Let's call these "Neptunian" or "Falstafian" referring attempts.) To say that Neptune or Falstaff doesn't exist is to say that such referring attempts do not succeed. This sounds strange. We seem to be talking about *Neptune* and *Falstaff*, not about kinds of attempted reference (notwithstanding the fact that there is no Falstaff to talk about). After all, the sentences we use consist in the name, "Neptune" or "Falstaff," with a predicate attached. The impression that Falstaff and Neptune are what we speak of is explained by the fact that we are pretending that this is so—or rather, we pretend to refer successfully by means of the names and to attribute properties to the referents.

In pretending to refer by means of the names, the speaker displays, shows, demonstrates, the kind of attempted reference she is talking about. (In the case of "Neptune exists" this is not *mere* pretense; the speaker actually makes an attempt of the kind she is talking about. Her attempt succeeds if what she says is true.)[62] In attaching the predicate, "exists" or "does not exist," she declares the kind of attempted reference indicated by the use of the name to be successful or unsuccessful; she *avows* or *disavows* attempts to refer of that kind. We can think of the existential claims like this. To say "Neptune exists" is to say:

Neptune: That was successful.

To say "Falstaff doesn't exist" is to say:

Falstaff: That didn't work.

In both cases the demonstrative "that" refers to the kind of attempted reference illustrated by the utterance of the name.

Other predicates besides "exists" and "does not exist" can serve the purposes of avowal and disavowal. "Is real" and "is actual" are used to attribute success to referring attempts. Predicates that may be used to say that referring attempts fail include: "is fictitious," "is a (merely)

---

[61] This is an instance of what some literary scholars call "free indirect discourse." See Walton (Walton 1990), p. 375 ff., especially pp. 379–380.

[62] I say more about how producing or indicating an instance of a kind serves to specify the kind in (Walton 1990), pp. 425–427.

fictional character," "is a mythical beast," "is feigned," "is counterfeit," "is a phantom (limb)," "is a (mere) toy," "is stuffed," "is a product of an overactive imagination," "is a trick of light" (Evans), "is an artifact of the experimental setup" or ". . . an artifact of the researchers' biases," "is a cultural artifact," "is a failed posit," "was invented by Walt Disney," and "is an empty concept." Some of these predicates have other uses as well. Some actual things are toys; to call a child's top or a Barbie doll a toy is simply to point out that it belongs to this category. But to say that *Barbie* is a (mere) toy (or "only a doll"), may be to say that a certain kind of referring attempt (attempts to refer to a *person*) fail. Walt Disney did invent some things, certain animation techniques, for instance, and one can point out that a certain technique was invented by him. Committees, governments, and laws are cultural artifacts, and can be described as such.[63] But to say that *Donald Duck* was "invented by Walt Disney" or that he "is a cultural artifact" is probably to say that there is no such thing, i.e. that Donald Duck-ish referring attempts fail. If Donald Duck is anything he is a *duck* (a talking duck); not an invention or a cultural artifact. Some concepts may be "empty;" the *concept* of Donald Duck (if there is such a thing) is one of them. But *Donald Duck* himself is not a concept.

In pretending to refer by means of a name such as "Falstaff" or "Santa Claus" or "Oedipus," speakers play along with, connive with, the pretense of the relevant fiction or myth. To attach the predicate, "does not exist," or "is a fictional character," or "is a mythical beast," is to continue the pretense further, pretending to attribute a property to the thing supposedly referred to, even while one actually declares the reference unsuccessful. This is a little bit like mom playing along with the bicycle game, pretending to advise Johnny not to ride the fence, while actually bringing him back to reality, warning about the dangerous traffic.

So it is part of the implied, unofficial fiction that some things exist and some things do not—rather, that "exist(s)" expresses a property which some things possess and others lack. Also, the fiction has it that, among "nonexistent" things, some are "mythical," others are "imaginary," "fictional," etc. and that some bears are made of flesh and blood, others are stuffed, and still others are painted or sculpted or "drawn with a very fine camel-hair brush." In *El Idioma de John Wilkins*, Jorge Luis Borges makes something like this unofficial game official. It is said that

---

[63]Whether there are such things as techniques, committees, governments, laws, concepts, etc., is not at issue here. I write as though there are, confident that in doing so I am saying something understandable, whether or not it is something about such entities. See Yablo (Yablo 2000).

"according to a certain Chinese encyclopedia" animals are divided into the following categories: (a) belonging to the Emperor, (b) embalmed, (c) tame, (d) sucking pigs, (e) sirens, (f) fabulous, (g) stray dogs, (h) included in the present classification, (i) frenzied, (j) innumerable, (k) drawn with a very fine camel-hair brush, (l) etcetera, (m) having just broken the water pitcher, (n) that from a long way off look like flies.[64] Ernst Gombrich can be understood to be recognizing a similar unofficial game when he speaks of a snowman as "a member of the species man, subspecies snowman," and when he suggests that "the museum turns images into art by establishing [a] new category, a new principle of classification that creates a different mental set. Take any object from a museum, say Riccio's Box in the Shape of a Crab. ... On the desk ... this object would belong to the species crab, subspecies bronze crab."[65]

It is fictional that one speaks truly when one says, "N is mythical," if (roughly) N-ish attempts to refer go back to a myth. This is the real world circumstance that makes this fictional. It is fictional that I speak truly in saying "Pooh is a stuffed bear" if the indicated referring attempts go back to a stuffed toy. It is fictional that I speak truly in saying "N doesn't exist" if N-ish attempts to refer fail, for whatever reason.

5.6   Comparisons with metaphor

Existence claims are like many metaphorical statements in that the speaker asserts what she does by engaging in pretense. She pretends to make an assertion of a particular kind, thereby actually asserting something of a different kind. She actually asserts that certain real world circumstances obtain, viz. those that would make it fictional in the implied make-believe that she speaks truly.

As in the case of some metaphors, there is no proposition which one pretends to assert, in making an existence claim. When I say "Neptune exists" or "Falstaff doesn't exist," I pretend to assert a proposition having the property of existence (as well as Neptune or Falstaff) as a constituent. But there is no such property, I claimed in (Walton 1990), and hence no such proposition. There is, however, the proposition that in speaking as I do I speak the truth. *This* proposition is fictional if Neptunian referring attempts succeed and Falstaffian ones fail, i.e. if it is fictional that "Neptune" (as used by the speaker on that occasion) refers to something which possesses a property denoted by "exists," and "Falstaff" refers to something which lacks it. What I actually assert is that Neptunian referring attempts do succeed, or that Falstaffian ones

---

[64] *Obras Completas*, p. 708. Thanks to David Hills.
[65] See Gombrich (Gombrich 1961), p. 100 and p. 114.

fail.

Metaphorical uses of language are usually or always guided—sometimes in mysterious ways, sometimes in obvious ones—by the literal meanings of the words used.[66] It is because we know and understand the literal meaning of "being infected by a virus" that we are able to use and understand the metaphorical description of a computer as infected by a virus. There is a semantic connection between the content of the speaker's pretended assertion and what, in so pretending, she actually asserts. This is so even when the content of what the speaker pretends to say consists in something less than a proposition. If there is no such property as being saddled with responsibility, and no proposition which I pretend to assert when I describe someone as saddled with responsibility, I am nevertheless pretending to assert a proposition having the property of being saddled and also the property of responsibility as constituents; I pretend that there is such a proposition and pretend to be asserting it. I pretend to be indicating a manner in which the person is saddled, and to be describing a relation that she bears to responsibility. It is by recognizing this pretense that hearers understand what I am actually asserting.

Is anything like this true in the case of existence claims? Does "exist(s)" have a "literal" meaning which guides its use in characterizing referring attempts? One's first reaction is likely to be this: the literal meaning of "exist(s)" just is its possessing the function of characterizing attempts to refer. Could there be *another* literal meaning that guides this one? There could be, but I doubt that there is.

Fred Kroon has argued that, since I deny that there are genuine properties which phrases like "is a (merely) fictional character," "is a failed posit," and "is a mythical beast," fictionally stand for, I cannot make sense of "the connection between what a sentence says in the scope of the pretense and what speakers assert when uttering the sentence," I cannot, he thinks, explain how we succeed in ascribing properties to attempted acts of reference through only pretending to ascribe properties to the referents of "Falstaff" and "Santa Claus."[67] He offers a useful example (which I modify in order to avoid possible confusions) to illustrate his worry.

Consider a game, inspired by Lewis Carroll's poem about the Jabberwock, involving an assortment of toy animals. Let's say that, as in the poem, it is fictional that some animals are "toves" and that others are "sneetches," i.e. it is fictional in the game that each of these words

---

[66]See, for example, Goodman (Goodman 1968) and Hills (Hills 1997).

[67]See Kroon (Kroon 1996), pp. 179–180.

picks out a property that some animals possess. But, as in the poem, there are no actual properties which, fictionally, they pick out. Suppose we adopt the arbitrary convention that animal figures made of wood represent "toves," and that figures made of plastic represent "sneetches." Now we know that Smokey is correctly called a "tove," in the fiction, if Smokey is represented by a wooden figure; in that case to say "Smokey is a tove" is, fictionally, to speak truly. There still is no property which the speaker is pretending to attribute in saying this, however; we merely pretend that there is one.

According to Kroon (I paraphrase his conclusion to accommodate my modification of his example), "the following ought to be clear: if we ... say 'Smokey is a tove' there is no sense—at any rate, no interesting sense—in which we thereby declare that a particular toy is made of wood." I answer that this could very well be what the speaker is asserting. (It is too much to ask that the sense in which this is true be an *interesting* one; a mundane sense will do.) Suppose the game is employed in a prop oriented manner. The plastic animal figures are suspected of being poisonous and must be removed from the nursery. I tell you that Smokey is a tove, meaning that the figure in question is made of wood and can safely remain. There doesn't *have* to be a semantic connection between what a speaker pretends to assert and what she actually asserts by engaging in the pretense. In this case there is no content at all to the speaker's pretended assertion. The speaker exploits a stipulated rule of make-believe governing the *words* used.

Singular existential statements may be something like this. There may simply be a brute convention to the effect that to attach the predicate "exists" or "does not exist" to a subject is to declare the indicated kind of referring attempt successful or unsuccessful. There does not have to be a property expressed by the predicate, a property one is pretending to attribute, which helps to determine what one actually asserts. A *grammatical form* is being used in a nonstandard way; the speaker is pretending to say something about the (pretended) referent of the subject expression. But we don't have to assume that she is using "exist(s)" or "does not exist" in a nonstandard or alternative or secondary way semantically, that she is pretending to use it with one meaning as a way of actually saying something different. The *only* meaning of the predicate that is involved may be the one consisting in its suitability for characterizing referring attempts as successful or unsuccessful.

What about predicates like "is a (merely) fictional character," "is a failed posit," "is a trick of light," "is a mythical beast?" As Kroon points out, these phrases serve not just to declare that the kind of attempted referrings indicated by the subject expression fail; they say something about how or why they fail. To describe something as mythical is different from describing it as imaginary, or as a failed posit. These predicates are composite, and it is clear that their components ("fictional," "mythical," "posit") have meanings which help to guide the use of the whole, which help to determine what is being said about the kinds of referring attempts the speaker is talking about. It does not follow that the predicate as a whole expresses a property which the speaker is pretending to attribute to something referred to by the subject expression. (We might allow that the predicate as a whole possesses a meaning, without insisting that its meaning consists in its expression of a property.)

Consider idiomatic expressions such as:

I'll fix your wagon,
He chewed her out,
She has a checkered past,
I am not prepared for the lecture; I'll have to wing it,
She made no bones about it,
He went bananas,
She chickened out,
He made a bee line for the refreshments,
She bent over backwards to be fair,
She blew her stack,
He is in the swim of things,
The computer went haywire,
He would have no truck with that proposal,
This behavior is beyond the pale,
She was beside herself with anger,
She stole his thunder.

These are familiar ways of saying things that, otherwise, have little, if any, salient connection with the standard literal meanings of the words used.[68] One would be hard pressed to predict the idiomatic uses of these sentences simply from the literal meanings and the context of utterance. Speakers must simply learn that pretending to assert that someone fixed someone's wagon, or pretending to assert this using these words, is, in English, a way of saying that the first person did the second one in, and that to "make no bones about" something is to be forthright about it. (This may be a reason not to classify such idioms as metaphors.) The literal meanings of the words probably do provide some guidance, however, in at least some of these cases. Knowing what "checkered," "chew,"

---

[68] Many of my observations about idioms here are discussed much more thoroughly in (Nunberg et al. 1994), pp. 491–538, and also (Davies 1983).

"wing," "cool," and "thunder," mean in other contexts surely helps one to learn and to remember the idiomatic uses of "checkered past," "chew him out," "wing it," "lose her cool," and "stole his thunder." But this is no reason to assume that the complex predicate as a whole expresses a property when its constituents are understood in the standard literal ways. Some of these predicates do, but others arguably do not. What would it be for a person, *literally*, to have a checkered past, or to wing a lecture, or to lose her cool, or to chew someone out?

That the standard literal meanings of the words in many of these phrases are operative in their idiomatic uses is clear from the fact that we can understand certain transformations of them on first hearing, for example:

> Make only a few bones about it,
>
> I wouldn't touch it with an 11 foot pole,
>
> I'll repair your cart,
>
> He has a wasp in his fedora,
>
> She found her cool,
>
> This gadget boasts a deafening cacophony of bells and whistles,
>
> [Geoffrey] Fieger has this tree-trunk of anger on his shoulder, which resonates among people who feel disenfranchised by the system. [69]

Understanding the above requires recovering the specific words of the relevant familiar idioms. In the last case, one must call to mind the phrase, "a *chip* on his shoulder." But what enables us to recover these words is a semantic link between, for example, the literal meaning of "chip" and the literal meaning of "tree-trunk."

It *might* be that "exist(s)" expresses a property, in some or all of its uses, even though the supposition that it does is not needed to account for its use in characterizing referring attempts. And it is possible that the sense it has in expressing this property guides its use in character-izing referring attempts in the way the literal meanings of metaphors guide their metaphorical uses. Gareth Evans and (I believe) Fred Kroon hold that existence is a universal property, one which everything pos-sesses by default. I claimed otherwise in (Walton 1990). (This is not an issue for me to stomp my foot about, however; none of the central fea-tures of my account of singular existential statements depends on it). Those who think there are nonexistent objects, of course, take it to be a discriminating property, one that some things possess and some things lack.

---

[69] *New York Times*, 3 August 1998.

If existence is a property necessarily possessed by everything, it is not the only one; self-identity is another. To say that existence is necessarily universal is not yet to specify what property it is. But suppose that existence *is* a universal property—never mind which one. How might it figure in a pretense account of singular existential statements?

The account would have it that in saying "Falstaff does not exist" the speaker pretends to describe the referent of the name as lacking this property, existence, and that in so pretending she asserts that Falstaff-ish referring attempts fail. The relevant pretense is one in which "exist(s)" expresses a discriminating property. So we will be pretending, of what we know to be a universal property, that it is actually a discriminating one; we will be pretending that there are things which lack it.

Something like this picture of the working of singular existential statements may fit some uses of other predicates. To assert:

Falstaff is not self-identical. (or Falstaff is not himself)

may be a metaphorical way of saying that Falstaff doesn't exist, that Falstaff-ish referring attempts fail. The speaker pretends to be claiming that an entity which she refers to as "Falstaff" lacks the property of self-identity; she pretends that some things are self-identical and some things are not. By engaging in this pretense, she genuinely asserts that Falstaff-ish referring attempts are unsuccessful. (The connection here is this: since, as we all know, nothing lacks self-identity, attempts to refer to things lacking self-identity are doomed to failure.) A corresponding metaphorical way of saying that Neptune exists is to assert:

Neptune is self-identical.

Are "Falstaff doesn't exist" and "Neptune exists" like these metaphorical claims? I am not sure, but I am sceptical.

A rather feeble reason for scepticism is the fact that "Falstaff doesn't exist" doesn't *feel* like "Falstaff is not self-identical." "Falstaff doesn't exist" doesn't sound to my ear like an indirect, or figurative, or metaphorical way of saying what is said. This impression might be explained by the hypothesis that "Falstaff doesn't exist" is a *dead* metaphor, one that is so familiar that, like "chair leg," "mouth of a bay," and "keep your eyes peeled," it has lost its aura of metaphoricality. But then I wonder if the metaphor was *ever* alive. Maybe it was dead on arrival. If so, was it ever a metaphor at all? (I don't rule out this possibility.)

A somewhat less feeble reason for scepticism is this: I can recapture the metaphorical character of "chair leg," "mouth of the bay," and "keep your eyes peeled," by attending to their obvious literal meanings. (In the case of "mouth of the bay" I suppose that this involves thinking of the opening of the bay as portraying or representing a mouth. It is harder to say what it amounts to in the other cases.) But it isn't at all clear that I can recapture—or capture for the first time—a way of hearing existence claims as metaphors. Presumably reviving the metaphor would require keeping in mind supposedly *literal* uses of "exists," cases in which it is used to express the universal property of existence. But are there any? Straightforward singular negative existentials are not such. Positive singular existentials, which serve the supposedly metaphorical function of characterizing referring attempts, *could* conceivably be functioning at the same time to attribute the universal property of existence to the subject, but it isn't at all clear that they are. Gareth Evans seems to think that "exists" has this "literal" sense in quantificational and modal contexts. I am not convinced.[70] In any case, this literal sense (if it exists) doesn't seem to be salient in ordinary existence claims. And I have argued that we don't need to suppose that it is operative in order to understand how by pretending to predicate "exists" or "doesn't exist" to (pretended) things, we manage to characterize referring attempts as successful or unsuccessful.

By contrast, "x is identical to y" has obvious uses when the success or failure of referring attempts is not in question. And so does "x is self-identical," at least in philosophical contexts. And it is clear that the sense identity statements have in these cases is being exploited when I say "Falstaff is not self-identical," meaning, metaphorically, that the guy *isn't*. [71]

I am not eager to offer a definition of "metaphor" or to pronounce on the limits of the category. But it seems reasonable to regard the dependence of what is asserted on distinct literal meanings of the words used, and the guiding function of the content of what the speaker (merely) pretends to say—as a necessary condition for an (assertive) utterance to be metaphorical. If this is a necessary condition, it looks as though we

---

[70]See Evans (Evans 1982), pp. 345–348. I think that "exist(s)" in such contexts can be understood convincingly without supposing that it has this sense. One who says "This might not have existed," for instance, utilizes the pretense that "exists" expresses a (discriminating) property and that there is a proposition to the effect that the object she refers to as "this" possesses this property. In saying what she does she pretends to be claiming that this proposition is possibly false. What makes it fictional that she speaks truly (if it is fictional that she does), and what she actually asserts to be the case, is something like the fact that it is possible that referring attempts of the kind exemplified by her utterance of "this" should have been successful.

[71] "Is identical to," understood literally, may not be what it seems to be—a predicate expressing a relational property which everything bears to itself and to nothing else. See Crimmins (Crimmins 1998) and Kroon (Kroon). Nevertheless, the literal sense of "Falstaff is not self-identical," whatever it amounts to, guides the metaphorical use of this sentence in asserting that Falstaff does not exist.

can escape the apparently bizarre thesis that "exist(s)," as it occurs in garden variety singular existential statements, is metaphorical.

Nevertheless, the fact that making an existential claim, like speaking metaphorically, is to engage in make-believe, the fact that the speaker utters her words in pretense, means that we do not have to take her apparent ontological commitments seriously. To claim that Falstaff doesn't exist is not to claim, seriously, that there is something, Falstaff, which lacks existence, any more than asserting what one does in saying "We are all in the same boat" is to claim that there really is a boat that we are all in, or the use of phrases like "raising hackles," "on pins and needles," "in seventh heaven," "beyond the pale," and "hold your horses" commits the speaker to the existence of (things called) *hackles, pins and needles, seventh heaven, the pale,* or *horses.*

5.7 Appendix: Logical Form (Reply to Peter van Inwagen)

Paraphrases must preserve the logical form of the statements they paraphrase and the entailment relations obtaining among them.[72] Peter van Inwagen has expressed scepticism about whether paraphrases like those I propose for statements concerning fiction satisfy this requirement.[73] Van Inwagen observes that

(1) There is a fictional character who, for every novel, either appears in that novel or is a model for a character who does.

appears to have a certain complex quantificational structure, a structure that validates the inference from (1) to:

(2) If no character appears in every novel, then some character is modeled on another character.

But none of the paraphrases of (1) and (2) that I recommended in my (Walton 1990) has these logical forms. On our primary model suggested there, both will be paraphrased by something of this form:

To engage in pretense of kind *K* is fictionally to speak truly in a game of such—and—such a sort.

(the relevant kind of pretense being different in the two cases). An alternative is to regard (1) and (2) as attesting to circumstances which, if present, would make it fictional of one who pretends in the relevant

---

[72]Reprinted by permission of the publisher from *Mimesis as Make Believe: on the foundation of the representational arts* by Kendall Walton, Cambridge Mass.: Harvard University Press, Copyright ©1990 by the President and Fellows of Harvard.

[73]See van Inwagen (van Inwagen 1985).

manner that he speaks truly (circumstances concerning the corpus of extant novels). Obviously we cannot expect any such paraphrases to mirror the quantificational structures exhibited by (1) and (2). Paraphrases of neither sort show (1) to entail (2) by virtue of logical form.

Not only can we live with this result; we will thrive on it. Recall, first, that what our paraphrases seek to capture is what speakers say in uttering the sentences cited, not what the sentences themselves mean or what propositions *they* express, if any. What speakers say simply does not have the logical forms indicated by the sentences they use. To assume otherwise would be question begging. But we do need to explain why people use sentences displaying logical forms different from those of what they assert in uttering them. And it certainly seems as though what is said by means of (2) follows deductively from what is said by means of (1); it is not easy to envisage accepting (1) while dissenting from (2). If the quantificational structures of what is said do not guarantee this entailment, what does? If the entailment does not hold, why does it seem to? Explanations are easily provided, but first let's say a little more about what speakers might assert by means of (1) and (2).

Utterances of (1) and (2) can be understood to involve unofficial games of a rather ordinary sort, ones with some approximation of the following features:

(a) All novels are props in them and most of what is fictional in any novel is fictional in them; the unofficial games combine the games authorized for each individual novel in a way familiar from (Walton 1990), section 10:4.

(b) It is fictional in these combination games that the universe is divided into realms corresponding to the various novels.[74] To say that "a character appears in a certain novel" is, fictionally, to locate a person in a certain realm.

(c) To write a novel of a certain sort is to make it fictional of oneself, in games of the implied sort, that one creates people ("characters") and endows them with certain properties. (Compare: "Jane Austen created Emma Woodhouse.")

(d) When, as we say, an author "models a character on some preexisting character," it is fictional that he creates someone to be like some other person, that he makes someone in the image of someone else. (In speaking of "characters" rather than "people"

---

[74]This is not an uncommon feature of unofficial games that combine other games, though there may be very little to be said about what, fictionally, realms are or what it is, fictionally, for things to belong to the same or different ones. See (Walton 1990), section 11.1.

the speaker *betrays* his pretense, but this does not affect the content of the assertion.)[75]

It is fictional in unofficial games of the kind implied, no doubt, that (1) and (2)—the sentences themselves—express propositions that have the logical structures they appear to have, ones by virtue of which (1) entails (2). And it is fictional of Ellen, if she utters (1) assertively while participating in such a game, that what she asserts entails, by virtue of logical form alone, what would be asserted by (2). This partly explains the impression that what Ellen actually asserts by means of (1) thus entails what would be asserted by (2).

What does Ellen genuinely assert by means of (1)? In the simplest and primary case (unlikely though it may be) she is participating in an unofficial game of the sort described and asserting that to pretend as she does is fictionally to speak truly. Her pretense is a kind of pretending to assert something of the form displayed by that sentence; it is fictional that she asserts a proposition of that form. So naturally she uses that sentence, even though what she actually asserts about this kind of pretense has a very different form.

If Ellen speaks of this kind of pretense without engaging in it, she still refers to it. If, rather than speaking about it she is pointing out the presence of circumstances by virtue of which to so pretend is fictionally to speak truly, it is by indicating the kind of pretense that she calls attention to the circumstances she claims to obtain. In either case the sentence she uses, (1), displaying the logical form it does, suits her purpose, since to pretend in the manner she refers to or indicates is fictionally to assert something of that form.

But it is *only* fictional, not true, that (1) has a quantificational structure such as to entail (2). And it is at most fictional, not true, that what is asserted by means of (1) entails by virtue of logical form alone what is asserted by (2). Nevertheless, one may be speaking truly in asserting

(3) (1) entails (2) by virtue of logical form alone.

Assertions of (3) can themselves be understood as we understand other statements concerning fiction. The speaker, in the primary case, indicates a kind of pretense—the pretense of asserting that (1) entails (2) by virtue of logical form alone—and claims that to so pretend in an unofficial game of an implied sort (the kind implied by (1) and (2)) is fictionally to speak truly. *This* claim is true, even though (1) does not entail (2) by virtue of logical form alone; (3) taken literally is false. The moral of the story, again, is that we must take care to distinguish be-

---

[75]See Walton (Walton 1990), section 11.1.

tween fictionality and truth, between what is the case and what is merely pretended to be the case.

The likelihood of confusion is enhanced by the fact that what is asserted by (1) probably does entail what is asserted by (2), though not by virtue of logical form alone. The principles constituting the implied games of make-believe are likely to be such that it cannot be fictional that to assert (1) is to speak truly unless it is fictional that to assert (2) is to speak truly. The unofficial games would have to be rather exotic logical fantasies for this not to be so. And the principles are likely to be such that the circumstances required to make it fictional that one speaks truly in asserting (1) are ones that make it fictional that one speaks truly in asserting (2). No wonder it is difficult to conceive of (1) being true and (2) false.

6

'Disavowal Through Commitment' Theories of Negative Existentials

FRED KROON

6.1 Introduction

Singular negative existential statements—"Hamlet doesn't exist," "Vulcan doesn't exist," "that ferocious monster doesn't exist," and the like—involve us in a famous quandary.[76] To all appearances, they involve the genuine use of referring expressions, and hence their truth or falsity should rest on the disposition of appropriate objects of reference: true if these are correctly described, false otherwise. Yet if what a negative existential says is true the expression featured can scarcely be allowed to have a genuine use: failing existence, there is no object of reference, so nothing true (or, for that matter, false) can be said about it. The problem of accounting for the truth of singular negative existentials in the face of this familiar prima facie contradiction I'll call the *negative existential problem*.[77]

There have been many and varied suggestions for a solution to the problem, from variations on an "object" theory like Meinong's which deny that a negative existential's subject-term lacks an object of reference, to variations on a "no object" theory like Russell's which deny that a negative existential's subject-term carries a commitment to objects of any kind. And then there are those who seem to want it both ways.

---

[76] A version of this paper was presented at a conference on "Empty Names, Fiction, and the Puzzles of Non-existence" (sponsored by the Center for the Study of Language and Information at Stanford University), on March 22. Thanks especially to Ken Walton, Ed Zalta, Stacie Friend, and Anthony Everett.

[77] I discuss the problem only as it involves allegedly "directly referential" expressions like names and demonstrative expressions, currently the most discussed version of the problem.

Empty Names, Fiction, and the Puzzles of Non-Existence.
Anthony Everett and Thomas Hofweber (eds.).

One such was the theologian Bernard Pünjer who, in an intriguing but little-known dialogue with Frege, argued that in a negative existential one represents a certain object as existing in order to deny that there is such an object, and hence one disavows the thought that there exists an object to be talked about by expressing a commitment to that very thought: what we might call a "disavowal through commitment" account.[78]

What is odd about the suggestion, of course, is that it seems to accept the premises leading to the prima facie contradiction just outlined, and so it is difficult not to feel a sense of impatience. Pünjer himself, in fact, does little to develop or defend the suggestion further, no doubt discouraged by Frege's objections. I want to urge, by contrast, that "disavowal through commitment" accounts have merit if developed in the right sort of way. After a brief excursus through Pünjer's comments, I'll spend the rest of the paper showing how the job might be done.

6.2 Frege vs Pünjer

The Frege-Pünjer dialogue is interesting for a number of reasons. For one thing, Frege's reply to Pünjer shows how close Frege seems willing to come to accepting "exists" as a genuine or logical first-level predicate. His actual view seems to be that "exists" is best viewed as a grammatical and not a logical predicate, "a mere auxiliary [that] language, feeling at a loss for a grammatical predicate, invented" in order to allow such sentences as "Men exist" or "something existing is a man."[79] "Exists," he seems to think, can't be a logical predicate if so used, for it does nothing substantial: it merely "predicates something self-evident, so that it really has no content" (ibid.). As Frege himself points out, however, the same is true of the predicate "is self-identical"[80] which presumably is a genuine predicate definable from the two-place predicate of identity. At any rate, Frege thinks that to the extent that "exists" is a first-level predicate—and it certainly is so grammatically—it predicates something that, as a matter of meaning, is true of anything whatsoever: a universal predicate.[81]

Pünjer himself initially comes across as a kind of proto-Meinongian, but one who shows none of the awareness that Meinong showed of the

---

[78] See his (Frege 1979). Pünjer intended his account to apply to plural negative existentials as well.

[79] See (Frege 1979), p. 62.

[80] See (Frege 1979), p. 65.

[81] Frege doesn't deny that we often intend singular existential statements to be non-trivial, but seems to think that such statements have then become covertly metalinguistic, see (Frege 1979), p. 60. See also Haaparanta, (Haaparanta 1986).

philosophical implications of his account. He claimed that all ideas have objects, but that some ideas are not "caused by something affecting the ego," and so their objects can't be experienced. This is true of the idea of the "this" (the idea that accompanies my utterance of "this table," for example) when the utterance and accompanying idea are caused by my hallucinating. Challenged by Frege, he agrees that the object of such an idea therefore doesn't exist. But Frege then deals what seems a death-blow to the view:

> Then it follows that there are objects of ideas—ideas which have not been caused by something affecting the ego—which do not exist. Now if you are using the word "exists" in the same sense as the expression "there is," then you have at the same time both asserted and denied the same predicate of the same subject.[82]

After Pünjer demurs that "there is" is wrongly used in this context, while admitting that no other expression would be any better, Frege declares that:

> So in your opinion we have here a contradiction in the nature of things—one to which reason is necessarily captive.[83]

Pünjer can do no better than agree, it seems. All he can say in response is that:

> before we deny the existence of anything whatever, we have to represent it as existing in order to go on to deny existence of it.[84]

(Call this *Pünjer's Thesis*). Perhaps wisely, he adds that "he doesn't think we shall get any further [by debating] along these lines."

I said that Pünjer comes across as a proto-Meinongian, but it seems difficult to sustain this view if we take his last claim (Pünjer's Thesis) seriously. For that claim clearly suggests that Pünjer is willing to accept Frege's admonition that if you regard "exists" as a predicate (and Pünjer clearly does) then it is a predicate satisfying the principle: everything there is, and nothing else, exists. Now maybe Pünjer was confused, and he should have resisted. But there is another interpretation. Maybe his remarks latch on to a rather different set of ideas, ideas that don't require him to acknowledge a sense of "there are" in which it is true that there literally are special objects that lack existence. Maybe there can be "dis-avowal through commitment" in other ways, and maybe Pünjer's Thesis

---

[82]See §79. of (Frege 1979), p. 59.

[83]See §83. of (Frege 1979), p. 59.

[84]See §84. (Frege 1979), p. 59.

gestures at these ways while failing to be explicit about the details.

6.3   Constraints on theories of negative existentials

That is the idea I want to explore. But to do so, there is merit in first laying out more clearly some of the reasons we might have for taking Pünjer's Thesis seriously. Let us begin by asking what we should look for in a viable solution to the negative existential problem: what sorts of constraints such solutions ought to meet, if only in the sense of being especially weighty conditions that have to be met if at all possible. This might at least cut the field down sufficiently to make it easier to choose among the remaining contenders and to see how Pünjer's suggestion fares. Here, I think, progress is indeed possible. As Saul Kripke insisted some time ago (and, following him, Gareth Evans),[85] an important element in the much-maligned Meinongian approach to negative existentials deserves strong endorsement. The Meinongian solution has in some sense set the standard for other solutions in its insistence that the terms in negative existentials are used rather than mentioned, exactly as grammar tells us, and furthermore are used as devices of reference, purporting to identify a referent rather than serving as shorthand for quantificational constructions that say what there is not. This constraint—call it "the constraint of *USE*"—disqualifies the historically important Russellian and metalinguistic solutions to the negative existential problem, for solutions of that stripe notoriously deny the identification of logical and grammatical form according to which a negative existential is simply an internally negated predication.

Given what *USE* implies, it is important that we understand why *USE* is so appealing as a constraint. What justifies it as an adequacy constraint is the fact that occurrences of terms in negative existentials pass exactly the same prima facie tests as occurrences of terms that count as paradigmatic uses. Aside from passing the surface-grammar test (the surface-grammar of a sentence like "Hamlet doesn't exist" is exactly that of a standard negative subject-predicate sentences like "Clinton doesn't smoke"), they also pass what we might call the term-resilience test—the requirement that if terms are genuinely being used then they, or their anaphoric proxies, should also have a use in surrounding contexts. After all, if a speaker takes herself to be talking about something, one would expect the ensuing discussion to extend to longer than a single sentence.

It is not hard to convince oneself that terms in negative existentials exhibit just this feature of resilience. Negative existentials, like ordinary

---

[85] Kripke's arguments were first presented in his (unpublished) *John Locke Lectures* of 1973. Evans's contribution occurs in (Evans 1982).

subject-predicate sentences, don't occur in a linguistic vacuum but routinely occur in the presence of other sentences that contain the same name (or an equivalent pronoun) in a context that is clearly a context of use. Note, for example, the triple occurrence of "Murphy Brown"/"she" in the following passage from *Time Magazine*:

> Murphy Brown does not exist. She is the TV character played by Candice Bergen. Murphy is a blond media anchor-goddess and wiseguy and now a defiantly unmarried madonna.[86]

Actually, we can formulate this point in a stronger form. Negative existentials are particularly apt to find themselves in this sort of company. Far from being a conversation-stopper, a negative existential is often just the beginning-point of a string of predications that clarify, explain, or enlarge on, what is said in the negative existential. Thus when *Time* announced that Murphy Brown did not exist, its readers naturally expected clarification of this point (after all, so much doesn't exist, and for so many different reasons—Vulcan, Hamlet, phlogiston, ...). Hence the continuation: "She is the TV character ..." Readers who wanted also to understand the reasons for Murphy's notoriety despite her non-existence were given further enlightenment in the very next sentence: "Murphy is a blond media anchor-goddess and wiseguy and now a defiantly unmarried madonna."

Suppose, then, that we agree to accept *USE*. This constrains us to see "exists" as a predicate, and so we need to ask what, if any, constraints we should place on "exists" as it occurs in negative existentials. The first thing to say is that the predicate must surely be assigned its standard meaning in negative existentials, the meaning it has in other existential statements (for instance, in the modal claim "I might not have existed"). In short, we must forego imputations of ambiguity—at least until we clearly have to. How might we characterize that meaning? Opinions will vary on this point. In particular, Meinongians will want to read "exists" as a discriminating predicate that partitions the class of all objects into those that have (spatio-) temporal location or concreteness, and those that don't. But the Meinongian view is arguably just a response to the problem of negative existentials; to adopt it now would be to give in too readily. Following Kripke and Evans, I prefer the simpler view that "exists" stands for a first-level property possessed by anything whatsoever; in fact, that saying that "exists" is true of everything is what uniquely fixes the meaning of "exists." (The latter is

---

[86]Time's answer to (Canadian ex-Prime minister) Mulroney puzzled question "Who is Murphy Brown?" after the furore surrounding Dan Quaile's attack on the show's alleged anti-family values (*Time International*, vol. 139, no. 22, June 1, 1992).

clearly a nod in the direction of Frege's view that "exists" is a "mere auxiliary," a sort of predicative shadow cast by the quantifiers.) If we call this the *simple* meaning of "exists," the proposed constraint is that the simple meaning provides the meaning of "exists" as it features in negative existentials (the constraint of *SIMPLICITY*).

I am not going to defend this constraint in any detail. It is enough for present purposes to point out that the simple meaning is implicitly accepted by many as a kind of default meaning—a meaning that

even Russell, for example, accepts when he argues that to say of something that it doesn't exist "would be nonsense, because you cannot have a constituent of a proposition that is nothing at all."[87] A view of this kind even allows us to generate the intended truth-conditions of quantified existential statements (for instance "Some tame tigers exists" and "No tame tigers exist"), to cope with tensed existence statements ("This hasn't always existed"), and to predict the ambiguity in a modal existential like "the first man in space might not have existed."[88] So *SIMPLICITY* seems a compelling constraint as well, at least on the surface and putting the negative existential problem aside.

6.4 Pretend-ways of satisfying the constraints

It is time to return to Pünjer. For it is not difficult to see Pünjer's Thesis as a rather blunt statement of how an analysis in conformity to the two constraints should parse negative existentials. But as Frege saw the matter, this simply left us with a contradiction "to which reason [as Pünjer thought] is necessarily captive" (See §83. (Frege 1979), p. 59); and Frege was not inclined to take this Kantian-sounding suggestion at all seriously since he had his alternative Kantian view that "exists" as a logical predicate really stands for a second-level property or concept. With hindsight, however, we see that the issue is more delicate. There seem to be weighty reasons for thinking that the constraints of *USE* and *SIMPLICITY* are conditions that ought to be satisfied if at all possible,

---

[87]In Russell's (Russell 1959b), p. 242. Russell continues: "[I]f Romulus himself entered into the proposition that he existed or did not exist, both these propositions could not ... be true, [or even] significant, unless he existed." Russell, of course, uses this argument to show that "exists" in ordinary negative existentials can't have the simple sense.

[88]These existentials are

discussed by Evans. Among those who explicitly admit "exists" as a predicate satisfying something like the simple view are Kripke in his (Kripke 1973), Evans in (Evans 1982), pp. 345–348, and Joseph Almog, (Almog 1986). Nakhnikian and Salmon had already argued much earlier that "[a]s a predicate, 'exists' is necessarily universal" ((Nakhnikian and Salmon 1957)), although they wrongly inferred that it was redundant (it is not redundant in modal existentials like "I might not have existed").

and hence weighty reasons for taking Pünjer's Thesis seriously. Yet there is no escaping the sense of contradiction once we do try to adhere to the constraints. Is there a way out?

It seems clear that there is no direct way of reconciling the two constraints: Frege's charge of inconsistency is just too difficult to turn aside. But there may be indirect ways. In this section I shall describe two. The first way was in fact first suggested by Meinong, who in his (Meinong 1983) proposed the view that a speaker who utters a negative existential assumes or pretends that something existent answers to the referring expression she employs:

> But what if someone intended something like "phlogiston," in order to make this judgment about it: that there isn't anything of that sort? ... [Assumptions to the effect that there is such a thing] play a quite essential role in the apprehending of objecta in such cases. This is also in thorough accord with the testimony of direct observation. It tallies with our clearcut experiences in many cases, that in order to give a thing some thought a person "places himself in the situation in which there is such a thing."[89]

In the case of "Vulcan doesn't exist," for example, a speaker pretends that the theory positing such a planet is true; in the case of "Hamlet doesn't exist," she pretends that the play *Hamlet* is known fact; and so on. In the scope of such an existential assumption or pretense, the speaker is then participating in a successful referential practice, using the expression to refer to an existent object, although in reality, of course, there may be no such object. According to the rest of the account, the speaker then proceeds to deny that this (pretended) object really exists, using something like the usual predicate of existence to do so. So Meinong too, in his own way, thinks that speakers can use negative existentials to disavow representations of the world that include the existence of certain objects, by first assuming or pretending that these representations of the world are correct.

Expressed this way, the view faces two immediate and seemingly devastating objections. The first is just Frege's inconsistency charge, transposed to the realm of pretense. How can a negative existential thus construed be true in *any* sense, given that the speaker assumes that there exists something to be referred to while also denying existence and thus expressing the baselessness of the assumption? Secondly, what in the world makes true negative existentials thus understood *genuinely* true, true in the sense of reflecting how things really are in the world

---

[89]See (Meinong 1983), p. 175.

as opposed to how things are pretended to be? For Meinong, both objections are in the end answered in terms of the traditional Meinongian commitment to non-existent objects. In negative existentials, existence is genuinely denied of the objects themselves, while the existential pretense is just a psychological aspect of our grasping and referring to these objects.[90]

So for Meinong, there is in the end no hope of fully satisfying the constraint of *SIMPLICITY*. The truth is that not all objects exist, and the constraint of *SIMPLICITY* turns out to be a constraint on our thinking only.

Meinong's way out, then, is far from being a whole-hearted acceptance of the two constraints. And it buys into ontic commitments—the full gamut of unreal objects—that we might well wish to do without. Is there an alternative?

In fact, by suggesting that pretense plays a pivotal role Meinong has, as in so much else, pointed the way to an alternative way of seeing the issues. Meinong himself relegates the defining role of pretense to the psychological, but at the time of the first edition of (Meinong 1983) he himself was inclined to see its role as more fundamental, as showing how there was no need after all to think of our ontic commitments as anything more than pretend-commitments.[91] And that way of seeing the issues has been given a new lease of life in modern appeals to make-believe or pretense, especially in the ground-breaking work of Ken Walton.[92] I'll call accounts like Walton's *austere pretense accounts* of negative existentials since they claim to be able to articulate the truth-conditions of such statements without relying on anything more than a pretend commitment to the existence of objects.

Let me begin by very cursorily describing the structure of austere pretense accounts before saying what is distinctive about Walton's own account. An account of this type claims that negative existentials feature referring expressions used in the scope of the pretense that the expressions genuinely refer. (As I understand it, Walton doesn't insist on this, allowing utterances of such statements in which there is only an allusion to pretense of this type.) *Pace* Meinong, this is not pretense *about* an object, but something much more austere: a kind of "as if" approach to use and reference on which speakers do "as if" they are successfully referring with a term. That is, speakers don't pretend, about a special fictional object Hamlet, that he exists and is a prince who resents his step-father. Instead, they pretend or imagine that *Hamlet* is a reliable

---

[90] See (Meinong 1983), pp. 170ff.
[91] So I argue in (Kroon 1992).
[92] See Walton, (Walton 1990).

record of actual events, and hence that its statements can be treated as linked to the world in the same way as genuinely reliable records. They thereby also pretend that occurrences of names like "Hamlet" genuinely refer to someone. Furthermore, it needn't be part of their pretense that only they are involved in reading about, and reflecting on, the events recorded in *Hamlet*. One game can encompass many players, and as a result, many and varied pretended attempts to refer can count as pretend-co-referential: this person's use of "Hamlet," that person's use of the anaphoric "he" or even of "the mad prince of Denmark," and so on. We might say that these are all pretended attempts to refer of the Hamlet-kind.[93]

I hope it is clear that *USE* is satisfied on this kind of account. Even though the account admits that the use of a term in a negative existential occurs in the scope of a pretense, that is surely enough; we had no right to demand more than this when we insisted on the constraint of *USE*. Let us now ask how an austere pretense account can explain the truth-stating capacity of negative existentials. How, in particular, can any such account do as well as a Meinongian account, with its straightforward claim that a negative existential is true just when the object implicated fails to have the property of existence?

Here the account that Ken Walton gives is of special interest, since there is a sense in which it replicates, in austere terms, the moves that Meinong makes in his pretense account.[94] According to Walton, a speaker who utters "Hamlet doesn't exist" is involved in an unofficial game of make-believe in which she plays along with the story of *Hamlet* and also pretends that "exists" expresses a property which some things possess and others lack: in short, a discriminating property, just like existence in Meinong's sense. The application-conditions for "exists" in this unofficial game are as follows: it is fictional that "*N* exists" is true if "*N*-ish" attempts at reference (where this marks out a relevant kind of attempt) successfully secure reference to something, and it is fictional that its negation "*N* doesn't exist" is true if "*N*-ish" attempts at reference fail to secure reference to anything. In particular, it is fictional that "Hamlet doesn't exist" is true if and only if all attempts at reference of the Hamlet-kind fail to secure reference to anything—roughly speaking, attempts to refer that from the perspective of the game successfully count as attempts to refer to Hamlet. Thus formulated, the account can make sense of both the content oriented make-believe on which it is fictional that Hamlet exists (from the perspective of the work, attempts

---

[93] See (Walton 1990), chapter 11 (and especially pp. 425–7, where Walton introduces the relevant notion of kind).

[94] See Walton's (Walton 2000) for a spirited account and defense of his views.

at reference do succeed) as well as the more salient prop oriented make-believe on which it is fictional that Hamlet doesn't exist (non-pretended attempts at reference of the same kind don't succeed).

We are, of course, primarily interested in the sense in which a speaker who says "Hamlet doesn't exist" speaks the truth. For Walton, however, the true claim that a speaker actually asserts with her utterance is not any proposition literally expressed by "Hamlet doesn't exist," for, absent a genuine Hamlet and even a genuine property of existence, there is no such proposition (Walton subscribes to a direct reference view of the relevant expressions). Rather, she asserts that certain real world circumstances obtain—the ones that make it fictional that "Hamlet doesn't exist" is true—and hence she declares the failure of all such genuine, non-pretended attempts at reference, using the device of pretending to refer successfully to do so. She speaks truly in saying "Hamlet doesn't exist" if what she thus declares is true.

I said that this account in a sense replicates, in admirably austere terms, Meinong's version of a pretense account. It even captures something we saw as important when discussing term-resilience as a reason for insisting on *USE*, namely the explanatory link that exists between certain sortal statements (e.g., "Murphy Brown is a TV character" or "Hamlet is a creature of fiction") and the corresponding negative existentials ("Murphy Brown doesn't exist" or "Hamlet doesn't exist"). Both Meinong and Walton make room for this explanatory link, but whereas for Meinong the link straightforwardly holds between the propositions expressed, for Walton the explanation is between the circumstances that make the one claim fictional and the circumstances that make the other claim fictional.[95]

This difference, of course, reflects another, more central difference. For Meinong, "exists" so used stands for a genuine property of things, but this is not so for Walton. Not only does Walton's account deny that "exists" stands for a universal property of existence (contra the constraint of *SIMPLICITY*); it even denies that "exists" stands for any property at all (it only does so in the pretense). It would be disappoint-

---

[95]Contrast

this with Evans's pretense account in (Evans 1982), which insists that "Really(Ft)" (uttered as a move in the relevant pretense) is true iff Ft, construed from outside of the pretense, expresses a proposition and this proposition is true. But given Evans's Russellian account of propositions and his commitment to *SIMPLICITY*, this means that "Really(Ft)" is true only if "Really(t exists)" is true. Such an account makes nonsense of the way negative existentials enjoy smooth explanatory links to other statements, often in terms of the contrast between how things are not *really* and how they *really* are—the way "Hamlet doesn't really exist," say, is explained by "Hamlet is really just a creature of fiction."

ing, in my view, if austerity came at so high a price. Can we do any better?

6.5   Negative existentials as (a kind of) metaphor

It is time we had another look at the resources available to an austere pretense account of negative existentials. I shall argue that an account of this type can be developed in such a way that the tension among *USE* and *SIMPLICITY*—the tension so graphically captured in Pünjer's Thesis—appears not only natural but almost inevitable from the point of view of the communicative purposes served by uttering negative existentials. In fact, tension of this kind is not only natural and inevitable; it is also relatively common.

Consider, in this connection, the class of what we might loosely call "quasi-paradoxical disclaimers," which use a conflict between subject and predicate to convey something else altogether. Suppose, for example, that we suddenly realize that a certain individual across the street is not what we thought "she" was. We say to others around us:

(1) That woman—the one wearing the smart red dress; look, she is turning this way again—is not really a woman at all; she is a man, and the red dress is really a red hunting-jacket (we are deluded by the light).

Note that the occurrence of "that woman" in (1) is not simply a referential rather than attributive use of a demonstrative description, for in (1) the speaker doesn't simply use a description (as it turns out, faulty) to identify a certain individual in order to say something about that individual. Any such construal leaves out of consideration an important reflective component in what the speaker communicates: the speaker deliberately uses the demonstrative description in order to declare its faultiness. In uttering (1), the speaker pretends for the sake of effect (where the effect includes providing her audience with recognizable clues for identifying a certain individual) that she and her audience correctly describe a certain demonstratively salient individual as a woman. She feigns the truth of this view in order to convey the thought that the view is false, and that the demonstrated individual is altogether different; and she does this by exploiting a certain interpretive tension that faces her audience. Since, in short, she can't realistically be claiming the truth of a contradiction, her audience will understand her allusion to "that woman" as pretended only.[96]

---

[96]Note that it would be a mistake to construe (1) as meaning something like "That individual you and others believe to be a woman is not a woman; that individual is a man." (1) doesn't talk about belief at all; relatedly, this reading destroys any

Note, by the way, that the speaker need not have used the qualifier "really" to generate this effect. In cases like (1), "really" is a pragmatic device that is used to highlight the contrast between a scenario X that is portrayed as expected or default and a different scenario Y that is endorsed in its place as the one that "really" happened. Hence: "It is really Sally whom John loves, not (contrary to what you have heard) Emma," or "John doesn't really love Emma; he really loves Sally." Often the expected scenario and the contrasting scenario are presented in a dramatic way that makes the former sound particularly compelling, almost a logical truth, and the latter particularly surprising, thereby creating an interpretive tension that needs resolution—for example, "that woman is not *really* a woman; she is really a man" or "that man is not *really* a man; he is really a mouse" (said of someone conspicuously lacking in courage). In such cases, however, the speaker can easily generate the same effect without using "really:" the interpretive tension is just too hard to miss.

One further feature of (1) needs emphasis: the second conjunct may be essential if the audience is to understand the speaker's full communicative intent. Here is an example of a quasi-paradoxical disclaimer that shares the first conjunct with (1) but is used to convey something quite different. Suppose, while he is trying to decide whether to venture out into heavy rain to catch a bus, you tell a friend: "There must be a bus coming; look, there is a woman waiting at the stop." If, after peering hard into the rain, he retorts:

(2) That woman is not [really] a woman; she is just a product of your imagination,

the speaker's audience again has no difficulty in understanding what is conveyed. What is conveyed is again conveyed by the speaker's exploiting a certain interpretive tension facing a literal construal of what is claimed; here what is conveyed includes the thought that in reality, as opposed to the pretense in which the speaker and his audience are watching a demonstratively salient woman, there is no individual to watch, that any thought to the contrary is the result of an imaginative reconstruction of such things as reflected light.

My account of the quasi-paradoxical disclaimers (1) and (2) was broadly pragmatic in nature. In neither case did it claim that the content conveyed was something like the truth-condition of the sentence. On the contrary: it was only through claiming that the sentences were used with

---

sense of semantic continuity between an utterance of (1) and other earlier uses of "that woman" on the part of the speaker's audience. (In addition, no such reading is possible in the case of (2) below.)

their ordinary meanings, and that the ordinary meanings generated an interpretive tension, that we were able to tell a story about what was conveyed. This is not unlike the mechanism of metaphor. (Think of certain cases continuous with (1) and (2) but more clearly metaphorical: for example, our earlier "That man is not really a man; he is really a mouse.") It seems apt, given all this, to think of quasi-paradoxical disclaimers as based quite generally on a special figurative use of language, broadly akin to metaphor.[97]

I think that there are analogous reasons for counting negative existentials as quasi-paradoxical disclaimers, and thereby as also broadly metaphorical in nature. In common with Walton's version of an austere pretense approach, let us agree that speakers utter them in the context of a pretense that the terms involved refer to something. Now assume that "exists" has its simple sense, and so stands for a genuine property of things, a property possessed by everything although presumably not an essential property of everything. But this means that negative existentials are used in the scope of a pretense that the terms refer to something existing. Danger looms, for we now seem to be back with the sort of inconsistent analysis encouraged in Pünjer's Thesis. This time, however, the complaint seems less urgent. For the complaint assumes that the language used in negative existentials is being used to ordinary effect, and that assumption is defeasible. Our quasi-paradoxical disclaimers (1) and (2) show, in fact, that we sometimes use inconsistency for pragmatic ends, to convey something that may well be true.

I shall argue that the utterer of a negative existential brings into play similar conditions for understanding the point of her utterance. Both "That woman is not [really] a woman" and "Hamlet doesn't [really] exist" force the speaker's audience to look beyond their evident, graphic falsity to other claims which are thereby made salient. In the former case, it is something like the claim that non-pretended attempts to refer to what in the pretense is a demonstratively salient woman do not in fact secure reference to a woman. In the latter case, it is—near enough—the claim that non-pretended referring attempts of the Hamlet-kind do not in fact secure reference to anyone.

This view, of course, is Walton's view in a different setting, presented this time not as a fact about the fictional application-conditions of "[doesn't] exist" but as a fact about what is saliently, even inescapably,

---

[97]The view of metaphor that perhaps best accounts for the way expressive tensions in language can generate a new content in this kind of case is the Gricean theory found in G. Nunberg's (Nunberg 1978). See also Walton's (Walton 1993), for a make-believe-based account of a large range of metaphors. I am unsure about the extent to which such theories are really in conflict.

implicated and conveyed by an utterance of the relevant negative existential. The view needs argument, of course; it is scarcely self-evident. One final point before I present the argument. For the purposes of the argument, I am going to follow Walton in assuming that names and demonstratives are devices of direct reference. Such an assumption is not only reasonable on its own terms, given the current semantic debate, but it also has the virtue of allowing us to present the account with as tough a test as possible.[98]

Assume, then, that the theory of direct reference is true. If so, the name "Hamlet" fulfils its semantic function of standing for a certain individual, at least within the scope of the pretense that the drama Hamlet is fact. This follows immediately from the "austere pretense" view that to pretend that *Hamlet* is fact involves pretending that there are standard referential connections between names used in *Hamlet* and objects in the world.[99] The semantic fact that "Hamlet" fulfils its semantic function is now enough to make "Hamlet exists" express a true proposition in the scope of the pretense; indeed, a kind of structural truth, assuming that structuralism about propositions is true, since existence is a universal property and hence a property of the constituent corresponding to "Hamlet" as well, so that the truth of the proposition is guaranteed by its structure alone. (This is all the case within the scope of the pretense, of course, not in reality).[100]

Suppose now that a speaker utters the negated existential statement "Hamlet doesn't exist," perhaps by itself, perhaps as part of a more complex statement ("If Hamlet doesn't exist then ...," etc.). If she understands this negation correctly as the negation of a trivial structural truth, then two things emerge. First, although she is speaking from inside the scope of a pretense her communicative aim is obviously not to express a thought about the world of that pretense even if her words do

---

[98] The theory of Direct Reference really stands for a cluster of theories, although all agree that there are such entities as singular propositions or singular truth-conditions. For a number of the speakers at the Stanford conference where this paper was read, the truth of the theory of direct reference is part of the (non-negotiable) background that makes the negative existential problem so troubling. Others who assume direct reference while insisting on the need for a "no object" solution to the negative existential problem include Braun, (Braun 1993), and Adams and Stecker, (Adams and Stecker 1994).

[99] But to pretend this way is not to pretend that all "names" occurring in *Hamlet* denote. Some apparent "names" are only fictional names in the play. This is true of "Gonzago," for example (*Hamlet*, act 3, scene 2), which denotes in the scope of the pretense that the play it features in is fact, but not in the scope of the pretense that *Hamlet* itself is fact (we can have games within games, as Walton reminds us in (Walton 1990)).

[100] See Almog, (Almog 1986), p. 236.

literally express a thought about this world. Instead, the conditions are in place for understanding her utterance as expressing a thought about the real world instead, which is the other direction her Janus-faced utterance is facing. (This is akin to Walton's distinction between content oriented and prop oriented make-believe.)

But what thought? The second thing to emerge is that, arguably, there is little or no contest. To see this, consider our other quasi-paradoxical disclaimers again. In the case of "That woman is not a woman," the interpretive tension is a broadly logical one, and so it seems easy to work out what is conveyed (unlike "That man is not a man but a mouse," say, which requires us to know contingent associations involving "man" as well as "mouse"). The speaker, it seems, is able to signify that she is "doing as if" a certain demonstratively salient individual is a woman (else no sense could be made of her speech act); this fact having become salient, she thereby also makes salient the claim that what is being referred to *outside* of this pretense is a man rather than a woman.

That, at any rate, is the speaker's intent in the case of (1). But note that the speaker doesn't have it all her own way. Before the utterance of the second conjunct of (1), there is an alternative interpretation, for having rendered salient the fact that she is pretending, "making as if," there is a demonstratively salient woman in front of her, the interpretive tension in "that woman is not really a woman" allows release in one of at least two ways. First, the speaker might be rendering salient a certain internal negation: the claim that the demonstratively salient individual in front of her—what she is referring to outside of the pretense that her demonstrative reference is to a woman—is not a woman at all. Secondly, she might be rendering salient an external negation only: the claim that it is *not* the case that there is a demonstratively salient individual in front of her who is a woman. The second, but not the first, is consistent with what the speaker manages to assert with (2), namely that there is no demonstratively salient individual at all, that any thought to the contrary is the result of deceptive light conditions. So the first conjunct of (1) and (2) suffers from a certain underdetermination. Absent other clues, the second conjunct is needed to clarify what is intended.

In short, our quasi-paradoxical disclaimers require context for their interpretation, even if they both convey what they do on the basis of a certain interpretive tension. Turn now to negative existentials, say "Hamlet doesn't exist" or even "That woman doesn't exist." Here, so I shall argue, the matter is far more straightforward.

For consider. A speaker uttering "Hamlet doesn't exist" intends her audience to recognize that she is pretend-referring to someone, that she is only *pretending*, *making as if*, she is party to a successful referential practice. She is able to communicate this intention by relying on a certain pragmatic problem facing the interpretation of any such negative existential—the fact that if it is involves a serious attempt at reference then it expresses at best a trivial structural falsehood, and hence a proposition that no-one would ever seriously contemplate: an unthinkable proposition, much like the proposition expressed by "That woman is not a woman" when the use of "that woman" is both serious and successful (if the attempts at reference fail, on the other hand, nothing is expressed).

Again as in the case of (1) and (2), there is now a salient and usable contrast between two different things where the speaker's words are concerned: how things are from the perspective of the pretense and how things really are. In the present context, this amounts to a salient and usable contrast between pretended attempts to refer to a certain individual using terms like "Hamlet," "that mad prince," "Ophelia's erst-while lover," and so on (judged from the perspective of the pretense, these attempts succeed) and non-pretended attempts of the same kind (attempts that use the same words, say, but this time rooted in the thought that *Hamlet* is fact).[101]

To see what the speaker conveys about such non-pretended attempts, recall that in the case of (1) and (2) the predicate "is not a woman" left things to a degree indeterminate: context was needed to clarify what was conveyed, because the contrast between internal and external negation generated one narrow reading and one wide reading. In the case of "Hamlet does not exist," there is no such problem and no such source of indeterminacy. Since there is nothing that doesn't exist, it can't be the speaker's intent to convey the narrow claim that the individual singled out by certain non-pretended attempts at reference fails to exist ((1), by contrast, was able to convey the narrow claim that the individual singled out by certain non-pretended attempts at reference was not a woman). The only remaining option is akin to (2). What is being conveyed is the wide claim that it is *not* the case that there is something that is singled out by genuine, non-pretended referring attempts of this kind and that also exists—in short, that nothing is singled out by genuine referring attempts of this kind (since, once again, everything exists). In the case of negative existentials, then, there is a particularly simple and direct way to determine the intended reading on the basis of the meaning of the predicate "exists."

Note, incidentally, that once the speaker has metaphorically declared

---

[101] See again Walton (Walton 1990), chapter 11. I'll assume, without further discussion, that the idea of "same kind" can be unpacked in something like the way Walton suggests.

a failure of reference of this kind, she may well want to go on to give the reasons for the failure. Hence the natural continuation "Hamlet is a creature of fiction" in the case of "Hamlet doesn't exist" and "That woman is a figment of your imagination" in the case of "That woman doesn't exist." The speaker here seems to rely on her audience's ability to exploit the literal meanings of words like "creature" and "imagination" in order to communicate via yet another kind of metaphor the way in which the failure of certain attempts at reference can be traced to the source of such attempts.[102] If this is right, the resilience of terms in negative existentials is the resilience of a broadly metaphorical way of speaking.

Note also the application of this kind of story to the case of affirmative existentials. Again relying on an interpretive tension, this time the triviality and pointlessness of "Hamlet exists" if it is assumed that the name is used simply to designate someone in order to ascribe the universal property of existence, it is possible to see the speaker's utterance of "Hamlet [really] exists" as conveying the claim that genuine referring attempts of the Hamlet-kind do secure reference to someone. Once again, there are other quasi-paradoxical disclaimers which suggest something like this story. When in *Shakespeare in Love* the Master of the Revels, Master Linley, bellows out "that woman is a woman!" upon finding Viola unlawfully playing the part of Juliet on the stage of The Curtain, none of us are in any doubt about what is being asserted. What is asserted, from within the pretense that he and the audience are watching a woman called "Juliet," is not some logical triviality but the substantive and legally consequential claim that, outside of the scope of the pretense that this demonstratively salient individual is a woman, the individual demonstrated is indeed a woman; the claim, we might say, that serious, non-pretended demonstrative referring attempts of a kind that in the pretense secure reference to a certain woman, secure reference to someone who is indeed a woman. The substantial claim conveyed by a speaker who attests that "Hamlet does exist" can be reconstructed from such a case. What is conveyed is the claim that serious, non-pretended referring attempts of the Hamlet-kind secure reference to someone who does indeed exist. But since everything exists, the addition of "exists" is, as before, an addition without a difference. That is why an utterance of "Hamlet exists" is naturally used to convey the claim that non-pretended referring attempts of the Hamlet-kind successfully secure reference to someone.

---

[102]I present this argument in my (Kroon 1996).

6.6   Concluding comments

Russell, I think, had it right: as soon as we can seriously entertain the thought that x (Hamlet, say) doesn't exist, the predicative reading we might otherwise have expected for this negative existential has to be replaced by something more congenial. The reason, as he reminds us, is that saying of something that it doesn't exist "would be nonsense, because you cannot have a constituent of a proposition that is nothing at all." But he chose the wrong method of replacement, concluding that ordinary names are not really names and, contrary to what he had just assumed, that "exists" is not really a predicate. By contrast, the account of the present paper retains the view that "exists" is a (universal) predicate and that ordinary names are names, while putting a wholly different spin on the idea that the predicative content we might have expected is not the content conveyed. On the present account, it is the speaker's own understanding of the tension in the literal, expected content that generates the conveyed, non-literal content.

We thus have a version of a "disavowal through commitment" that comports well with Pünjer's Thesis in the form attacked by Frege, yet seems coherent despite its air of incoherence. In this concluding section, I'll consider some important objections to an account of this type (well aware that these are far from being the only objections), before describing one final consideration in its favor.

> *First objection.* Negative existentials don't *sound* like metaphors. Surely this is as much a datum to be respected as *USE*, and (rather more so) *SIMPLICITY*.

> *Reply.* But the account explains why negative existentials will sound non-metaphorical. For it claims that there is something almost unavoidable about the non-literal reading a negative existential delivers. Once we have the ability, no doubt largely unreflective, to make the sort of pragmatic moves also required for an understanding of other quasi-paradoxical disclaimers, accessing this non-literal reading doesn't rely on additional imaginative capacities, but only on an understanding of the simple meaning of "exists." Nothing like this is true, as I suggested earlier, in the case of "That man is not a man but a mouse," say, or even "that woman is not a woman."[103]

---

[103] It need not even be true in the case of statements that use some other necessarily universal predicate. Take "That woman is not herself/is not self-identical," which uses another such predicate, that of self-identity, but is more easily heard as a psychological metaphor. On a metaphorical interpretation of Pünjer's Thesis, there may well be differences between what "N doesn't exist" and "N is not self-identical" are naturally

So to the extent that negative existentials rest on something akin to metaphor, it is a peculiarly direct, unimaginative kind of metaphor.

Still, I don't think we should say it is a dead metaphor (it may be closer to a frozen metaphor). There are times when the interpretive tension that generates the intended reading for a negative existential becomes almost palpable. Thus there is something deliberately odd and unsettling about the use of "exists" in a sentence like "Look at that woman—the one standing in the rain over there. Sadly, she doesn't exist; she is just a trick of the light," an oddness I have tried to capture in terms of the tension created by the juxtaposition of a demonstrative attempt at reference and "doesn't exist." Even if other explanations are possible, furthermore, a metaphorical explanation might well recommend itself on grounds of greater generality. Quasi-paradoxical disclaimers like "that woman is not a woman" need explanation as well, and in their case there seems little doubt that literal meanings are exploited to a broadly metaphorical end—if I am right, an end which has much in common with that of negative existentials. (We might even combine the two kinds of expression: "Look at that woman—the one standing in the rain over there. Sadly, she is not a woman at all; she is just a trick of the light and doesn't really exist.")

Second objection. Following Walton, although for different reasons, the metaphor account claims that negative existentials are used to convey the failure of a class of non-pretended referring-attempts. But if "Non-pretended referring attempts of the Hamlet-kind don't succeed" is just a literal expression of the metaphorical content of "Hamlet doesn't exist," we should expect to find the first expression, or something like it, used as a way of literally saying what the latter conveys in a metaphorical fashion. This never happens, however.

Reply. Answering this question requires both a reminder and a disclaimer. The metaphor account claims that what is conveyed is generated by interpretive tensions exploited by the speaker in order to signal the failure of a class of referring attempts. My Waltonian reading didn't stress one aspect enough, however: the indexical character of the claim conveyed. For what the speaker conveys she conveys by pretending that she is successfully referring with "Hamlet," and what she disavows are non-pretended attempts at reference

_____
used to convey.

that include—here's the indexical element—her own attempt at reference with "Hamlet," now understood from outside the scope of the pretense that it succeeds.

Now for the disclaimer. So far I have been content to follow Walton in my talk of the success or failure of a certain class of non-pretended attempts at reference. But that was in part because I have wanted to be neutral on the question of what determines success or failure. I doubt that we can afford to be too neutral, however. In particular, we need to ward off deflationists about reference who will say that talk of the referential failure of "Hamlet" is simply disguised talk of the non-existence of Hamlet.[104] Let's assume for the moment that what determines reference for the tokening of a name is possession of (enough) associated properties, in the case of "Hamlet" properties like being called "Hamlet," being someone whom the speaker is acquainted with through her reading of such-and-such a text and whom she takes to be a Prince of Denmark, etc. (The causal theorist will, of course, tell a different story about referential mechanism.)[105] Then what a speaker conveys in saying "Hamlet doesn't exist" is that, outside of the scope of the pretense that the very reference-determining properties she thus relies on successfully single someone out, these same properties don't single anyone out.

In short, by talking about someone in the scope of the pretense, she manages to say that there is not anyone she is talking about! But our pretense is shared pretense, of course, a game of make-believe that many can play, and so the failure of my associated properties will also mean the failure of your associated properties. It is therefore tempting to let the claim conveyed by the speaker include the claim that related properties on the part of other speakers—properties that single out the same individual in the scope of the shared pretense—will also fail. Such an addition is perhaps not strictly necessary, but we need not decide the issue here. Whatever the best story of this type might be, our earlier talk of non-pretended referring attempts of this or that kind can now be construed as code for whatever is needed according to this story.

I shall conclude with one final point in favor of the account defended in this paper. Most of us have the intuition, honed by Kripke's remarks in (Kripke 1980), that in so far as Hamlet and Santa Claus don't exist,

---

[104]See, for example, Hartry Field, (Field 1994), esp. p. 261ff.

[105]Frank Jackson offers a good defense of such a descriptivism in (Jackson 1997). Kripke's (Kripke 1980) is the locus classicus for a causal account.

they just *couldn't* have existed. I think this is right, but that it neglects another intuition most of us have (or used to, before Kripke), namely that even though Hamlet and Santa Claus don't exist, they *might* have existed, that our childish hope that Santa Claus exists was not an impossible one.[106] Where there are two such readings, there must be a complexity in the underlying form that encourages such readings.

The present account encourages the following story. Where modality comes into play, we need to focus on the previously redundant occurrence of "exists" in the underlying form of what is conveyed. When we attend to the conveyed claim that there is no x such that non-pretended attempts at reference of a certain kind—in particular my present attempt, now understood from outside of the pretense that it succeeds—secure reference to x (and x exists), the modalized statement "Hamlet might have existed" is naturally taken in two ways. First of all, given the (non-epistemic) sense in which the play *Hamlet* might have been historical fact, we may wish to emphasize the possibility of successful reference to a person referred to in that work as "Hamlet." It is then natural to take "Hamlet might have existed" as conveying the claim that:

1. (i) possibly, there is an x such that (actual) non-pretended referring attempts of the Hamlet-kind, including the speaker's own attempt, secure reference to x and x exists
   (i.e., $\Diamond(\exists x(\text{Non-pretended attempts at reference of the Hamlet-kind secure reference to } x \,\&\, x \text{ exists}))$).

And that, presumably, is true. Hamlet might indeed have existed in sense (i).[107]

---

[106]See (Kripke 1980), pp. 157–8. For an intriguing attempt to capture both senses in terms of an "abstract object" solution to the negative existential problem, see Ed Zalta, (Zalta 1988).

[107]But recall my emphasis above on the notion of underlying referential mechanism. The following case, brought to my attention by Anthony Everett, shows the importance of referential mechanism if readings like (i) are to work. Take the ovum from which I developed and one of my father's sperms which, though real and actual, failed to fertilize that egg. It seems plausible to suppose that had that ovum and sperm united they would have produced a determinate human being. Call this imagined person "X." Now X does not really exist, but he might have done. Indeed, the following stronger claim seems true: "Possibly (no language is ever used and X exists)". In that case, the account on offer seems in trouble, since it suggests that what is conveyed is the inconsistent: "Possibly (no language is ever used and genuine attempts at reference of the X-kind secure reference to someone)." But if we stress the role of underlying referential mechanism, we can characterize what is conveyed as follows: "Possibly (no language is ever used and the very property hereby used to pick out a person [viz. X] in the scope of the pretense that the property does single someone out [the property of being the unique individual that results from a certain sperm and egg] also singles someone out when this same referential mechanism is understood

Secondly, we may wish to keep Hamlet's non-existence in focus. It is then natural to let the interpretation of "Hamlet might have existed" be determined as follows. If Hamlet doesn't exist—if, that is, it is not the case that there is an x such that non-pretended attempts at reference of the Hamlet-kind secure reference to x (and x exists)—then it is also not the case that:

1. (ii) there is an x such that non-pretended attempts at reference of the Hamlet-kind secure reference to x and x *possibly* exists ($\exists x$(Non-pretended attempts at reference of the Hamlet-kind secure reference to x & $\Diamond(x$ exists)).

But Hamlet doesn't exist, so (ii) is indeed false. Hence there is also a clear sense in which Hamlet could not have existed.

---

from outside of the pretense)." The latter claim, clearly, is not only consistent but true; given what we know of "X" it is equivalent to "Possibly (no language is ever used, and the ovum and sperm in question combined to form a determinate individual)." It is a cumbersome claim, of course; but that just underscores the genius of existential locutions which allow a far more elegant expression of claims of this kind.

7

The Road Between Pretense Theory and Abstract Object Theory

EDWARD N. ZALTA

7.1 Introduction

In this paper, I attempt to reconcile two different theoretical approaches to the philosophy of fiction, namely, the theory of abstract objects (hereafter "object theory")[108] and pretense theory.[109] I think that the seminal insights of both theories are, for the most part, consistent with one another. To make this idea plausible, I spend a large part of what follows both correlating the basic notions of pretense theory with those of object theory and showing how pretense-theoretic notions can be systematized within the framework of object theory. At the end of the paper, I consider a point of apparent inconsistency between the two theories. This concerns the question, do names such as "Zeus" and "King Lear" denote objects? Object theorists believe they do, while pretense theorists think not. However, there is a way to reconcile these opposing answers to some extent, namely, by showing that the formalism of object theory has an interpretation on which fictional objects become entities that a pretense theorist already accepts. So if a pretense theorist is already committed to the existence of such entities, they should accept that names such as "Zeus" and "King Lear" denote, for this offers a more systematic analysis of language. Or so I hope to show.

The key to the reconciliation of object theory and pretense theory will involve an appeal to a Wittgensteinian approach to the meaning of names of stories and fictional characters. The traditional Wittgen-

---

[108]The principal development of object theory occurs in Zalta (Zalta 1988) and (Zalta 1983).

[109]The principal development of pretense theory occurs in Walton (Walton 1990).

Empty Names, Fiction, and the Puzzles of Non-Existence.
Anthony Everett and Thomas Hofweber (eds.).

steinian approach to the meaning of the names of fiction takes the meaning of a term like "Holmes" to be constituted by its pattern of use. But such accounts typically don't allow us to get very precise about the patterns in question. Notice that, at the very least, such an approach quantifies over, and is committed to the existence of, *patterns*. I shall argue that the formalism of object theory, in its application to fiction, can be interpreted as systematizing such patterns. The "abstract objects" of the formal metaphysical theory are reconceptualized as patterns of use and patterns of behavior in general. The semantic analyses of fictional discourse which are constructed in terms of object theory then take on new significance, for names of fiction will denote entities that the pretense theorist already accepts. Thus, we will have forged not only a way of making the Wittgensteinian view about meaning more precise, but also a way of reconciling two approaches to the philosophy of fiction that seem to be heading off in different directions.

I'll follow the same strategy that the pretense theorists follow, namely, engage initially in talk of abstract and fictional objects (such as stories and characters) and at the end show how to reconceive this talk in an acceptable way. So, as I correlate the notions of pretense theory with object theory, I'll help myself to all of our usual talk about fictional objects.

7.2 Some data to be explained

Before we begin our rapprochement, it is worthwhile to set out clearly before us just what it is we are trying to explain. I shall suppose that the data fall into four principal groups. The first group consists of certain historical facts:

- The ancient Greeks worshipped Zeus.
- Sherlock Holmes still inspires modern criminologists.
- Holmes is more famous than any real detective.
- Ponce de Leon searched for the fountain of youth.
- If you had asked Ponce de Leon what he was doing in the swamps of Florida, he would have said that he was searching for something.
- Teams of scientists have searched for the Loch Ness monster, but since it doesn't exist, no one will ever find it.

The second group of data consists of the ordinary valid inferences we derive from the above:

- Ponce de Leon searched for the fountain of youth.
  Therefore, Ponce de Leon searched for something.

- The ancient Greeks worshipped Zeus.
  Zeus is a mythical character.
  Mythical characters don't exist.
  Therefore, the ancient Greeks worshipped something that doesn't exist.

The third group of data consists of facts about what goes on in a fiction:

- In Dostoyevsky's *The Brothers Karamazov*, Dmitri, Ivan, and Alyosha Karamazov are brothers.
- In Günther Grass's *The Tin Drum*, Oskar Mazerath decides to stop growing at the age of 3.

The final group of data consists of ordinary statements that someone might make in the context of thinking about fictions:

- Some fictional characters are interesting because they find themselves in situations in which they appear to be able to choose their identity, though it sometimes turns out that factors beyond their control, antecedent to the moment of choice, have already determined the kind of person that they would be.
- There are fictional characters that no one admires.
- Thinking about the lives of fictional characters helps us to reflect on the roles one might assume in real life, helps to inform us about the nature of evil so that we may be better prepared to do battle with it, helps us to understand and sympathize with others, and enables us to come to grips with our own feelings about certain situations in which we might find ourselves.
- All of the characters in this novel are fictional and any similarity between them and real individuals is purely coincidental and not intended by the author.

I take it that we shall have given an explanation of these data if we can analyze them in a systematic way. Such an analysis has to obey certain constraints. (1) It should preserve the truth values and logical consequences of the original. For example, a regimentation which analyzes the descriptions of fictional entities the first group of data (e.g., "the fountain of youth") in terms of Russell's theory of descriptions would not obey this constraint, since such an analysis would turn truth into falsehood. Similarly, no Russellian analysis of names in terms of definite descriptions would be acceptable. (2) It has to discriminate the truth of "The ancient Greeks worshipped Zeus" from the falsity of "The ancient Greeks worshipped Sherlock Holmes." (3) It should not make sentences such as the last example in the fourth group vacuously true; any systematization that represents "All of the characters in this novel are fictional ... " as vacuously true (on the grounds that there are no fictional characters) will get the wrong truth value for the sentence "All of the characters of this novel are both aliens from Mars and natural numbers" (for it will say that this sentence is true instead of false). (4) The systematization should not analyze such 'intensional' verbs as "search for" in one way when they appear in such sentences as "Bill Clinton searched for Hillary Clinton" and in a different way when they appear in such sentences as "Ponce de Leon searched for the fountain of youth." Similarly for comparative verbs like "is more clever than" and "is more famous than."

The systematization described in what follows in fact obeys these constraints. It clearly delineates fact from fiction, but allows us to talk about the latter. The basic notions of "story," "according to the story," "character," "fictional," etc., have been defined in terms of a few basic notions. Moreover, many of the intuitions that pretense theorists have about these notions are preserved in the definitions. To establish this, we now track some of the basic features of pretense theory.

7.3 Tracking features of pretense theory

In his intriguing book *Mimesis as Make-Believe*, Kendall Walton develops a conceptual framework for discussing fiction. He asserts numerous claims about fiction that are couched in terms of this framework. By reviewing the main claims, we will get a good sense of the notions that are involved in the conceptual framework:

> The propositions fictional in the world of a game are those whose fictionality is generated by virtue of the principles and props of the game—the propositions which, because of the principles in force and the nature of the props, are to be imagined by participants in the game. (p. 59)

> Each fictional world is associated with a particular class or cluster of propositions—those propositions that are fictional in that world. (p. 64)

> ... classes [of propositions] constituting fictional worlds, unlike those constituting possible worlds, need not be either consistent of complete. (p. 66)

> What is important is various properties that propositions sometimes possess: the property of being fictional and that of being fictional in a particular representational work or game of make-believe or dream or daydream. It is natural to express these properties with the help of phrases appearing to refer to fictional worlds ..., and so for convenience, I will often do so. But my

explanations of these properties do not presuppose any such reference. (p. 67)

A prop is something which, ..., mandates imaginings. Propositions whose imaginings are mandated are *fictional*, and the fact that a proposition is fictional is a *fictional truth*. Fictional worlds are associated with collections of fictional truths; what is fictional is fictional in a given world—the world of a game of make-believe, for example, or that of a representation work of art. (p. 69)

Works of fiction are simply representations in our special sense, works whose function is to serve as props in games of make-believe. (p. 72)

Napoleon is an object of *War and Peace*. ... A thing is an object of a given representation if there are propositions about it which the representation makes fictional. (p. 106)

A proposition is fictional in the world of a game just in case there is a prescription that it is to be imagined by appreciators. (p. 208)

From this selection, it is clear that Walton's conceptual framework includes the following notions: game, make-believe, participant, prop, imaginings, proposition, and a variety of forms of the notion of fiction. In the above quotations and in various other places in Walton's book, we find: (a) "fiction" used as a noun, (b) "fictional" used as an adjective (as in "fictional world" and "fictional truth"), (c) "fictional" used as a predicate adjective (as in "...is fictional"), (d) "is fictional in" used as a part of a verb phrase (e.g., when something is said to be "fictional in a game, work, or world"), (e) "it is fictional that" used as a sentential adverb, and (f) constructions such as "...is, fictionally, ..." (as in "The saddle of a mountain is, fictionally, a horse's saddle") and "...make it fictional..." (as in "The cloud is a prop which makes it fictional that there is an angry face"). It is not easy to work out just how to organize and analyze these various uses. The variety of uses appears to be somewhat unsystematic, and there is a danger that the various forms of the word "fiction" may start to lose their sense.

Nevertheless, there is much to be gained in approaching fiction fundamentally in terms of the notions of game, make-believe, and props. I'll return to the discussion of these particular notions in the final section of this paper. However, in the next section, I'll focus upon the regimentation of the various notions of fiction, story, and character. In my previous work, I have developed a way of precisely regimenting these notions. I now want show how this regimentation can be correlated with Walton's language and claims. I hope to establish that the regimentation captures a certain systematicity in Walton's use of these notions and so falls within the spirit of pretense theory.

In what follows, I shall presuppose that the reader has some basic familiarity with object theory. In this theory, the notions of n-place relation ("F^n"), property ("F^1"), proposition ("F^0" or "p"), abstract object ("$A!x$"), ordinary object ("$O!x$"), encoding ("xF"), and exemplification ("$F^n x_1 \ldots x_n$") have all been regimented within the framework of an axiom system. There are axioms that assert the existence of relations, properties, and propositions, as well as an axiom that asserts the existence of abstract objects. And there are conditions that state when relations F and G, propositions p and q, and objects x and y, are identical. Those readers unfamiliar with the theory will find a sketch of the basic ideas in the Appendix to the present paper. In the next section, I presuppose that the reader knows why it is that for every proposition p, there exists a corresponding property *being such that p* ("$[\lambda y\, p]$"). I also presuppose that the reader knows that: (1) there are abstract objects (namely, situations) that encode only propositional properties, (2) that a proposition p is true in situation s ("$s \models p$") just in case s encodes the propositional property being such that p (i.e., just in case $s[\lambda y\, p]$), and (3) that these ideas yield a derivative sense of "encode" in which abstract objects (and, in particular, situations) encode propositions.

7.4 Correlating pretense theory and object theory

In previous work,[110] the theory of fiction was constructed with the aid of three special theoretical notions. The first is the authorship relation. We use "Axy" to assert that x authors y. The second is a relation of temporal precedence. We use "$p < q$" to assert that p obtained before q. The third is the logical notion of relevant entailment. We use "$p \vdash_R q$" to assert that q is relevantly implied by p. Work in tense logic and relevance logic gives us a pretty good idea of what the latter two notions amount to—we need not commit ourselves in this paper to a particular tense logic or relevance logic. We shall assume that the reader has both an intuitive grasp of the authorship relation as well as a grasp of the role it plays in pretense theory.

According to pretense theory, when someone authors a story, they produce certain sounds or marks ("representations") which serve as props that somehow mandate or prescribe that listeners/readers imagine certain propositions as being fictional in "the world of the story" None of this, however, tells us what a story or work of fiction is. The following

---

[110]See Zalta (Zalta 1983) pp. 91–99, and (Zalta 1988) pp. 123–129, and 143–150.

definition fills in the blank:[111]

>x is a *story* $=_{df}$ x is a situation that is authored by some concrete object.

In formal terms, we have:[112]

$$Story(x) \ =_{df} \ Situation(x) \ \& \ \exists y(E!y \ \& \ Ayx).$$

Since this definition identifies a story as an abstract object, it follows that stories are individuated by the propositional properties they encode. Indeed, given our derivative sense of "encodes," we may say that stories are individuated by the propositions they encode.[113] Since we have defined stories as a subspecies of situation, we may define the story operator "According to story s, p" in the same way that we defined the notion "p is true in situation s," namely, as $s \models p$.

Now the first point of correlation between object theory and pretense theory concerns the way our identification of stories can be reconciled with Walton's talk about "fictional worlds." Whereas Walton takes fictional worlds to be constituted by (classes of) propositions (pp. 64, 66), our stories encode propositions. However, I think it preferable to talk in terms of "stories" instead of "fictional worlds." Typically, a "world" is a complete and consistent situation, where:

$$Complete(s) \ =_{df} \ \forall p(s \models p \ \lor \ s \models \neg p).$$
$$Consistent(s) \ =_{df} \ \neg \exists p(s \models p \ \& \ s \models \neg p).$$

At least, *possible* worlds are complete and consistent in these defined senses.[114] But when Walton speaks of "fictional worlds," he relaxes our conception of worlds in two ways, one of which is innocuous and the other of which is problematic. First, he allows that (the propositions constituting) fictional worlds can be inconsistent. Insofar as "fictional world" is supposed to be more inclusive than "possible world," this is

---

[111]What follows is equivalent to the definition constructed in Zalta (Zalta 1983), p. 91.

[112]Readers unfamiliar with object theory should note that the predicate "*E!*" stands for the property of being spatiotemporal or concrete. In the Appendix, you will find that we have defined ordinary objects to be the kind of thing that could be spatiotemporal, and defined abstract objects as: not the kind of thing that could be spatiotemporal.

[113]If you are a pretense theorist and are feeling uneasy about this identification of stories with abstract objects, remember that at this point, we are helping ourselves to talk about abstract objects. We will, in due course, discharge this talk in terms of talk that may be more acceptable to you.

[114]In object theory, we have defined a possible world to be a situation x that (encodes only propositional properties and) *might* have encoded all and only the true propositions. This implies that possible worlds are complete and consistent, in the senses just defined. See Zalta (Zalta 1993).

innocuous enough. Moreover, object theory can make sense of this kind of talk. We can precisely define *impossible worlds* and identify inconsistent fictional worlds in terms of these worlds. Impossible worlds are those situations that are complete but not consistent (in the above senses). This notion has been the focus of recent work.[115]

However, Walton also relaxes the notion of world in a problematic way, by supposing that there are fictional worlds which are not complete. This strikes me as somewhat inappropriate. The notion of "world" should be reserved to refer to a complete situation. It therefore strikes me as improper to use the term "world" to talk about "the world of a game of make-believe" (as Walton does on p. 69 and elsewhere). There are just too many worlds that can be correlated with a given consistent story. For example, if we assume for the moment that the Conan Doyle novels are consistent (in the sense defined above), then there are numerous possible worlds "consistent with" those novels. There is no such thing as *the* world of the Conan Doyle novels.

So, in what follows, we shall assume that possible worlds are complete and consistent, and that stories are (typically) incomplete and sometimes inconsistent. Accordingly, we shall not employ the notion of "the world of a fiction." However, if we operate under the translation scheme that "the world of story s" in pretense theory correlates with "story s" in object theory, we can reconcile the two apparently distinct theoretical languages. Under this translation scheme, we preserve the truth of the Walton's claims on pp. 64, 66, and 69, for the claims which result under the substitution are, respectively:

> Each story is associated with a particular class or cluster of propositions—those propositions that are fictional in that story.
>
> ... classes [of propositions] constituting stories, unlike those constituting possible worlds, need not be either consistent of complete.
>
> ... Stories are associated with collections of fictional truths; what is fictional is fictional in a given story—the story of a game of make-believe, for example, or that of a representation work of art.

I take it that the pretense theorist would be able to accept the above. Moreover, we may regiment the pretense theoretic notion "fictional in" as follows:

$$p \text{ is fictional in } s \ =_{df} \ Story(s) \ \& \ s \models p.$$

---

[115] See Zalta (Zalta 1997) and some of the other theories of impossible worlds described in the special volume of the *Notre Dame Journal of Formal Logic* which contains Zalta (Zalta 1997).

This definition forges another link between the notions of pretense theory and our framework for fiction.[116] A simple generalization of this last definition regiments Walton's notion "p is fictional":

p *is fictional* $=_{df} \exists s(Story(s) \ \& \ s \models p).$

In other words, p is fictional if it is true in some story. This corresponds to Walton's claim (p. 69) that what is fictional is fictional in a given world. Of course, this is a rather weak sense of what it is for a proposition to be fictional, for it allows true propositions to be fictional. But the definition can be strengthened if there is a need to do so.[117]

Next, we can appeal to pretense-theoretic notions to flesh out the authorship relation. As noted above, the authorship relation was taken as primitive in object theory, but pretense theory seems like a good place to look for its analysis. Given the quotations from pp. 59 and 69 of Walton's book, it seems natural to suggest the following analysis of the authorship relation:

x *authors* s iff x produces a work (prop) such that every proposition that the work mandates us to imagine is true in s.

We can make the form of the definition a little clearer if we give it more structure and use one of our regimented notions. We first define:

y *is a prop for* s iff y is a prop $\&$ for any proposition p, if y mandates that p is to be imagined, then $s \models p$.

Now we may define:

x *authors* s iff $\exists y[x$ produces $y \ \& \ y$ is a prop for $s]$.

This reformulated definition does show that the notions of pretense theory and object theory can serve to inform one another. This definition allows us to derive one of the basic claims of pretense theory, namely, that if a prop of story s mandates that proposition p is to be imagined, then p is fictional in s. For suppose that y is a prop for story s and that y mandates that some proposition, say q is to be imagined. Then our definitions tell us that $s \models q$. But since s is a story and $s \models q$, it follows from a previous definition that q is fictional in s. Notice that this is Walton's claim on p. 69, where he says that propositions whose imaginings are mandated are fictional.

Despite these interesting consequences of our definition of the authorship relation, it leaves several open questions. For one thing, it gives

---

[116]Note that we can now define the notion "s is a *true story*" as follows: every proposition fictional in s is true.

[117]If we wish to excludes facts from being classified as fictions under this definition, we conjoin the clause $\neg p$ to the definiens.

us no indication as to what kind of thing a prop is. It seems reasonable to assume that props are concrete objects of various sorts and we shall proceed on that assumption. This seems consistent with pretense theory. A second question that the definition of authorship forces us to consider is the theoretical status of the notions of "x produces y" and "y mandates that p is to be imagined." These seem to be taken as basic and not further defined in pretense theory. Consequently, if the above definition of authorship is to be added to the definitions of object theory, "x produces y" and "y mandates that p is to be imagined" will have to replace "x authors y" as primitive. It is always good to know what primitives are employed in your theory.

A third question that arises in connection with the definition of authorship is how a (representational) artifact or prop for a story mandates which propositions are true in the story. Presumably, this will be different for different media. However, in the case of ordinary novels produced in a print medium, the manuscript or other copy of the novel will contain (tokens of) linguistic expressions which themselves designate some (but not necessarily all) of the propositions true in the story. An exact specification of the relationship between the props and the group of propositions true in the story goes beyond the present essay, but we can give some indication of how this goes. The basic idea involves the notion of relevant entailment (which we mentioned earlier). As we read each sentence S in a manuscript or other copy of a novel, we typically conclude that the proposition p that S designates is true in the story s which is being presented by this novel (since we typically assume that this is one of the propositions that the prop mandates us to imagine). However, we don't conclude only that $s \models p$, but also that any proposition relevantly entailed by p is also true in s. In previous work, I have suggested that the following Rule of Closure is operative:

> *Rule of Closure*: All of the relevant consequences of propositions true in s are true in s.

In formal terms:

> If (a) $s \models p_1 \,\&\, \ldots \,\&\, s \models p_n$, and (b) $p_1, \ldots, p_n \vdash_R q$, then $s \models q$.

Alternatively, this rule could be recast in terms of Walton's notion of "mandates that p is to be imagined" as follows: if a prop y mandates that p is to be imagined and q is a relevant consequence of p, the y mandates that q is to be imagined. Surely the logic of fiction will include some such formulation of this rule. The exact nature of this logic of fiction is one of the more interesting open philosophical questions.[118]

---

[118]See Parsons (Parsons 1980), pp. 175–182, for an excellent discussion of the issues

Despite the fact that the definition of authorship leaves open certain questions, it nevertheless does seem to capture an insight which connects the two theoretical frameworks under discussion. One last group of connections concerns the notion of a "character." In object theory, this notion is first defined relative to a story:

> *x is a character of s* $=_{df}$ there is some property F such that the proposition that x exemplifies F is true in s.

In formal terms, this becomes:

> $Character(x, s) =_{df} \exists F(s \models Fx)$.

This definition allows all manner of animate and inanimate objects to be characters of stories. Nor does it exclude concrete, spatiotemporal objects from being characters of stories. I take it that our definition of "character of" corresponds to Walton's claim (p. 106) that a thing is an *object of* a given representation if there are propositions about it which the representation makes fictional. Here again, then, is a point at which we can correlate the notions of pretense theory with the regimented notions of our object-theoretic approach to fiction.[119] Of course, we may say that an object x is a character just in case there is some story s such that x is a character of s:

> $Character(x) =_{df} \exists s[Character(x, s)]$.

It is important here to distinguish "character" in this sense from "fictional character," which we have not yet defined.

We may conclude this series of observations correlating pretense and object theory by focusing on the distinction between a proposition p being fictional (in a story), which was defined above, and a character being fictional. As we saw above, a proposition's being fictional is simply a matter of its being true according to some story. However, for a character to be fictional, it must "originate" in some story. In previous work, we have defined this notion of "originates" in terms of our tense-theoretic primitive (mentioned above) as follows:

> *x originates in s* $=_{df}$ *x* is an abstract object that is a character of s and x is not a character of any earlier story.

In formal terms, this becomes:

> $Originates(x, s) =_{df} A!x$ & $Character(x, s)$ &
> $\forall y \forall z \forall s'((Azs' < Ays) \rightarrow \neg Character(x, s'))$.

---

involved here.

[119]Note also the similarity with Parsons definition "x occurs in s" in his (Parsons 1980) (p. 57).

So whereas Holmes originates in the Conan Doyle novels (since he is an abstract character of the stories and is not a character of any earlier story), London does not (it is not abstract). Similarly, Gregor Samsa originates in Kafka's *The Metamorphosis*.

With this definition of "originates," we may say, of a *character*, that it *is fictional* whenever the character originates in some story or other:

> x is a *fictional character* $=_{df}$ x is a character and x originates in some story.

In formal terms, this becomes:

> $FictionalCharacter(x) =_{df} Character(x) \,\&\, \exists s(Originates(x, s))$.

This distinguishes the notion of "fictional" as it applies to characters from Walton's notion of "fictional" that applies to propositions. Presumably, this regiments another of the many different ways in which he uses the notion "fictional" and shows how the fictionality of characters is conceptually dependent upon the fictionality of propositions, among other things. Indeed, we can also regiment our talk of "fictional detectives" (as in "Holmes is a fictional detective"), "fictional student" (as in "Raskolnikov is a fictional student") as follows:

> $Fictional\text{-}F(x) =_{df} \exists s \exists x [Story(s) \,\&\, Originates(x, s) \,\&\, s \models Fx]$.

So if "S" stands for the property of being a student, and "r_{CP}" stands for the Raskolnikov of *Crime and Punishment*, we may analyze the fact that Raskolnikov is a fictional student as:

> $Fictional\text{-}S(r_{\mathrm{CP}})$.

In what follows, I shall assume that for any property F, there is a property that corresponds to *Fictional-F*, even though this is not strictly guaranteed by the axioms we have employed so far.[120]

We conclude this section by reminding the reader that in object theory, the comprehension principle for abstract objects is used to identify characters as abstract objects only when the character is fictional. The following claim has the status of an axiom:

> Axiom: If character x originates in story s, x is (identical to) the abstract object that encodes all and only the properties F such that according to s, x exemplifies F.

In formal terms:

> Axiom: $Originates(x, s) \rightarrow x = \imath y[A!y \,\&\, \forall F(yF \equiv s \models Fx)]$.

---

[120]In other words, I shall suppose that we can consistently add the claim that there is such a property. I don't think too much will hang on this claim should I turn out to be wrong.

It follows from this axiom that if x originates in s, then x encodes a property F iff according to s, x exemplifies F. Consider then, what follows from the fact that Sherlock Holmes originates in the Conan Doyle novels. If we introduce the name "Holmes$_{CD}$" to indicate that we are referring to the Sherlock Holmes of the Conan Doyle novels, we may infer the following biconditional from the previous fact given our axiom:

Holmes$_{CD}$ encodes F if and only if according to the Conan Doyle novels, Holmes exemplifies F.

(In the above and in what follows, we drop the subscript on "Holmes" relativizing the name to the corresponding story only in those contexts where it is clear what the relevant story is.) In formal terms, this becomes:

$$h_{CD}F \equiv CD \models Fh.$$

Of course, we may disagree with one another about which properties are in fact attributed to Holmes in the Conan Doyle stories. But our disagreement is grounded in a more fundamental agreement, namely, that Holmes is in fact constituted by (i.e., encodes) those properties attributed to him in the novels, whichever ones those turn out to be. That fundamental point of agreement is captured by our axiom.

In what follows, we shall assume that the true sentences of the form "According to the Conan Doyle novels, Sherlock Holmes is (a(n)) F" ("CD $\models Fh$") have been added to object theory as facts. The facts asserted by these "prefixed story-operator" sentences serve to orient us philosophically to the analysis of a wide variety of other facts. For example, consider ordinary sentences of English such as "Sherlock Holmes is a detective," which are unprefixed by a story-operator but for which truth is preserved when the relevant story-operator is prefixed. It is an *auxiliary hypothesis* of object theory that the copula "is" (in such sentences) is ambiguous between encoding and exemplification predication. The true reading of the English will be:

$$h_{CD}D.$$

This is now provable as a consequence of the theory. The false reading will be:

$$Dh_{CD}.$$

Holmes is an abstract object and so doesn't exemplify the property of being a detective, or any other property that would imply that he has a spatiotemporal location.

In what follows, I shall assume that the reader can use the foregoing ideas to analyze the data described in Section 1. For the most part, this is straightforward. Some of the more subtle issues affecting the analysis have been discussed in Zalta (Zalta 1988) and (Zalta 1983).[121] If the project in the final part of the present paper is successful, then the analyses of these data in object theory should be acceptable to a pretense theorist, for we hope to justify the *referential* use of names of fictional characters from the point of view of pretense theory. None of the special paraphrases that pretense theorists offer for the kinds of data discussed in Section 1 will be necessary. Before we turn to the final part of the paper, however, it would serve well to examine a subtle and interesting class of data which we didn't discuss in Section 1. This discussion will show how awkward the pretense theoretic paraphrases can become when names of fictional characters are treated as "empty."

7.5 Special problem cases for pretense theory

There are some very interesting issues that arise in connection with the analysis of (the logical consequences of) sentences involving comparatives. Consider the following two sentences:

(GC) Pinkerton is as clever as any fictional detective.

(GF) Pinkerton is as famous as any fictional detective.

("GC" and "GF" abbreviate "general clever sentence" and "general famous sentence," respectively.) Suppose both that "Pinkerton" names a real detective who is still alive and that these two sentences are true.[122] Now given the fact:

(1) Sherlock Holmes is a fictional detective,

(GC) and (GF) imply the following, respectively:

(SC) Pinkerton is as clever as Holmes.

(SF) Pinkerton is as famous as Holmes.

(We may think of (SC) and (SF) as the "specific clever sentence" and "specific famous sentence," respectively.) Clearly, these are valid consequences of our data.

The two interesting puzzles concerning (SC) and (SF) are: (a) how do we analyze them so as to deal with the subtle difference that in (SC), Pinkerton's (exemplified) degree of cleverness is being compared to the degree of cleverness that Holmes exemplifies *in the story*, whereas in

---

[121]See Zalta (Zalta 1988), pp. 123–129, and 145–150; and (Zalta 1983), pp. 91–99, and 50–52.

[122]The second sentence is probably false of Allan Pinkerton (1819–1884), the famous Scottish-American detective who was appointed the first city detective in Chicago in 1850 and who made his reputation when he recovered a large sum of stolen money and discovered a plot to murder Abraham Lincoln in 1861.

(SF), Pinkerton's (exemplified) degree of fame is being compared to the degree of fame that Holmes exemplifies *simpliciter*; and (b) how do we analyze them so that, together with fact (1), they are consequences of (GC) and (GF), respectively. These puzzles become more acute when we consider the pretense-theoretic analyses of these sentences. Let us consider these first.

I shall assume that any analysis of our data must begin with a certain uncontroversial ordinary-language definition of the comparative relation. I shall formulate this definition in terms of the variable "G," which ranges over those properties that can be subject to comparisons of this kind. Henceforth our property variable "F" will now be used as a *constant* which denotes the property of being famous (this will make its appearance shortly). Here, then, is a reasonably uncontroversial understanding of the comparative relation:

(A) x is as G as y iff there is a degree d_1 of G and a degree d_2 of G such that: (1) x is G to degree d_1, (2) y is G to degree d_2, and (3) d_1 is comparable to d_2 (i.e., $d_1 \geq d_2$).

The variable "G" can range over such properties as intelligence, tallness, fame, etc. If we let G be the properties of cleverness ("C") and fame ("F"), respectively, and we use $As\text{-}G\text{-}As(x, y)$ to represent the apparent logical form of "x is as G as y," then we have the following two examples of (A):

(AC) $As\text{-}C\text{-}As(x, y)$ iff there is a degree d_1 of cleverness and a degree d_2 of cleverness such that: (1) x is clever to degree d_1, (2) y is clever to degree d_2, and (3) $d_1 \geq d_2$.

(AF) $As\text{-}F\text{-}As(x, y)$ iff there is a degree d_1 of fame and a degree d_2 of fame such that: (1) x is famous to degree d_1, (2) y is famous to degree d_2, and (3) $d_1 \geq d_2$.

We may refer to (AC) and (AF) as the "analysis of comparative cleverness" and the "analysis of comparative fame," respectively. If we ignore fictional objects, then presumably (AC) and (AF) offer us a general analysis of the relations *as clever as* and *as famous as*, respectively.

Notice that since a pretense theorist takes the name "Holmes" to be empty, he or she can't proceed to get an analysis of (SC) and (SF) by applying (i.e., instantiating the variables of) (AC) and (AF) to the objects Pinkerton and Holmes$_{CD}$. Since there is no such thing as Sherlock Holmes, Pinkerton can't bear a relation to him. At best, a pretense theorist might say that we can apply the relations to the objects Pinkerton and Holmes$_{CD}$ only within a certain kind of pretense. But whereas we might agree that (SC) does require that the comparison take place within a kind of pretense, (SF) is rather different. Although (SF) is a statement that presupposes that there is a pretense, the comparison is not being made within that pretense. But since a pretense theorist might even refuse to accept this, let us put the issue aside. Presumably, a pretense theorist can suggest that we can think of (AC) and (AF) as sentence schemata that can be applied to the *names* "Pinkerton" and "Holmes" and that when they are so applied, the right-hand sides of the resulting biconditionals give the true analysis/logical form of the ordinary English. That is, the pretense theorist can approach the analysis of our data by first applying (AC) and (AF) to the names "Pinkerton" and "Holmes$_{CD}$" as follows:

(AC$_i$) As-C-As(Pinkerton, Holmes$_{CD}$) iff there is a degree d_1 of cleverness and a degree d_2 of cleverness such that: (1) Pinkerton is clever to degree d_1, (2) Holmes$_{CD}$ is clever to degree d_2, and (3) $d_1 \geq d_2$.

(AF$_i$) As-F-As(Pinkerton, Holmes$_{CD}$) iff there is a degree d_1 of fame and a degree d_2 of fame such that: (1) Pinkerton is famous to degree d_1, (2) Holmes$_{CD}$ is famous to degree d_2, and (3) $d_1 \geq d_2$.

The pretense theorist can then proceed by focusing on the right sides of these applications of (AC) and (AF), arguing that the left sides of the resulting biconditionals are only the apparent logical form of the sentence in question. (SC) and (SF) don't assert that a simple relationship holds, but rather assert more complex sentences involving quantifiers.

Let's consider, then, the right-hand side of (AC$_i$):

(RS$_c$) There is a degree d_1 of cleverness and a degree d_2 of cleverness such that: (1) Pinkerton is clever to degree d_1, (2) Holmes$_{CD}$ is clever to degree d_2, and (3) $d_1 \geq d_2$.

(RS$_c$) ("right-side of the applied clever analysis") is *not yet* the proper pretense-theoretic analysis of (SC), for it hasn't yet addressed the fact that the second clause refers to the degree of cleverness that Holmes has in the Conan Doyle novels.

Crimmins (Crimmins 1998) suggests how to do this, for he offers a pretense-theoretic analysis of a sentence very similar to (SC).[123] His analysis of (SC) would be as follows:

(2) The degree of cleverness that actually is such that in the Sherlock Holmes stories there is portrayed there being a person named "Holmes" with that degree of cleverness, is such that Pinkerton's degree of cleverness is comparable to the former.

---

[123]Consider sentence (2) on p. 3 of Crimmins (Crimmins 1998).

Since I am unable to determine what Walton's analysis of (SC) would be, let us focus on Crimmins' analysis.

So how are we supposed to derive (2) from (RS_c)? Well, it will not do any real violence to (2) if we reparse it a little as follows:

(2′) There is a degree d_1 of cleverness and a degree d_2 of cleverness such that: (1) Pinkerton is clever to degree d_1, (2) in the Conan Doyle novels there is portrayed there being a person named "Holmes" who is clever to degree d_2, and (3) $d_1 \geq d_2$.

Let us, then, take (2′) instead of (2) as Crimmins' analysis of (SC). It should be clear that Crimmins can derive (2′) from the analysis (RS_c) if he supposes (as it seems he does) that the proper pretense-theoretic analysis of the second clause:

Holmes$_{\text{CD}}$ is clever to degree d_2,

is:

In the Conan Doyle novels there is portrayed there being a person named "Holmes" who is clever to degree d_2.

Now it is unclear why the latter should be considered an acceptable analysis or paraphrase of the former. But let us put to one side the serious problem lurking here. Moreover, let us presume that the subscript on the name "Holmes" is the marker which tells us that in (RS_c) we should paraphrase the second clause and not the first.

If the above is a correct understanding of the pretense theoretic account of our data, then our two puzzles (a) and (b) remain unsolved. We can't generalize this entire procedure to produce an analysis of (SF). For if the pretense theorist were to follow the same steps as we just followed, he or she would produce the following analysis of (SF):

There is a degree of fame d_1 and a degree of fame d_2 such that: (1) Pinkerton is famous to degree d_1, (2) in the Conan Doyle novels there is portrayed there being a person named "Holmes" who is famous to degree d_2, and (3) $d_1 \geq d_2$.

But this, of course, is the wrong analysis, for (SF) does not compare Pinkerton's fame with the degree of fame Holmes enjoys *within* the fiction, but rather with the degree of fame Holmes enjoys outside the fiction, in his guise as a well-known fictional character.

The second puzzle also remains: it is unclear how the pretense theoretic analyses of (GC) and (1) are supposed to imply the pretense-theoretic analysis of (SC). Although a pretense theorist might claim that (AC) is to be recast as a schema that can be applied to the "empty names" of fiction, or that we can pretend to apply (AC) to Pinkerton and Holmes, these moves won't help us here, for we have a genuine (non-pretend) *valid* inference to account for. It is just a simple fact that (GC) and (1) together imply (SC). The same goes for (GF), (1), and (SF). It is unclear whether the pretense-theoretic analyses (or paraphrases) of the premises will imply the pretense-theoretic analysis (or paraphrase) of the conclusion. Even though we haven't discussed here how the pretense theorist would paraphrase (GC) and (1), there is a *prima facie* problem already apparent if (2′) is the alleged analysis (paraphrase) of (SC), for it is no longer clear what rule of inference is going to move us from the paraphrases of (GC) and (1) to (2′).

This last problem is a very general one. As far as I have been able to discover, no pretense theorist has been able to give an account of the inference (described in Section 1) from:

> The ancient Greeks worshipped Zeus,
> Zeus is a mythical character,
> Fictional characters don't exist,

to:

> The ancient Greeks worshipped something that doesn't exist.

This inference, and numerous others like it, are not part of any pretense. These are facts about our pretheoretic notion of logical consequence, and as such, should be preserved on a proper logical representation of the data. A pretense-theorist has to show that the pretense-theoretic paraphrases of the premises imply the pretense-theoretic paraphrase of the conclusion. This hasn't been done. By contrast, an analysis is available in object theory.[124]

Let us return to and complete our discussion of comparatives by considering how object theory conceives and analyzes the comparatives data. (A) is accepted as a general analysis of comparatives, yielding (AC) and (AF) when the variable G is instantiated to *cleverness* and *fame*. The variables x, y in (AC) and (AF) are regarded as objectual, and range over the objects Pinkerton and Holmes$_{CD}$. When these variables are instantiated in a straightforward manner, the right-side of the resulting biconditional is (RS$_c$), which we repeat here for convenience:

(RS$_c$) There is a degree d_1 of cleverness and a degree d_2 of cleverness such that: (1) Pinkerton is clever to degree d_1, (2) Holmes$_{CD}$ is clever to degree d_2, and (3) $d_1 \geq d_2$.

Notice, however, that the auxiliary hypothesis of object theory (mentioned in the penultimate paragraph of §4) now predicts that the sec-

---

[124]See Zalta (Zalta 1988), p. 128.

ond clause in (RS_c) is ambiguous between the philosophical claim that Holmes$_\text{CD}$ exemplifies being clever to degree d_2 and the philosophical claim that Holmes$_\text{CD}$ encodes being clever to degree d_2. If we let "C_{d_2}" be the predicate representing the property of being clever to degree d_2, we have the following two readings of the second clause of (RS_c), the first of which is an exemplification predication and the second of which is an encoding predication:

$$C_{d_2} h_\text{CD},$$
$$h_\text{CD} C_{d_2}.$$

In this case, the correct reading is the encoding predication, for the exemplification predication is false. Abstract objects do not exemplify the property of being clever (to any degree). So the proper analysis of (SC) in object theory is:

(B) There is a degree d_1 of cleverness and a degree d_2 of cleverness such that: (1) Pinkerton exemplifies being clever to degree d_1, (2) Holmes$_\text{CD}$ encodes being clever to degree d_2, and (3) $d_1 \geq d_2$.

This, I suggest, is the proper understanding of (SC). Note also that it is a theorem of object theory that Holmes$_\text{CD}$ encodes the property of being clever to degree d_2 if and only if according to the Conan Doyle novels, Holmes exemplifies being clever to degree d_2:[125]

$$h_\text{CD} C_{d_2} \equiv \text{CD} \models C_{d_2} h.$$

This is a consequence of the fact that Holmes$_\text{CD}$ encodes all and only those properties that Holmes exemplifies according to the Conan Doyle novels. So the second clause of our analysis of (SC) is equivalent to the claim:

According to the Conan Doyle novels, Holmes exemplifies being clever to degree d_2.

Substituting this into our analysis (B) of (SC), we get the following claim, which is equivalent:

(B') There is a degree d_1 of cleverness and a degree d_2 of cleverness such that: (1) Pinkerton exemplifies being clever to degree d_1, (2) according to the Conan Doyle novels, Holmes exemplifies being clever to degree d_2, and (3) $d_1 \geq d_2$.

Both (B) and (B') can be rendered into our formal notation in the way demonstrated above. Note that from (B'), we can predict Crimmins' analysis (2') if one accepts the controversial idea that the second clause

---

[125]Remember that we drop the subscript on "Holmes" in those (formal) contexts that are relativized to the Conan Doyle novels.

in (B′) can be rendered "In the Conan Doyle novels there is portrayed there being a person named 'Holmes' who is clever to degree d_2."

Our representation and analysis of (SC) avoids the two puzzles connected with the proper representation of our data. With respect to the first problem, it makes the right prediction in the case of (SF). To analyze (SF), we follow the same steps we followed in analyzing (SC). These steps allow us to move from (AF) to (RS$_f$):

(RS$_f$) There is a degree d_1 of fame and a degree d_2 of fame such that: (1) Pinkerton is famous to degree d_1, (2) Holmes$_{\text{CD}}$ is famous to degree d_2, and (3) $d_1 \geq d_2$.

Again our theory predicts an ambiguity in the second clause of (RS$_f$) between Holmes exemplifies being famous to degree d_2 and Holmes encoding being famous to degree d_2. However this time, the correct analysis is the exemplification reading:

$$F_{d_2} h_{\text{CD}}.$$

With this as our reading of the second clause of (RS$_f$), we obtain the following analysis of (SF):

There is a degree d_1 of fame and a degree d_2 of fame such that: (1) Pinkerton exemplifies being famous to degree d_1, (2) Holmes$_{\text{CD}}$ exemplifies being famous to degree d_2, and (3) $d_1 \geq d_2$.

So our theory solves the first puzzle involving comparatives. A simple ambiguity in the copula infects our everyday, ordinary understanding of comparatives, insofar as they are applied to fictions. Once the ambiguity is resolved, the proper analyses can be given.

Before we discuss the second problem, the ambiguity must be removed from our notation for the comparative relation $As\text{-}G\text{-}As(x, y)$. English sentences of the form "x is as G as y" can be disambiguated in one of three ways. If one of the relata is a fiction and it is the degree of G that that relatum has *in the fiction* that is in question, we disambiguate our formal notation by marking the variable with a "+." This will serve to indicate that the encoding reading for that relatum is in play. So, in what follows, we shall distinguish the following four biconditionals:

$$As\text{-}G\text{-}As(x, y) \equiv \exists d_1 \exists d_2[G_{d_1} x \,\&\, G_{d_2} y \,\&\, d_1 \geq d_2],$$
$$As\text{-}G\text{-}As(x, y^+) \equiv \exists d_1 \exists d_2[G_{d_1} x \,\&\, y G_{d_2} \,\&\, d_1 \geq d_2],$$
$$As\text{-}G\text{-}As(x^+, y) \equiv \exists d_1 \exists d_2[x G_{d_1} \,\&\, G_{d_2} y \,\&\, d_1 \geq d_2],$$
$$As\text{-}G\text{-}As(x^+, y^+) \equiv \exists d_1 \exists d_2[x G_{d_1} \,\&\, y G_{d_2} \,\&\, d_1 \geq d_2].$$

Thus, for example, the last of these would be appropriate for the analysis of the English sentence "Holmes is as clever as Poirot," since this compares Holmes' cleverness within the Conan Doyle novels with Poirot's cleverness within the Agatha Christie ("AC") novels. So the formal representation:

$$As\text{-}C\text{-}As(\text{Holmes}^+_{\text{CD}}, \text{Poirot}^+_{\text{AC}}),$$

is equivalent to:

$$\exists d_1 \exists d_2 [h_{\text{CD}} C d_1 \ \& \ p_{\text{AC}} C d_2 \ \& \ d_1 \geq d_2].$$

This asserts that there are degrees d_1 and d_2 such that: (1) $\text{Holmes}_{\text{CD}}$ encodes being clever to degree d_1, (2) $\text{Poirot}_{\text{AC}}$ encodes being clever to degree d_2, and (3) d_1 is greater than or equal to d_2. Given the equivalences in object theory discussed at the end of Section 4 and even more recently, we know that this representation of the English "Holmes is as clever as Poirot" is yet again equivalent to:

> There are degrees d_1 and d_2 such that: (1) according to the Conan Doyle novels, Holmes exemplifies being clever to degree d_1, (2) according to the Agatha Christie novels, Poirot exemplifies being clever to degree d_2, and (3) d_1 is greater than or equal to d_2.

I take it this is the correct way to understand the English.

It is now easy to see that the second puzzle we have been tracking has been solved as well. Our representation and analysis of (SC) demonstrates that (SC) is a simple consequence of (GC) and (1), in which the inference is a simple application of universal instantiation and modus ponens. Our representations of (GC) and (1) are, respectively:

$$\forall x[Fictional\text{-}D(x) \to As\text{-}C\text{-}As(p, x^+)],$$
$$Fictional\text{-}D(h_{\text{CD}}).$$

From these two claims, it follows that:

$$As\text{-}C\text{-}As(p, h^+_{\text{CD}}).$$

The inference in question is the simple one that we know it to be. Note, however, that the corresponding representation of the inference from (GF) and (1) to (SF) does not use a "+-marked" variable x. From:

$$\forall x[Fictional\text{-}D(x) \to As\text{-}F\text{-}As(p, x)], \text{ and}$$
$$Fictional\text{-}D(h_{\text{CD}}),$$

it follows that:

$$As\text{-}C\text{-}As(p, h_{\text{CD}}).$$

Again, the inference here is a simple case of universal instantiation and modus ponens.

One final point about these representations and analyses. Those well-versed in object theory will recognize that the +-marked $As\text{-}G\text{-}As$ conditions do not automatically constitute relations. We must explicitly assert that these conditions constitute relations. I believe that we can consistently add such claims to object theory, but I will not pursue the consistency question here. If the resulting theory is consistent, then we can regard the new +-marked *As-G-As* notation not simply as defined notation but as notation which reveals the true logical form of the English. If not, then we are no worse off than the pretense theorists, since they do not regard comparative expressions as capable of asserting genuine relations between real individuals to fictions.

7.6   Reconceptualizing abstracta

It is time now to "discharge" our talk of abstract objects. So far, we have seen that many of the notions of pretense theory correspond to regimented notions of object theory but that pretense theory has difficulty analyzing comparative (as well as intentional) relations between real objects and fictions. Presumably, a pretense theorist will not accept the object-theoretic analyses of these sentences that we proposed in the previous section. This seems to be the point at which the two theories are inconsistent with one another. An object theorist identifies fictions as abstract objects and accepts that names such *"The Tin Drum"* and "Raskolnikov" denote such objects. A pretense theorist rejects this.

In this section, I hope to show that a pretense theorist can accept our analyses of the data by showing that our quantification over abstract objects is harmless from the point of view of pretense theory. To make this point, my strategy will be to develop an interpretation of the formalism of object theory that should be acceptable to a pretense theorist, given that the interpretation quantifies only over entities that a pretense theorist already accepts. Since I think such an interpretation is simple to state, reasonably clear, and easily grasped, I plan to be brief.

Let me begin by inviting the reader to think about the formalism of object theory "from the bottom up." From a "naturalized" point of view, how are we to understand a theory that simplifies the logical analysis of the data but at the cost of invoking high-level generalizations that assert the existence of abstract objects. I suggest that when looking at those high-level generalizations "from below," they can be reconceived as quantifying over patterns of properties that are connected with behavioral patterns of various kinds. These include the patterns of pretense behavior involved in producing a prop and the subsequent dispositions to engage both in pretense behavior and in certain related patterns of speech and "manners" of speaking. So, I suggest that we reinterpret the instances of the comprehension principle for abstract objects (which appear to assert the existence of stories and fictional characters) as asserting the existence of natural patterns of properties. The (kind of) property pattern that is asserted to exist depends on the nature of the condition used to define the pattern.

If this idea can be sustained, then we will have an interpretation of object theory that should be acceptable to a pretense theorist. Even a pretense theorist must accept that pretense behavior and speech within and about pretense falls into rather large-scale, general *patterns*. So I simply suggest that we make the implicit quantification over patterns in pretense theory explicit, and then interpret object theory in the resulting ontology.

Let us make this plan a little more precise. Here are two instances of the comprehension principle. The first appears to assert that there is an abstract object which encodes just the properties that are constructed out of propositions true in the *The Tin Drum* ("TD") and the second appears to assert that there is an abstract object that encodes just the properties that Holmes exemplifies in the Conan Doyle novels:

$$\exists x (A!x \;\&\; \forall F(xF \equiv \exists p(\text{TD} \models p \;\&\; F = [\lambda y\, p]))),$$
$$\exists x (A!x \;\&\; \forall F(xF \equiv \text{CD} \models Fh)).$$

To interpret these claims so that they are consistent with pretense theory, we simply need to offer an acceptable interpretation of the predicate "$A!$" and the formal claim "xF." As to an acceptable interpretation of "$A!$," I suggest: *being a pattern of properties*. Under such an interpretation, these two formal claims assert the existence of patterns. As to an acceptable interpretation of "xF," I suggest: F is an element of the pattern x. Under this interpretation, our two formal claims simply tell us about the nature of the pattern.

Now to carry the idea one step further, let us ask what is it in the natural world that grounds these patterns of properties? The answer is: human behavior (including speech behavior). Consider the first of our two formal claims. The source of this particular pattern of properties is the game of make-believe created by Günther Grass and institutionalized by his production of a manuscript (prop) which, subsequent to copying and dissemination, served to identify (many of) the propositions whose imaginings are prescribed by the game. The resulting prescriptions and rules affect anyone who takes part in the game, creating thereby large-scale patterns of behavior, including the disposition to utter the token "*The Tin Drum*" in various well-regulated ways in certain situations. The first of the above formal claims asserts the existence of a pattern of properties grounded in the production of the prop which regulates this behavior. This pattern of properties involves (encodes) those properties of the form *being such that p*. Our disposition to make and judge as true claims of the form "According to *The Tin Drum*, *p*" traces back to the production of the prop. So the first formal claim simply asserts the existence of a pattern of properties which is defined by those properties *F* of the form *being such that p* which are constructed out of propositions fictional in *The Tin Drum*.

The individual elements of the pattern are clear enough. They include properties such as: being such that Oskar Mazerath decided to stop growing at the age of 3, being such that on Oskar's first day of school when (his teacher) Miss Spollenhauer damaged his drum, he let loose a piercing shriek which literally pulverized both lenses of her spectacles, and being such that Oskar felt responsible for dispatching his mother, Jan Bronski, his uncle, and his father (i.e., most of his loved ones) to their graves. Ultimately, our disposition to judge these claims to be true in the novel is grounded in the production of the prop, and this latter, in turn, grounds the existence of the property pattern. The instance of comprehension simply quantifies over this property pattern and objectifies it, so that it can be the subject of discourse. As such, the pattern may *exemplify* properties. For example, it might exemplify a relation to the pattern we would identify with Heinrich Böll's novel *Group Portrait with Lady*. When we say that the former is a more widely-known post-war German novel than the latter, this can be construed as an exemplification claim relating two patterns.

Now consider the second of our two formal claims. The source of this particular property pattern is the game of make-believe created by Conan Doyle, and institutionalized by his production of manuscripts (props) which, subsequent to copying and dissemination, served to identify (many of) the propositions whose imaginings are prescribed by the game. The resulting prescriptions and rules affect anyone who takes part in the game, creating thereby large-scale patterns of systematic behavior. The production of the prop established a pattern of properties, and this pattern in turn grounds a subpattern of subsequent dispositions to utter sentences like "Sherlock Holmes is *F*" in certain situations. Anyone who engages in the pretense (i.e., plays the game) accepts that the elements of the property pattern are constitutive of Holmes, even though they may disagree as to which properties are elements of the pattern. The property pattern that is established when the prop is produced becomes embodied again in the subsequent dispositions to assent to "Holmes is *F*" in contexts where the pretense is accepted (e.g., in a literature class).

So the second of the above formal claims therefore asserts the existence of a certain property pattern, namely, one which is grounded in the production of a prop that regulates behavior such as our disposition to make and judge true such claims as "According to the Conan Doyle novels, Sherlock Holmes is F." The elements of this pattern are such properties as: being a detective, living in London, and being extremely clever. The instance of comprehension simply quantifies over this property pattern and objectifies it, so that it can be the subject of discourse. As such, the pattern may *exemplify* properties. For example, when we say "Holmes still inspires modern criminologists," we may take this to be a property that the pattern exemplifies. As a pre-theoretic, untutored claim of ordinary language, the sentence "Holmes doesn't exist" can be read as saying that nothing exemplifies all the elements of the Holmes pattern (this, of course, is consistent with saying that the pattern Holmes does exist). To say "Holmes might exist" is to say that something could exemplify all of the properties that Holmes encodes.[126]

So we have our interpretation of object theory that is consistent with pretense theory. The commitment to fictional objects, when they are conceived in this way, is a commitment that pretense theory already makes, for such objects are subpatterns among the behavioral patterns which constitute the phenomena being investigated and which are presupposed to exist.

7.7   Observations about the road between

The fundamental claims of pretense theory, which involve such notions as "make-believe," "game," "imagination," "prop," etc., (which we temporarily put aside in the penultimate paragraph of Section 3) should now be consistent with object theory, under our new interpretation. One such

---

[126] Actually, there is a fruitful area for further investigation here. There is an argument which suggests that Holmes couldn't exist, given this definition. For one of the properties that Holmes encodes is being a friend of Watson. However, if Watson is an abstract object or pattern, then since no ordinary object could possibly exemplify the property of being a friend of some pattern, Holmes couldn't possibly exist. The fruitful area for further research is to develop the definitions under which we can truly say that Holmes might have existed. One strategy is to Ramseyfy, as suggested in Currie (Currie 1990). We suppose there is a finite sequence of formulas $\phi_1, \ldots, \phi_n$, which constitute the truths of the Conan Doyle novels. We then conjoin all of these sentences. We then existentially generalize (using a distinct variable) on each name n of a fictional character other than Holmes to produce a multiply quantified conjunction of formulas. We make sure that "relevant entailment" is defined so that this "Ramsey sentence" is relevantly entailed by the propositions true in the novels and so will itself be true in the novels. As such, Holmes will encode the property that is denoted by the λ-expression that is formed by dropping out all of the occurrences of "Holmes" from the Ramsey sentence and replacing them with a single variable bound by the λ. Call the resulting property "the individual concept of Holmes" (the truth of the Ramsey sentence in the novels should relevantly entail that Holmes exemplifies the individual concept of Holmes in the novels; so this is a property that Holmes encodes). The sense in which "Holmes *might exist*" is true, then, is that there might be some ordinary object which exemplifies the individual concept of Holmes.

claim is that when someone authors a work of fiction, they produce a prop which mandates imaginings in a game of make-believe. There is no conflict between this seminal idea and the conceptual framework of object theory. Indeed, given our new understanding of this framework, the existence of the stories and characters becomes a contingent matter which is ontologically dependent on the behavior of authors. Stories and characters, as patterns, *supervene* on the author's storytelling, prop-producing, and game-institutionalizing behavior. We can produce instances of the comprehension principle (i.e., apply the framework to produce specific existence claims) only when there is genuine data to be explained, i.e., only when authors do in fact behave in certain ways.

Since we now have an interpretation of our formalism on which the comprehension principle quantifies over contingently existing patterns, we can truly say that the Conan Doyle stories and the character of Sherlock Holmes *didn't exist* before Conan Doyle engaged in certain behavior. This puts to rest a traditional objection to the identification of fictions as abstract objects. It has been claimed that the identification of fictions with abstract objects does not account for the sense in which fictions are "contingently created."[127] This has led Thomasson, for example, to develop a theory of "dependent abstracta."[128] Of course, if we take only the Platonic interpretation of our comprehension principle, where abstract objects are conceived to be timeless and eternal objects which exist necessarily and always, then this objection to object theory has some *prima facie* force.[129] But under our new interpretation, we may focus on the fact that the comprehension principle can be invoked to assert the existence of patterns only when we have data of the form "According to story s, x is F." The existence of this data is a matter that depends contingently on behavior of a certain kind and so is the existence of the property patterns discussed in the previous section. Thus we have an understanding of fictions that accounts for the intuition that they are contingent entities.

This sense of contingency for fictions (i.e., patterns) doesn't imply

---

[127]For a nice discussion of this problem, see Deutsch (Deutsch 1991).

[128]See Thomasson (Thomasson 1998a).

[129]It is important to note, however, that even under the Platonic interpretation of the theory, there is a response that can be made to this objection. For even if we construe abstract objects as existing necessarily and always, we can still say that the fact that an abstract object is a story is a *contingent* fact, for example. For the abstract objects that satisfy our definition of "x is a *story*," do so contingently! And if it is a contingent fact that certain abstract objects are stories, it is a contingent fact that certain other abstract objects are characters in those stories.

Of course, under the new interpretation of object theory described in this paper, this defense of object theory is unnecessary.

that they are anything like concrete objects. There is still a categorial difference between fictions and ordinary, concrete objects. Patterns of properties and the behavioral patterns they supervene on are not concrete or spatiotemporal in the same way that ordinary objects and individual instances of behavior are concrete or spatiotemporal. A pattern of properties or behavior is fundamentally different in kind from the individual instances of behavior. Indeed, our new interpretation of object theory offers us a new, almost *deflationary* conception of "abstract objects," on which the "mind-independence" and "objectivity" of such objects is to be contrasted with that of ordinary objects. But this is a matter for a different paper.

Since pretense theorists already accept behavioral patterns and the property patterns that supervene on them into their ontology, they need no longer refuse to treat names such as "Holmes" and "Zeus" as denotational. They can now accept the straightforward analysis of certain data without invoking awkward paraphrases. Intentional relations such as x fears y, x worshipped y, x searched for y, etc., can be accepted as such. There is no need for them to try to defend the idea that such things as "pretend-fear," "pretend-worship," or "pretend-searches," account for the data in question. Ponce de Leon was not pretend-searching for the fountain of youth. We do not pretend fear when we wake up screaming in the middle of the night, having dreamed about a monster. Indeed, we have now a sense in which the dream object "is" a monster. Such a sense is all that is needed to explain why fear can be appropriately directed towards such an object!

Nor do we have to invoke the notion of "pretend-reference" to account for this data.[130] The notion of "pretend-reference" is certainly worthwhile if we want to describe the author's use of names *during* a storytelling. A storytelling (prop-production) could be understood as an extended "naming baptism," for once the storytelling is complete, a property pattern will have been defined.[131] The pretense theorist should be able to accept that real reference to patterns can subsequently take place. The present interpretation of our formal theory requires nothing more than that. The notion of reference can be analyzed causally in the way Kripke (Kripke 1980) and others suggest as long as we amend the

---

[130] See Walton (Walton 1990), pp. 391ff, and pp. 422–425, where an appeal to pretend-reference is made. However, see Kroon (Kroon 2000), for an excellent, and more subtle, discussion of how pretend-reference might be used to understand negative existentials from a pretense theoretic point of view. Also, there is unpublished work by Kripke in which "pretend-reference" plays a role.

[131] This suggestion was developed in my short article "Referring to Fictional Characters: A Reply," which was translated into German and published as Zalta (Zalta 1987).

causal theory slightly in the case of names of fiction. Recall that in the case of names of ordinary objects, the causal chain of uses of a name with an intention to refer traces back to an initial "baptism" in which the named object is ostended. However, in the case of names of fictions, the causal chain of uses of a name with the intention to refer trace back to a property pattern grounded in a storytelling, i.e., a property pattern grounded in the production of prop that mandates imaginings in a game of make-believe. Unfortunately, a full discussion of this issue has to be reserved for a different occasion.

Under the interpretation of object theory we have just proposed, property patterns grounded in behavioral patterns constitute the meaning (semantic significance) of names like "Holmes," "Zeus," etc. It seems clear that the new interpretation of object theory proposed here reflects a kind of Wittgensteinian approach to meaning. It is intriguing that a Wittgensteinian approach to meaning provides an interpretation of our formal metaphysical theory and of the analyses constructed in terms of that theory. While the Wittgensteinian approach to meaning offers a naturalized interpretation of the formal metaphysical theory, the formal theory in return makes the Wittgensteinian approach to meaning more precise. Since pretense theory has been developed in the spirit of a Wittgensteinian theory of (language) games, the road from pretense theory to object theory is therefore a short one and more easily navigated than one might have expected.

7.8 Appendix:
A sketch of object theory for the uninitiated

Readers unfamiliar with object theory may find it useful to know that the theory distinguishes between abstract objects and ordinary objects. We say that an object x is ordinary ($"O!x"$) just in case x might have been concrete (i.e., just in case $\Diamond E!x$). When x and y are ordinary objects, then $x = y$ just in case necessarily, x and y exemplify the same properties (i.e., just in case $\Box \forall F(Fx \equiv Fy)$). In the language of object theory, we use "Fx" to represent the fact that object x exemplifies property F and "$F^n x_1 \ldots x_n$" to represent the fact that objects $x_1, \ldots, x_n$ exemplify the relation F^n.

An object x is *abstract* ($"A!x"$), by contrast, just in case x isn't the kind of thing that could be spatiotemporal (i.e., iff $\neg \Diamond E!x$). Abstract objects both *encode* properties as well as exemplify properties. (It is an axiom that ordinary objects don't encode properties.) From the point of view of object theory, Sherlock Holmes is an abstract object that encodes being a detective, being clever, living at 221B Baker Street in London, etc. That is, it encodes all and only the properties attributed to Sherlock Holmes in the Conan Doyle novels. However, Holmes exemplifies being more famous than any real detective, being thought about by Conan Doyle, being admired by, and an inspiration to, modern criminologists, etc.

As a second example, object theory identifies the fountain of youth as an abstract object that encodes being a fountain, producing waters which confer everlasting life when consumed, being located somewhere in Florida, etc. The fountain of youth exemplifies, however, such that Ponce de Leon searched for it, being mythical (assuming there is such a property), etc. Similarly, object theory identifies the monster I dreamed about last night as an abstract object that encodes being a monster, having three heads, having breathed fire, etc. The monster I dreamed about last night, however, exemplifies being a dream object, being frightening, being such that I hope that I never dream about it again; etc.

In the language of object theory, we use "xF" to represent the fact that (abstract) object x encodes property F. We say that abstract objects x and y are identical if and only they necessarily encode the same properties. In formal terms, this would be written:

$$A!x \ \& \ A!y \rightarrow [x = y \equiv \Box \forall F(xF \equiv yF)].$$

The ordinary sentences of natural language having the form "x is F" are ambiguous between Fx and xF. So "Holmes is a detective" receives two readings when analyzed in the language of object theory. When analyzed as "Holmes encodes detectivehood" it is true; when analyzed as "Holmes exemplifies detectivehood," it is false. So the present theory can explain why the monster I dreamed about last night frightened me. There is a sense of "is" on which the monster I dreamed about *is* a monster.

Object theory is applied to the theory of fiction with the help of two interesting features, namely, its underlying theory of properties and theory of propositions. The main principle of the underlying property theory is that for every condition on objects expressible without encoding subformulas, there is property that is exemplified by exactly those objects satisfying the condition.[132] We may denote such complex prop-

---

[132] In formal terms, this principle asserts:

$\exists F \forall x(Fx \equiv \phi)$, where ϕ has no free Fs and no encoding subformulas.

This, of course, has numerous instances, among which are the following:

$\exists F \forall x(Fx \equiv \neg Gx)$,
$\exists F \forall x(Fx \equiv Gx \ \& \ Hx)$,
$\exists F \forall x(Fx \equiv Gx \ \lor \ Hx)$,
$\exists F \forall x(Fx \equiv \exists y Ryx)$,
etc.

When we add more expressive power to the language of object theory, we get a

erties using λ-notation. The expression $[\lambda x\ \phi]$ (where ϕ has no encoding subformulas) denotes the property *being an x such that ϕ* and the principal axiom governing this expression is that an object y exemplifies $[\lambda x\ \phi]$ iff y satisfies ϕ.[133] We say that properties F and G are identical just in case, necessarily, they are encoded by the same objects (i.e., $F = G \equiv \Box\forall x(xF \equiv xG)$. Though the theory of (existence and identity conditions for) properties can be generalized to that of relations, we omit the discussion of the more general theory from this brief introduction.

If we take propositions to be 0-place properties, then the main principle of the underlying theory of propositions is a special case of the principle for properties. The main principle of the theory of propositions is that for every condition expressible without encoding subformulas, there is a proposition that is true iff that condition holds. Basically, any formula ϕ in the language of object theory which doesn't involve encoding subformulas can be used in a term of the form "*that-ϕ*" ("$[\lambda\ \phi]$"). The principal axiom governing this term is a simple one: *that-ϕ* is true iff ϕ. This is the "degenerate" case of λ-Conversion; from it, one can prove the existence of a wide variety of propositions.[134]

Now the principles governing the existence of properties and propositions interact with each other. Every proposition p corresponds with a propositional property of the form *being such that p*. The following claim is a consequence of our formal theory:

$$\forall p \exists F \forall x(Fx \equiv p).$$

In other words, for every proposition p, there is a property that objects exemplify iff p is true. In what follows, we refer to these propositional

---

wider variety of properties. See Zalta (Zalta 1988) (which adds tense operators) and (Zalta 1993).

[133] In formal terms:

$$\forall y([\lambda x\ \phi]y \equiv \phi_x^y).$$

This axiom, in fact, implies the main principle of the underlying property theory.

[134] By existentially generalizing on $[\lambda y\ \phi]$, we can derive the main principle of the theory of propositions (mentioned just previously in the text) from this axiom:

$$\exists p(p \equiv \phi), \text{ where } \phi \text{ has no free } ps \text{ and no encoding subformulas.}$$

As a result, we have the following instances of this theorem schema:

$$\exists p(p \equiv \neg q),$$
$$\exists p(p \equiv q \ \& \ r),$$
$$\exists p(p \equiv q \ \vee \ r),$$
$$\exists p(p \equiv \exists x Mx),$$
$$\exists p(p \equiv \forall x(Gx \to Fx)),$$
etc.

As we add expressive power to the language of object theory, we get a wider variety of propositions. Already, however, the language has enough expressive power to represent a wide spectrum of our ordinary talk about fictions. See Zalta (Zalta 1988) and (Zalta 1993).

properties using λ-notation as $[\lambda x\,p]$. We read this term as follows: being such that p. Of course, such terms obey the axiom discussed previously: an arbitrary object y exemplifies $[\lambda x\,p]$ iff p.[135] These propositional properties allow us to state identity conditions for propositions: p and q are identical if and only the property of being such that p is identical to the property of being such that q (where identity for properties has already been defined). In formal terms, we would write: $p=q \equiv [\lambda y\,p]=[\lambda y\,q]$.

Given that our theory of properties and propositions asserts the existence of propositional properties of the form *being such that p*, the theory of abstract objects then asserts that there are abstract objects that encode such properties. In what follows, we can extend the notion of encoding so that we may talk of abstract objects encoding *propositions*. We shall say that an abstract object encodes p ('$\Sigma_x p$') whenever x encodes the property *being such that p*. In formal terms:

$$\Sigma_x p \ =_{df} \ x[\lambda y\,p].$$

Note that it now follows that there is a distinguished subdomain of abstract objects which encode *only* propositional properties. They are called *situations*:

$$Situation(x) \ =_{df} \ A!x \ \& \ \forall F(xF \rightarrow \exists p(F=[\lambda y\,p])).$$

When s is a situation, we may then define "p is true in s" ("$s \models p$") as s encodes p:

$$s \models p \ =_{df} \ \Sigma_x p.$$

With this notion, we are just a step away from defining the notion of a story. Before we turn to this latter notion, it is important to note that it now follows in object theory that if the same propositions are true in situations s and s', then $s=s'$; i.e., $\forall p(s\models p \ \equiv \ s'\models p) \rightarrow s=s'$.

---

[135]In formal terms:
$$\forall y([\lambda x\,p]y \equiv p).$$
This is an instance of the axiom:
$$\forall y([\lambda x\,\phi]y \equiv \phi_x^y),$$
which we discussed above.

8

Making up Stories

HARRY DEUTSCH

8.1 Introduction

"The world," said Santayana, "is not a myth, to be clarified by a little literary criticism."[136] Yet the blunt truth of Santayana's statement seems to have been lost amidst recent anti-realist manifestos. For example, in a chapter entitled "The Fabrication of Facts," Goodman denounces the common sense ground of the fact/fiction (world/myth) distinction:

> Of course, we must distinguish falsehood and fiction from truth and fact; but we cannot, I am sure, do it on the ground that fiction is fabricated and fact found.[137]

Goodman thinks that facts are as much a fabrication as is fiction. He views the adage that facts are found and fiction fabricated as a tenet of "fundamentalism"—the view that there is but one true "world version." But he acknowledges that we must distinguish fact from fiction, which he proposes to do largely in terms of literal truth and falsity. According to Goodman, fiction is literal falsity: "Literal falsity distinguishes fiction from true report."[138] Not so: Fiction need not be false. A fictional story may be, as a matter of pure coincidence, true. And not all falsehood is fiction. The fact that the earth is not flat is not the same as a fiction in which the earth is depicted as flat. The common sense adage begins to look more plausible, and I think it can be explained in such a way as not to imply fundamentalism. However much we may want to steer clear of naive fundamentalism, we cannot be left without a sharp distinction between fact and fiction. The distinction is too important to us. To

---

[136] See (Santayana 1948).
[137] See (Goodman 1978), p. 91.
[138] See (Goodman 1978), p. 124.

Empty Names, Fiction, and the Puzzles of Non-Existence.
Anthony Everett and Thomas Hofweber (eds.).
Copyright © 2000, CSLI Publications.

borrow Walton's example, in *Dr. Strangelove* the world is destroyed by a nuclear holocaust in the early 1960's, but the world was not actually destroyed by a nuclear holocaust in the 1960's. As Walton says: "The difference is enormous and nothing could matter more."[139] Let the facts be fabricated just as certainly as fiction. Then they must be fabricated differently in some sense and we advert to this difference when we say that the facts are found whereas fiction is fabricated. What is needed is an account of the ground of the distinction that is consistent with anti-realism, and for that matter, with fundamentalism.

I wish to suggest an account that grounds the distinction in the difference between two abstraction or comprehension principles—in the logician's sense: one governing the realms of fact and the other the realms of fiction.[140] Meinongian object-theorists will see the relevance of comprehension principles to a discussion of fiction, but they seem to have missed the point that such principles have explanatory force when it comes to understanding the distinction between fabrication and finding or creating and discovering.[141] Let these concepts be intermingled as much as you like. Let there be fabricating in finding, discovery in creation, fiction in fact. Let the facts be as theory laden as can be. There

---

[139]See his (Walton 1990), p.101.

[140]Roughly speaking, comprehension principles are ontological principles specifying the variety of objects of various logical types. For example, the naïve set-theoretic comprehension principle says that corresponding to any condition on objects, there is a set whose members are exactly those objects satisfying that condition. Similarly, the naïve object-theoretic comprehension principle states that corresponding to any condition on properties there is an object having exactly the properties satisfying that condition. Both of these naïve comprehension principles are contradictory. For example, the set-theoretic principle gives rise to Russell's Paradox. Various sorts of restrictions may be applied to yield what are very likely consistent principles. (The qualification "very likely" is encouraged by Gödel's Second Incompleteness Theorem.) I leave it to the reader to derive a contradiction from the object-theoretic principle.

[141]See below. In the present paper I do not discuss the "creation problem" dealt with at length in (Deutsch 1991), touched on in (Deutsch 1985), and touched on again in (Deutsch 1998). The creation problem is to say what creating such things as novels and fictitious characters comes to, since these things either already exist prior to any creative activity or else do not exist even after such activity. Lest it be thought that this problem is easily resolved by adopting an anti-platonist stance, I would point out that anti-platonism about allographic works, combined with common assumptions about identity, existence, and creating things, yields the result that two persons could not independently create the same allographic work. This patently absurd notion is enthusiastically affirmed by Kit Fine and Jerrold Levinson, to name but two of many philosophers who have succumbed to a naïve historicism about the identity of works and which is claimed to have the approval of none other than Jorge Luis Borges, see (Fine 1982) and (Levinson 1980). I demur in (Deutsch 1991) p. 24. In (Deutsch 1998), I argue that the problem is one of many instances where a plausible metaphysics clashes with a concept of identity appropriate enough for mathematics but inappropriate for the metaphysics of contingent reality.

is still the "enormous" difference Walton mentions.

The fact/fiction distinction is one of a family of related distinctions: fiction versus reality, fabricated versus found, created versus discovered, fiction versus non-fiction, and my favorite: the distinction between making something up ("out of whole cloth") and finding something out. These distinctions are allied and intertwined. Walton thinks it is impossible to link the fiction/reality (fact/fiction) distinction to the fiction/non-fiction distinction, though he never says why.[142] Common sense links the two—not that I am always a staunch supporter of common sense. Walton abandons the fiction/reality distinction, despite its enormous importance, and the fiction/nonfiction contrast turns out on his account to be largely a matter of style or the use to which a text is put. According to Walton, for example, New Journalism—even when not deliberately fabricated—counts as fiction.[143] I will have more to say about Walton's view below, but here I can only comment that I do not easily recognize my concept of fiction—or yours—in Walton's.[144]

---

[142]Walton remarks that "Notions of fiction akin to ours, in the library and bookstore spirit, are in many discussions intertwined irresponsibly with fiction-reality contrasts, with chaotic results," see (Walton 1990), p. 75. What are these "many discussions" and their "chaotic results?" Walton doesn't say. In spite of these animadversions, Walton himself notices an important connection between the fiction/non-fiction contrast and the fiction/reality distinction. See footnote 5 below.

[143]See (Walton 1990), p. 80. There is an uneasy tension between this view and Walton's notion that fictional works "prescribe imaginings," though Walton seems unconcerned. I comment further on this matter below. Also, Walton disputes the popular idea that purely fictional discourse is necessarily non-assertive, but acknowledges that there is a "simple but important truth" underlying the idea—namely, that fiction *need not* be assertive, see (Walton 1990), p. 81. I would point out, however, that non-fiction need not be assertive either. For example, a non-fictional work might consist of a series of commands, as in the case, say, of the *Ten Commandments*. The mere possibility of being non-assertive hardly helps to distinguish fiction from non-fiction.

[144]Nevertheless, apparently as an afterthought, Walton uncovers an important part of the truth about the fiction/nonfiction distinction: "One fundamental difference between the real world and fictional ones, if both are somehow man-made, lies in the manner in which we make them. A particular work of fiction, in its context, establishes its fictional world and generates the fictional truths belonging to it. A particular biography or history does not itself establish the truth of what it says or produce the facts it is concerned with. What generates facts, if they are our own creations, is not individual pieces of writing but something more like the whole body of a culture's discourse." ((Walton 1990), p. 101) Walton says too little to allow an evaluation of this last statement, (Why in theory couldn't everything that appears in "the whole body of a culture's discourse" also appear in an "individual piece of writing?"), but it is certainly true that a particular biography or history, "does not itself establish the truth of what it says," whereas in some sense a work of fiction does establish the (fictional) truth of what it says. The problem is to give substance and clarity to this distinction. That is what I try to do below.

I am going to borrow freely from the vocabulary of contrasts mentioned above, with two qualifications. First, the word "fiction" is sometimes used to mean a falsehood widely believed to be true, or one we accept provisionally for the sake of convenience (a "useful fiction"). Set this sense of the word aside. Secondly, the words "create" and "discover" are often used in normative senses whereby to discover something is to evince originality and to create something is to show creativity. I am using "discover," however, as I use it when I say that I have discovered a dead cat in the garden. That does not require originality.

The case of "create" and "fabricate" is trickier. As I am using these words here, to create something is to make it up, dream it up, invent it out of whole cloth or thin air. The part about whole cloth is important because creation/invention out of whole cloth contrasts with the more obviously useful sort of invention such as the invention of the wheel. Inventions of the latter sort may or may not work; but inventions out of whole cloth always work, since there is nothing to prevent them from working. Yet even so, a creation/invention out of whole cloth need not be any good, need not manifest any creative talent. However bad a fictional story or storytelling may be, it still counts as a creation in this sense.

In what follows, I first present an account of fiction and the fictional in terms of an analysis of the concept of making something up (section 2). I claim that the key to understanding fiction and the fictional is not the concept of make-believe, but rather the concept of making something up out of whole cloth. I acknowledge that both fiction and lies are "made up" and that the sincere poet "never lieth." [145] But I do not see this as a difficulty for the view that at the heart of the concept of fiction is the notion of making something up. I maintain that sometimes fiction is put forward as fact, but it is still fiction. Thus, the poet who puts fiction forward as fact does indeed lie. When the poet pretends not to be a poet, and hides the pretense, she lies, but she is still a poet. There is room for conflict here with the views of Gregory Currie.

In section 3, I raise certain objections to Currie's and Walton's analyses of fiction in terms of the concept of make-believe, and I argue that my own account in terms of making something up better explains key features of the phenomenon of fiction.

In section 4, I comment critically on the dominant view that our relations to fictional things, our fearing and pitying them, our referring to them, our making assertions about them, are not the real thing, but rather pretended, mock, or make-believe relations.

---

[145]See Sir Philip Sidney's, *Apology for Poetry or The Defense of Poesy.*

8.2 Creation and comprehension

In the opening pages of F. Scott Fitzgerald's *Tender is the Night*, we find the following beautiful passage:

> At the hotel the girl made the reservation in idiomatic but rather flat French, like something remembered. When they were installed on the ground floor she walked into the glare of the French windows and out a few steps onto the stone verandah that ran the length of the hotel. When she walked she carried herself like a ballet dancer, not slumped down on her hips but held up in the small of her back. Out there the hot light clipped close her shadow and she retreated—it was too bright to see... Below the balustrade a faded Buick cooked on the hotel drive.

The passage takes the form of a literal description of things and events at Gausse's Hotel des Etrangers on a June morning in 1925. Of course, it is no such thing. If it were, Fitzgerald might have been wrong about this or that detail, or about the whole of it. Suppose we ask: Did he get it right? Was it a faded Buick, rather than, say, an Oldsmobile, that cooked on the hotel drive? The question is clearly absurd. Fitzgerald could not have been wrong about the make of the car. He was in charge of such details. An author can make mistakes, aesthetic mistakes, factual mistakes, but not *this* kind of mistake. Similarly, it would be absurd for the reader to wonder about Rosemary's whereabouts (Rosemary Hoyt is the girl mentioned in the passage) between the time she first meets Dick Diver on the beach, and lunch with her mother a half hour later, when she announces that she has fallen in love with Diver. To my astonishment, literary critics have sometimes actually wondered about such things. Ellen Terry, in her lectures on Shakespeare, wonders where the boy in Henry V learned to speak French: "Robin's French is quite fluent. Did he learn to speak it from Prince Hal, or from Falstaff in London, or did he pick it up during his few weeks in France with the army?" And the eminent critic A.C. Bradley wonders about the whereabouts of Hamlet at the time of his father's death! A colleague of Terry's, L.C. Knights, wrote a delightful paper on (among other things) such absurd musings, entitled "How Many Children Had Lady Macbeth?" The play tells us she had some children but not how many, and it is no use wondering what the number is. There is no such number. Probably the sharpest rebuke to critics who thus reify fictional characters is Dover Wilson's: "Critics who speculate upon what Hamlet was like before the play open....are merely cutting the figure out of the canvass and putting it into a doll's house of their own invention."[146] Such reification of the fictional is a familiar phenomenon: Consider the case of the man who leaps onstage to save the fictional heroine. We are all unabashedly guilty of indulging in this sort of logically questionable behavior when we shout (or just *think*) "look out" as the villain sneaks up on the hero.

What accounts for an author's immunity from error, both of commission and omission? (It cannot be the case both that Lady Macbeth has exactly *n* children, and Shakespeare *neglected* to mention that "fact" in *any* draft, partial or not, purely mental or not.) The answer, one wants to say, is that since the author makes up the story, it is up him or her and open to him or her to determine what goes on in it. Yet this does not help very much. Apart from the unanalyzed reference to making something up, it amounts to no more than the idea that the author determines what goes on in the story. But, likewise, the theorist or textbook writer determines what goes on in the theory or textbook, and they *can* be wrong.

Let us consider the matter in the following way: The passage from *Tender is the Night* takes the form of a literal description of things and events at Gausse's Hotel des Etrangers on a June morning in 1925. But it is logically impossible for the describer of these things and events to misdescribe them. We should not lose sight of this basic fact just because it is true that an author can misdescribe matters in a number of other ways. For example, what an author puts down on the page can run counter to his or her own intentions. It nevertheless remains the case that a third party with no knowledge of Fitzgerald's intentions cannot fault him for misdescribing the make of the car cooking on the hotel drive.

The question is this: What would the world have to be like were the description of Rosemary's actions at the hotel fully veridical and it were— *is*—logically impossible for Fitzgerald to have misdescribed the event? (By "fully veridical" I mean, among other things, that the description is not true purely coincidentally.[147] I suggest that the answer is that the world would have to be a *plenitude*: It would have to contain every sort of object and event imaginable, and then some.[148] It would

---

[146]Terry's comment on Robin is quoted in (Knights 1947), p. 16. See the reference therein to Terry's *Four Lectures on Shakespeare*. Reference to A.C. Bradley's remarks may be found in (Knights 1947) as well, pp. 17–18. See the reference therein to Bradley's *Shakespearean Tragedy*. Dover Wilson's comment is quoted in (Currie 1990), p. 60. It comes from John Dover Wilson, *Introduction to Hamlet*, Cambridge: Cambridge University Press, 1936, xlv–xli.]

[147]An analysis of non-coincidental truth is beyond the scope of this paper.

[148]A plenitude is an abundance, as in "a plenitude of food." I am appropriating it to mean a maximal variety of objects.

be a Meinongian jungle with a vengeance, for its objects would not be tame, timid abstracta, but wild and woolly concreta! In other words, in writing the passage quoted above, Fitzgerald enjoyed immunity from error precisely because *whatever* description he had recorded would have been equally correct. On the admittedly rather bizarre supposition that his descriptions were logically guaranteed to be veridical, this would imply that the world would have to be any and every way possible—and impossible.

The odd supposition that Fitzgerald's description was (non-coincidentally) true, was solely for the sake of argument. As I've said, the passage from *Tender is the Night* takes the form of a description of things and events at Gausse's Hotel des Etrangers on a June morning in 1925. Yet it is no such thing. What, then, *is* it a description of? Most would say "nothing." They would claim that "Rosemary," as used in subsequent passages to "refer" to the girl described in this passage, is an "empty name" that in fact refers to nothing.

I want to propose almost exactly the opposite point of view. I grant that the fictional description is linked at best accidentally to concrete reality, but I claim that it is linked *necessarily* to what I call the "fictional plenitude." The latter may be thought of simply as the universe or domain of discourse—to borrow some terminology from logic—relevant to fictional discourse. The fictional plenitude is defined by a logical comprehension principle that says, in effect, that the domain contains any and every variety of object and event imaginable—and then some. Every aspect of concrete reality is a part of the fictional plenitude as is every aspect of any other possible concrete reality. Whatever other aspects of any possible reality there may be are also aspects of the fictional plenitude. In addition, the fictional plenitude contains an enormous variety of impossibilities. The technical details regarding fictive comprehension and the fictional domain can be worked out along the lines of recent object theories such as Zalta's or Parsons'.[149] In fact, the comprehension principles of these theories can be viewed as generating certain accounts of the fictional plenitude with which, however, I disagree.[150] These matters need not detain us. For present purposes, the crucial point is that the description of Rosemary's actions at the Hotel des Etrangers is very far from being an "empty description" and "Rosemary" as used in *Tender is the Night* is very far from being an "empty name." Both necessarily denote and/or describe elements and aspects of the fictional plenitude. A description recorded in the course of making up a story cannot fail to

---

[149] See (Zalta 1983) and (Parsons 1980).
[150] See (Deutsch 1985).

describe something and it cannot be a misdescription of anything. Whatever the descriptions describe, the King of France, the round square, the
girl in the lobby of Gausse's Hotel des Etrangers on a June morning in
1925, there is such a thing in the fictional plenitude-which, I hasten to
add, is not the same as saying that there is such a thing *simpliciter*.

More explicitly: We have on the one hand the fictional discourse,
such as the passage from *Tender is the Night*. On the other hand, we
have a domain of discourse defined by a rather free wheeling comprehension principle. We may view the discourse as consisting of descriptions
(in a general sense of "description"—not all are *definite* descriptions).
We imagine that these descriptions are evaluated attributively over the
domain. Thus, if I write a story that includes the sentence "The man
drinking the martini was sitting at the piano," this necessarily describes
a fictional character that is a man seated at a piano drinking a martini.
In cannot happen, as it can in discourse about reality, that I am using
the description "the man drinking the martini" to refer to someone who
in fact is not drinking a martini. It follows from the joint assumptions
that (a) the fictional descriptions are evaluated attributively over the
domain, and (b) the domain is a plenitude, that the descriptions are always proper (in the broad sense that there is always something that they
fit) and that they never misdescribe their referents.[151] Briefly, then, to
make something up is to record attributive descriptions of aspects of the
fictional plenitude. Here the descriptions in question need not be verbal
descriptions. More on this in due course below.

The following are not full-fledged comprehension principles for stories
and their objects. I simply want to indicate to the skeptical reader or
one not familiar with the object-theoretic literature, how the idea of the

---

[151]The requirement that the descriptions be attributive may be too strong. It is intended to rule out the possibility of an author using a description to refer *unwittingly*
to an object the description does not fit, as in the standard examples of referential
use. But I can imagine an author introducing a character by means of the description
"the man seated at the piano drinking a martini" but such that we later find out
that the man was not "in fact" drinking a martini. Yet this still doesn't seem to be
a straightforward case of referential use. The relevant description seems to be the
following attributive one: "the man seated at the piano who is at first presumed to
be drinking a martini but who in fact is not drinking a martini." In any event, I do
not mean to preclude the possibility of the referential use of descriptions in fiction.
A consideration of the case may well shed some light on the referential/attributive
distinction. Certainly descriptions can be used referentially by characters in dialogue.
Moreover, requirement (a) applies directly only to "canonical" descriptions, i.e. descriptions used to introduce or focus attention initially on an object of the fiction.
Canonical descriptions sometimes consist of little more than proper names—as in the
case of the description of the cast of characters in a play, as in: "*Characters,* Sir
Claude Mulhammer, Eggerson," etc., from T.S. Eliot's play *The Confidential Clerk*.
In that case, requirement (a) is otiose.

fictional plenitude may be given logical legitimacy. I call the following principles "principles of poetic license."

(P1) Let C be any condition on properties. Then there is an object in the fictional plenitude *FP* that has, in *FP*, all the properties satisfying C.

(P2) Let C be any condition on properties. Then there is a story in which some object has all of the properties satisfying C.

(P3) Let C' be any condition on propositions. Then there is a story in which all of the propositions satisfying C' are true.

I may seem to have landed squarely in the company of Meinongians, which I don't mind in the least. However, the view I am attempting to articulate is weaker than Meinongianism. Notice first that P2 and P3 make use only of the primitive notions of a story and truth in a story, (along with the notions of proposition, and property). These are (more or less) pre-theoretical notions not confined to Meinongianism. P2 postulates a story-in-the-abstract (i.e. one not necessarily yet composed) in which there is an object having the properties satisfying C. Not much there for the ontologically challenged to grumble about, except, perhaps, the idea of a story "in the abstract." But the wary reader is welcome to read the quantifier "there is" in the principles of poetic license as "there could be" or "there is potentially" or using some other suitable modal qualifier. Secondly, and this next point proves to be of crucial importance, P1 does not say that there is an object possessing the properties in C. It says that there is such *in the fictional plenitude FP*; and furthermore, it's not simply that the object in *FP* possesses the properties satisfying C. That would be contradictory: Just let C be the condition of being the property of not being in *FP*. It's rather that the object in *FP* possesses the properties *in FP*. It may help to think of *FP* as one big totally incoherent "story" which says whatever can be said about anything imaginable (and then some)![152] Then what P1 says is that there is an object in the "story" *FP* that has the properties satisfying C in the "story" *FP*. Thus, suppose I write a story in which FDR never existed. The proposition that FDR never existed is true in *FP*, and hence is true in my story. But FDR does "exist" *in FP*, in the sense that when we quantify over *FP*, we quantify over FDR. Then how can the proposition that FDR never existed be true in *FP* when FDR does exist in *FP*? The answer is that *every* proposition about FDR is true in *FP,* including the proposition that FDR does not exist, (and the proposition that he does exist) and indeed, including the proposition that FDR does not exist *in*

---

[152]Cf. Borges' story "The library of babble" in *Ficciones*.

FP. Third, I have little or no commitment regarding the exact nature of the things in *FP*. By modifying the principles of poetic license, the elements of *FP* could be the descriptions themselves, and the "describes" relation would then be the identity relation. That would be something of a nominalist approach. Or they could be taken to be the senses of the descriptions, whence the "describes"-relation would be the "expresses"-relation. Alternatively, the elements of *FP* might be actual and possible "abstract artifacts" of the sort discussed by Salmon in (Salmon 1999). The "describes"-relation would relate the description to the content of the artifact. At the realist extreme, the elements of *FP* are, straightforwardly, the referents of the descriptions. As usual, it proves to be far less cumbersome to talk the realist talk rather than the nominalist or any intermediate talk, and I will continue in that vein.

Notice that P1 does not say that there is (in *FP*, etc.) an object that possesses *exactly* the properties satisfying C. It is consistent with P1 that any object possessing the properties satisfying C might possess others as well; e.g. properties entailed by properties satisfying C. The stronger principle—that corresponding to C, there is an object with all and only the properties satisfying it—would give a full-fledged object-theoretic comprehension principle. As things stand, P1 does not determine a unique object corresponding to C. But the stronger principle leads to an interesting paradox, and thus invites the imposition of restrictions. I have argued elsewhere that the restrictions imposed, in particular, by Parsons' object theory, are inconsistent with the idea that absolutely anything can be made up out of whole cloth. And I have suggested that consistent comprehension principles can be obtained by requiring that the sets of properties or propositions corresponding to C or C' be logically closed. I have even sketched a proof that if closure under classical consequence is required, then the paradox is blocked. Of course, classical consequence does not seem appropriate in the context of stories, and in several papers published in the 1980's I have investigated systems of "analytic" relevant consequence that are more appropriate.[153]

In (Salmon 1999), Nathan Salmon seems to contradict all that has just been said about fictional comprehension: "One should not suppose that to every improper definite description there corresponds a fiction, or mini-fiction, in which the description is proper. Even pulp fiction is not that easy to write."[154] But I protest that pulp fiction *is* that easy to write. Give me any improper description and I will immediately "conjure up" a story in which that description describes something. It may

---

[153]See, for example, (Deutsch 1979) and (Deutsch 1984).
[154]See p. 306.

not be that easy to write good fiction, even good pulp fiction, but that is another matter. At the point in (Salmon 1999) at which this remark occurs, Salmon has backed himself into a corner. He has just argued, quite persuasively, that fictional things are existent "abstract artifacts," and that most of the things stories say about these artifacts are literally false. Thus, for example, it is literally false that Sherlock Holmes is a detective, since literally speaking, Sherlock Holmes is an abstraction. Salmon applies this same doctrine to the likes of Vulcan, Babinet's hypothesized planet. Then does every improper description give rise to a corresponding abstract artifact? Salmon says "No." He argues in effect that Noman, the counterfactual product of specific gametes, is a possible but non-existent person rather than an existent abstract artifact like Sherlock Holmes. The confusion here has to do precisely with the difference between making something up and not making something up. If the description, "the product of gametes S and T," is recorded in the course of non-fictional discourse about reality, then it is improper and the sentence "Noman does not exist" is true exactly because the name "Noman" fails to refer to anything in reality. If, however, the description is recorded in the course of making up a story, then it is proper and it refers to a particular denizen of the fictional plenitude—which, if you like, we may take to consist of actual and possible abstract artifacts of the sort Salmon favors.

The principles of poetic license guarantee that Fitzgerald cannot have been wrong about the make of the car cooking on the hotel drive. And as noted already, an author's descriptions are definitive in yet another respect. Why is it absurd for Ellen Terry to wonder where Robin learned to speak French? Similarly, why is it absurd to leap on the stage to save the fictional heroine? The reason, of course, is that Robin has no history, no life of his own apart from Shakespeare's descriptions of him, and likewise for the fictional heroine and the descriptions of her. It may be replied that *of course* Robin has no life of his own; he has no existence at all, since he is purely fictitious. This misses the point. Even real objects have no independent history in the stories in which they appear. Suppose I write a story that ends with the protagonist accidentally falling from the Eiffel Tower. It would make no sense to wonder whether subsequently the authorities put up better guard rails. That they did or didn't is not part of the story. (The authorities might take a hint from the fiction and put up better guard rails, but that is irrelevant.) The point is that it is nonsense to wonder about an untold part of the fictional history of even a real object. There are no such untold parts.

We can appeal again to the fundamental fact that the fictional domain is a plenitude to explain why Terry's musings about Robin are

nonsense and why it is absurd to leap on the stage to save the heroine. If there were some untold part in which Robin learns French while
in the Army but not from Falstaff in London, then it would have been
possible for Shakespeare to have been mistaken about that. Since that
is not possible, there can be no such untold part. And here by "untold
part" I certainly do *not* mean some detail the author thought of including but didn't. I mean literally something the author completely omitted
from any draft but that was nonetheless true of the character or other
fictional object. Moreover, if it were possible to save the heroine from
her fate by coming to her rescue, there would be an untold part of the
story—namely, the part in which someone comes to her rescue, and such
untold parts do not exist.

A variation on this theme: It is often remarked that fictions are "incomplete." The play tells us that Lady Macbeth has children but it
doesn't say how many. No proposition of the form: "Lady Macbeth has n
children" is true in the play. (This sort of incompleteness is not the same
as that known to logicians as "ω-inconsistency," nor the notion known as
"ω-incompleteness."[155] Some have drawn certain rather startling conclusions from the premise that a description in fiction may be incomplete.
From the fact that the description of Sherlock Holmes is incomplete,
Kripke infers that Holmes is not any particular possible object (for if
so, which?); and David Lewis infers that Holmes is "plural." Different
possible objects play the role of Holmes in different possible worlds.[156]
Yet it may seem that neither inference is strictly valid, since both ignore
the "possibility" that only our information about Holmes, not Holmes
himself, is incomplete—that there are untold parts of the stories about
Holmes. Apparently, Kripke and Lewis assumed that this "option" is not
a live one, but they never say why it should be ruled out. According to

---

[155] I mention this because some commentators have said otherwise. A formal system,
S, whose variables may be interpreted as ranging over the natural numbers and
which contains some mechanism for forming the numeral n corresponding to any
natural number n, is ω-*inconsistent* if there is a formula $F(x)$ in one free variable,
x, such that $\exists x F(x)$ is provable in S and yet all formulas of the form $\neg y F(n)$ are
also provable in S. The situation with Lady Macbeth's children is not an instance
of—nor even a close analogue of—ω-inconsistency (substituting the notion of truth
in the play for provability in S) since it is not the case that *any*, much less *all*, of the
sentences of the form "It is not the case that Lady Macbeth has n children" is true
in the play. Currie claims that both belief and fictional truth are "ω-incomplete,"
and that he is here "adopting the terminology of the logicians." Currie is thinking
of ω-inconsistency not ω-incompleteness. S is ω-incomplete if $\forall x F(x)$ is *not* provable
although $F(n)$, for any number n, is provable. There are consistent systems that are
ω-inconsistent. ω-inconsistency implies ω-incompleteness but the converse is not true.
See (Smullyan 1992) for a very readable discussion of these notions.

[156] See (Lewis 1983), and (Kripke 1980).

the epistemic theory of vagueness, there are necessarily untold parts to the story about, say, baldness. This theory holds that there is a sharp dividing line between the bald and the non-bald, but we cannot know what it is. Could fictional incompleteness be such a "blindspot?" The answer is: Absolutely not. If the number of hairs on Holmes' head were an untold part of the stories, it would have been possible for Conan Doyle to have been mistaken about that. Had he hazarded a guess, he might have been wrong; but he couldn't have been wrong. The very nature of fabricating fiction rules out such a "possibility." More precisely, what rules it out is the fact that the fictional domain is a plenitude. The epistemic alternative is simply not available in the case of fictional incompleteness.

It seems to me that the unreality of fictional things has little to do with their mode of being or non-being. Rather, it has to do with the features of fictional discourse to which I have been attempting to draw attention: Robin's unreality is a function of the fact that Shakespeare's descriptions of him cannot be misdescriptions, and that he cannot exceed the boundaries of those descriptions (lest it be possible to misdescribe him). So understood, the Eiffel Tower of my story is as unreal as Robin. That is not to say that the Eiffel Tower of my story is anything other than *the* Eiffel Tower. On the contrary, *the* Eiffel Tower figures in my story. But it is unreal in that it can no more exceed the boundaries of its descriptions than Robin can exceed his. Furthermore, it is not possible for me to misdescribe the Eiffel Tower of my story, though of course my descriptions may well not be true of the real Tower. If I were to say in my story that the Eiffel Tower was built in 1888, a year earlier than it was in fact built, that would be a mistake if my intention had been to state the year the Tower was in fact built. But it need not have been a mistake. Whether it was a mistake or not would be up to me, not you. If I insist that the mistaken date of origin is integral to my story, than that's that. Of course, if my descriptions of the Tower stray too far from the truth, then the Tower itself no longer figures in my story.[157] So, there are some constraints, but they are minimal. Such is the price of importing real objects into the unreal world of a story.

The unreal, then, need not be non-existent. Meinongians who hold that unreality consists in non-existence will be hard pressed to explain the unreality of the Eiffel Tower of my story—unless, implausibly, they take it to be an object distinct from the Eiffel Tower. Some non-Meinongians also equate unreality with non-existence. Salmon, after developing the idea that fictitious characters and other fictional objects originating

---

[157] Perhaps not. Could the Tower be, fictionally, a gigantic insect?

in fiction are abstract artifacts, is faced with explaining their unreality. If Holmes is an existent artifact, then what are we saying when we say that he does not exist, or that he is "only" a fictional thing. Salmon concludes that we mean by this that there is no object that is both Holmes-the-artifact and just like the detective depicted in the stories, i.e. "Holmesesque." So, when we say that Holmes is only fictional we are asserting the non-existence of an impossibility—for it is impossible for Holmes-the-artifact to have practically any of the properties Holmes is depicted as having in the stories. Now, I am inclined to agree with Kripke that purely fictional things are not possible things, and that when we say that Holmes does not exist that is literally to assert a necessary truth.[158] But I do not think that is what we mean when we say that Holmes is merely or purely fictional, unreal, and "does not exist." I think we mean that the stories about Holmes are fictional, that they are not history or biography or news of any sort. We can detect, so to speak, the sheer fictionality or unreality of even real objects in fictional stories by reminding ourselves of the oddity and absurdity of such questions as: When exactly did Sherlock Holmes finally expire? (Conan Doyle killed him off once but brought him back by popular demand.) Or, did the authorities finally, after the tragic accident, put up higher guard rails in the Tower? Or, where *did* Robin learn to speak French? Similarly, we detect the unreality of the fictional heroine by contemplating the absurdity of leaping onstage to save her. These reminders take us closer to the source of the unreality than does straightforward philosophical thinking about ontology. Who cares whether purely fictional things literally exist or not? What is important is to understand their fictionality.

Another way to "detect" the unreality of fictional things is this: Such things are tied much more intimately to their descriptions than are real things. (These remarks concern only *purely* fictional things, although I would argue that even the Eiffel Tower of my story is tied more intimately to the fictional descriptions of it than is *the* Eiffel Tower tied to the non-fictional descriptions of it.) Fitzgerald's canonical descriptions of Rosemary literally create the possibility of reference to her. No canonical description, no Rosemary, no reference. No description, however, creates the possibility of reference to me. I do that by my very presence. Such is the power of the real.[159]

Some would argue that reference to Rosemary is not real reference to a fictional thing but only a fictional kind of reference, a pretense to re-

---

[158] See below for discussion of Kripke's "coincidence argument."

[159] This remark reminds me of Russell's priceless comment that "if no one had thought of Hamlet, that would be the end of it, but if no one had thought of Napoleon, he would soon have seen to it that someone did," see (Russell 1919).

fer, an act of pretending or make-believe. There are a number of distinct proposals along these lines by Kripke, Searle, Walton, Currie, and others. This is not the place to mount a full scale attack on the reliance, in recent philosophy of fiction, on the notions of pretense, pretending, and make-believe, though I address some of the problems with such views in the next sections. Here I wish to remark that the idea that in the passage from *Tender is the Night* there is no genuine *reference* to Rosemary or to the Buick cooking on the Hotel drive represents a methodological mistake seriously affecting both the theory of reference and the philosophy of fiction. Such passages should be treated as raw data to which the theory of reference and the philosophy of fiction must conform. If we start with a theory of reference that allows reference to obtain only between touchable labels for touchable things, we are ignoring the data. To suppose that reference to Rosemary is mock reference or pretended reference is like supposing that riding a bicycle is pretending to drive a car. You are not really driving a car because you've got no engine, so you must be pretending to drive one! I intend to address this matter in more detail elsewhere. (See below, section 4, for related discussion.)

What now of the fact/fiction distinction and its relatives? I promised two comprehension principles—one governing the realms of fact. It is not possible, however, to state a comprehension principle governing actuality, since much of what passes for actual is contingently so. It is not true that corresponding to a consistent and complete class of properties that is compatible with actual scientific law, there is an object with those properties. What there is for the most part just happens to be what there is. If Laplacean determinism were true, we might be able to "generate" all the facts that hold, past, present and future, from those holding at a particular time, but that would not constitute an application of abstraction or comprehension. Nevertheless, the difference between the comprehension principle generating the merely possible objects—or better, the merely scientifically possible objects—and fictive comprehension is all we need. The realms of possible facts (i.e. possible worlds) are not plenitudes; the realm of fictional things is a plenitude. That is the difference between (possible) fact and fiction. This is not a difference that implies fundamentalism. There is no suggestion that there is but one true world version of found out fact. There may be many, but each must be consistent, complete, and scientifically coherent. Goodman wants to count fictional world versions among the versions that constitute our visions of reality. He remarks, for example, that while "Don Quixote" does not literally label anything, it constitutes a metaphorical label of ourselves as engaged in our quixotic endeavors. I like the idea of metaphorical reference far better than that of pretended reference. But

I would insist that the full story about our quixotic endeavors, if true, must be consistent, complete, and compatible with scientific law.

The important idea introduced above is that of the fictional plenitude. My skeptical colleagues will probably insist that this idea commits one to Meinongianism. However, I must insist that I am not a strict Meinongian. I am what Rorty once termed a "casual Meinongian," and so are you.[160] Our talk about fictional things and that of authors, often takes the form of descriptions of things and events, such as the things and events at Gausse's Hotel des Etrangers on a June morning in 1925. These can be any things and any events, whether actual or not. So such talk invokes, perhaps naively, a Meinongian-like domain of discourse. That is just a fact; and to acknowledge it is to acknowledge that we are all "casual Meinongian's." Perhaps the philosopher is right to rule that casual Meinongianism is naïve, that "strictly speaking" it is false, etc, etc. Yet remarkably enough, once casual Meinongianism is articulated properly (i.e. in terms of comprehension) it turns out to have considerable explanatory power. Here is one further illustration of that power.

Kripke has observed that the discovery of creatures just like those described in the myth about unicorns would not mean that the myth was about the real creatures, or that the extension of "unicorn" would contain the real creatures, so that they would be unicorns. If the myth was made up out whole cloth, then the relation between the term "unicorn" and the real creatures would be far too adventitious to constitute reference. Reference is no coincidence.

The foregoing argument should be carefully distinguished from the one discussed above which derives the impossibility of unicorns from the incompleteness of their descriptions. Kripke claims that the irremediable incompleteness of the descriptions of unicorns implies that they are no particular unique possible species, and of course he's right. But that doesn't show that unicorns are not possibilia, since, for all this argument shows, they might be plural possibilia, i.e. they might be any number of possible species, as Lewis would suggest. Does the coincidence argument rule against the idea that unicorns are plural possibilia? I would have thought so. For the argument seems to show that unicorns couldn't be actual; whence, they couldn't be possible, if by "possible" is meant "possibly actual" as it does on the indexical theory of "actual." Why is this not an acknowledged criticism of Lewis' theory? The reason is that Lewis' theory does not recognize the myth about unicorns as a myth. Lewis' theory treats the myth as if it were a record of known fact. By this means, Lewis seeks to render Kripke's point irrelevant. The point

---

[160]See (Rorty 1970).

sticks nonetheless. According to the coincidence argument, the names of (purely) mythical species and of (purely) fictional characters are not names of possibilia, plural or otherwise; and by extension, (purely) mythical species and (purely) fictional characters are not possibilia, plural or otherwise. According to Lewis' theory they are. Thus, Lewis' theory is mistaken.[161]

It must be admitted, however, that the coincidence argument is rather peculiar. There surely could be creatures just like those described in the myth about unicorns. Why aren't the latter the former? Why would the connection between the latter and the former be purely coincidental? Quick answers such as that there would be no causal or historical connection between the latter and the former are unsatisfactory. (This is Kripke's own quick answer. See the appendix to (Kripke 1980).) There need be no such connection between a name and its nominatum. If I call the tallest martian "Fred," supposing there is one, "Fred" is its earthly name though there is no natural connection, save a purely semantic one, between Fred and its earthly name.

The correct answer has to do precisely with the nature of making things up. The picture I have been sketching is that of a fictional domain containing anything imaginable. That the fictional domain contains creatures just like those described in the myth about unicorns is not a mere happenstance. They are there of necessity and the fictional descriptions of them necessarily describe them. By contrast, membership in the domain corresponding to contingent reality is largely a matter of happenstance. Now, however, we run into an interesting and potentially troublesome development. Suppose that the descriptions of unicorns in the myth were complete down to the last detail but that they were nonetheless made up out of whole cloth. Such a supposition is highly implausible but not, I take it, inconsistent. Furthermore, suppose that there were actually such creatures in existence. Then the casually Meinongian view entails that these same actual creatures are denizens of the fictional plenitude and that the fictional descriptions and the term "unicorn" apply to them. But this seems to contradict the coincidence argument which concludes that the term "unicorn" as well as (I assume) the fictional descriptions of unicorns, i.e. the descriptions actually occurring in a text of the myth, do not apply to these actual creatures.

This difficulty is only apparent, however. Let us look back at a distinction I drew earlier when discussing the principles of poetic license. I pointed out that P1 does not assert that objects in *FP* have properties corresponding to C; rather, objects in *FP* have properties corresponding

---

[161]See below for another, though related, criticism of Lewis' theory.

to C *in FP*. This is analogous to the idea that an object in a story has properties *in the story*. The relativization of propertyhood to *FP* is crucial: Without it we get a contradiction. Likewise, a fictional description or name applies to an object in *FP* only relative to *FP*. This should not seem mysterious. One of the interesting consequences of casual Meinongianism is that one of the relata of the reference relation is the relevant domain of discourse. But certainly domains can overlap. Fictional discourse invokes the fictional domain; literal or non-fictional discourse invokes the domains of the actual and possible. These domains overlap. In fact, every domain is a subset of *FP*. Accordingly, the point that emerges from the coincidence argument is that, speaking non-fictionally, the actual unicorn-like creatures would not be unicorns, and would not be properly so called. Equivalently, relative to non-fictional domains, the actual unicorn-like creatures are not unicorns and are not properly so called. However, from the standpoint of the fictional domain evoked by the casually Meinongian incantations of ordinary fictional discourse, the de facto actual unicorn-like creatures would be unicorns. Equivalently, speaking fictionally, rather than non-fictionally, the actual unicorn-like creatures would be unicorns and would be properly so-called.

It is thus not quite true that unicorns could not have been actual, for what are fictionally unicorns could have been actual creatures. But there could not have been real unicorns; that is, there could not have been creatures that are non-fictionally unicorns. Unicorns are ineluctably fictional. At work here is a distinction of discourses corresponding to a distinction of domains. Descriptions in fictional discourse describe the fictional domain. Descriptions in non-fictional discourse describe some non-fictional domain, canonically, the domain of actuality, and if there are modal elements present, they may describe domains of pure possibility as well.

Some may view the need to relativize reference to domain as merely an *ad hoc* way to dodge the contradictions to which casual Meinongianism is susceptible. But I would point out that relativization of reference to domain is a familiar idea from logic. It is not terribly surprising that the analysis of fictional discourse should require such relativization if it is also required by other intensional notions such as logical validity. Furthermore, the relativization helps explain in just what sense the fictional descriptions are not about the actual unicorn-like creatures. In fact, the fictional descriptions could be about the actual creatures, if such existed. The point is rather that the fictional descriptions, i.e. the descriptions that occur in a text of the myth, are evaluated with respect to the fictional domain. Since this domain contains the actual creatures, the fictional descriptions would indeed be about the actual creatures, if such existed. But the descriptions occurring in the myth are not evaluated with respect to non-fictional domains, and hence are not about anything in those domains. This is the crucial point. As you read along in the text of the myth you come across some description. What is that description about? Answer: Something in the fictional plenitude. Nevertheless, the very same description type can be used to describe something in a non-fictional domain. It seems, however, that exceptions to this are the names ("Sherlock Holmes") or name-like terms ("unicorn") that originate in fiction. The purely fictional term "unicorn" could not, without further ado, be used in non-fictional discourse to refer to unicorn-like creatures or to anything else. Of course, there might be some further ado. We might decide to use "unicorn" in non-fictional discourse to refer to the unicorn-like creatures we just discovered living in the French countryside. But then it would probably be best to view the fictional term "unicorn" and its non-fictional twin as homonyms.

The situation here is a bit delicate, but the upshot is clear: Speaking of the real world, the coincidence argument dictates that the actual unicorn-like creatures are not literally or non-fictionally unicorns. But speaking of the mythical world, casual Meinongianism dictates that the actual unicorn-like creatures are in the fictional extension of "unicorn" as used in the text of the myth and serve as the referents of the descriptions occurring in the text of the myth (and in our discourse about mythical unicorns).

8.3 Making-up versus making-believe

I claim that a document or other form of communication is fiction if it is a token of a type that was made up out of whole cloth, perhaps with generous amounts of the fabric of fact woven in as well. By "made up out of whole cloth" ("thin air" will do as well) I mean specifically that the author of the document recorded descriptions that are to be understood (philosophically) as describing elements of the fictional domain. I assume that this domain of discourse is a plenitude in the sense given by the principles of poetic license.

This account of the essence of fiction is very different in both content and character from the influential theories of Currie and Walton. Neither of these philosophers discusses the notion of the creation of fiction in their well-known books on fiction. Words such as "create," and "fabricate" are not even in the indices of these books. I seem to recall that both Currie and Walton use phrases similar to "makes up a story," but they don't seem to think that the notion requires analysis or that such an analysis may contribute to our understanding of the notion of fiction. Both Walton and Currie discuss principles that they claim generate fictional truths. But this project does not concern the creation of fiction. In a sense it does not even concern fiction as such. The project is roughly the same as Lewis' project in (Lewis 1983). Lewis undertakes to formulate truth conditions for an operator that he proposes to read as "In the fiction F." Now in the many years this article has been read and discussed, it has not, as far as I know, been noted that Lewis' various proposals work equally well or poorly for an operator of the form "In D" where D is just about any sort of document, not necessarily a work of fiction! (Remember that what is true in some non-fictional document D need not be true.) For example, one proposal Lewis considers is to take a proposition p to be in F, or true in F, just in case if all of F were true, then p would be true. This works equally well or poorly for "In D" where D is, say, a biography. A proposition p is true in the biography D, just in case if all of D were true, then p would be true. Perhaps we would want to strengthen the counterfactual conditional to indicative entailment, but the effect is virtually the same. The basic problem with Lewis' approach, and the reason it can't offer much by way of a distinction between truth in fiction and truth in biography, is that Lewis views the difference between the actual and the fictional as the same as the difference between the actual and the possible. His only nod in the direction of what is unique to truth in fiction is the requirement that the worlds relevant to determining what is true in the fiction be worlds in which the story is "told as known fact." Lewis adds this condition in response to the Kripkean point discussed at the end of section 2 above. This is rather ironic, however, since now Lewis' fiction operator might as well be a non-fiction operator! Furthermore, adding the requirement that the fiction be told as known fact makes absolutely no significant difference to what propositions turn out to be true in the work. For every world in which the fiction "comes true," i.e. where everything is as the work says it is, there is a corresponding world in which it comes true and is told as known fact.[162] It follows that the same propositions turn out to be true in fiction on the amended account as turn out to be true on the simpler account that says that what is true in fiction is what is true throughout the set of worlds in which the work of fiction comes true. But that condition is just as appropriate for biography as it is for fiction. It is just as appropriate for any sort of document, whether a treatise or a story. It turns out to be a bad account of truth in biography because it entails a descriptions theory of names. Of course, Lewis

---

[162]Well, almost. The teller cannot report as known fact that no one lives to tell the tale. But apart from this difference, I stand by the statement in the text.

defends a descriptions theory of fictional names. So he might point to this difference as an important difference between "In F" and "In D;" but surely truth in fiction and truth in biography differ more sharply than that. Lewis' project, it seems to me, sheds little light on the concept of fiction as such, and likewise for the variations on Lewis' theme found in Currie's and Walton's work. This is not to say, however, that these efforts shed little light on the notion of *truth in fiction*. A work of fiction is a document and so these various analyses of what amounts to truth according to some document are highly relevant. They are just not relevant, in my view, to an analysis of the fictionality of a document.

Walton and Currie do offer additional accounts of what fiction and fictionality are, appealing chiefly to the concept of make-believe and completely ignoring the concept of fictional fabrication, i.e. the concept of making something up. In my opinion, which I will defend shortly, this is a two-fold mistake. To ignore the concept of making something up and its casually Meinongian nature, is to do without an important explanatory construct; and to rely so heavily on the concept of make-believe is to psychologize the concept of fiction. This concept is a logical one not a psychological one.[163] I do not deny that making-believe and making-up are related activities; both are activities of the imagination. They are clearly conceptually connected, as is apparent in Dover Wilson's conceit quoted above and worth repeating: "Critics who speculate upon what Hamlet was like before the play opens... are merely cutting the figure out of the canvass and putting it into a doll's house of their own invention." The "canvass" invokes whole cloth and the doll's house invokes make-believe. But the two concepts are very different, as is already apparent from the fact that make-believe need not involve any making-up at all. When I was a child I sometimes made-believe that I was Audie Murphy heroically battling the Germans. I didn't make up the idea of Audie Murphy heroically battling the Germans, he really did do that and I knew it. Moreover, doesn't make-believe necessarily involve inserting oneself or a character one is playing into the action? Perhaps, then, make-believe comes in on the side of reader rather than author. That is what both Currie and Walton think.

Currie argues in (Currie 1990) that a document is fiction if it meets the following two conditions: (a) It is the product of "fictive intent," and (b) it is "at most accidentally true." Roughly speaking, "fictive intent" refers to the author's intention that the reader make-believe the story,

---

[163]The concept of fiction doesn't even have to do with art *per se*. Walton takes himself to be discussing matters bearing on the "representational arts," but the fact that a work of fiction is high art (as is *Tender is the Night*) has to do with features of it other than its basic fictionality.

where to do the latter is to make-believe that the story is "told as known fact." Walton's view (developed in (Walton 1978) and (Walton 1990)) is less easily encapsulated, but for present purposes it may be sufficient to say that Walton holds that the essence of fiction lies in the notion of make-believe. All our relations to fictional things can be reduced, according to Walton, to make-believe relations. Charles' fear of the slime racing toward him on the movie screen is make-believe fear, and our pity for Anna Karenina is not the real thing. It is mock pity. We make-believe that we pity her. Similarly, to say that Anna Karenina threw herself under a train is to say that it "is fictional" in a game of make-believe with Tolstoy's novel as a "prop" that she did so. A document is fictional if it serves as a prop of a certain sort in games of make-believe and the fictionality of a proposition "consists in the fact that imagining it is prescribed by a rule of the game." See (Walton 1990), p. 40. This last notion—the fictionality of a proposition—is the fundamental one. It seems obviously similar to Currie's notion of "fictive intent" in that on both accounts the reader ("appreciator" is Walton's rather barbarous general term) is enjoined to make-believe or imagine something. I find Walton's stress on the reader's imagination ironic. The traditional emphasis in literary studies, at least since Coleridge, has been on the writer's imagination. The concept of making something up takes us back to the writer's imagination.[164]

Let us consider Currie's views first. It is not true that authors of fiction must have "fictive intent" as Currie claims. A few years ago a Washington Post reporter named Janet Cook wrote a series of articles on a child heroin addict for which she was awarded the Pulitzer Prize in journalism. The prize was rescinded, however, when it was discovered that she had made the whole thing up.[165] Obviously, Janet Cook's articles were fiction but she did not have "fictive intent."

Currie anticipates this sort of objection. He cites the case of Daniel Defoe who is reputed to have insisted that Robinson Crusoe was a true story. Currie says that if Defoe did so insist, "then his was a lying utterance," where the utterance in question is not the one in which Defoe insists his story is true, but rather Defoe's utterance in writing Robinson Crusoe. Currie then adds:

> ... there is no firmer doctrine in the poetic tradition than the doctrine that fiction makers do not lie in the act of making

---

[164]It is a sad coincidence that while the analytic philosophers of fiction ignore the imagination of the author, the postmodern philosophers ignore, in fact, efface, the author altogether.

[165]See *The Washington Post* for Sunday, September 29, 1980, and for Sunday, April 19, 1981.

fiction. If we discovered that Defoe's intention had been assertive rather than fictive, we would conclude that Robinson Crusoe was not, after all, fiction." [166]

This is highly implausible. When Janet Cook and Daniel Defoe insist that their stories are "true stories" (i.e. not fictional), they are lying! Some lies consist in putting fiction forward as fact. Hence, it cannot be constitutive of fiction that it be put forward as such, or that the author intend that it be treated as fiction, by making-believe it, or whatever. Janet Cook did everything a storyteller would do. [167] She made up characters, she made up a plot, she supplied motives for actions, she gave her characters attitudes and emotions, and so on. After doing all this and before publishing the results in the newspaper, had she then fabricated fiction? Currie would insist that if she put her text forward as fact, as she did, she had fabricated a lie, not a fiction. Well then, what did the lie consist in? Currie's answer must be that she lied in that she asserted propositions she knew to be false. That is not so, however. Janet Cook believed that many of the propositions she asserted in her story were true; and for all she knew, they were true. The falsity of her stories seems irrelevant to the character of her lie. Had she conducted an assiduous investigation, but was mislead by her sources, we would not accuse her of having perpetrated a deception. She deceived us not by getting us to believe things she knew to be false (or didn't know, or even believe, to be true) but by getting us to believe things she made up out of whole cloth. In any case, the intuition is very strong that Janet Cook produced what would otherwise count as fiction were it not for its mode of publication. That seems to me to suffice for it to count as fiction, period. Some lies consist in putting fiction forward as fact.

Not only can fiction be put forward as fact, fact can be put forward as fiction. One might do this for political reasons. It very likely has happened. In such a case there is fictive intent but no fiction. Currie realizes this too. In fact, that is why he requires that fiction be "at most accidentally true." So there is a curious and surely untenable asymmetry in Currie's views: He allows the possibility that fact might be put forward (e.g. published) as fiction, but not that fiction might be put forward as fact.

There is a further difficulty with the idea of "fictive intent." Currie requires not only that readers make-believe that the story is true, but also that they make-believe that the story is "told as known fact." It

---

[166] See his (Currie 1990), p. 37.
[167] However, she didn't "go beneath the surface" or else she would have been found out. See the discussion of Wayne Booth's commentary below.

is not entirely clear why Currie needs this requirement except that he deems it important that the set of fictional truths generated by a work of fiction has many of the characteristics of the set of beliefs of a cognitive agent. Furthermore, in describing the reader as involved in a pretense that they are being informed of known facts, Currie is following Kaplan and Lewis. There is, however, a very striking difficulty with this view. Unless it is part of the artifice itself, as it is in first-person narratives, there is, in the communication from author to reader, no illusion that the author (or a "fictional author") is passing on information in their possession. Much of this information is simply not the sort of information that a cognitive agent, short of an omniscient God, *could* know: e.g. information about the inner lives and moral stature of individual people. Wayne C. Booth makes this neglected but important point on the very first page of his classic study of fiction (Booth 1983). Quoting from the beginning of the *Book of Job* (which Booth treats as fiction), Booth writes:

> "There was a man in the land of Uz, whose name was Job; and that man was perfect and upright, one that feared God and eschewed evil." With one stroke the unknown author has given us a kind of information never obtained about real people, even about our most intimate friends. Yet it is information that we must accept if we are to grasp the story that is to follow. In life, if a friend confided his view that his friend was "perfect and upright," we would accept the information with qualifications imposed by our knowledge of the speakers' character or of the general fallibility of mankind. We never trust the most reliable of witnesses as completely as we trust the author of the opening statement about Job.

Previous to this, Booth makes the following trenchant comment:

"Whatever our ideas may be about the natural way to tell a story, artifice is unmistakably present whenever the author tells us what no one in so-called real life could possible know." ((Booth 1983), p. 3)

Thus, Booth observes not only that authorial information is often of a kind not accessible to finite minds, and hence not the sort of information that can be known, in any ordinary sense of the word, but also that the presence of such information is an "unmistakable" sign that it is fictional information. The Kaplan-Lewis-Currie view is not even in the ballpark. I think I can say with confidence that when I read a story, I do not even come close to doing what Currie claims I must be doing. I do not make-believe that I am being informed of known facts; for I am well aware that much of the information in question is not information that can be known, and I am certainly not making-believe that it can be known. If I am making-believe anything, it is not that. Am I, then, making-believe that my source of information is an omniscient knower? Critics have sometimes spoken of "the omniscient author." And, of course, some believe that the ultimate source of the information in the *Book of Job*, is the omniscient mind of God—but that, of course, is just an irrelevant artifact of Booth's chosen example. But if the author is omniscient, why do I need to make-believe that? Clearly, in general, the author is not literally omniscient, assuming that the notion of literal omniscience makes sense at all. The author does not know everything, just everything about the fiction. Nor does the reader make-believe that the author is omniscient in this more limited sense. There is no need for pretense here, since the author really is omniscient in this more limited sense. Perhaps the idea is that we as readers make-believe that we are being told known fact from a literally omniscient source or at least a source that is omniscient about a certain part of reality—the part that includes the lives and inner lives and moral stature of Rosemary, Nicole, Dick Diver and the others. I am to suppose, then, that in reading *Tender is the Night*, I make-believe that the information is coming to me from a "fictional author" who possesses one of the perfections of God! But not even such a one could "know" about the many fantastic and impossible things that can happen in stories: talking horses, never never lands, the Jedi, round squares. Since I know that such things cannot be known of, I am not inclined to make-believe that they are told about as known fact. The reader does not make-believe that the source of information is either literally omniscient or omniscient in the limited sense. Nor does the reader make-believe that information is being passed along from an ordinary knowledgeable source. It looks as though make-believe does not enter the picture at all. Nor does knowledge. To say that the author is omniscient about the fiction is not to say that he or she possesses a special epistemological relation to it. Authorial authority does not derive from what the author knows, but from what the author *does*. The author records—perhaps only mentally at first—various descriptions. These are attributive descriptions of a plenitude, and this is what grounds our trust in the accuracy of the author's pronouncements. They cannot help but be accurate. Assuming that the *Book of Job* is fiction, we "completely trust" (as Booth puts it) the author when we are told that Job is "perfect and upright" not because of what the author knows about Job, one cannot know such things as that Job is "perfect and Upright," but because the author has made the thing up out of whole cloth. As I have been at pains to explain, making something up is a matter concerning descriptions and what they describe, not knowers and what they know. Furthermore, it appears that it is the notion of making something up, not that of making-believe, that proves in the end to be illuminating, as was just illustrated by the answer to the question of why we "completely trust" the author.[168] Currie's notion of a "fictional author" who speaks to us even in third-person narratives is particularly suspect. The voice we "hear" when we read fiction is less like that of a knowledgeable informant and more like that of our own inner voice. If I make-believe anything when I read a third-person story it is that I am a lone observer of the things and events I am reading about. I certainly don't imagine that there is another participant (distinct from the author) whose opinions and reactions to the things and events unfolding might or might not be similar to my own.[169]

Let us turn to Walton's views. According to Walton, "a fictional truth consists in there being a prescription or mandate in some context to imagine something." ((Walton 1990), p. 39.) This is so general it is difficult to interpret. Who is to do the imagining? Where does the mandate come from? As I've indicated, I interpret it to mean that the *audience* is enjoined to imagine something. Certainly the author does not order himself or herself to imagine something. He or she just does it. As some slight evidence for my interpretation, I cite the following statement: "Readers of Gulliver's Travels imagine that there are six-inch tall people." ((Walton 1990), p. 37) This suggests that for Walton at least one of the requirements of the fictionality of a proposition is that the audience imagine it. But this view is as easily refuted by the Janet Cook case as is Currie's requirement of fictive intent. Janet Cook's audience was enjoined not to imagine but to believe. On the other hand, since Walton holds that New Journalism is fiction, perhaps he doesn't set much store by the difference between the injunction to imagine, and the injunction to believe! Seriously, however, I fail to see how Walton's account of fictionality squares with his view that New Journalism counts as fiction. New Journalism, despite its fiction-like style, does not enjoin the audience to imagine its propositions, instead there is an injunction to believe them. If believing is adjudged a form of imagining, or if the injunction to believe is presumed to be compatible with the injunction to imagine, then, by Walton's criteria, any proposition counts as fictional

---

[168] After writing this section it came to my attention that Alex Byrne has recently developed a similar criticism of Currie's view, but without reference to Wayne Booth.

[169] Currie remarks that the Menard story illustrates the idea that difference of fictional author is in itself sufficient to generate different fictional truths. Yet, if, as I have insisted, Borges has his tongue in his cheek, then the Menard story illustrates exactly the opposite point: that a difference of fictional author is *not* sufficient in itself to generate a different set of fictional truths!

and any text as fiction.

Another difficulty with Walton's view is that, as mentioned, it can and has happened that an author will put fact forward as fiction. Thus, the audience is enjoined to imagine the proposition (or entire work) but it's not fiction. Currie notices this point and thus requires that for a proposition or work to be fictional it must be at most accidentally true. Walton's failure to acknowledge this point is, it seems to me, a result of his excessive concentration on the imagination of "appreciators" to the exclusion of that of authors, or makers. If one focuses on the imagination of authors, then the concept of making something up will loom large.

Finally, it is interesting to compare Walton's and my own explanations of why leaping onstage to save the heroine is absurdly inappropriate (and ineffectual). Recall that my account is that if it were possible to rescue the heroine by leaping onstage, that would constitute an untold part of the story, and there are no untold parts in the sense intended.[170] It's a bit hard to tell what Walton's explanation is. He says he's got one, but I, for one, can't quite tell what it is. Walton says: "Some will be impatient for the theory developed in Part One to rescue us from these embarrassments. It does suggest an easy way of dealing with Henry's challenge to the supposed physical isolation of fictional worlds from the real world, and one which I endorse." ((Walton 1990), p. 194) What is this "easy way?" Is it just that intruders from the real world are not welcome in the game of make-believe going on in the playhouse? But it is unclear what work the notion of make-believe is doing. We already know that such intrusions are unwelcome. Adverting to make-believe adds nothing. Perhaps it's that the fictional heroine does not exist and for that reason cannot be rescued; or perhaps she does exist *qua* abstract artifact and for that reason cannot be rescued. Such notions miss the point. The play might be a fiction about a real person. It still doesn't make sense to leap onstage, and the reason it doesn't is that the fictional fate of this real person is unreal. We can detect its unreality by contemplating the absurdity of the act of leaping onstage. Walton says something very peculiar about this act. He says that it succeeds in "making it fictional" that the heroine survives! I would have thought that it succeeds only in halting the performance. In the play (as opposed to such and such performance of it), the fictional heroine continues on, impervious to the disruption, to meet her fate, and survives or doesn't as the case may be.

---

[170]There are plays that have audience participation built in. A recent example is "Shear Madness," an amusing whodunit in which the audience votes on who the culprit is. In such cases, the members of the audience are extended characters in the play, even if, as in "Shear Madness," they retain their role as members of the audience.

Walton appears to momentarily confuse play with performance.

8.4 Postscript on fear and pity

Is it possible to pity Anna Karenina as well as Bill Clinton? It's not only possible, I should think, but easier to pity Anna Karenina than Bill Clinton. Many philosophers would dispute this. The prevailing view seems to be that one cannot pity what one knows not to exist. One cannot pity a poor relation one knows not to exist. And similarly one cannot pity or grieve for Anna Karenina (who throws herself under a train). She does not exist and we know that so we cannot pity or grieve for her. This is but one argument that our pity/grief for Anna is unreal. Another is that our pity/grief for Anna does not cause us to act—or even be inclined to act—in ways appropriate to or conventionally associated with real pity or grief. For example, we are not inclined to send letters of condolence to Count Vronsky. Similarly, one cannot really fear a fiction. Real fear involves the belief that there is a threat, and however shook up Charles may be watching the onslaught of the slime on the screen, he perceives no threat, since he knows that the slime on the screen is unreal.

Walton proposes that our attitudinal and semantic relations to fictional things be analyzed in terms of the notion of make-believe. Charles does not fear the slime, he makes-believe that he does; and our pity for Anna is a pretended pity, which is part and parcel of a game of make-believe we play using the novel as a prop. But this description of Walton's view does not do justice to its force and sweep. Walton's idea is that the problems and puzzles concerning our discourse about fictional things may be resolved if we descend to the level of the fictional things themselves; if our statements and actions come within the scope of "fictionality." We do not find it particularly puzzling that one character can fear or pity another. It is *our* pitying or fearing a character that we (supposedly) find puzzling. Well, then, we may regard ourselves as characters in a fantasy, a game of make-believe, such that "it is fictional that" we pity Anna, and fictional that Charles fears the slime. As Walton puts it (see his (Walton 1990), p. 23):

> On my theory we accomplish the "decrease of distance" [between ourselves and fictional things] not by promoting fictions to our level but by descending to theirs. (More accurately, we extend ourselves to their level, since we do not stop actually existing when it becomes fictional that we exist.)...Rather than somehow fooling ourselves into thinking fictions are real, we become fictional. So we end up "on the

same level" with fictions.

Walton's target here seems to be casual Meinongianism, which, as Walton interprets it, would elevate fictional things to our level thus affording us the opportunity to fool ourselves into thinking such things are real. But this is unfair. Although casual Meinongianism acknowledges our ability to refer to fictional things, and does not question the non-fictional nature of our pity for Anna or Charles' fear of the slime, it nonetheless recognizes the unreality of fictional things. In fact, casual Meinongianism offers the best explanation of the absurdity of Terry's musings about Robin and similar telltale mistakes having to do with the unreality of fictional things. If it can do that, why should we suppose that it might tempt us to think that fictional things are real?

In this connection, it is worth mentioning that from the fact that certain sorts of interactions with fictional things are impossible—such as rescuing the fictional heroine—it does not follow that all are. In particular, the rule appears to be that fictional things can have an effect on us, but we cannot have an effect on them. Leaping onstage has no effect on the fictional heroine's fate, but that fate can cause us consternation. Walton seems to suggest that these two sorts of relations to fictional things are of a piece: Just as it is futile to try to save the fictional heroine, so it is futile to try to pity her. Pity for her is as unreal as she is. But I would point out that the explanation of why it is futile to try to save her does not extend to explain why it is futile to try to pity her, if that is indeed the case. This is at least one bit of evidence that our pity for her may not be all that unreal.

Call a relation to fictional things resistant if it cannot be traded in for a mock or make-believe counterpart. That is, a relation to fictional things is resistant, if it cannot be in effect eliminated by descending to the level of fictional things, and placing it within the scope of fictionality. There are a great variety of resistant relations and this fact surely poses a prima facie problem for Walton's theory. Walton seems at least partially aware of the problem. He devotes a whole chapter to the treatment of two resistant relations, namely, the properties (unary relations) of being fictional and not existing, both of which are non-fictional properties of some fictional things. Walton suggests that when we say that Anna is fictional or non-existent, we pretend to refer to "her" and then we betray (i.e. reveal) that pretense, by affirming it using the predicates "fictional" and "non-existent." That does seem to be a somewhat plausible account of the puzzling negative existentials involving fictional names. Unfortunately, There are many other resistant relations and I don't see how Walton's account generalizes to cover them all. For example, there are what appear to be causal relations to fictional things. The antics of fictional things can make you laugh, make you ill, turn you on, move you to tears. It is not fictional or make-believe that these things happen; they really do happen. Then there are numerous meta-relations to fictional things that arise out of our discourse, including our philosophical discourse, about them. For example, there is the three-place relation that holds between myself, Walton, and Anna in virtue of our disagreement as to whether my pity for Anna is genuine. This is not a fictional disagreement.

Philosophers are prone to pound the table about the causal relation. Fictional things cannot cause anything to happen in the physical world, for that would (for one thing) violate the principle of the conservation of energy! In fact, however, all it violates are certain prejudices about the causal relation parallel to the prevailing prejudices about reference. Caught up in these prejudices, it might be suggested that it is not Anna that evokes our feelings of grief or Iago that produces very physical feelings of revulsion, but rather the descriptions of these things—or rather the reading of these descriptions. Well, all right, if that helps. As I said earlier, for some purposes we might as well identify fictional things with the descriptions of them. But I don't see how Walton's theory can handle the three place relation just mentioned, and the like, and there are still other resistant relations.

One very important example is the creates-relation, i.e. the makes-up-relation. Fitzgerald created Rosemary and Tolstoy created Anna. These things are literally true. Nor do they commit us to the proposition that Fitzgerald brought Rosemary into existence. They do not even commit us to the proposition that Fitzgerald brought the descriptions of Rosemary into existence. The sheer existence of the descriptions is on a par with the sheer existence of sequences of numbers. Creating Rosemary was a matter of making her up out of whole cloth; and that was a matter of recording descriptions of things from amongst a plenitude of them. In recording the descriptions of Rosemary, Fitzgerald faced a daunting plenitude of choices. That is what made his activity creative. Walton does not treat the matter of creation, and I hesitate to attribute a view to him, but it seems false to say that in creating Rosemary, Fitzgerald made-believe that he was referring to and describing a real person. That would be something the pathological Janet Cook might have done. Or such fantasizing may be one technique some authors employ. But it doesn't seem to be something authors must do in order to create. In fact, it doesn't seem to have anything to do with creation at all. I suspect that Walton views our talk of creating fictions with the same skepticism with which he views our fearing them. Whatever he may take our talk of creating fictions to "really mean" it is not fictional that we create fictional things.

Finally, I want to give voice to two not entirely unfounded suspicions concerning the make-believe theory. It is probably best that the reader treat these as open questions, since I am not prepared to fully document the issues here. First, I suspect that research in psychology does not and will not bear out the make-believe theory. The issue is whether fearing fictions (for example) is to be conceived of as a kind of real fear or as pretended fear or "quasi-fear." Since fear of fictions can be quite intense and can involve somatic and other physiological phenomena associated with fear, psychologists are likely to view it as a variety of real fear. In fact, psychologists often use fiction in an experimental setting to evoke emotions and attitudes such as fear and pity for study. The emotions and attitudes so evoked are surely regarded as the real thing. Furthermore, there is evidence suggesting that phobia therapy using only descriptions and/or imagery rather than real objects (e.g. pictures of snakes as opposed to real snakes) is as effective as therapy using the real thing. This certainly suggests that the emotions evoked by the "non-threatening" descriptions and imagery are the genuine article and not some quasi variety or mock version.[171] As far as I can tell, there is little reference to research in psychology in the philosophical literature on fiction and make-believe.[172] The open question, then, is whether this research confirms or disconfirms—or just ignores—the make-believe theory.[173]

Secondly, I suspect that the make-believe theory does not supply an adequate answer to the question of why fiction is important to us. Walton's idea that its importance derives from the psychological importance of games of make-believe does not do justice to the mature experience of fiction. Among literary scholars, the word "poetry" used to mean imaginative literature of a certain quality, but of any kind, including novels

---

[171]I have been unable to find *any* books or papers in psychology specifically about our emotions towards fictional things, but then I have not done an exhaustive search. But see (Beck 1985) for the point about phobia therapy.

[172]Currie notes the "vast amount" of theorizing in psychology on emotions and says that it is difficult "to assimilate to acknowledged philosophical perspectives." See his (Currie 1990), p. 191, n. 13. Try to imagine some philosopher saying this about the vast amount of theorizing about motion in physics! If scientific results cannot be assimilated to some philosophical perspective, so much the worse for the perspective.

[173]One bit of evidence in favor of the make-believe theory is the fact that even the "unpleasant" emotions caused by fictions can be pleasurable. But perhaps the pleasure Charles feels when fearing the slime is due not to the fear itself but to the relief he feels knowing that the threat is unreal. In any case, Walton, for one, does not take the line that Charles' fear is unreal because it's pleasurable. Walton recognizes that real "unpleasant" emotions can be pleasurable in certain ways. See (Walton 1990), p. 257.

and short stories. The make-believe theory makes a mockery (pun intended) of our experience of poetry in this sense. The critic I. A. Richards once commented on just this point (long before the notions of pretense and make-believe became so prominent in the philosophy of fiction):

> Make-belief is an enervating exercise of fancy not to be confused with imaginative growth. The saner and greater mythologies are not fancies; they are the utterance of the whole soul and, as such, inexhaustible to meditation.[174]

By "greater mythologies" Richards means "poetry" in the broad sense. The vocabulary of the make-believe theory is completely inadequate to describe our experience of poetry (which to my mind includes much "popular" fiction, e.g. science fiction), and hence is inadequate to explain why it is important to us. If you want to know why poetry is important to us, forget the games of make-believe and consult Sartre's "Why Write" or Wallace Stevens' "The Noble Rider and the Sound of Words." (This essay may be found in (Stevens 1942).) From these works we learn that we turn to poetry for the same reasons we turn to science: to make sense of things and to help us live our lives.

The open question here is likely to remain open indefinitely, since answering it requires nothing less than articulating the nature of poetry. Philosophy is a rather dull tool in this enterprise; at least it has been in the past. A good example of this dullness is the problem we have been discussing. The very way the problem of emotions and fiction is posed by the philosopher is maddening to the non-philosopher, especially the poet and literary scholar. Currie states, for example, that on a certain construal of emotions, having emotional reactions to fictions seems to be "impossible" ((Currie 1990), p. 183.)

Reading this, the poet is likely to think that such a construal of emotions, whatever it is, must be totally implausible, since it is completely inconsistent with our experience. Similarly, when Radford says "I can only be moved by someone's plight if I believe that something terrible has happened to him," (quoted in (Currie 1990), p. 183), the poet is likely to agree and to point out that terrible things happen to people in fiction all the time; and if you ask a reader of *Anna Karenina* whether they believe that something terrible happens to Anna, they will say that they do. If the poet suspects that the analytic philosopher is able to grieve only for real persons, she will conclude that such philosophers are not capable of grief in the fullest sense. If the philosopher suggests that our grief for Nicole or Dick Diver falls short of the real thing, the poet will conclude that the philosopher hasn't the slightest idea what

---

[174]See (Richards 1969), p. 171.

the real thing is.[175]

The "problem" of emotions and fiction is one of those problematic problems, (a pseudo problem!) one of those trumped up issues deriving from strictures laid down by logical positivists and other "hard headed" philosophers claiming to have an especially robust sense of reality. But as Wallace Stevens says with no small contempt: "We feel, without being particularly intelligent about it, that the imagination as metaphysics will survive logical positivism unscathed." The imagination for Stevens is the poet's imagination, not the reader's, and it is unclear that it has survived recent philosophy of fiction unscathed. It seems to have disappeared, eclipsed by the imagination of "appreciators." I propose that it be revived.[176]

---

[175]There need not be only one variety of the real thing. Aesthetic grief is no doubt different from grief for a dying loved one.

[176]A portion of this paper was presented at a philosophy colloquium at Rutgers University in February of 1999. I wish to thank the faculty and students who attended that colloquium for many comments many of which led to substantial improvements and revisions. Special thanks are due to Max Deutsch for numerous helpful conversations on these topics.

9

Real People in Unreal Contexts, or Is There a Spy Among Us?

Stacie Friend

9.1 Introduction

Recent decades have seen an increase in interest among analytic philosophers in the problem of fictional reference. Philosophers of language are concerning themselves more and more with our discourse about fiction, including statements of what is "true in fiction," assertions about our responses to fiction, true nonexistence claims, and so on. The rise of "direct reference" theories of names is in large part responsible for this trend, since the use of Fregean senses or Russellian descriptions are not available to deal with our apparently meaningful use of empty names (names that seem to lack referents). The names of fictional characters, being among the most commonly used empty names, therefore present a challenge to theories of language that utilize direct reference. A number of philosophers, concerned not only with truth and reference but also with the phenomena surrounding intentionality, have concluded that such issues require us to find room in our metaphysics for some type of fictional object. In opposition to this line of thinking are theories that explain fictional discourse without appealing to fictional objects, among which are theories that invoke purely linguistic solutions (paraphrase, quantification, etc.), as well as various pretense, or make-believe, theories.

For the purposes of this paper, I am going to assume that there are only two diametrically opposed camps in the theory of fictional reference: make-believe theories and fictional-object theories.[177] The fictional-object

---

[177]See Parsons (Parsons 1974), (Parsons 1975), and (Parsons 1980), Thomasson (Thomasson 1996), van Inwagen (van Inwagen 1977) and (van Inwagen 1983), Wal-

Empty Names, Fiction, and the Puzzles of Non-Existence.
Anthony Everett and Thomas Hofweber (eds.).
Copyright © 2000, CSLI Publications.

theories take our talk about fictional characters to involve genuine reference to real, usually nonexistent, objects of one sort or another. Ed Zalta's theory invokes abstract objects, and Terence Parsons' theory invokes incomplete Meinongian objects. In contrast, Kendall Walton's make-believe theory denies that there is genuine reference to fictional objects. On this theory, such talk involves make-believedly referring to an existent object. We pretend that there are such people, and then within the context of this pretense, but not outside it, we refer to them. These are the views I will be contrasting throughout most of this paper. Walton's theory attempts to explain all features of our talk about fiction without countenancing any fictional objects; Zalta's and Parsons' views attempt to explain all such talk with as little pretense as possible. There are, however, some "mixed" views of fictional reference, such as Peter van Inwagen's and Amie Thomasson's, which countenance a type of fictional object, but which require pretense to explain many of our responses to fiction. I will return to these below.

While both the make-believe and the fictional object theories seem to account equally well for some of our talk about fiction, there are certain areas of our discourse that look better for one side or the other. Here I want to address an area that has been taken as a significant point against Walton's theory: discourse about our attitudes in response to fiction. These are the feelings and emotions we experience when we are engaged with a piece of fiction. We may admire Sherlock Holmes, feel compassion for Anna Karenina, fear Freddie Kruger, and so on. It is interesting that such attitudes have sometimes been invoked as evidence for the fictional object theory. For instance, one might maintain that if it is true that real detectives admire Sherlock Holmes, then it follows that there is someone real detectives admire.[178] In the debate over such inferences it appears to be an assumption that real detectives really admire Holmes. But coming from a different perspective, what appears problematic here is the attitude itself. How can we have such emotional responses to fictional characters? This has been the subject of heated controversy in the aesthetics of fiction for some time.[179] It is the answer to that question which will occupy me for the rest of this paper.[180]

Let's focus on the statement "I pity Anna Karenina." Both the make-

ton (Walton 1990), and Zalta (Zalta 1983) and (Zalta 1988).

[178]This case comes from Zalta, who uses versions of it in (Zalta 1988) p. 4 and pp. 123–129, and in Zalta (Zalta 2000).

[179]See Walton (Walton 1990), especially chapters 5 and 7, and the bibliography. See also Hjort and Laver (M. and Laver 1997).

[180]I am going to be discussing what Kroon (Kroon 1992) calls "*reflective* appreciator attitudes," which one has toward a person might affect one directly (e.g. fear, jealousy).

believe and the fictional object theories share the assumption that in this statement there can be no genuine attitude if there is no real object of the attitude. According to the fictional object theory, there is such a real object, so the attitude is genuine. On that view the analysis of "I pity Anna Karenina" is straightforward: it is true so long as I pity Anna, who in some sense has the property of having suffered.[181] But on the make-believe theory there is no such object as Anna; I only make believe that Anna exists, and I only make believe that she has suffered. As a result, I cannot literally pity Anna. Rather, this must be make-believe, or fictional, or pretend, or imagined, or quasi-pity. And the same goes for other such attitudes.

Now the claim that my pity for Anna is not genuine, but only make-believe or imagined pity, has met with a great deal of resistance.[182] For example, the claim seems to deny the phenomenology of my attitude: my pity of Anna does not feel any less genuine than my pity of actual people. It doesn't *feel* as though I am pretending to pity. Furthermore, the whole notion of "make-believe" or "pretend" pity seems to imply that I am play-acting. But clearly I am not pretending to pity Anna in the sense that an actor pretends to have an attitude or emotion. Now, Walton never calls these attitudes "make-believe" or "pretend" attitudes himself, although that is how they are usually discussed in the literature. But Walton's terminology does not make matters that much better.[183] Calling my attitude "quasi-pity" also implies that it should feel different from genuine pity. Saying that "it is fictional that I pity Anna" makes it sound as though I am part of the fiction. And Walton's most preferred terminology—"I am imagining myself pitying Anna"—still sounds too deliberate, when my compassion seems spontaneous. To some extent the criticism of Walton's theory has rested on confusion over the implications of the terminology. However, at the risk of perpetuating that confusion, I will for the remainder of the paper refer to the attitudes in question as "make-believe" attitudes, for reasons that will become clear below.

Given this resistance to positing apparently strange and implausible make-believe attitudes, the fictional object theory may look more attrac-

---

[181]Defining in what "sense" Anna Karenina has the property of having suffered differentiates Parsons' and Zalta's theories. Zalta argues for a distinction between two ways of having properties, so that the abstract object "encodes" the properties it has according to the story, while it "exemplifies" such properties as being a fictional character. In contrast Parsons distinguishes two kinds of properties that objects can have, "nuclear" and "extranuclear." See Kroon (Kroon 1992) for a discussion of the differences. Van Inwagen (van Inwagen 1977) and (van Inwagen 1983) draws a distinction between "having" and "holding" properties that appears to parallel Zalta's.

[182]Walton addresses his critics on this issue most recently in Walton (Walton 1997).

[183]Walton makes use of this terminology in (Walton 1990) and (Walton 1997).

tive. But I don't think it is. I think make-believe attitudes have gotten a bad rap. So the objective of this paper will be to persuade you that make-believe attitudes are not nearly so bizarre as some have thought. The purpose is *not* to argue that the make-believe theory is better than the fictional object theory, although of course my conclusions will have consequences for the debate. However, since the implausibility of make-believe attitudes is often seen as a reason to prefer the fictional object theory, then if I can make such attitudes seem more respectable, this reason loses its force.

The impact of this argument for the more general debate among theories of fictional reference is in a sense not very substantive, since it is a negative conclusion. However, it should be clear by the end that I believe the make-believe theory offers a more promising picture of our emotional responses to fiction than the fictional-object view. And although I approach this issue from a different angle than does Walton himself, I take myself in this paper to be defending his basic view. As for my own view, I am not sure that Walton's precise proposals will, in the end, be entirely satisfactory, but I do think that the pretense approach to fiction is truer to our experience with fiction than other approaches.

9.2   Strategy

My strategy will be to develop and analyze one case in which make-believe attitudes are not only plausible, but also quite explanatory. This case, unlike those usually discussed, involves our responses to a piece of fiction containing so-called "real" names. These are names like "Napoleon" and "London," which, in contrast to so-called "fictional" names, have concrete, existent referents in ordinary contexts. Since this terminology has unwanted implications for the metaphysical status of the names themselves, I will use different terms. I call the names "connected" and "unconnected" names. "London" and "Napoleon" are connected to actual, concrete objects in ordinary contexts; "Anna Karenina" and "Sherlock Holmes" are not. I will claim that in the example I analyze, the connected names refer to their ordinary referents. I will argue that this is the case, not only in statements about what is true in the fiction, but also in statements of our attitudes. In other words, my claim is that our attitudes in response to this particular piece of fiction are directed toward the real people mentioned in the story. I will show that objections to this claim, including one proposed by Fred Kroon, are unsuccessful.[184] Based on that conclusion, I will argue that we need some notion of make-believe attitudes to account for this reference to real peo-

---

[184]See Kroon (Kroon 1994).

ple. This will be a very minimal notion of make-believe attitudes, one that does not yet cover the rich range of emotional responses we have to fiction. I will return to the issue of emotional complexity after I have defended the minimal notion.

Since my conclusion does not follow unless I can show that our attitudes in response to fiction really *can* be directed at real people, the bulk of the paper will be devoted to showing that they can. This is no small task, because the claim is highly controversial. For example, suppose that in response to reading Shakespeare's play, I say, "I despise Richard III for murdering the princes." Now, historians tell us that Richard most likely did not murder the princes. Let's suppose he didn't, and that I don't believe that he did. Then how can I really despise the actual Richard for something he didn't do? The fictional-object theorist would say that the name "Richard" in the statement of my attitude is disconnected from the real person, and instead refers to a fictional character. However, as we will see when we come to Kroon's argument, there is a different way to interpret the position that the name is disconnected, more in line with the make-believe theory. But until we get there I will talk as if the disconnection of names like "Richard III" involves the claim that they refer to fictional objects. Which interpretation you prefer does not matter, since I will argue that these names are not necessarily disconnected. At the end I will bring the discussion back to make-believe attitudes.

Let me turn now to the example I will be discussing. It takes the form of a short story. This story was first told at the Empty Names Conference at Stanford University's Center for the Study of Language and Information (CSLI). The story is about one of the organizers of the conference, named Anthony Everett, who was present at the talk.

> Anthony Everett, whom you all know as one organizer of this conference, isn't just a philosopher. It turns out that he is also a secret agent with Great Britain's MI6, code-named "Periwinkle." For many frustrating years, British agents were tracking the clever and deadly spy from Italy known only as "Porcini." Several years ago there was a breakthrough when the Brits discovered the secret of Porcini's success in eluding them: his disguise as a well-known philosopher of language. The agency recruited Everett because they needed someone who could infiltrate the underworld of philosophy espionage. On Everett's side, this was an opportunity, not only to be a real-life, jet-setting James Bond, but also—considering the academic job market—to make sure he had a more secure career to fall back on. Now all that Everett had to go on,

apart from knowing about Porcini's evil deeds, was that the Italian has never been known to tell a joke or to laugh at one. So it has taken years for Everett to track him down. Over these years Everett has come to despise Porcini more and more. It is precisely Porcini's brilliance that causes Everett's contempt, since he can find nothing admirable in intelligence used for evil. So Everett can think of nothing else but his goal: to rid the world of the most diabolical spy it has ever known. In fact, this search has become an obsession, and the only person who cannot see the pitiful wreck he's made of the rest of his life is Everett himself. Now, finally, the Empty Names Conference is the culmination of Everett's master plan to trap the elusive Porcini. The trap has been set in CSLI. If anyone can catch this grim, deadly man, it's Everett. But will he succeed? You'll have to wait and see. The End.

So much for the story itself. Notice that I used several connected names in telling it, for example "Everett" and "CSLI." But most of what I said was made up, and I didn't expect you to believe it. It is not true that Everett is a secret agent chasing a spy named Porcini, that there is a trap set in CSLI, that Porcini never tells a joke, and so on. All of these are statements of what is true *in the story*, not of what is actually true. Reports of what is true in the story are not usually the kinds of statements that enter into the debate over whether or not connected names remain connected.[185] Fictional object theorists, such as Parsons and Zalta, agree that in these statements, the names refer to their ordinary referents. This does not endanger the truth of such statements for the object theorist, because we can just prefix them with an "in the fiction" operator. Then it might just be true that *in the story* Everett is chasing an Italian spy, even though it is not true *simpliciter* that Everett is chasing an Italian spy. I will leave aside here the question of whether or not "truth in the story" is really any species of truth.[186]

---

[185] At least, not among philosophers of language and metaphysicians concerned with fiction. Those who come from aesthetics or literary theory are more likely to question whether any names in works of fiction refer to reality. I think arguments against the claim that works of fiction never refer to reality are unsuccessful for a variety of reasons.

[186] Kroon (Kroon 1992) discusses the various positions on this question on p. 516, footnote 22. Zalta takes the unprefixed statements to be literally false and the prefixed ones to be literally true. The issue is more complicated on the pretense theory.

9.3   Responses to the story

The prefix will not help, however, with the discourse about fiction that concerns me here, which involves reports of how *we* respond to what we imagine based on the story. I follow Walton in thinking of statements of what is true in fiction, like those above, as prescriptions of what we are to imagine.[187] Works of fiction are not created so that readers and audiences can assess and tally what is true in some distant fictional world. Rather, the audience is expected to engage imaginatively with the work. In short, the proper response to the fiction is to *imagine*, to *make believe*, that what is true in the fiction, really is true, that the events it narrates really have taken place, and so on. We imagine that we are discovering the facts about real people and events, and we respond to these. Applying this to the story, I might report some of my responses as follows:

(1) I envy Everett because he's living the life of a jet-setting secret agent.

(2) I pity Everett because he is too obsessed with Porcini.

I will call such statements as (1) and (2) "Attitude-Reason Statements." The question is whether or not the name "Everett" in (1) and (2) remains connected to the real Everett. Notice that, in contrast to statements of what is true in the fiction, these statements about my attitudes cannot be prefixed by an "in the story" operator, because I am not in the story. The problem is the same as the one I brought up at the beginning about Richard III: how can I really envy or pity the actual Everett for such reasons?

It is crucial to recognize that the problem is not the same as the worry over how I can pity Anna Karenina. That was a concern about the nature of the object of my pity. In the case of Everett, there is no problem with the object—he's an ordinary, concrete, existent person. Certainly I can envy or pity him. Rather, the problem is that the reasons for my attitudes are not the sort of reasons that justify, or explain, genuine attitudes toward Everett. This will be better understood if we divide each Attitude-Reason Statement into two parts:

1a. I envy Everett [because]

1b. Everett is living the life of a jet-setting secret agent.

2a. I pity Everett [because]

2b. Everett is too obsessed with Porcini.

---

[187]This is Walton's proposal in (Walton 1990). For Walton, this involves entering into a "game of make-believe" with the work of fiction as prop.

I call (1a) and (2a) the "Attitude Reports," and I call (1b) and (2b) the "Reason Reports." The Reason Reports provide the fictional character-istic of the object that explains the Attitude Reports. Since Everett is a perfectly respectable object of envy and pity, there is no evident prob-lem with the Attitude Reports by themselves. So it must be the Reason Reports that determine whether or not the name "Everett" remains connected to the real person.

To see what the problem with the Reason Reports might be, let's consider ordinary attitudes in ordinary, non-fiction contexts. Say that I like Everett because he is easy-going (I do). We can divide this claim into an Attitude Report and a Reason Report as well:

3a. I like Everett [because]

3b. Everett is easy-going.

Clearly there's no doubt that the object of my liking is Everett, and that this attitude is explained by my belief that Everett is easy-going. Notice that it is *not* explained by the truth of the statement, "Everett is easy-going," but rather by my *belief* that he is.[188] Suppose I have a false belief about Everett, for instance that he spread rumors about me. Then I might well be angry with him, and this anger would be explained by my belief, even though the belief is false.[189] Therefore, if the Reason Reports in (1) and (2) are problematic, that must be because I *don't* believe them. Since the correct response to a fictional story is that we imagine that what is fictionally true really is true, my reasons are statements of what I *make* believe, not of what I believe. I am *imagining* that Everett is a jet-setting secret agent, and I am *imagining* that he is obsessed with capturing Porcini. But of course I don't believe either of these claims. The reasons for my attitudes come from the way Everett is portrayed in the fiction, and fictional reasons are not the kinds of reasons that could justify a genuine attitude directed at the real person. That is why it cannot be straightforwardly true that I envy Everett because he is a jet-setting secret agent: *not* because there is no Everett, but because I do not really believe the reason that explains my attitude.

We have seen that the question of whether or not the real Everett is the object of my attitude hinges on whether or not it is the real Everett

---

[188] There is some debate over the claim that a genuine attitude requires belief, which usually comes up in this context with the issue of fearing fictions. Do we literally fear movie monsters, even though we don't really believe that we are in danger? Walton (Walton 1990) discusses this issue in Chapter 7. Whatever one might say about such possibly irrational attitudes as fear, I think it remains clear that for those attitudes that require a reason (the reflective attitudes), this reason must be believed.

[189] This is, for example, why the Greeks' worship of Zeus is not at issue here. More on this below.

to whom I make reference in my reason for the attitude. That means we need to look more closely at the Reason Reports. Take (1b). I am imagining that Everett is a jet-setting secret agent, and I am reporting the content of what I imagine. Is this a case of imagining, *of* the actual Everett, that he is as described in the story? Or is it imagining that a fictional character, the "Everett-of-the-story," is as the story describes him to be? The contrast is between a case of *de re* imagining about the real person, and a case of imagining about a fictional character.[190] If we are imagining *de re* about the real Everett, then we can infer that "Everett is such that we imagine, of him, that he is a secret agent."[191] In such a case, the parallel between make-believe and belief is evident. In this report of the content of our imaginings, as in a *de re* belief report, the name "Everett" can be replaced with any co-referring expression.[192] Of course none of this is to say that the Everett-of-the-story would be completely unrelated to the real Everett. Presumably the Everett-of-the-story would be based on the real Everett in some close way. Even with that caveat, it seems to me that this is clearly a case of imagining *de re* about the real Everett.

Assume that you are at the Empty Names Conference, listening to the story. You would probably look at Everett while I tell it. If you did not take the story to be about the real person, one of the organizers of the conference, you would not find it so amusing. The fact that what I've said of Everett in the story isn't true of him should not be a problem. After all, though Everett may not really be a secret agent, it is not so difficult to imagine that he is (he's British, he travels a lot, etc.). In fact, if you know Everett well, you are probably imagining even more than what is true in the story. Perhaps you are considering how Everett

---

[190]Walton discusses imagining *de re*, and the generation of *de re* fictional truths about real objects, in Walton (Walton 1990), especially Chapter 3.

[191]It should be noted that on Thomasson's theory, imagining what is prescribed by the story involves *de re* imagining about fictional characters. For Thomasson, Sherlock Holmes is an abstract cultural artifact that has such properties as having been created by Conan Doyle, being anchored in certain texts, being a fictional character, etc. In the Holmes stories, other properties are "ascribed" to Holmes: being a detective, being a man, living in London, etc. We imagine, of Holmes, that he has these properties, apparently in much the same way we imagine, of Everett, that he has the properties ascribed to him in the story. See Thomasson (Thomasson 1998a) and in particular (Thomasson 1996).

[192]In their (Lamarque and Olsen 1994) Lamarque and Olsen dispute this claim. They argue that reference to real objects in fiction is only under the modes of presentation authorized by the fiction. I do not find their argument convincing for a variety of reasons, most importantly its practical obliteration of the difference between reference to real people and reference to fictional characters, especially in terms of our attitudes.

has managed to keep up his secret agent skills right under your noses. Consider some other responses you could have. After the story is told, you might go up to Everett, and in a joking tone inquire as to whether he's caught any spies lately. Similarly, just as a tourist might go to Baker Street in London to be on the street where Holmes lived, you might be imagining yourself in the very building (CSLI) where there is a spy trap. In these cases it looks as though the imaginative engagement with the story is an engagement with the real person and the real place mentioned in the story. Now, I don't want to overestimate what these examples show. They are intuition pumps, not knockdown arguments. If you prefer the fictional object theory, you can probably reinterpret these points in terms of fictional objects related in the right ways to the real things. But I do think the examples at least make it quite plausible, pre-theoretically, that you are imagining about the real Everett and the real CSLI, rather than about fictional objects based on them.

To sum up where we are right now. As we have already seen, since there is a real object for the attitudes, the Attitude Reports are unproblematic. So if we are to say that the name "Everett" is disconnected from the real Everett in (1) and (2), that would have to be because it is disconnected in the Reason Reports. But consideration of how we respond to the story indicates that it is the *real* Everett about whom we are imagining, and therefore that it is the *real* Everett to whom the Reason Reports refer. It will turn out that if it is, indeed, the real Everett about whom we are imagining, it is most plausible to think of our attitudes as make-believe attitudes. But before I explain why, I will turn to some objections to what I have said so far.

9.4   The Porcini objection

I have argued that it is the real Everett about whom we are imagining in response to the story. Now I want to focus on an objection to this claim that arises from conflicts in our abilities to imagine what is fictionally true. Broadly speaking, this objection points to cases in which, *if* we assume that in the Reason Reports we are imagining about real objects, we cannot explain how it is even possible to imagine what is true in the fiction. After I have dealt with a counterexample to my claims along these lines, I will show how my analysis applies to interesting and related cases brought up by Fred Kroon. To illustrate the objection, let's suppose that in response to the story I say this:

4. I dislike Porcini because he never tells a joke.

Now allow me to let you in on a part of the story I didn't tell. I am sure you have been wondering who Porcini really is. Suppose that we add to the story the following sentence: "Little did Everett know, Porcini was really his own advisor at Stanford, the author of a number of influential works in the philosophy of language: John Perry." If Porcini is Perry, then my Attitude-Reason Statement would be:

5. I dislike John Perry because he never tells a joke.

As usual, we divide the Attitude-Reason Statement into an Attitude Report and a Reason Report:

5a. I dislike John Perry [because]

5b. John Perry never tells a joke.

Once again there is no problem with the Attitude Report, because Perry is a perfectly respectable object of dislike. But the Reason Report appears problematic. Remember that the Reason Report states what you imagine that explains the attitude. That means you are being asked to make believe that *John Perry* is a diabolical Italian spy who has no sense of humor and never cracks a joke. Even if you can get yourself into the imaginative frame of mind that Perry is an Italian spy, you may be hard-pressed to think of him as someone who has never cracked a joke. Perry is well known for his joke-telling propensities. So, the objection goes, if you *can* imagine that Porcini never tells a joke, that must be because Porcini is not the real Perry, but only the John-Perry-of-the-story. If the only way to imagine what is true in the fiction is to imagine about a fictional character, then it must be fictional characters about which we are imagining. And, since what we imagine is the Reason Report that explains the attitude, then the attitude should also be to a fictional character. Call this the "Porcini Objection."

I think the Porcini Objection does not entail this conclusion, although it points to an interesting phenomenon. You found the sentence I added to the story amusing precisely because it's supposed to be Perry you are making believe never tells a joke. If I took out the connected names in the story, a good part of the humor would have been lost. It is pretty clear that this story was designed for a certain audience who would appreciate the allusions. So if we deny that we are supposed to be imagining, of Perry, that he never tells a joke, or of Everett, that he is a secret agent, then it seems as if we lose the point of the story altogether. So I think that the difficulty we have in imagining that about Perry, while apparently an objection to my view that the names remain connected in our attitudes, actually provides support for my claim. It is precisely *because* you recognize that you are supposed to be imagining, of *John Perry*, that he never tells a joke that you experience a kind of humorous tension. My proposal will be that such obstacles to imagining what is true in this fiction are problems for the *psychology* of our imagining, and not for the semantics of the reports of what we imagine. We can make perfect sense of the problem in (5b) without saying that the name "John Perry" is disconnected from the real Perry.

We can see this if we consider the response of someone who does not know Perry well enough to be aware that he tells a lot of jokes. The difficulty many of us have in imagining (5b) would not even arise for this person. Unless you think that the reference of a name is secured by the descriptions or conceptions associated by a speaker with a name—and I don't—it is safe to say that someone can refer to John Perry without knowing that he tells lots of jokes. So such a person can certainly imagine, *de re*, of Perry that he never tells a joke. Why should the difficulty of those of us who know Perry well preclude others from imagining this about him? It seems evident that what is at issue here is a conflict between modes of presentation of Perry.[193] The reason we have difficulty imagining (5b) is that many of us think of Perry in a certain way: as someone who tells a lot of jokes. This mode of presentation of Perry, if it is in the front of our minds, will interfere with our thinking of Perry under the mode of presentation of the fiction. The fiction presents Perry in a way exactly opposed to the way we normally think of him. But the conflict here is psychological, not semantic. Certainly it is no part of the meaning of his name that Perry tells jokes. And we don't have to be thinking of Perry in exactly the same way, for it to be Perry we are imagining about. Someone who doesn't know that Perry tells jokes will presumably be thinking of Perry in some other way that does not conflict with the portrayal in the fiction. Two more points need to be made. First, the fact that many of us usually think of Perry as a joke-teller, does *not* mean that we cannot still imagine of him that he never tells jokes. To do that requires, as Walton has suggested, that we not explicitly, or occurrently, keep in our minds our knowledge of Perry.[194] This is a purely psychological maneuver, and the fact that we may resort to it just shows that we recognize that we are supposed to be imagining about the real Perry. The psychological conflict would not arise unless it was Perry who was the referent in the Reason Report. And second, the point of this particular story depends on the expectation that we won't resort to this maneuver. If we manage to suppress the way we normally think of Perry, the story wouldn't be as amusing. This is a case where we are sacrificing illusion for the sake of humor.

---

[193]I will discuss "modes of presentation" in more detail below.

[194]Walton draws the distinction between occurrent and nonoccurrent imaginings in Walton (Walton 1990). pp. 16–21. He suggested, in correspondence, applying this notion to Kroon's argument.

Let me add that such psychological obstacles to imagining what is true in a fiction are not unique to this particular story. In fact, the phenomenon is quite pervasive. It happens, for example, when you see bad movies, where the special effects cause you to laugh rather than fear the aliens. Or in a work intended to be realistic, but where the inaccuracies are too blatant. This is not to say that we are *never* able to imagine what is unreal, but merely that in some cases what is too unrealistic can interfere with our imaginings. I suggest that the same thing may occur when we know enough about a particular subject or person that is portrayed in a work of fiction, such as John Perry. In such cases the crucial point is that this happens not in spite of, but *because*, we recognize that we are supposed to imagine about a real person. For instance, historians of England often have trouble buying into some of Shakespeare's plays. If a historian has in the front of her mind the knowledge that Richard III really wasn't so evil, she may not be able to enter fully into the make-believe. Similarly, if Hitler were portrayed as a loveable, misunderstood fellow in a movie, it might still be very difficult for us to imagine him that way. But again, it is because we recognize that we are supposed to be imagining about the real Hitler that we have this difficulty.[195]

So, far from showing that connected names are disconnected in the Reason Reports, it turns out that the Porcini Objection lends *support* to this view. Maintaining that these names remain connected explains the psychology of the situation better than the denial of this claim. The obstacles to imagining would not come up if the referent were not the real person. But before we conclude that we are imagining about the real people, and that our Reason Reports refer to the real people, I want to consider another objection.

9.5 The Kroon objection

This objection, which I call the "Kroon Objection," involves versions of two puzzles offered by Fred Kroon (Kroon 1994). Kroon uses his puzzles to show why make-believe theorists should give up the assumption that connected names in attitude reports refer to real people. Wherever the fictional object theorist would say that the disconnection of the names involves reference to fictional objects, Kroon himself would interpret such claims in terms of pretend-reference. So he handles the name "Everett" in the same way as Walton handles the name "Anna Karenina,"

---

[195] Of course, as Anthony Everett pointed out to me, in the Hitler case the problem might be a moral disdain for imagining this way, rather than an inability to imagine it. However, this moral disdain is itself evidence that we recognize it is Hitler about whom we are supposed to imagine.

except that we can bring in more information about the real Everett in our imaginings.[196] I want to indicate how I think my analysis of Reason Reports handles Kroon's Objection as well.

Here is the first puzzle. Since, according to the story, Porcini is brilliant in diabolical scheming, I imagine that he is such. And, since I admire brilliant people, regardless of the use to which they put their intelligence, I may have the following attitude in response to the story: "I admire Porcini because he is brilliant in diabolical scheming." Now consider Everett, who is listening to the story right along with you. Perhaps he too finds himself admiring this clever spy for the same reason. So we can report his attitude as follows: "Everett admires Porcini because he is brilliant in diabolical scheming." But now we have a problem, since according to the story, Everett *despises* Porcini for his brilliance in diabolical scheming. In fact, the story is *explicit* that Everett cannot bring himself to admire Porcini for just this reason. If we maintain that in both attitude reports, the names refer to the actual people, then we seem to have a contradiction:

6. Everett admires Porcini because he is brilliant in diabolical scheming, and Everett despises Porcini because he is brilliant in diabolical scheming.

The problem here is not with the object of the attitude, of course, since Porcini is John Perry. Rather, the puzzle is that we have the very same fictional reason giving rise to contradictory attitudes.

The second case is even more complex. According to the story, the rest of Everett's life has been ruined by his obsession with Porcini. Everyone except Everett pities Everett, but Everett is too blinded even to pity himself. Let's say that I particularly pity people who cannot manage to pity themselves, they are so wretched. So I have the following attitude in response to the story: "I pity Everett because Everett does not pity himself." Once again consider the real Everett listening to the story. Perhaps he feels just the same way. So we can report his attitude like this:

7. Everett pities Everett because Everett does not pity himself.

---

[196]This qualification turns out to be rather significant, so significant, in fact, that it is sometimes hard to tell if we are really disagreeing. In Kroon (Kroon 1994), he proposes to explicate this idea by saying that the pretend reference to a real object, which imports information about the real object into the game of make-believe, can be seen as "relative reference." Kroon says "we might say that there is a real person [Everett], whom the speaker refers to *relative to, or from the perspective of, that [the story] yields reliable information* (p. 219). However Kroon has since given up this explication in favor of an appeal to the idea of "shallow pretense," as proposed in Crimmins (Crimmins 1998).

Now the contradiction is even more blatant. It is not merely that Everett has two conflicting attitudes grounded on the same reason, but that the reason for the attitude appears to contradict the attitude itself. We analyze it this way:

7a. Everett pities Everett [because]
7b Everett does not pity himself.

The Attitude Report (7a) is supposed to be explained by the Reason Report (7b), but surely that does not happen here. As usual the Reason Report is a fictional reason, since it is according to the story that Everett does not pity himself. But that is no bar to the Attitude Report's making reference to Everett, as we have seen. So what is the problem?

Kroon suggests rephrasing (6) and (7) along the following lines:

6* Everett admires Porcini because he is brilliant in diabolical scheming, and *in the story* Everett despises Porcini because he is brilliant in diabolical scheming.

7* Everett pities Everett as *he is in the story* because *in the story* Everett does not pity himself.

When we rephrase this way, it looks as though in each case the first occurrence of "Everett" refers to the real Everett, while the other occurrences of the name refer to a fictional Everett, the Everett-of-the-story. In other words, we get rid of the contradiction in (6) if we say that that the first "Everett" refers to the *real* Everett admiring the *fictional* John Perry, much any reader might admire Sherlock Holmes. Then we would say that the second "Everett" refers to the *fictional* Everett despising the *fictional* John Perry, just as Holmes might despise Moriarty. Similarly, when we rephrase (7), it looks as though Everett is pitying a fictional character, rather than himself. In both cases Kroon reinterprets this to mean that only the first occurrence of the name "Everett" refers in the standard way to the real person; in the other cases it pretendedly-refers (and the same goes for "Porcini"). So, if we said that the name "Everett" is disconnected from the real person in all but the first occurrence in (6) and (7), we would seem to get rid of the contradiction. But we do not need to do that.

Once again I want to say that although there may be psychological difficulty in Everett's imaginings, it is not a semantic difficulty. There is a simple way to account for the semantics, while retaining the position that in every occurrence in (6) and (7) the name "Everett" remains connected to the real person. I will number the occurrences of the name to make this clear:

6. Everett$_1$ admires Porcini because he is brilliant in diabolical schem-

ing, and Everett$_2$ despises Porcini because he is brilliant in diabolical scheming.

7 Everett$_3$ pities Everett$_4$ because Everett$_5$ does not pity himself.

There is no doubt on anyone's part that "Everett$_1$" and "Everett$_3$" refer to the real person, since he's the person doing the imagining in response to the story. The doubt is raised by "Everett$_2$," "Everett$_4$," and "Everett$_5$," and of course the "himself" refers to whatever "Everett$_5$" refers to. If I am going to say that all of these occurrences of the name remain connected to the real Everett, I will have to provide an account that explains the difference between the two sets of names, while dealing with the apparent contradictions.

Following Walton, and along the lines of my response to the Porcini Objection, we just distinguish the modes of presentation of the real Everett. So "Everett$_1$" and "Everett$_3$" refer to the real Everett under whatever mode of presentation you are thinking of the real Everett. This would probably be a *de re* mode of presentation, a perceptual one if you were at the Empty Names Conference. "Everett$_2$," "Everett$_4$," and "Everett$_5$," then refer to the real Everett under the mode of presentation of the fiction. We think of Everett as he is portrayed in the fiction. As for Everett himself, in (6), Everett thinks of himself *de se* as admiring Porcini, and *de re* re as despising Porcini. In (7), Everett thinks of himself *de se* as pitying someone, and the someone he pities is himself, thought of as presented by the fiction. In other words, Everett himself would report his attitudes as follows:

8. I admire Porcini because he is brilliant in diabolical scheming and Everett despises Porcini because he is brilliant in diabolical scheming.

9. I pity Everett because Everett does not pity himself.

In these statements, the occurrences of the name "Everett" refer *de re* to the real Everett, of whom Everett is imagining that he is as described in the story. Notice that the rest of us would report our attitudes in just the same way.

A word should be said about the use to which I am putting these various "modes of presentation." I do not have a theory about what modes of presentation are: abstract objects, concrete particulars, etc. However, it should be clear what they are not: part of the semantics of the names used in reports of what we imagine. That is why the conflict that arises for some of us when we try to imagine John Perry as someone who has never told a joke is a psychological conflict, rather than a semantic contradiction. That is a conflict between whatever way we normally think of Perry, and the way the story presents—or rather, represents—him. In the cases described by Kroon, another important distinction is between *de re* and *de se* modes of presentation. The *de se* mode is marked by immunity to error through misidentification, to use Shoemaker's term.[197] In (7), for example, Everett cannot be wrong that it is he who is imagining, though it is conceivable that he could be mistaken that he is the object of his imaginings (e.g., he might be wrong to think that he is the Everett the story is about). That is why the other occurrences of "Everett" cannot refer to him *de se*, even though it is the real Everett of whom he is imagining.

However, distinguishing between first- and third-person modes of presentation will not suffice to resolve the puzzle in Everett's situation. Consider the following (non-fiction) scenario. Ellen is a poor student who lives in pitiful conditions. However, she does not realize what she is missing, and so she does not pity herself. When she overhears her teachers talking about her situation, she learns for the first time that she is someone to be pitied. She comes to pity herself in a third-person way, looking at herself "from the outside," so to speak. But even if that is the route to Ellen's recognition of her own situation, if she understands that it is she who is being discussed, she will come to think of *herself* as pitiable, in the first-person way. If Ellen fails to make the transfer between the third-person perspective and the first-person perspective, then she has not recognized that she is the subject of the conversation. This failure of recognition gives rise to the puzzles Perry and Kaplan use to show that there is a difference between the first and third persons, as when one says, "that man's pants are on fire," without realizing that one is looking in a mirror.[198]

Things are different with the Everett case. As noted above, if there is a fictional portrayal of a person there is always the possibility that one might not recognize that one is being portrayed. But that is not the situation in this example; Everett knows perfectly well that it is he who is being described in the story. So it would seem that within the pretense Everett should be doing what Ellen does in the non-fiction case: making the transfer from the third person to the first. But Everett cannot do that, because to do so would be for him to think of himself in a contradictory manner. If he is aware, in the course of his imaginings, that it is *he himself* who both pities and does not pity himself, he will not be able to imagine as the story prescribes. But once again this is a psychological difficulty, not a semantic one. As Walton has suggested, he might not be able to imagine both at the same time occurrently, to keep

---

[197]See Shoemaker (Shoemaker 1968). Walton discusses *de se* imagining in his (Walton 1990).

[198]See Kaplan (Kaplan 1989) and Perry (Perry 1993).

both in the front of his mind. He can imagine both that he pities Everett, and that Everett does not pity himself, so long as he doesn't explicitly imagine that he and Everett are the same person. The fact that Everett has to resort to this psychological trick, the fact that he experiences this tension between the two ways of imagining, again supports the claim that he is supposed to be imagining about himself.[199] I return to the disanalogy between the non-fiction case and the fiction case below.

9.6   Back to make believe attitudes

We have seen that the issues that arise in the Porcini Objection and the Kroon Objection can be resolved without saying that the names are disconnected. To assume otherwise would force us to give up some basic intuitions, and would not explain why we have trouble imagining some of what is fictionally true. But it is not merely the case that we can, if we want, maintain the view that the names are connected. Rather, I think this story indicates that we should maintain that view. That is because the justification for denying that our attitudes directed at the real people would be that my *reasons* for these attitudes do not make reference to the real people. But we have seen that that is not the case—clearly it is *Everett* about whom I am imagining, in response to this story. So it would be rather strange, I think, to say that although it is *Everett* about whom I am imagining that he is a jet-setting secret agent, it is *not* Everett of whom I am envious. To say that would mean to say that my response is like this: First I imagine that the real Everett is a jet-setter. Then I envy a fictional character for being a jet-setter. Surely that is not the correct explanation. If it is Everett who is the jet-setter of my imaginings, then it is Everett, thought of as a jet-setter, of whom I am envious.

But then we return to the original problem. If this reason is not

---

[199]Kroon has recently suggested (in correspondence) that the distinction between modes of presentation indicates "shallow pretense," as proposed in Crimmins (Crimmins 1998). For example, when we talk about Hammurabi's beliefs about Hesperus and Phosphorus, we are pretending (in a very shallow way) to talk about two different things; the pretense is that thoughts about Venus under the Hesperus-mode are thoughts about different things from thoughts about Venus under the Phosphorus-mode. The pretense account is then utilized to determine the truth conditions of these statements. If all that Kroon means by saying that the reference to Everett is pretend-reference is that it involves shallow pretense, then the difference between our views is negligible, since shallow pretense is invoked in cases where we are clearly referring to one thing (e.g., Venus) in ordinary belief contexts. The fact that we imagine about things under modes of presentation does not preclude genuine reference to those things. What interests me in the paper is how Kroon's argument might be used to deny this genuine reference to real objects, even if Kroon's own understanding of it goes in a different direction.

something I believe, then how can I *really* envy the real Everett? I don't think I can. Notice that this question has two parts: either I *really* envy a *fictional* Everett; or the attitude isn't *real* envy. Since it's not the first, it must be the second. In other words, if it isn't a fictional Everett I'm really envying (which I have argued it is not), then it must be that the attitude isn't genuine envy. Let's think of this non-genuine attitude as one of Walton's make-believe attitudes. My argument is not how Walton himself derives his account, but I think what I've said indicates a way to understand such attitudes so that they are perfectly plausible. The reason the attitudes are make-believe, does not necessarily have to do with the phenomenology of my attitude, nor am I play-acting that I envy Everett. Rather, what it means to say that I make-believedly envy Everett is merely this: My envy depends on a reason that I don't believe, but only imagine. There is a two-stage process: first I imagine Everett, the real Everett, to be a jet-setter. Then, with that presupposed, in the context of my imagining, I envy him. This envy, once again, cannot be genuine envy because it is not explained by my beliefs about the real person. Since it is explained, rather, by my make-beliefs, it is in just that sense *make*-believe envy.

Of course the parallel between belief and make-belief is not so straight-forward. It is well known that problems for the theory of reference arise in consideration of belief attributions. To recycle an old example, it seems that "Ken believes that Phosphorus is rising" could be true while "Ken believes that Hesperus is rising" was false, even though "Hesperus" and "Phosphorus" refer to the same thing (Venus). Similarly, it seems that "Everett imagines that Everett is pitiful" could be true while "Everett imagines that he himself is pitiful" is false, even though "Everett" and "he himself" refer to the same person. The difference is that if Ken finds out that Hesperus is Phosphorus, he will adjust his beliefs so as to avoid the contradiction. If Ken were to suppress this knowledge and continue believing as before, he would be irrational. But not only does Everett already know that he is the object about whom he is imagining, it is not irrational for him to suppress this knowledge. In fact, he needs to suppress this knowledge in order to imagine as the fiction prescribes.

Furthermore, in the case of ordinary belief attributions, one might say that the same belief content is believed (or not) under different modes of presentation. So Ken believes that Venus is rising under one mode of presentation, but not under another. I have talked as though, in the Everett case, the fiction provided just another mode of presentation along the same lines. If that were so, it would seem that Everett could simply *believe* that he is a secret agent under that mode of presentation. But the fictional mode of presentation clearly changes the attitude in question from belief to make-belief. There is no mode of presentation under which Everett believes that he is a secret agent; he only imagines that he is. The same applies to anyone else's imagining that of Everett. And reports of what we imagine, I have claimed, are *de re* in the sense that we can substitute co-referring expressions for "Everett." We imagine of *Everett* (thought of however you might think of him) that he is a secret agent. But then, when we envy him for this, we envy him under the mode of presentation of the fiction (i.e., our envy is grounded on make-belief rather than belief), since it is only thought of as a secret agent that we would envy him.

Since genuine envy, pity, and so on (reflective appreciator attitudes) require a belief that the object possess the trait that explains the attitude, we have make-believe attitudes wherever we have make-beliefs as the explanation for the attitude. This is a very minimal notion of these attitudes, and tells us nothing about the richness or complexity of our emotional responses to fiction. For all that I have said, our make-believe pity of Everett could be just as intense, if not more intense, than any genuine pity for a real person might be. It could feel exactly like genuine pity.[200] I have argued simply that there is a condition on an attitude's being a make-believe attitude: that it be grounded on what we imagine rather than what we believe. This is so no matter what the outward aspect of our emotions may be, how deeply we feel them, and so on. It is a minimal requirement, but it rules out cases that are clearly not make believe, for example the Greeks' worship of Zeus. Presumably the Greeks believed (falsely) that Zeus was an existent, powerful god. Therefore, their worship was not make-believe worship.

Considerations of connected names, then, show that some notion of make-believe attitudes is viable and useful. It seems, in fact, that we need such attitudes to explain at least the story I have discussed, a case where there are connected, rather than unconnected names. If I am right that the best explanation of such a case is one that invokes make-believe attitudes, then it looks as if any theory of fiction would make use of these attitudes, since connected names occur throughout fiction. Let's assume the fictional object theorist grants that make-believe attitudes have a place in a theory of fiction when it comes to explaining our responses to some stories with connected names. He still could maintain that our attitudes toward purely fictional characters, such as our pity of Anna Karenina, are genuine, on the grounds that these characters really have the properties that explain our attitudes. That would be the case

---

[200] See Walton (Walton 1997) for a discussion of the intensity and variety of our emotional responses to fiction.

on Zalta's and Parsons' views (especially for Parsons, since the sense in which Anna suffers is exactly the same sense in which any actual person might suffer). In contrast, since for Thomasson Anna does not literally have the property of having suffered, we cannot genuinely pity her. Van Inwagen also argues that our attitudes toward fictional characters are pretend attitudes, on the grounds that one does not admire, or pity, or envy things that are non-rational, non-sentient beings (such as abstract objects).[201] It seems to me that it would be a more consistent treatment of our responses to fiction to extend the make-believe analysis to purely fictional characters. In this respect Thomasson's account would be more consistent than Parsons' or Zalta's. On her view, our imagining of Everett that he is a secret agent and our make-believedly envying him for that, would be just like our imagining of Anna Karenina that she suffers and our make-believedly pitying her for that.

Pushing this line far enough could lead one to see how the make-believe theory becomes more attractive as an explanation of other aspects of our discourse about fiction.[202] Of course there are other considerations that may favor a fictional object theory, and I do not claim to have addressed all such considerations. Even so, I hope I have make clear that make-believe attitudes are not implausible. Therefore we should not view the commitment to these attitudes as a drawback for the pretense theory of fiction, or as a particular reason to favor a fictional object theory.

---

[201] This is although van Inwagen does not appear to agree with Thomasson that we only imagine Anna to have the property of having suffered. He makes a distinction in line with Zalta's, between "having" (exemplifying) properties and "holding" (encoding) them. But Zalta thinks our attitudes toward abstract objects based on the properties they encode are genuine, while van Inwagen thinks attitudes based on the properties such objects hold are pretend attitudes.

[202] Kroon (Kroon 1992) argues that Meinong held a mixed view involving pretense about non-existent objects, and that he should have abandoned the commitment to non-existent objects in favor of a pure pretense account. The point is once make believe is doing the explanatory work in one's theory, there is little point in positing such objects. But this is, of course, a very contentious claim.

10

Semantic Pretense

MARK RICHARD

Kendall Walton says that talk ostensibly about fictional objects involves pretense.[203] For example, in a typical utterance of

(1) Only Ishmael survived the wreck of the Pequod,

we engage in the kind of imaginative pretense involved in reading or appreciating *Moby Dick*, pretending to refer to a man named "Ishmael" and a ship named "the *Pequod*," further pretending to say that the one is related in a certain way to the other. The purpose of engaging in this pretense is to allow us to talk about it; crudely put, to utter (1) is (normally) to say, of the kind of pretense in which we're engaged, that it is one in which readers of *Moby Dick* are supposed to engage. How is it that uttering (1) is making such a claim? According to Walton, the mechanism is of the same kind as that which allows "[a] native of an exotic culture [to] inform his alien guests that the snake livers are to be eaten with the parrot's nest sauce by going ahead and doing so. ...Doing something is sometimes a way of claiming that it is proper or acceptable to do so" (Walton 1990), p. 399.

This account allows for the truth of ordinary talk about fiction without implying that what there is includes, not only *Moby Dick*, but Moby Dick. For there doesn't have to *be* such a thing as Moby Dick in order for me to pretend to refer to such. An additional advantage of the account is its (logico-) syntactic conservativeness. When I utter (1) in pretense, I do not refer to, or pretend to refer to, the novel *Moby Dick*, or to the property of being fictionally true. Rather, I simply pretend to make the references which (1)'s surface syntax suggests its literal utterance would involve. If, as Walton suggests, uttering (1) is (typically) a case

---

[203] Most notably in (Walton 1990).

Empty Names, Fiction, and the Puzzles of Non-Existence.
Anthony Everett and Thomas Hofweber (eds.).
Copyright © 2000, CSLI Publications.

of "saying by doing," we do not have to suppose that uses of (1) which say something true are uses of a sentence whose surface or logical form involves a covert operator "it is fictional that;" indeed, we need not suppose that (1)'s apparent syntactic form is in any way misleading as to its logical form.

Mark Crimmins says that talk about propositional attitudes also exploits pretense,[204] though the pretense involved and the mode of exploitation are somewhat different from those invoked by Walton. According to Crimmins, a typical utterance of

(2) Hammurabi believes that Hesperus is a star,

is embedded in the pretense, that Hesperus and Phosphorus are different things, and that therefore holding a belief "under the Hesperus mode" is believing something about one thing, holding a belief "under the Phosphorus mode" is believing something about another thing. *Relative to such a pretense*, what makes (2) true is that Hammurabi has a belief under the Hesperus mode; *relative to such a pretense*, what makes

(3) Hammurabi believes that Phosphorus is a star,

true is that Hammurabi has a belief under the Phosphorus mode. Crimmins' idea (very roughly) is that a typical use of (2) says the conditions, which would make (2) true in the pretense, in fact obtain. That is, in uttering (2), we are typically saying (something true if and only if) Hammurabi has a belief, under the Hesperus mode, that what it presents is a star. On this view, we engage in pretense, not to talk about the pretense itself, but (again, roughly put) to talk about the truth conditions which the pretense associates with our utterance.

The payoffs here are kindred to those of Walton's account. Crimmins can be conservative about the logical syntax of (2) and (3). He can deny that they involve reference to modes of presentation or expressions; he can accept that their semantics is Millian through and through. Still, if we are exploiting pretense as Crimmins proposes, then our intuition, that what we say with (2) is different from what we are say with (3), is not only explained; it is validated. And Crimmins' account can apparently explain how a sentence such as

(4) Daphne believes that Zeus is a god,

can have robust truth conditions (and ones different from that of "Daphne believes that Ahura Mazda is a god"), even though there is no such thing as the proposition, that Zeus is a god. For we can *pretend* that there is such a proposition, and make it true, in our pretense, that someone

---

[204]Most notably in (Crimmins 1998).

believes it just in case they are suitably related to the "Zeus mode of presentation."

Walton's original idea about (1) is a clever one, as is Crimmins' variation thereon. But neither, I shall argue, is adequate to the data it sets out to explain. In section 1, I exposit Walton's account of "ordinary" talk about fiction (e.g., typical utterances of (1)). Section 2 argues that obvious facts about speakers' "low level" semantic beliefs (for example, about when a sentence says something meaningful) imply that speakers will find the mechanism of pretense an unnecessary complication, in assertive uses of sentences like (1); thus, there is no reason to suppose that speakers make use of pretense in using sentences such as (1). Section 3 exposits Crimmins' view; the following two sections criticize it. Section 4 argues that, Crimmins' protests notwithstanding, the pretense account is not able to give a coherent account of the truth conditions of attitude ascriptions whose content sentences contain the identity predicate or the apparatus of quantification. Section 5 discusses what a pretense theory such as Crimmins' would have to say, about the semantics of expressions like "it is fictionally true." It argues that the sort of problems about logical syntax the pretense account is supposed to solve for sentences such as (2) re-emerge for this operator, and that this fact counts against the pretense account. Finally, section 6 examines Walton's and Crimmins' accounts of denials of existence, such as "Santa doesn't exist." I argue that neither account is acceptable.

1. When we play a game of make believe—Cowboys and Indians, say—we "explicitly pretend" certain things—that I am a cowboy, that you are an Indian, that this orchard is a plain filled with warriors. What is thus pretended true is "true-in-our-game," "fictionally true"—where to say that p is fictionally true in a game is to say that p is something that someone playing the game is supposed to imagine true.[205] Things other than what we explicitly pretend will be true in our game, in virtue of various states of affairs actually obtaining (or in virtue of actually obtaining states of affairs and fictional truths). If, for example, you creep across the orchard and roll under the pear tree, it will be true in the game that an Indian is preparing a surprise attack.

---

[205] This needs to be qualified in certain ways which are irrelevant to present purposes. It should be mentioned in passing that *fictional truth* is something of misnomer. To say it is fictionally true that p sounds a little like saying that there is some world, situation, or such at which p is true. This is not what Walton (or Crimmins) takes fictionality to be; as said in the text, p is fictional in such and such a game just in case (roughly) one is supposed to imagine p in the game.

What makes it fictional, that an attack is imminent? Walton speaks of the *principles of generation* associated with a game or fiction. These may be thought of as rules to the effect that if circumstances of kind C in fact obtain, then a proposition of a kind related thus and so to C is fictionally true. For example, in our game it might be a rule that if one points a finger in direction *d* and says "pkkch," it is fictionally true that one has fired a gun in direction *d*. Principles of generation may be explicitly laid down, but that would surely be unusual. They are typically implicitly presupposed: "what principles of generation there are [for a particular game of make believe] depends on which ones people accept in various contexts. The principles that are in force are those that are understood, at least implicitly, to be in force." (Walton 1990), p. 38.

According to Walton, associated with a work of fiction such as *Moby Dick* are various games of make believe, which involve imagining various things explicit and implicit in the fiction to be true. On this picture, a novel or story is a sort of "prop" in the games associated with it; its purpose in these games is to make various propositions fictionally true. Reading a novel or story involves participating in such a game. Thus, associated with *Moby Dick* is a game, the playing of which requires, among other things, imagining that the only survivor of certain wreck (that of the ship "the *Pequod*") is the person telling one a story. Part of the games associated with *Moby Dick* involves uttering, or at least thinking, sentences such as

(1) Only Ishmael survived the wreck of the Pequod.

Relative to such games, such an utterance is appropriate, for *Moby Dick* makes it fictionally true that only Ishmael survived the wreck of the *Pequod*. Thus, relative to *Moby Dick*, if one utters (1), one makes it fictionally true that one has spoken truly.

A typical utterance of (1) strikes most of us as saying something true; Walton concurs. What is genuinely asserted is that in a game of the relevant sort, the kind of pretending involved in uttering (1) is OK— engaging in that kind of pretense is making it true of oneself, in the game, that one has spoken truly. Slightly more precisely: Call the games for which *Moby Dick* has the function, of making various claims fictionally true, games that are *authorized* for *Moby Dick*. In uttering (1), one engages in a certain sort K of pretense, in which one pretends to refer to someone name "Ishmael" and to a boat name "the *Pequod*," and say of the first that only he survived the wreck of the second. What one genuinely asserts, in uttering (1) is

(5) If you engage in a pretense of kind K in a game authorized for *Moby Dick*, then you make it true of yourself, in the game, that

you speak truly.[206]

2. According to Walton, when one utters a sentence such as (1), one is (normally) talking about a certain kind of pretense. Exactly what kind? "When there is no apparent reference to purely fictitious entities...there is a purely descriptive way of specifying the relevant pretense." (see Walton, (Walton 1990), p. 401). If there is no such apparent reference— if the sentence uttered is something like

(6) Only one man lived to tell of how a white whale sank a ship with a one legged captain

—then a proposition (p call it) is expressed. In such a case, the relevant kind of pretense is simply: pretending to assert p. So, what's said by an utterance of (6) is

(7) If you pretend to say that only one man lived to tell of how a white whale sank a ship with a one legged captain, in a game authorized for *Moby Dick*, then you make it true of yourself, in the game, that you speak truly.

Now, as Walton observes, there seems to be a much simpler paraphrase of the relevant uses of (6). What, after all, makes (7) true? Well, it's the fact that, according to *Moby Dick*, only one man lived to tell of how a white whale sank a ship with a one legged captain. So, a gloss of an utterance of (6) "which, although not strictly equivalent, is near enough for many purposes" is

(7.1) It is fictional[ly true] in *Moby Dick* that only one man lived to tell of how a white whale sank a ship with a one legged captain.

"This gives the same result as the familiar suggestion that [in uttering (6) the speaker] has merely omitted, left implicit, some such phrase as 'it is fictional [in *Moby Dick*] that,' or 'it is true [in *Moby Dick*] that.'"[207] Why does Walton resist the claim that (6) is simply an elision of (7.1)? Well, one wants there to be a fairly strong "affinity"[208] between what's said by (1) and what's said by (6) (when each is uttered as a report about *Moby Dick*). If (6) elides (7.1), (1) elides

(1.1) It is fictional in Moby Dick that only Ishmael survived the wreck of the *Pequod*.

---

[206]See (Walton 1990), section 10.3, esp. p. 400. I have not slavishly followed Walton's phrasing of what is said by utterances like that of (1).

[207](Walton 1990), p. 401. I have changed the example under discussion.

[208]"affinity" is Walton's term for the relation between the statements made by the relevant uses of sentences related as are (1) and (5); see (Walton 1990), p. 402.

More generally, if (6) elides (7.1), then an utterance of sentence S as a report about what happens in a fiction *f* is an elision of (something of the form) *it is fictional in f that S*. But this "does not solve our problem, of course. [In a case like that of (1) and (1.1)] the longer statement retains the apparent reference to [Ishmael and the *Pequod*]...." (Walton 1990), p. 397). The problem is that a sentence in which a name of a fictional character is used can't *literally* say anything at all, since (on Walton's view) fictional names are empty names ((Walton 1990), pp. 385–400), and sentences in which empty names are used don't literally say anything. Since "Ishmael" is presumably used in a literal utterance of (1.1), treating (1) as (1.1)'s elision gets us no purchase on the problem of how (1), containing an empty name, can be used to say anything at all.

So far as I can see, Walton's principal reason for resisting the idea that *all* "ordinary" discourse about fiction—all utterances which, like (1) and (6), simply purport to recount what happens in the fiction— is paraphrasable *á la* (7.1) is that many such utterances don't literally say anything, because they involve the use of names of merely fictional characters. I think that if we reflect a little, we will agree that this is really a very bad reason for supposing, either that Walton's account of such sentences is correct, or that an across-the-board paraphrase of ordinary discourse about fiction, *á la* (7.1), would be incorrect. This is so, even if we begin by accepting Walton's account of the role of pretense in the appreciation of fiction.

The problem is that there is no reason to think that the linguistic behavior of normal speakers does or should reflect the (possibly correct but highly theoretical) claim that sentences such as (1) do not literally say anything. The claim, that if there there is no such thing as Ahab, then there is no such thing as the claim that Ahab was a sailor, borders on conventional semantic wisdom, in these post-Kripkean times. But this was not always so; what consensus there is has been reached only after a few dozen years of reflection on a variety of arguments and theoretical considerations. The foot soldiers of illocution—the ordinary men and women down in the trenches, doing the dirty work of saying, suggesting, and so forth—would find the idea, that strictly speaking one can't say (or think) that Ahab was a sailor, plainly incredible, perhaps even more incredible than the idea, that to say that Hesperus is Hesperus is to say that Hesperus is Phosphorus.

Suppose that you are such a non-theorist, and are reading *Moby Dick*. How, if you thought about it, would you describe your activity, as you read the Epilogue, whose epigraph is *Job*'s "And I only am escaped alone to tell thee?" Quite probably, you would agree with Walton that you were imagining certain things. You might naturally say something like

> When I read "The drama's done. Why then does any one step forth?—Because one did survive the wreck," I imagine that Ishmael is telling me that he is the only person who escaped the wreck of the *Pequod*.

You would also find it natural to say that according to the novel, Ishmael survived; you would allow that the novel says that he survived. You would recognize no discontinuity among sentences such as

> "Snow is white" says that snow is white.
> Mary said that the rain in Spain falls mainly on the ground.
> In Moby Dick, it says that only Ishmael escaped the wreck of the *Pequod*.

There will be nothing about your usage or linguistic behavior which would justify thinking that you (or your "language module") perceives the last sentence to differ in some semantically significant way from the first two. There will be nothing that suggests that you see the last sentence as requiring special or exceptional treatment, if its assertive use is to be successful.

Suppose that I am correct about this, and that Walton is correct about the nature of works of fiction and their aesthetic appreciation. That is, suppose that Walton is correct in thinking that: associated with a work of fiction such as *Moby Dick* are various games of make believe, which involve imagining various things true in the fiction to be true; *Moby Dick* is a sort of "prop" in such games, whose purpose is to make various propositions fictionally true; central to reading the novel (and appreciating it) is participating in such a game. What earthly reason could there be, for thinking that when a speaker utters a sentence such as (1) or (6), she performs the quite complex task of engaging in pretense in order to discuss the pretense performed, instead of straightforwardly trying to say, of what's said by (1) or (6), that it's "true in *Moby Dick*?" Why think that "the familiar suggestion," that a fictionality operator is elided, doesn't give a perfectly correct account of account of how we (are disposed to) think that utterances of (1) and (6) come to say whatever it is that they do say? The theoretical fact, if it is a fact, that (1) doesn't say anything seems perfectly irrelevant. Not only is the fact not in our pre-theoretical ken, it seems to be one which we (obviously) disbelieve. Certainly we can't appeal to it, to explain why the utterer of (1) engages in pretense, for the utterer, as just observed, rejects the theoretical fact. From the speaker's perspective, the suggestion that one needs to engage in pretense, in order to make a claim in uttering (1) or (6), seems an utterly unnecessary complication. After all, if (1) is not semantically defective,[209] then the reason that (5)—Walton's gloss of normal uses of (1)—is true is simply that readers of *Moby Dick* are supposed to imagine that only Ishmael survived the *Pequod*'s wreck. So if (1) is not semantically defective, the complex performance—pretending to use (1) assertively and, in doing so, signaling to one's audience that what one is doing is sanctioned by a game associated with the novel—seems little more than a very complicated way of signaling that, according to the novel, only Ishmael survived. And one can signal that, if (1) is not semantically defective, simply by uttering "According to the novel, only Ishmael survived." For to say that relative to *Moby Dick*, p is the case, is to say that some of the rules of generation associated with the novel prescribe imaging p. So, since, from the perspective of the speaker, (1) non-problematically says that only Ishmael survived, there is no reason, in uttering (1), to depart from what is presumably standard illocutionary practice, of using declarative utterance to assert what is literally expressed—and eliding the (presumably contextually obvious) "according to *Moby Dick*."

But then why think that speakers *do* depart from normal assertive practice in uttering sentences such as (1)? As Walton himself admits, what the speaker means to convey by uttering (1) would be "near enough for many purposes" to what would be literally conveyed by "According to *Moby Dick*, only Ishmael survived the wreck of the *Pequod*," if only sentence (1) said something to begin with. But *we* (normal speakers) think it does say something. There doesn't appear to be anything which we believe, inchoately suspect, or sub-doxastically register which would tend to make us think that an utterance of (1) (involving an elision of "According to *Moby Dick*") would not say exactly the thing which we intend to say, in uttering (1). So we can be expected to believe, of (1) and that which (on all accounts) we are trying to get across with (1)'s utterance, that a literal utterance of the first expresses the second (or something equivalent, for all purposes, thereto). Why would the language module be so inefficient that it invented a novel mechanism for using sentence S to assert p, when it already took S to literally say p (and so could use S to assert p simply by conforming to standard assertive practice)?

3. Among the principles of generation in a game of make believe will (typically) be ones to the effect that uttering a sentence of such and so a kind makes it fictionally true that one has asserted a proposition of so

---

[209]That is, if its literal, unembedded use makes a truth evaluable claim.

and such a kind. For example, in Cowboys and Indians, we may have a principle of generation along the lines of

(P1) If one utters "some cowboys are behind that ridge," pointing to a mound of dirt, it is fictionally true that a ridge at which one points is such that one has asserted that some cowboys are behind it.

Suppose I point to a pile of dirt and say "some cowboys are behind that ridge." Whether I have, in the context of the game, spoken truly will depend on (a) what principles of generation besides (P1) operate in the game, and (b) what states of affairs in fact obtain. Suppose, for example, that the *only* other relevant principle of generation is

(P2) If Bill, Tiny, or Jessica is behind a mound of dirt, then it is fictionally true that it [the mound] is a ridge behind which are some cowboys.

Then it will be fictionally true that I spoken truly iff the condition

(C) Bill, Tiny or Jessica is behind the demonstrated dirt,

actually obtains. Let us say that when a game f, an utterance u, and state of affairs s are thus related—s is a situation which must really obtain for u to be a true utterance in f (and whose really obtaining suffices for u to be a true utterance in f)—that s *is a real world truth condition of u, relative to f.* [210]

Suppose we are playing Cowboys and Indians, and it is fictionally true, of our belts, that they are holsters. Then the real world truth condition of an utterance, addressed to you, of "your holster is unbuckled" is, of course, that your belt in unbuckled. Now suppose that I notice that your belt is unbuckled and, worried that your pants are headed south, utter "your holster is unbuckled." The point of my utterance is not so much, to engage in the pretense that you are a cowboy whose holster is unbuckled and that I am a fellow cowboy saying that this is so, as to convey to you that the real world truth condition of my utterance—that your belt is unbuckled—in fact obtains. My utterance is intended to be construed, and indeed is correctly construed, not merely as part of a

---

[210]That is: s is a real world truth condition of u relative to f iff (1) it is true in f that u is the assertion of a proposition, and (2) in the context of f, that s obtains is necessary and sufficient, for it to be fictionally true that u is the assertion of a true proposition. The second clause of this is, of course, less than pellucid. Various remarks of Crimmins' suggest that we might replace (2) with something like: The principles of generation of f entail that (it is fictionally true in f that u is the assertion of a true proposition) iff s obtains. (See, for example, the discussion of sentences (2) and (3) at (Crimmins 1998), p. 6.)

I will generally speak of *the* real world truth condition of an utterance (relative to a fiction), in order to avoid agonizing prolixity.

game of make believe in which I *pretend* to make an assertion, but as an act which in fact involves making an assertion. When I utter "Your holster is unbuckled," it seems, I *pretend* to say that your holster is unbuckled and I *in fact* say that your belt is unbuckled. Let us call this sort of thing—making an utterance *u* within a pretense in which *u* has a real world truth condition *c*, thereby actually asserting a proposition which is (in fact) true iff *c* obtains—*piggy backing*.[211]

Crimmins holds that a good deal of discourse is accompanied by one or another sort of pretense, off of which the discourse's assertive utterances piggyback. In particular, he holds that propositional attitude ascription involves piggy backing. According to Crimmins, when we talk about what someone believes, we pretend that different modes of presentation present different objects.[212] In discussing Summarian astronomical beliefs, for example, we pretend that there are two objects, one named "Hesperus" and presented by the mode of presentation [Hesperus] actually associated with that name, the other named "Phosphorus" and presented by the mode [Phosphorus] actually associated therewith. The pretense employs principles of generation along the lines of

(P3) If (and only if) someone has a thought involving [Hesperus], then it is fictionally true that they have a belief about the object named "Hesperus,"

(P4) If (and only if) someone has a thought involving [Phosphorus], then it is fictionally true that they have a belief about the object named "Phosphorus."

Given the game we are playing, when I utter

(2) Hammurabi believed that Hesperus was a star,

it becomes fictionally true that I have said that Hammurabi believed, of the object named "Hesperus," that it was a star. Given the operative principles of generation, the real world truth condition for my utterance—the condition that must actually obtain, in order for it to be fictionally true that I have said something true—is that Hammurabi had a belief involving [Hesperus], which was an ascription to a thing of the property of being a star. (Following Crimmins, we abbreviate this as follows: the real world truth condition of my utterance is that Hammurabi believed <[Hesperus], being a star>.)

Call this sort of pretense—in which modes of presentation associated with different names are pretended to present different things bearing

---

[211] The term "piggy backing" is mine, not Crimmins' or Walton's.

[212] Crimmins is non-committal about the nature of modes of presentation; I shall be, too.

those names, and principles of generation such as (P3) and (P4) are employed—*attitude pretense*. We engage in attitude pretense, Crimmins says, in order to piggy back: My utterance of (2) is the assertion of a claim true iff Hammurabi believed <[Hesperus], being a star>.[213] The general pattern is that, in talking of attitudes, we pretend that different modes of presentation present different objects and adopt the obvious principles of generation. The upshot is that we are able to piggy back an utterance of

> So and so believes that ... n ... ,

into the assertion of something that is true iff

> So and so believes <[n], the property of being an x such that ..x...>.

What work does the postulation of semantic pretense? Well, suppose we have been convinced, by arguments concerning semantic innocence, the coherence of quantifying in, or whatever, that the logical syntax of a belief ascription is what the Millian or neo-Russellian would have us believe. We thus think that (2) literally says, of Hammurabi and the Russellian proposition that Venus is a star, that the one believes the other. We think that the behavior of the words in the complement is, semantically, in no way extraordinary; in particular, "Hesperus" there names Venus, and does nothing else. However powerful the arguments for this view of (2)'s semantics, it seems to sit poorly with truth conditional intuitions: Speakers see the truth of (2) turning on whether Hammurabi conceived of Venus in a particular way.

If, however, utterances of (2) generally involve piggy backing, the view of logical syntax and our intuitions concerning truth conditions can both be correct. Given the view of the logical syntax, uttering (2) makes it true in the pretense that one has said that Hammurabi believed a certain singular proposition, whose constituents are the property of rising in the west and the object named by "Hesperus." The real world truth condition of this utterance is that Hammurabi believed <[Hesperus], being a star>—that is, he believed the proposition that Venus is a star "under the Hesperus mode." So, given that the utterance of (2) involves piggy backing, such an utterance is actually true iff Hammurabi believed the proposition that Venus is a star "under the Hesperus mode." Russellian logical syntax, Fregean truth conditions; the Holy Grail is found, the Fisher King is healed.

---

[213]It is not supposed to be the assertion of the claim that this condition obtains. As Crimmins is aware, this would assign the wrong modal truth conditions to utterances of (2). See the discussion in section 6.

4. Roughly, and to a first approximation, in piggy backing, I play a game g in which it is fictionally true that I say that p, so that I may exploit the fact, that it is c's obtaining which makes p true in g, in order to say that c obtains. This means that when p is something which simply can't be true in the context of the game, there will be little point in trying to piggy back off the fictional truth that I say that p.

Now, on Crimmins' account, when we ascribe an attitude, we begin by pretending that every mode of presentation presents something, and that no two modes of presentation present the same thing.[214]

---

[214]This seems to be Crimmins' intention. But it is too strong. One thinks that it will be fictionally true that if Hesperus is the heavenly body most discussed by philosophers, then it will be fictionally true that Hesperus is identical with Hesperus, the heavenly body most discussed by philosophers. In many attitude pretenses, the antecedent will be fictional. So—assuming modus ponens in this instance preserves fictionality, we have a case in which distinct modes of presentation fictionally present the same thing. (The modes must be distinct, because they won't present the same thing at a world where no one discusses Hesperus.)

There seems to be serious trouble lurking here. For example, it will presumably often be fictional that an object o is the unique possessor of a property F and the unique possessor a property G, F and G independent. (This would be so, for example, in a case where we are discussing someone who knows that Twain alone wrote *Tom Sawyer* and *Huck Finn*, but doesn't realize that he alone wrote *The Mysterious Stranger*.) Since we can presumably rely on the fictional truth of principles such as

If o is the F, then what $[o]$ presents is what $[o$, the $F]$ presents,

as well as modus ponens preserving fictionality, it will be fictional that

What $[o]$ presents is what $[o$, the $F]$ presents, and what $[o]$ presents is what $[o$, the $G]$ presents.

But one would think that we should also be able to rely on the fictionality of principles such as

If o is the F, then what $[o$, the $F]$ presents is what $[$the $F]$ presents.

So, again assuming that modus ponens preserves fictionality, it will be fictional that

What $[o$, the $F]$ presents is what $[$the $F]$ presents, and what $[o$, the $G]$ presents is what $[$the $G]$ presents.

But as long as banalities such as

If one thing is identical with a second and with a third, then the second is identical with the third

are fictional, and universal specification preserves fictionality, it will be fictional that

what $[$the $F]$ presents is what $[$the $G]$ presents.

So if we are thinking apart $[$the $F]$ and $[$the $G]$, it will be fictional that what $[$the $F]$ presents is and is not what $[$the $G]$ presents.

Generally, attitude pretense will be logically incoherent in this way. I am not completely sure whether this a problem; fiction is often enough logically incoherent. But this certainly *looks* problematic. Crimmins wants the likes of

Hammurabi believed the planet most discussed by to be a star, but he didn't believe the planet which rises over there to be a star,

to be such that it can be true even when we suppose that Hesperus has both the relevant properties (as we would if, for example, in the discourse as a whole we are

Relative to such a pretense, a sentence such as "Hesperus is Phosphorus" apparently says something impossible, for it apparently says something true only if the modes of presentation [Hesperus] and [Phosphorus] present different things while also presenting the same thing. So, since "Hesperus is Phosphorus" says something which can't be fictionally true, it says something which, relative to the pretense, can't be known. So there is apparently no (possibly obtaining) condition c which is the real world truth condition for a sentence such as

(8) Hester knows that Hesperus is Phosphorus.

So, apparently, we can't appeal to piggy backing to explain how this sentence can be used to say something possibly true and interestingly different from "Hester knows that Hesperus is Hesperus."

Crimmins is aware of this problem, and suggests a fix. He notes that when we speak of identity, we speak as if it is a relation which can hold between distinct objects ("when two objects are identical, any property of one is a property of the other"). He suggests that such talk involves the pretense that "with certain of our linguistic devices that normally express identity, we can express a relation which can hold between distinct objects" (Crimmins 1998), p. 35. Call the relation *ickdentity*. Suppose that in attitude pretense we (a) pretend that our use of the "is" of identity expresses ickdentity; (b) pretend that ickdentity holds between the objects presented by modes m and m', if in actuality m and m' present the same thing; (c) assume principles of generation such as

P5: If (and only if) Hester knowingly believes <[Hesperus], identity, [Phosphorus]>, then it is fictionally true that Hester knowingly ascribes ickdentity to <what is named by "Hesperus," what is named by "Phosphorus">.

Then, when I utter (8), it will be fictionally true that I have said, of what "Hesperus" and "Phosphorus" fictionally name, that Hester knows that they are ickdentical. And this piggy backs into saying something true

---

discussing two people, one who knows that Hesperus has both properties, one who thinks that different things have them.) Presumably banalities like

If one thing is identical with a second, and Hammurabi believes the first to be F, then Hammurabi believes the second to be F,

will be fictional. But then we have

Hammurabi did and did not believe the star which rises over there to be a star,

being fictional, given that semantic pretense involves principles of generation such as

It is fictional that one believes the star which rises over there to be a star iff one believes <[the star which rises over there], being a star>.

just in case Hester knows under the relevant modes that Hesperus is Phosphorus.

The fix, then, is that attitude pretense involves re-interpretation of the identity predicate. But this seems to cause problems with sentences in which the the apparatus of quantification or counting is used. Recall how an attitude pretense about Venus and the Summarian gets going: We "make believe that Hesperus and Phosphorus are two things...[so that] it is fictionally true that there are two things to which we can refer as 'Hesperus' and 'Phosphorus,'" (Crimmins 1998), p. 9. Consider the most basic fact about the determiner phrase "two things":

(F1) *two things F* is true if and only if there is an x and a y such that x is not identical with y, x Fs, and y Fs.

Do we carry this fact into the fiction or not? That is, is (F1), as uttered within the fiction, true? Suppose it is. This will certainly force the following to be true, as uttered in the fiction:

(F2) (There are two things to which we can refer, respectively, as "Hesperus" and "Phosphorus") iff (there is an x and a y such that x is not identical with y, we can refer to x as "Hesperus" and we can refer to y as "Phosphorus"),

Now, assuming that we aren't pretending that "Hesperus" and "Phosphorus" are ambiguous, the following will be fictionally true:

(F3) (There is an x and a y such that x is not identical with y, we can refer to x as "Hesperus" and we can refer to y as "Phosphorus") iff (Hesperus is not identical with Phosphorus and we can refer to Hesperus with "Hesperus" and we can refer to Phosphorus with "Phosphorus").

But Crimmins' solution to the problem with (8) was to hold that in attitude pretense, we pretended that "is identical to" expressed ickdentity, and so "Hesperus is identical with Phosphorus," within the fiction, says something true! So the right side of (F3)'s biconditional is fictionally *false*; so its left side is too; so, chasing this consequence up the F's, it is fictionally false that there are two things to which we can refer as "Hesperus" and "Phosphorus." Since it is fictionally true that the names refer, this drags in its wake the fictional equivalence of claims that someone believes Hesperus to be F to claims that she believes that Phosphorus is. And this is something the pretense account cannot allow.

To avoid this one must deny that (F1) is carried into the fiction. It is not clear that it makes sense to suppose this—(F1) is, if anything is, analytic. But let us for the moment entertain the idea that attitude pretense involves a sort of uncoupling of "two" (and thus of "one," "three," and the rest of the numerals) from the identity predicate, at least to the extent that both of

(Y) Hesperus is identical with Phosphorus,

(N) Hesperus and Phosphorus are two things, not one,

can both be fictionally true—as they would have to be, if we can have an attitude pretense in which it is true that Hester knows that Hesperus is identical with Phosphorus, but in which we begin by "thinking Hesperus and Phosphorus apart"—i.e., making it fictionally true that Hesperus and Phosphorus are two things, not one.[215]

It now becomes quite obscure, what are an attitude pretense's principles of generation—obscure, that is, what principles tell us which real world conditions make which sentences fictionally true. We are told that attitude pretense makes use of principles of generation along the lines of

(F4) It is fictionally true that Hester believes that Hesperus is a planet iff Hester believes <[Hesperus], being a planet>.

Now, to truly believe p is to believe p while p is true; whatever it is that *Hester truly believes that S* says, it had better not say something which can be true when (what) S (actually says in fact) is not. So, given that the likes of (F4) are principles of generation, we are committed to principles of generation on which *Hester truly believes that S* is fictionally true just in case what S says is *actually* true, and it is *fictionally* true that she believes S. In particular, we have

(F5) It is fictionally true that Hester truly believes that Hesperus and Phosphorus are two things, not one iff (it is true that Hesperus and Phosphorus are two things not one, and Hester believes <[Hesperus], being two things, not one, [Phosphorus]>.

Surely, however, fictional truth is "closed under triviality," so that (all instances of) the schema

(F6) It is fictionally true that H truly believes that S iff it is fictionally true that S, and it is fictionally true that H believes that S),

are true.[216] All this cannot be. Suppose Hester believes that Hesperus and Phosphorus are two things, not one, and does this "under" the mode

---

[215]There is, in fact, a fairly strong argument that Crimmins must say that in an attitude pretense it is fictional that Hesperus is Phosphorus, and it is fictional that Hesperus and Phosphorus are two things, not one. For he holds that the "is" of identity fictionally expresses ickdentity, and the makes it fictional that Hesperus is Phosphorus. And we *are* supposed to pretend that "Hesperus" and "Phosphorus" name **two** different things.

[216]Such instances must be true so long as instances of

(T) It is fictionally true that [H truly believes that S iff (S, and H believes that S)]

of presentation [Hesperus and Phosphorus are two things, not one]. Then she believes <[Hesperus], being two things, not one, [Phosphorus]>. So it is fictionally true that she believes that Hesperus and Phosphorus are two things, not one. And it is fictionally true that Hesperus and Phosphorus are two things, not one. So, by (F6) and (F5), Hesperus and Phosphorus are two things, not one. But this, of course, is not so. I find it hard to believe that a pretense account of attitude ascription can correctly assign truth conditions to claims about knowledge, true belief, or any of the other "factive attitudes."

5. Making believe and pretending would seem to be propositional attitudes: One makes believe *that Hesperus is not Phosphorus*; one pretends *that this is an apple pie*.[217] Making believe and pretending are, furthermore, generators of fictional truth: When we pretend that *p*, then, relative to our make believe, it is fictionally true that *p*.

Now, fictional truth is presumably a property of the object of pretense and make believe; the latter being a proposition, it follows that fictional truth is a property of propositions. If fictional truth if a property of propositions,[218] what are we saying when we say (for example) that it is fictionally true that Hesperus is a star? The *natural answer* is: We are saying, of the proposition that Hesperus is a star, that it is fictionally true. But much of the point of adopting a pretense account of attitude ascription is to allow us to maintain a broadly Russellian account of propositions, on which the proposition that Hesperus is a star is the proposition that Phosphorus is, given that Hesperus is Phosphorus. So, given the natural answer, if it is fictionally true that ...Hesperus..., then it is fictionally true that ..Phosphorus.... This, of course, sounds wrong. In an attitude pretense about Hammurabi, it is supposed to be fictional that he sees Hesperus in the evening; it's not supposed to be fictional that he sees Phosphorus in the evening.

In thinking about what is going on here, we need to carefully distinguish

---

are true and "fictional truth is closed under biconditional elimination"—i.e., so long as the inference *FT[A iff B], FT[A], so FT[B]* is valid. (Ok, ok, you also need to be able to infer FT[B iff A] from FT[A iff B].) It is difficult to credit the claim that either (T) or closure under biconditional elimination fails.

[217]This is a bit too simple, actually. If I pretend to do something, more than a propositional attitude is involved. Still, a propositional attitude *is* involved; if I am not *imagining* that I am serving you a pie, I'm not pretending that I am.

[218]Well, this isn't exactly correct. Fictional truth is relation, between a fiction or game and the bearer of fictional truth: It may be true in one game of capture the flag that this tree is the Pentagon and not the Lincoln Memorial, while in some other game it may be fictional that the tree is the Memorial, not the Pentagon. In what follows, I suppress the relativization, to reduce prolixity.

(a) The proposition in fact expressed by S being fictionally true,

(b) The literal truth of the sentence *it is fictionally true that S*.

Even if fictional truth is a property of propositions, (a) and (b) might come apart: They might, for example, if, for some ('non-homophonic') function f from sentences to propositions, *it is fictionally true that S* said, of $f(S)$, that it had the property of being fictionally true. In order to facilitate distinguishing (a) and (b), let us write **FT[S]**, where S is replaced by a sentence, to abbreviate *it is fictionally true that S*. (So "FT[Hesperus is a star]" abbreviates "it is fictionally true that Hesperus is a star.") And let us write **FIC[S]**, where S is replaced by a sentence, to say, of the proposition in fact expressed by S, that it is fictionally true.[219]

What we called the natural answer, to the question *What are we saying in saying that it is fictionally true that S?*, must be rejected. That answer—that we are saying of the proposition S expresses, that it is fictional—commits us to instances of

(A) FT[S] iff FIC[S],

at least when S is a sentence which expresses a proposition. But it does not seem likely that we could avoid endorsing instances of

(B) FT[An utterance of "S" is true] iff FT[S],

at least when S is a sentence which expresses a proposition. After all, in pretending that Hesperus isn't Phosphorus, we are not pretending away banalities about meaning. Indeed, our pretense exploits the usual rules for making assertions and surely involves assuming / pretending that, save for the difference in the sense and reference of certain names and other expressions, the language we speak is just as it normally is. And (B) is nothing more than a reflection, within the pretense, of the banality expressed by instances of

(D) An utterance of "S" is true iff S.

(To see this, note that (B) follows from

(D') FT[An utterance of "S" is true iff S],

so long as "fictional truth is closed under biconditional elimination"—see note 219 above.) But since the Russellian proposition that Hammurabi believes that Hesperus is a star is the Russellian proposition that he believes that Phosphorus is, the relevant instances of (A) and (B) imply

---

[219]Throughout what follows, I pretend that context sensitivity doesn't exist. Understand me to be speaking of some particular case of semantic pretense, in which someone utters "Hammurabi believes that Hesperus is a star."

(E) FT[An utterance of "Hammurabi believes that Hesperus is a star" is true] iff FT[An utterance of "Hammurabi believes that Phosphorus a star" is true].

But this is disastrous for the pretense account, since the account depends on utterances of the sentences having non-equivalent fictional truth conditions, in order to explain how one sentence may be used to say something true without the other sentence being such that its use would be a true one.

We must reject (A), and with it the natural answer to our question about "it is fictionally true." This strikes me as a very odd result. For one thing, it makes the nature of fictional truth opaque: What is it, for it to be fictionally true that Hesperus is a star, if it is not that this—that Hesperus is a star—is fictionally true? Somewhat less question beggingly, the result rings false, if we think about more mundane instances of make believe. In ordinary make believe, the players use various props—cups of mud, their fingers, garbage pail covers—to represent various things—pieces of pie, guns, shields. Such pretense is usually a matter of pretending, of the prop, that it is so and so: a game of mud pies, in which a cup of mud with a leaf on top is pretended to be a slice of apple pie a la mode, is a game in which the participants are pretending, with respect to it, the cup of mud, that it is a piece of pie. And pretending, of x, that it is F, seems to be pretending that x is F. In this case, its being fictional that this [imagine me pointing to a cup of mud] is a piece of pie seems to be a matter of our pretending-true the proposition that this [the mud] is a piece of pie. And this suggests that, in this most basic case, its being fictional that this [the mud] is a piece of pie is simply a matter of the proposition, that this is a piece of a pie, having the property of being pretendedly—i.e., fictionally—true. Why isn't the same thing true in semantic pretense? Hesperus, after all, is just as much a prop of the semantic pretense, involved in pretending to say of Hesperus, that Hammurabi believes that it is a star, as the cup of mud is a prop of the game of mudpies.

One might claim, in defense of rejecting (A), that it couldn't be true across the board, anyway. For, the argument goes,

(F) FT[Zeus is a god] iff FIC[Zeus is a god],

must fail: There will be fictions relative to which its left hand side is true; but, since there is no proposition that Zeus is a god, its right hand side cannot be true.

This strikes me as a disingenuous defense of the pretense account. Recall that the point of the pretense account is to allow us to treat sentences of the form *Hammurabi believes that S*, and of allied forms, as "innocent" constructions, whose logical form is exactly as the neo-Russellian or Millian says it is. The pretense account is supposed to show us how something like

(G) Daphne believes that Zeus is a god iff the proposition that Zeus is a god is such that Daphne believes it,

can be a *consequence* of a correct semantics for English, and its left hand side can be used to say something true, *even though* there is no such thing as the proposition that Zeus is a god. That is, adopting BT[S] as an abbreviation for *Daphne believes that S*, BEL[S] as a abbreviation for *the proposition that S is such that Daphne believes it*, the pretense account is supposed to reconcile the claims that:

(G') BT[Zeus is a god] iff BEL[Zeus is a god]

is a consequence of a correct semantics of English; its left side can be used to say something true; there is no such thing as the proposition that Zeus is a god.

One would have thought beforehand that, at the level of logical form, the syntactic structures *FT[S]* and *BT[S]* would both pick out relations to (Russellian) propositions if either did. Thus, it is rather dumbfounding to be told that "Daphne believes that" picks out a relation to a proposition, that there is no such thing as the proposition that Zeus is a god *but still* "it is fictionally true that Zeus is a god" may be true. Obviously, if this is so, "it is fictionally true" doesn't pick out a relation to a Russellian proposition. One of course now wants to know exactly what its semantics is—for one suspects that if we understood it, we would be able to validate our intuitions about attitude ascriptions without invoking semantic pretense.

Let us take stock. We began this section wondering what it could be, on the pretense theorist's view, for it to be fictional that (say) Hesperus is a planet. We argued that the pretense theorist could not adopt the natural answer—fictionality is simply a property of a proposition; *it is fictional that S* is true iff the proposition expressed by S is fictional—because of the way the pretense theorist ties what uses of attitude ascriptions convey to fictionality. But, as we just saw, the pretense theorist is under some theoretical pressure to accept the natural answer. At this point, it may occur to one that the pretense theorist might treat fictionality and "it is fictional that" in the way he treats belief and "Daphne believes that": He might claim that while fictionality is a property of propositions, and the literal truth conditions of *it is fictional that S* are simply a matter of the relevant proposition having the property of being fictional, our uses of these sentences involve pretense in more or less the same way that attitude ascriptions do.

How might this go? Consider

(I) It is fictionally true (in pretense p) that [an utterance of "Hammurabi believes that Hesperus is a star" is true iff Hammurabi believes that Hesperus is a star].

One might say that a normal utterance of this involves a rather elaborate pretense: One pretends to refer Hammurabi, Hesperus, and the sentence "Hammurabi believes that Hesperus is a star," while pretending to say that the last is true iff the the first believes that the second is a star. Call this elaborate pretense P; what one normally conveys by uttering (I) is that if one is engaged in P, then performing P makes it the case, in P, that one has spoken truly. The upshot is that when we utter (I), we are not trying to convey the fictionality of the proposition expressed by its embedded sentence; instead we are claiming that certain behavior (engaging in P) will, in certain circumstances (my participating in P), make a certain proposition (namely, the proposition that I say something true) fictionally true.

This is all very well, and it does perhaps explain how, on pretense theoretic terms, "it is fictional that Zeus is a god" can convey a truth. But it is of absolutely no help in dealing with the problem set out at the beginning of the section. That problem was that if the pretense theorist admitted the truth—i.e., the literal truth—of all instances of

(A) FT[S] iff FIC[S],

as well as the truth of

(D') FT[An utterance of "S" is true iff S],

then he was committed to the disastrous

(E) FT[An utterance of "Hammurabi believes that Hesperus is a star" is true] iff FT[An utterance of "Hammurabi believes that Phosphorus a star" is true].

As we observed, rejecting (D') seemed unlikely, given that semantic pretense presumably presupposes banal facts about meaning. And the current proposal just *is* that all instances of (A) *are literally true* . The fact that typical utterances of sentences about fictional truth might be intended to convey something other than what they literally convey is simply irrelevant to the problem on the table.

Perhaps the pretense theorist, given that she is going to assert all instances of (A) must in the end deny that claims such as those made by

"Hesperus is a star" is true iff Hesperus is a star,

An utterance of "Hammurabi believes that Hesperus is a star" is true iff Hammurabi believes that Hesperus is a star,

are fictionally true in attitude pretense. But how could these fail to be fictionally true? Well, one might suggest that our pretense is not really about Hesperus at all. We pretend that there is *something named "Hesperus,"* but we don't really pretend anything about Hesperus. This would make

(K) " 'Hesperus is a star' is true iff Hesperus is a star" is true,

fictional without making

(K') "Hesperus is a star" is true iff Hesperus is a star,

so. And really, all we need to make it fictionally true that I speak truly, when I utter "Hesperus is a star," is (K),

(K") "Hesperus is a star" is true,

and some mundane facts about the biconditional. On this way out, the pretense theorist effectively denies that Hesperus stands to an attitude pretense about Hesperus and Hammurabi, as the mudpie stands to a game of mudpies. In the latter, we pretend that the mudpie is a pie; in the former, however, we do not really pretend anything about Hesperus at all.

This doesn't solve the general problem. So long there is *something* about which we pretend, in attitude pretense, some instances of

(A) FT[S] iff FIC[S],

(D') FT[An utterance of "S" is true iff S],

will jointly generate troubles. For example, notice that in attitude pretense the speaker pretends that *he* is saying something, about the beliefs of others. If Mark Twain were to utter "Dreiser believes that I wrote *Huck Finn*," he would be pretending of himself that he said that Dreiser believes that he wrote *Huck Finn*. Such an utterance would thus make it the case that, literally construed,

FT(Twain said that Dreiser believes that he wrote *Huck Finn*),

is true. But then, *if* "it is fictionally true" and "Dreiser believes" are innocent, then literally construed, such things as

FT(Twain said that Dreiser believes that Twain wrote *Huck Finn*),

and

FT(Twain said that Dreiser believes that Clemens wrote *Huck Finn*), will be true. But this seems to show that if the fictional truth condition for an utterance by Twain of "I said that Dreiser believes that I wrote *Huck Finn*" obtains, then the fictional truth condition for "Twain said that Dreiser believes that Clemens wrote Huck Finn," and that for "Twain said that Dreiser believes that Twain wrote Huck Finn" as uttered by anyone obtains. For the fictional truth condition of the latter (presumably) does not vary from attitude pretense to attitude pretense. But since one can say that ... Twain ..., without saying that ... Clemens ... , this is just this sort of thing which the pretense theorist needs to avoid.

6. Crimmins motivates what he says, of sentences such as "Hester knows that Hesperus is Phosphorus" with a discussion of accounts of statements about non-existence which can be extracted from the work of Walton and Gareth Evans.[220] As Crimmins summarizes these accounts, in uttering

(9) Santa does not exist

(i) one pretends that every mode of presentation presents something, and further,

(ii) pretends that all and only those things which *really* exist have the property ascribed by "exists"; thus,

(iii) the real world truth condition of a sentence of the form *a does not exist* is that the mode of presentation associated with *a* does not present anything, (Crimmins 1998), p. 33.

However, Walton and Evans do not appeal to piggy backing in their accounts. According to Walton, in uttering (9) we engage in the sort of pretense just outlined, and pretend to refer to something called "Santa." But the point of this charade is not to piggy back to something true iff our utterance is fictionally true. Instead, the point of the charade is to *disavow* our pretended attempt to refer; according to Walton, what is said, in uttering (9), is that an attempt to refer of *this* kind [where the kind in question is exemplified by the pretended reference to Santa] would not be successful.[221]

---

[220] Walton's discussion is in (Walton 1990), Chapter 11. Evans' is in Chapter 10 of (Evans 1982). Crimmins characterizes Walton as tentatively suggesting various aspects of the following account; I shall, perhaps a bit misleadingly, simply call the account discussed in this and the next paragraph "Walton's account."

[221] Actually, Walton holds that we may not need to pretend to refer with the utterance of "Santa," but may instead "allude" therewith to a pretense in which such an act of pretended reference occurs. The qualification is for the present purposes irrelevant.

As Crimmins notes, there is a problem. Crimmins assumes—rightly, I think—that the modes of presentation associated with proper names generally present what they present (or fail to present anything at all) contingently. On many natural ways of understanding the notion of a mode of presentation, this seems guaranteed to be true. For example, the mode [Hesperus] presumably doesn't present anything in a situation in which (on Earth) nothing which looks remotely like Hesperus is visible in the western sky at the times Venus in fact is. Given this assumption— and the assumption that what a sentence says determines its modal truth conditions—Walton's account has the absurd consequence that, if Hesperus could exist without appearing from earth as it in fact does, then what's said by

(10) Hesperus doesn't exist,

could be true even if Hesperus existed. If, furthermore, we understand the notion of a mode of presentation so that it is only a contingent matter that [Santa] doesn't present anything, Walton's suggestion would require us to say, *contra* conventional Kripkean wisdom, that (9) is only contingently false.

Crimmins suggests a correction to Walton's account; to understand it, we need to briefly digress, to discuss the issue of modal content. The pretense account of attitude ascription as thus far presented is not an account of what is said by uses of attitude ascriptions: It does not assign anything like a Russellian proposition, Fregean thought, or even a set of possible worlds or truth supporting situations to such uses. Rather, it is a proposal about utterance truth conditions, purporting to associate, with each possible utterance of an attitude ascription (or, at least, with each such utterance paired with a pretense) a necessary and sufficient condition for the utterance's being true. As it stands, the pretense account, for example, tells us that

(U1) When accompanied by a normal attitude pretense, an utterance in world w of:

> (2) Hammurabi believed that Hesperus is a star
>
> says something that is true in w iff in world w Hammurabi believed <[Hesperus], being a star>.

In and of itself this tells us nothing about the conditions under which the utterance correctly describes an arbitrary possible world—it does not tell us how a world w^* must be, in order that an utterance of (2) *in* w be true at w^*. As Crimmins remarks, "the modal content of an utterance and the utterance's truth conditions [i.e., the rule which tells us the conditions under which the uttered sentence, as uttered in w, is true in w] have to agree about the utterance's truth *value* (they have to "agree at the actual world"), but the truth condition of an utterance need not be equivalent to its modal content," (Crimmins 1998), p. 27.

For an actual, piggy backing utterance of (2) to say something which is actually true, the utterance must, actually, be fictionally true. For such an utterance to say something which is counterfactually true, true at a world w, the utterance must be, relative to w, fictionally true. So Crimmins says. He continues

> But what can it mean for an utterance to be fictionally true in relation to another really possible world? I suggest that we need the notion of genuine possibilities generating fictional possibilities. This notion is needed anyway, since even ordinary pretenses...extend modally. [In a game in which you and I pretend that a certain hill is Mount Olympus and that we are gods] it is fictionally true that I *might* have pushed a god and made him fall, and this fact about fictional possibility is generated by the real possibility that I should have pushed you and made you fall. Just as real-world facts about the Hesperus-mode make it fictionally true that there are facts "about Hesperus," so certain genuine possibilities make it fictionally true that there are certain sorts of possibilities "for Hesperus." [An utterance of an] attitude report correctly describes just those possible worlds that generate fictional possibilities that, fictionally, are described truly by the utterance, (Crimmins 1998), p. 30.

It is not altogether clear how we are supposed to determine the conditions under which a really possible world w generates, relative to fiction f, a fictional possibility.[222] But for present purposes we can ignore most

---

[222]What is it, for a world w to generate a fictional possibility, relative to a pretense f? Crimmins offers no definition, but there is a

> Very Natural Answer: Relative to a pretense, world w generates p as a fictional possibility iff something happens in w which, according to the rules of the pretense (its principles of generation) is sufficient for p's being fictionally true.

Let me state the answer more precisely. Identify fictional truths with certain propositions (those which are true relative to the fiction). Identify fictional possibilities with those propositions p such that p's possibilization is fictionally true. (This is to say, very roughly, that every instance of

> Relative to f, it is fictionally possible that S just in case, relative to f, it is fictionally true that p could obtain,

is true.) For the actual world to generate, relative to pretense f, a fictional truth p—for the actual world to make p fictional—is for the actual world to contain a state of affairs s and f to contain a principle of generation g such that, according to g, if c obtains, then p is fictionally true. So, presumably, for a counterfactual world to

of the details. All we need to remark is that the proposal Crimmins
makes involves the claim

---

generate, relative to f, a fictional possibility p—for w to make p fictionally possible—
is for w to contain a state of affairs s and f to contain a principle of generation g such
that, according to g, if c obtains, then p is fictionally true.

If this is what generating a fictionally possibility comes to, then the principle offered
in the last sentence of the citation comes to this

(U2) Relative to pretense f, an utterance u (as it occurs in a world w) is true at w^*
iff there are propositions p and q such that: p is true at w^*; there is a principle
of generation g for f such that, according to g, p's truth is sufficient for q's
being fictionally true (relative to f), and it is fictionally true (relative to f)
that if q is true, then p is true.

Recall that one of the principles of generation in our pretense about Hammurabi
is that

(P3) If (and only if) someone has a thought involving [Hesperus], then it is fictionally true that they have a belief about the object named "Hesperus."

According to (P3), it is necessary and sufficient, for its being fictionally true that
Hammurabi believed that Hesperus is a star, that he believed <[Hesperus], being a
star>. So, given the Very Natural Answer, it would seem that

(U4) An utterance in world w of "Hammurabi believed that Hesperus is a star," is
true in w^* iff in world w^* Hammurabi believed <[Hesperus], being a star>.

But, as Crimmins acknowledges, this gets the truth conditions wrong, at least given
the assumption that [Hesperus] could have presented something other than Hesperus.

> ...which real possibilities generate fictional possibilities in which there
> are attitudes "about Hesperus"...? [That is, which are ones which a
> sentence such as (1), as used in semantic pretense, correctly describes,
> relative to the pretense?] The argument from
>
> (2) Hammurabi believed that Hesperus is visible in the evening,
>
> to
>
> (3) There's a real thing such that Hammurabi had a belief attributing
> evening visibility to it,
>
> fails to exhibit an entailment in modal content if we answer this question
> in a particular way: by deciding that *all* possibilities in which there are
> attitudes involving the Hesperus-mode generate fictional possibilities
> involving attitudes "about Hesperus". ...But clearly this cannot be the
> right answer. Instead, the contours of our pretense seem normally to
> be such that only possibilities that both involve the Hesperus-mode
> *and are about Venus* generate fictional possibilities concerning attitudes
> "about Hesperus". Plausibly, this is a reflection within the pretense of
> the rigidity of names ((Crimmins 1998), pp. 30–31, numbering altered).

It is not altogether clear what the methodology is here. It seems as if the proposal
is that we simply look at our modal intuitions about utterances of sentence (2), in
order to determine what worlds would be, from the perspective of semantic pretense,
correctly described by (2)'s utterance. That is, we consult our modal intuitions about
the conditions under which what (2) says is true, and identify (2)'s modal content
with what they yield. The disadvantage of this methodology is that it is painfully *ad
hoc*.

(a) If an utterance u involves piggy backing relative to a pretense f, the modal content of u is the set of possible worlds w such that, relative to f, u is fictionally true at w.

Notice that (a) apparently implies what Crimmins observes, about utterance truth conditions constraining modal content:

(b) If an actual utterance u involves piggy backing relative to fiction f, and it is fictional relative to f that u is true, then the actual world is a member of the modal content of u.

And this, in turn, means that if a pretense involves pretending that a sentence S's utterance would be the utterance of something true, then one cannot piggy back, using the pretense and an utterance of S, to the saying of something necessarily false. For in this case, whatever is said must be, in actuality, true.

Now, let us return to the issue of denials of existence. How, exactly, are we to understand them, if we are not to understand them as Walton would have us? Well, we could understand them as involving piggy backing. Relative to the pretense (i)–(iii), an utterance of (9) piggy backs to a claim true just in case [Santa] doesn't present anything. So, as a mater of fact, what (9) says on a piggy backing account is true. What about counterfactually?

> ... we need to ask which real possibilities make it fictionally true that there are possibilities in which "Santa exists." I believe that the following ... [is] defensible: normally, ... no possible world makes it fictionally true that there is a possible world in which "Santa exists" (so that (9) normally expresses a necessary content despite having a contingent truth condition) ... (Crimmins 1998), pp. 34–5, numbering altered.

Let's just grant that, relative to the pretense (i) through (iii), there is no situation which makes it fictional that Santa exists. There is still a problem: (9) is not the only way we might say that there is no such thing as Santa; we might also utter

(11) There is no such thing as Santa,

to get this across. Indeed, if we are arguing with someone with more or less Meinongian tendencies, the best, and perhaps only, way for us to express our disagreement is to utter (11), for she who "distinguishes existence from being" may well agree with (9).

If the general strategy of piggy backing is to apply not just to (9) but to (11), it must be possible for (11) to be fictionally true. But relative to the pretense framed by (i) through (iii) (11) cannot be fictionally true: *The point* of the pretense is to set things up so that sentences like (11) are guaranteed to be fictionally false. As Crimmins puts it

> [In the context of such a pretense] when the speaker says "There are some things that do not exist," I would say, she is relying both on the genuine universal property of existence (which informs "there are") and the pretended discriminating property (which informs "do not exist"). Within the pretense, this might be described as the distinction between *being* and *really existing* ((Crimmins 1998), p. 34).

To indulge in the pretense outlined by (i) though (iii) is to pretend that an extreme form of Meinongianism is correct, and thus to pretend that any denial of being is false. Relative to the pretense, "there is [no]" serves to (fictionally) ascribe the universal property of being something or other (so that if a has a sense, *there is no such thing as a* is fictionally false); "[does not] exist" serves to (fictionally) ascribe the pretense's pretend property of existing (so that if a presents nothing, *a does not exist* is fictionally true). So (11) is false relative to the pretense outlined by (i) through (iii). The current account, then, seems to be unable to explain how a sentence such as (11) can be used to convey something true. Indeed, this account has the incredible implication that what we normally intend to get across with the sentence "There is no such thing as Santa" is not only *false* but *trivially and obviously false*. For, if the account is correct, then our normal use of this sentence is a piggy backing use of the sentence within a pretense whose rules of generation (i.e., whose rules for fictional truth) make the sentence false provided the name "Santa" has some mode of presentation or other associated with it. But it is a trivial, obvious fact that the name is senseful.

There is a response which needs be considered, namely that idioms such as "there is" and "exists" have multiple uses within the sort of pretense we are considering.[223] On this response, "there is [no]" may be "informed" by either the genuine property of existence or the pretend discriminating property; likewise for "[does not] exist"; thus, there is a use of (11) on which it is true in the pretense if (and only if) [Santa] presents nothing, as well as the use on which the just lodged objection capitalizes. Thus, it is perfectly possible to use (11) to express a truth.

Suppose we grant that there is *a* pretense bound use of (11) on which what is said is true. This doesn't erase the incredible implication that (11) has a use on which it says something trivially and obviously false. Neither does it erase the incredible implication that the dominant, de-

---

[223]Crimmins made the following response in correspondence.

fault use of (11) is one on which it says something trivially and obviously false.[224] Indeed, the problem is exacerbated, since it now turns out that there is a use of "Santa *exists*" (the one on which "exists" is "informed" by genuine, not pretend, existence) on which it says something trivial and obviously true.[225] It seems absolutely incredible to think that any linguistic practice in which we routinely engage is one on which this sentence can (naturally!) be used to say something *trivially and obviously* true.

Interestingly, Walton's view is not liable to the objection just lodged, for on it the truth condition of—indeed, the proposition expressed by— an utterance of (9) does not turn on the fictional truth conditions of its utterance. In fact, Walton's account does not even require the pretense that there is a property of existing possessed by some but not all of what there is: Since the point of the utterance of (9) is simply to disavow that a certain kind of pretended reference could actually succeed, all one has to do is to pretend that such a reference is possible. One could do this within the scope of a pretense that every mode of presentation presents something which exists. And there seems to be no reason one could not, within the scope of such a pretense, also utter (11) in order to disavow that the relevant sort of attempt to refer could be successfully carried off. Walton's account gets the *truth conditions* of (11) right, but it gets the modal content wrong.

---

[224]The implication is a result of the fact that the principles of generation for the fiction framed by (i) through (iii)—i.e., the principles which determine truth in that fiction—explicitly make it fictionally true that every senseful name names something, and thus (since it will be fictionally true that "Santa" is senseful and "Santa" names something iff a use of (11) is true) make it fictionally true that a use of (11) is true.

[225]This is the use on which "exists" is functioning as "there is" normally does, so that *a exists* says something which agrees in truth value with (a normal use of) *there is such a thing as a.*

Part III

Ontology

11

Quantification and Fictional Discourse

PETER VAN INWAGEN

This paper is an application of what is sometimes called "Quine's criterion of ontological commitment" to some questions about the ontology of fiction. Having begun with this statement, I must immediately record my conviction that there is an important sense no such thing as Quine's criterion of ontological commitment. That is, there is no proposition, no *thesis*, that can be called "Quine's criterion of ontological commitment"—and this despite the fact that several acute and able philosophers have attempted to formulate, or to examine possible alternative formulations of, "Quine's criterion of ontological commitment."[226] Insofar as there is anything that deserves the name "Quine's criterion of ontological commitment," it is a strategy or technique, not a thesis.

Strategies and techniques can be applied in various contexts. Let us concentrate on the context supplied by a debate, an ontological debate, a debate between two philosophers about what there is. Argle, let us say, contends that there are only concrete material objects. Bargle points out that Argle has asserted that there are a great many holes in this piece of cheese, and calls Argle's attention to the fact that a hole does not seem to be describable as a "concrete material object." I trust you know how this story goes.[227] It is, as its authors intended it be, a paradigm of the application of Quine's strategy. It has, however, a special feature. One of the characters in the dialogue (Bargle) is, as we might say, forcing the application of the strategy; but the other character (Argle) cooperates;

---

[226] See for example Church (Church 1958) and Cartwright (Cartwright 1954).

[227] I allude, of course to David and Stephanie Lewis's classic paper (Lewis and Lewis 1970).

Empty Names, Fiction, and the Puzzles of Non-Existence.
Anthony Everett and Thomas Hofweber (eds.).
Copyright © 2000, CSLI Publications.

Argle does not dispute the legitimacy of the questions that Bargle puts to him. Other philosophers might not be so cooperative as Argle. Consider, for example, the late Ernest Gellner. In an article now about twenty years old, Gellner gave a very nice description of Quine's ontological strategy, and, having paused briefly to identify himself as a nominalist, went on to say

> The dreadful thing is, I haven't even tried to be a serious, card-carrying nominalist. I have never tried to eliminate "quantification" over abstract objects from my discourse. I shamelessly "quantify over" abstractions *and* deny their existence! I do not try to put what I say into canonical notation, and do not care what the notation looks like if someone else does it for me, and do not feel in the very least bound by whatever ontic commitments such a translation may disclose.[228]

In an ontological debate with someone like Gellner, one would have to apply different strategies from those that are appropriate in a debate with someone like the admirable Argle. But I shall not further consider philosophers like Gellner. I have a lot to say to them, but I will not say it in this paper. Here I will simply assume that Gellner's confession comes down to this: I don't mind contradicting myself if figuring out how to avoid contradicting myself would require intellectual effort.

Those philosophers who, like Argle, admit the legitimacy of Quine's strategy in ontological debate will, I think, mostly be willing to accept the following thesis: The history of ontological debates in which all parties admit the legitimacy of Quine's strategy shows that it is harder to avoid tacitly asserting the existence of things like numbers, sets, properties, propositions, and unrealized possibilities than one might have thought it would be. If, for example, you think that there are no numbers, you will find it difficult to recast all you want to say in the quantifier-variable idiom (and to do so in sufficient "depth" that all the inferences you regard as valid will be valid according to the rules of first-order logic) without finding that the sentence

$$(\exists x)(x \text{ is a number}),$$

is a formal consequence of "all you want to say." It may be possible in the end for you to do this—for you to "avoid ontological commitment to numbers"—but you will not find it a trivial undertaking.

I have argued in several essays that it is very difficult to say all that we want to say and to avoid ontological commitment to "creatures of

---

[228] See (Gellner 1979), especially p. 203.

fiction"—fictional persons, buildings, cities, and so on.[229] In this paper, I want to confirm this conclusion by displaying it as an all but inevitable consequence of a correct understanding of quantification.

What is the correct understanding of quantification—of the symbols "∃" and "∀" (or of whatever symbols we use for the quantifiers) and the variables with which they interact? Let me give two examples of how someone might answer this question. The first, in my view, is right, the second wrong.

My first answer to the question, What is the correct understanding of quantification? proceeds by showing how to introduce variables and the quantifiers into our discourse as abbreviations for phrases that we already understand.[230] (This, I believe, is the *only* way—other than ostension—in which one can explain the meaning of any word, phrase, or idiom.) It will be clear that the quantifiers so introduced are simply a regimentation of the "all" and "there are" of ordinary English.

We begin by supplementing the pronominal apparatus of English. We first introduce an indefinitely large stock of third-person-singular pronouns, pronouns whose use carries no implications about sex or personhood. These pronouns are to be orthographically and phonetically diverse, but semantically indistinguishable. Let three of them be: "it_x," "it_y," and "it_z;" let the others be of the same sort.

Now let us call the following phrases *universal quantifier phrases*:

It is true of everything that it_x is such that ...
It is true of everything that it_y is such that ...
It is true of everything that it_z is such that ...
Etcetera...
Etcetera...

Call the following phrases *existential quantifier phrases*:

It is true of at least one thing that it_x is such that ...
It is true of at least one thing that it_y is such that ...
It is true of at least one thing that it_z is such that ...
Etcetera...
Etcetera...

Any reader of this paper is likely to have a certain skill that will enable him or her to turn complex general sentences of English into sentences whose generality is carried by quantifier phrases and pronouns. For example:

---

[229]See (van Inwagen 1977), (van Inwagen 1983), and (van Inwagen 1985).

[230]The following account of quantification is modelled upon, but does not reproduce, the account presented in Quine (Quine 1940).

Everybody loves somebody;

It is true of everything that it_x is such that if it_x is a person, then it is true of at least one thing that it_y is such that it_y is a person and it_x loves it_y.

Such sentences, general sentences whose generality is carried by quantifier phrases and a multiplicity of third-person-singular pronouns, may be hard to read or even ambiguous because of uncertainty about where the "that"-clauses that follow "everything" and "at least one thing" and "such" end. This difficulty is easily met by the use of brackets:

It is true of everything that it_x is such that (if it_x is a person, then it is true of at least one thing that it_y is such that (it_y is a person and it_x loves it_y)).

When we put this miscellany of devices together, we have a supplemented and regimented version of English. (The only features of the sentences of this new "version" of English that keep them from being sentences of ordinary English are the "new" pronouns and the brackets. If we were to replace each of the subscripted pronouns with "it" and were to delete the brackets from these sentences, the sentences so obtained would be perfectly good sentences of ordinary English—perfectly good from the grammarian's point of view, anyway; no doubt most of them would be stilted, confusing, ambiguous, unusable, and downright silly sentences.) This supplemented and regimented English is obviously a bit cumbersome, in large part because of the unwieldiness of our "quantifier phrases" and the difficulty of writing or pronouncing all those annoying subscripts. We can to some degree remedy this defect by introducing a few systematic abbreviations:

- Abbreviate subscripted pronouns by their subscripts, italicized and raised to the line. (Call these abbreviated pronouns "variables.")
- Abbreviate "it is true of everything that (x is such that ..." by "$\forall x(...$"—and similarly for the other variables.
- Abbreviate "it is true of at least one thing that (x is such that" by "$\exists x(...$"—and similarly for the other variables.

Our example, so abbreviated, is:

$\forall x(\text{if } x \text{ is a person, then } \exists y(y \text{ is a person and } x \text{ loves } y))$.

What we have now, of course, are quantifiers and variables. We have, or so I claim, introduced quantifiers and variables using only the resources of ordinary English. And to do this, I would suggest is to *explain* quantifiers and variables.

We may attribute to Frege the discovery that if the pronominal apparatus of English (or German or any reasonably similar natural language) is supplemented in this way, then it is possible to set out a few simple rules of syntactical manipulation—rules that can today be found in any good logic textbook—such that a truly astounding range of valid inference is captured in the sequences of sentences that can be generated by repeated applications of these rules. It is these rules that give quantifiers and variables their point. The odd-looking, stilted, angular rewriting of our lovely, fluid English tongue that is the quantifier-variable idiom has only one purpose: to force all that lovely fluidity—at least insofar as it is a vehicle of the expression of theses involving universality and existence—into a form on which a manageably small set of rules of syntactical manipulation (rules that constitute the whole of valid reasoning concerning matters of universality and existence) can get a purchase. But while it is these rules that provide the motivation for our having at our disposal such a thing as the quantifier-variable idiom, they are not the source of the meaning of that idiom, the meaning, that is, of sentences containing quantifiers and variables. The meaning of the quantifiers is given by the phrases of English—or of some other natural language— that they abbreviate. The fact that quantifiers are abbreviations entails that we can give them the very best definition possible: we can show how to eliminate them in favor of phrases that we already understand.

If our explanation of the meaning of the quantifiers—and of the existential quantifier in particular—is correct, the sentence

$$\exists x(x \text{ is a dog}),$$

is an abbreviation for

> It is true of at least one thing that it_x is such that it_x is a dog.

That is,

> It is true of at least one thing that it is such that it is a dog.

That is,

> It is true of at least one thing that it is a dog.

That is,

> At least one thing is a dog.

That is,

> There is at least one dog.

The existential quantifier therefore expresses the sense of "there is" in ordinary English. (As an opponent of any form of Meinongianism, I would say that the existential quantifier is appropriately named—for the reason that, in expressing the sense of "there is" in English, it *thereby* expresses the sense of "exists" in English. But that is another story.)

I turn now to the second promised answer to the question, What is the correct understanding of quantification? Since this explanation is rather complicated, I am going to present it very informally, by means of an example. A real presentation of this explanation would be a generalization of the example. Consider the sentence

$$\exists x \forall y \exists z (x \text{ is taller than } y \text{ and } y \text{ is taller than } z).$$

What does this mean? Well, first, if this sentence is meaningful at all, then the open sentence "x is taller than y and y is taller than z" must have an *extension*, a set-theoretical object whose ultimate members are drawn from a certain domain of quantification. The extension of a sentence that, like the one we are now considering, contains three free variables, would normally be understood to be a set of ordered triples: in the present case the set containing all and only those triples whose first element is taller than their second element and whose second element is taller than their third.[231] (The members of the triples must belong to the domain of quantification. In the sequel, I'll leave it to you to supply appropriate references to a domain of quantification.) The result of prefixing "$\exists z$" to this open sentence is a new open sentence

$$\exists z (x \text{ is taller than } y \text{ and } y \text{ is taller than } z).$$

If our original open sentence had an extension, this one does too, and its extension is determined by the extension of the original: on the particular (and usual) set-theoretical understanding of "extension" that we have employed, the extension of this sentence is the set of all ordered pairs whose first member is taller than their second member and whose second member is taller than something. The result of prefixing "$\forall y$" to this second sentence is a third open sentence

$$\forall y \exists z (x \text{ is taller than } y \text{ and } y \text{ is taller than } z).$$

The extension of this third sentence is determined by the extension of the second sentence: it is the set of all objects that are taller than *everything* that is taller than something (and this will of course be the empty set, since, given that there are things taller than something, nothing can be

---

[231]The objects in each triple in the extension do not have to be deployed in the order tallest-intermediate-shortest. They could as well be deployed in the reverse of that order or even in the order intermediate-shortest-tallest. What is important is that they be deployed in the same order in each triple and that, if the are deployed in, say, the order intermediate- shortest-tallest, the variable "x" in the open sentence be correlated with the third member of each triple, the variable "y" with its first member, and the variable "z" with its second member.

taller than all of them, owing to the fact that nothing can be taller than itself).

Finally, prefixing "$\exists x$" to this sentence produces a fourth sentence, (not, this time, an *open* sentence) whose extension is "truth" if *something* belongs to the extension of the third sentence and "falsity" otherwise—for it is useful to stipulate that closed sentences have extensions, and that their extensions are their truth-values. And, since the extension of "$\forall y \exists z\, x$ is taller than y and y is taller than z" is, as we saw, the empty set, the extension of our final sentence is falsity—that is, it is false.

This demonstration that "$\exists x \forall y \exists z\, x$ is taller than y and y is taller than z" is false by a sequential examination of the extensions of the sentences

- x is taller than y and y is taller than z,
- $\exists z\, x$ is taller than y and y is taller than z,
- $\forall y \exists z\, x$ is taller than y and y is taller than z,
- $\exists x \forall y \exists z\, x$ is taller than y and y is taller than z,

and an explanation of the way in which the extension of each succeeding sentence is determined by the extension of its predecessor, displays the meanings of the quantifiers. Each of the quantifiers is an extension-transforming operator. (Or, to be pedantic, each quantifier-*phrase*—a quantifier followed by a variable—is an extension-transforming operator.) To explain the meaning of a quantifier is to explain how it transforms extensions.

In my view, there is a lot of truth in this second account of what the quantifiers mean. The quantifiers *are* normally extension-transforming operators, and I think that this account is precisely right about what extension-transforming operators they are. I say that the quantifiers are *normally* extension-transforming operators because there are undeniable cases in which they are meaningfully prefixed to sentences the haven't *got* extensions. Consider, for example, the sentence "if x is an ordinal number, then y is an ordinal number and y is greater than x." This sentence has no extension, and neither has

$\exists y$(if x is an ordinal number, then y is an ordinal number
and y is greater than x).

But the sentence

$\forall x \exists y$(if x is an ordinal number, then y is an ordinal number
and y is greater than x),

is just true.

Nevertheless, it seems evident to me that our second answer to the question, "What is the correct understanding of quantification?" does give a correct account of how the quantifiers transform extensions *when that is what they do*. My problem with the second answer is simply that it isn't an answer to the question that it is supposed to be an answer to: It doesn't provide an *understanding* of quantification. It doesn't tell us what the quantifiers *mean*. It just tells us how they transform extensions. And that wouldn't be an explanation of what the quantifiers meant even if it weren't for the difficultly raised by the fact that they are sometimes meaningfully employed when there are no extensions to be transformed. The first answer, however, *does* explain what the quantifiers mean: it tells us how to turn sentences containing quantifier-variable constructions into sentences not containing these constructions, sentences containing only words and constructions of which we have a prior grasp. Someone may protest that the first account of the meaning of a sentence containing quantifiers does not, in the words of David Lewis, tell us "the first thing about the meaning of the. . . sentence: namely, the conditions under which it would be true."[232] But, really, the conditions under which a sentence would be true, are not the first thing about the meaning of a sentence. The first thing about the meaning of a sentence is what the sentence means. And that's just what the first account tells us about sentences containing quantifiers—at least it tells us this about a given sentence containing quantifiers if we know what all the other items (all the predicates and connectives and so on) in the sentence mean.

If you want to be told the conditions under which a sentence containing quantifiers is true (or, if it's an open sentence, under what conditions it has which extensions), the second proposed answer to our question—which I say is not an answer to our question at all—provides a very beautiful (if, as we have seen, incomplete) answer to your request for information. I think that it's the correct answer—as far as it goes: when it does tell you that a sentence containing quantifiers is true or is false, it will be right. (And that is a useful thing to have. If we know how the quantifiers transform extensions, we can use this knowledge to prove that that "manageably small set of inference rules" I referred to earlier are in technical but intuitive and useful senses valid and complete. No doubt the fact that so many logicians and philosophers of logic have thought that the way to explain the meanings of the quantifiers is to show how they transform extensions is explained by the fact it is the extension-transforming powers of the quantifiers—this feature of the quantifiers and no other—that plays a role in model-theoretic proofs of theorems about logical systems whose language contains quantifiers.)

---

[232]Lewis's complaint was directed at the "semantic marker" method of doing semantics for natural languages, see his (Lewis 1970).

Instead of calling the second answer to our question by the incorrect name "the second answer to our question," let us call it the objectual truth-theory for quantifier-sentences. There are, of course, alternative truth-theories for quantifier-sentences. There is the substitutional truth-theory for quantifier sentences. There are also truth-theories for sentences containing quantifiers in a more general sense—things that look a lot like quantifiers but which bind "variables" that have the syntax of sentences or predicates. I cannot discuss these here. [233]

Now assume that our first answer to the question, What is the correct understanding of quantification? is right. What are the consequences of this assumption for an understanding of fictional discourse? Since our time is limited, I will proceed straight to a special part of fictional discourse, the part I think is of the greatest ontological interest. By fictional discourse I mean not the sentences that are contained in works of fiction but rather sentences spoken or written about works of fiction— whether they issue from the pen of F. R. Leavis or from the mouth of the guy sitting beside you on the plane who is providing you with an interminable defense of his conviction that Stephen King is the greatest living novelist. The sentences of fictional discourse that I want to discuss are those that have the following four features:

(i)   they are existential quantifications, or at least look as if they were;

(ii) they have complex quantificational structures (e.g., $\exists \forall \exists$)—or look as if they do;

(iii) the inferences from these sentences that standard quantifier logic endorses for sentences that have the quantificational structures these sentences appear to have are valid—or at least appear to be;

(iv) they contain not only predicates such as you and I and our friends might satisfy (predicates like "is fat," "is thin," "is bald," "is the mother of") but also "literary" predicates like "is a character," "first appears in chapter 6," "provides comic relief," "is partly modeled on," "is described by means of the same narrative device the author earlier used in her more successful depiction of," and so on.

Here is an example:

There is a fictional character who, for every novel, either appears in that novel or is a model for a character who does.

---

[233]But see my (van Inwagen 1981) Unfortunately, I can't refer you to my paper, *Why I Don't Understand Quantification into Non-nominal Positions* because I haven't written it. I could talk you through it, though.

(This sentence would express a truth if, for example, Sancho Panza served as a model for at least one character in every novel but Don Quixote itself.) This sentence is (i) an apparent existential quantification; (ii) complex in its apparent quantificational structure; (iv) contains the literary predicates: "is a fictional character," "appears in," and "is a model for." Moreover, (iii) it certainly appears that the inferences licensed by quantifier logic for sentences with the apparent quantificational structure of the above sentence are valid. It appears, for example, that we can validly deduce from the above sentence the sentence

> If no character appears in every novel, then some character is modeled on another character.

Many philosophers deny the reality of fictional characters. Kendall Walton is a good example, and I will use him as one.[234] (But the questions I direct to him are meant to be directed at anyone who denies the reality of fictional characters. Walton is, by the way, my source for the words "deny the reality of fictional characters;" at any rate he contends that one of the selling points of his own theory of fiction is that it does not "threaten to force the reality of fictional characters upon us.") I would ask Walton three questions. First, how would he paraphrase these two sentences? Secondly, does his paraphrase of the former allow the deduction of the latter by quantifier logic alone—or, at any rate, by quantifier logic plus a few intuitive rules governing the logic of his special operator?—for his answer to the "paraphrase" question involves the introduction of a special operator, a "fictional truth" operator. Thirdly, if his paraphrase of the former sentence does not allow the formal deduction of the latter, how will he explain this?

In short, I am asking Walton for a way of paraphrasing complex existential quantifications that appear to assert that there are fictional characters, and I am asking that either his method of paraphrases be "valid-inference-preserving," or else that he tell us why it is all right for it not to be valid-inference-preserving.

I do not by any means want to contend that Walton and other philosophers who deny "the reality of fictional characters" cannot meet this challenge. But, so far as I can see, none of them *has* met it. From my point of view, the matter is very simple. The first sentence obviously entails the second, and the explanation of the obvious fact is that the two sentences can be correctly translated into the quantifier-variable idiom as follows:

$\exists x(x$ is a fictional character $\& \forall y(y$ is a novel $\rightarrow (x$ appears

---

[234]See his (Walton 1990), especially chapters 10 and 11.

in $y \vee \exists z(z$ is a fictional character $\&z$ appears in $y\&x$ is a model for $z))))$.

$\exists x(x$ is a fictional character $\&\forall y(y$ is a novel $\to x$ appears in $y)) \to \exists x \exists y$ (y is a model for x.)

And the second sentence is a formal consequence of the first. And the thesis that these two translations are correct does not seem to be in any way implausible or far-fetched. They certainly *look* correct.

A second formal consequence of the first sentence is "$\exists x \, x$ is a fictional character"—that is to say:

It is true of at least one thing that it is such that it is a fictional character.

Or, more idiomatically, "There are fictional characters." And, since fictional names like "Mr Pickwick" and "Tom Sawyer" (when they occur in what I am calling fictional discourse) denote fictional characters if there are fictional characters, Mr Pickwick and Tom Sawyer are among the things that are—an assertion that we anti-Meinongians regard as equivalent to the assertion that Mr Pickwick and Tom Sawyer are among the things that exist. (It should be noted that, at least in certain circumstances, ordinary speakers are perfectly willing to apply the word "exist" to fictional characters. Consider: "To hear some people talk, you would think that all Dickens's working-class characters were comic grotesques; although such characters certainly exist, there are fewer of them than is commonly supposed." "Sarah just ignores those characters that don't fit her theory of fiction. She persists in writing as if Anna Karenina, Tristram Shandy, and Mrs Dalloway simply didn't exist.")

There is an obvious objection to this conclusion. It might be stated as follows: There are characters in some novels that are witches—for example, in John Updike's *The Witches of Eastwick*. Van Inwagen's line of argument, therefore, would lead us to accept

It is true of at least one thing that it is such that it is a fictional character and a witch,

which, of course, formally entails that there are witches—and there are no witches. For an adequate reply to this objection I must refer you elsewhere.[235] The essence of the reply is that we must distinguish between those properties that fictional characters *have* and those that they *hold*. Fictional characters have only

(a) "logical" or "high-category" properties such as existence and self-identity,

---

[235] See (van Inwagen 1977) and (van Inwagen 1983).

(b) properties expressed by what I have called "literary" predicates—
being a character in a novel, being introduced in Chapter 6, being a
comic villainess, having been created by Mark Twain, being modeled on Sancho Panza, and so on.[236]

Properties that strictly entail the property "being human"—being a res-
ident of Hannibal, Missouri, being an orphan who has a mysterious bene-
factor, being a witch—they do not have but *hold*. (Of course, if a fictional
character holds the property F, then it has the literary property "holding
the property F.") It is therefore not true in, as they say, the strict and
philosophical sense, that any fictional characters are witches—or that
any of them is human, female, or a widow who lives in Eastwick, Rhode
Island. What we should say in, as they say, the philosophy room, is this:
some of them *hold* the properties expressed by these predicates.

But what about our firm conviction—everyone's firm conviction—
that, e.g., Tom Sawyer and Sherlock Holmes do not exist? Let us consider
two cases in which someone might use the sentence "Sherlock Holmes
does not exist." Consider, first, a frustrated detective who says in ex-
asperation, "It would take Sherlock Holmes to solve this case, and unfortunately Sherlock Holmes doesn't exist." Consider, next, an amused
London cop who is responding to a flustered tourist who can't find
221B Baker Street ("You know, Officer—where Sherlock Holmes lived").
"Lord bless you, sir, Sherlock Holmes doesn't exist and never did. He's
just a chap in a story made up by someone called Conan Doyle." It seems
to me that the first use of "Sherlock Holmes does not exist" expresses
the proposition

> No one has all the properties the fictional character Sherlock
> Holmes holds (nor has anyone very many of the most salient
> and striking of these properties).

The second use of "Sherlock Holmes does not exist" expresses—I would
argue—something like the following proposition.

> Your use of the name "Sherlock Holmes" rests on a mistake.
> If you trace back the use of this name to its origin, you'll
> find that it first occurs in a work of fiction, and that it was
> not introduced into our discourse by an "initial baptism."
> That is, its origin lies in the fact that Conan Doyle wrote a

---

[236]Or, rather, these are the only properties they have other than those that may
be prescribed by a specific theory of the nature of fictional characters. Compare:
"Numbers have only logical properties like self-identity and arithmetical properties
like being prime or being the successor of 6." There is no doubt a sense in which this
is true, but we must recognize that a specific theory about the nature of numbers
may ascribe further properties to them—like being an abstract object or being a set.

story in which one of the characters held the property "being named "Sherlock Holmes," and we customarily refer to fictional characters by their fictional names. (That is to say: if x is a name, and if a fictional character holds the property of being named x, we customarily use x as a name of that character.) You have mistaken this story for a history or have mistaken discourse about a fictional character for discourse about an historical figure—or both.

The difference between these two examples is this: In the first example, both the speaker and the audience know that Holmes is fictional and the speaker is making a comment that presupposes this knowledge in the audience; in the second, only the speaker knows that Holmes is fictional, and is, in effect, informing the audience of this fact. The lesson I mean to convey by these examples is that the non-existence of Holmes is not an ontological *datum*; the ontological datum is rather that we can use the sentence "Sherlock Holmes does not exist" to say something true. (Or something false. I can imagine cases in which it was used to say something false.[237]) Different theories of the ontology of fiction will account for this datum in different ways. According to one ontology of fiction, the reason we can use this sentence to say something true is that "Sherlock Holmes" does not denote anything. According to another, the reason is that "Sherlock Holmes" denotes something non-existent. I prefer a third account, the rather more complicated account I have briefly outlined. These ontologies should be compared and evaluated not simply by seeing how well they explain our reactions to special and isolated sentences like "Sherlock Holmes does not exist;" they should be compared and evaluated by seeing how well they explain our reactions to the whole range of sentences we use to talk about fiction—and our ability to integrate these explanations with an acceptable philosophy of the quantifier and an acceptable general ontology.

---

[237] It is five hundred years in the future. Sally is being examined on her Ph.D. thesis, *The Detective in British Popular Fiction before the First World War*. A pompous (and ill-informed) examiner speaks as follows: "This thesis appears most impressive. But it is concerned largely with the appropriation by the popular imagination of a fictional detective called Sherlock Holmes. I know the popular fiction of the period well, and I'm sorry to have to tell you that Sherlock Holmes does not exist. Conan Doyle never created any such character. The author simply made him and his supposed popularity with the public up. Apparently she believed that no one on this committee would, know the period well enough to expose her fraud."

12

Quantification and Non-Existent Objects

Thomas Hofweber

12.1 Non-existent objects

Whether or not there are non-existent objects seems to be one of the more mysterious and speculative issues in ontology.[238] To affirm that there are non-existent objects is to affirm that reality consists of two kinds of things, the existing and the non-existing. The existing contains all of what is in our space-time world, plus all abstract objects, if there are any. Most people, it seems fair to say, would think that this is all there is. For them the only real question in ontology can be what kinds of existing things there are. However, followers of Meinong maintain that this isn't all there is. There is also another kind of things, those that do not exist. And to say this, the Meinongians continue, is to accept that reality is divided into two basic kinds of things, the existing and the non-existing. Whether or not reality contains two basic categories of things, existing and non-existing, or only one, existing, is what the debate about non-existent objects is all about. And as such it seems to be the most speculative of the debates in ontology. How could we human beings possibly decide it? One might think that to find out whether or not there are abstract objects is hard to decide, since they are not in space and time, causally inaccessible, unobservable, etc.. But whatever difficulty there might be to answer the question whether or not there are abstract objects, it has to be even harder to decide whether or not there are non-existent objects. Abstract objects, if there are any, at least exist. non-existent objects at best seem to fill out the space of what there is.

---

[238]Thanks to Johan van Benthem, Sol Feferman, John Perry and Ed Zalta for comments on earlier drafts.

Empty Names, Fiction, and the Puzzles of Non-Existence.
Anthony Everett and Thomas Hofweber (eds.).

To affirm that there are such things seems to engage one in ontological speculation of the highest kind.

Reasonable as this might be, it on the other hand seems to be quite trivial to argue that there are non-existent objects. To accept that there are non-existent objects doesn't seem to come down to much more as to accept such trivialities as that, say, Santa Claus doesn't exist. To illustrate this, let's first consider the question whether or not there are non-cooperative objects. This, it seems, is easily answered by the fact that Fred does not cooperate. That Fred doesn't cooperate can be said in many different and more or less direct ways. Consider:

(1) Fred is doesn't cooperate.

(2) Fred is non-cooperative.

(3) Fred is a non-cooperative person, (or thing, or object).[239]

To say that Fred doesn't cooperate is, modulo subtleties, the same as to say that Fred is a non-cooperative person, (or thing, or object). These are just different ways of saying the same thing. So, since Fred is a non-cooperative object, doesn't that answer the question whether or not there are non-cooperative objects? And similarly for the case of Santa's non-existence. That Santa doesn't exist can also be said in many different ways:

(4) Santa does not exist.

(5) Santa is non-existent.

(6) Santa is a non-existent person, (or thing, or object).

So, isn't it trivial to decide whether or not there are non-existent objects? After all, Santa doesn't exist, and to say that Santa is a non-existent object seems to be no more than a fancy way of saying that Santa doesn't exist.

To be sure, one can believe that the acceptance of non-existent objects is implicit in accepting that Santa doesn't exist. But this might not be taken to settle the issue about non-existent objects. One can simply claim that all this shows is that Santa's non-existence is to be taken to be an equally controversial and difficult issue as there being non-existent objects. This is certainly an option, but not one that seems to be very attractive to take. After all, a philosopher's claiming that the existence or non-existence of Santa Claus is an open and substantial philosophical problem isn't usually taken to shed a favorable light onto contemporary

---

[239]Of course, in ordinary discourse "object" is often contrasted with "person". However, I will use the word "object" to be more general than "person", as it is commonly used in debates about ontology.

philosophy. Usually, but not always, the participants in the debate are happy to concede that Santa doesn't exist, but they don't take this to answer the question whether or not there are non-existent objects. This question isn't answered by this because it doesn't answer the question whether or not there is a Santa Claus. Only if we knew that

(7) There is a Santa Claus.

and in addition that

(4) Santa doesn't exist.

would we have an answer to the question whether or not there are non-existent objects. This reasoning thus might grant that Santa doesn't exist, but transfers the real issue of deciding whether or not there are non-existent objects into the issue of deciding whether or not there is a Santa Claus. Thus the issue gets transformed into an issue about the truth of statements involving quantifiers. And to get the truth value of such quantified statements as (7) right is the really tricky case, or so the common line.

This, again, seems perfectly reasonable, but also quite problematic. Can the move to quantified statements really be that central? Consider again the question whether or not there are non-cooperative objects. Suppose we agree that

(1) Fred is doesn't cooperate.

and thus that

(3) Fred is a non-cooperative person, (or thing, or object)

Could it really be that we might reasonably have a substantial disagreement about whether or not

(8) There are non-cooperative objects.

is true? It might seem reasonable to say that this last issue has been resolved by example: of course there are non-cooperative objects, and Fred is one of them. Similarly for the case of non-existent objects. If we agree that

(4) Santa does not exist.

and thus that

(6) Santa is a non-existent person, (or thing, or object).

how can it still be a substantial question whether or not there are non-existent objects? Again, this question seems to have been answered by example. Thus it seems to be a trivial inference to conclude form

(6) Santa is a non-existent person, (or thing, or object).

that

(9) There is a non-existent object, namely Santa.

If one would want to deny that inference one would have to deny that there is a tension or inconsistency between

(10) Santa is a non-existent object.

and

(11) Nothing is a non-existent object.

But these sure seem to be in conflict with each other, and it will need quite a bit of philosophical sophistry to explain that away.

So, we are in a dilemma, a dilemma with the following two horns:

a) One the one hand, it seems reasonable that in order for us to decide the ontological dispute about non-existent objects we have to look at the truth value of statements with quantifiers that range over non-existent objects. To do this is to engage in a substantial and possibly quite speculative philosophical project.

b) One the other hand, it seems that it follows trivially from the uncontroversial facts like that Santa doesn't exist that there are non-existent objects. This inference can go as follows:

(4) Santa Claus does not exist.

(10) Santa is a non-existent object.

(9) There is a non-existent object, namely Santa.

To understand this dilemma better is to gain a better understanding of the debate about non-existent objects, and about ontology in general. This paper is supposed to shed some light on how this dilemma is to be resolved. To do so we have to have a closer look at quantification.

12.2 Quantification

The standard debate about whether or not we should accept an ontology of non-existent objects is very closely connected to the debate whether or not we should or accept quantification over non-existent objects. In fact, it is a classic "one person's modus ponens is another person's modus tollens" debate. It is commonly agreed upon among the members of that debate that

(I) If there are statements that are literally true and that contain quantifiers that range over non-existent objects then reality consists of two kinds of things: the existing and the non-existing.

However, it is controversial whether or not we should accept such quantified statements. On the one side (the Meinongean, or modus ponens, side) are people who point out that we do in practice use such quantified statements and that therefore we should just accept that reality contains more than we naively thought. On the other side (the anti-Meinongean, or modus tollens, side) are people who think that such an ontology is absurd and that therefore we should not quantify over non-existent objects, unless, of course, we are not trying to make a literally true statement.[240]

12.2.1 Quinean and non-Quinean quantifiers

It seem that there is very good reason to believe that (I) is true and that therefore one either has to reject all quantification over non-existent objects, or accept a Meinongean ontology. To see if this is indeed so we shall have a look at how (I) is motivated.

First, an observation that leads to some useful terminology. Those who accept quantification over non-existent objects basically accept that quantifiers come in two kinds. There are ordinary quantifiers, as they occur in ordinary utterances of

(12) Someone ate my sandwich.

and there are the one's that apparently require an ontology of non-existent objects, as in

(13) Someone is smarter than any real detective, namely Sherlock Holmes, but unfortunately he doesn't really exist.

The first kind can be explicitly modified with "which/who exists" without change of truth conditions. Only things that exist are relevant for the truth of the utterance. After all, to say:

(14) Someone ate my sandwich, but he doesn't exist.

is more than odd. When quantifiers are used in the way in which they apparently range over Sherlock and the like, such an explicit modification without change of truth conditions does not seem possible. (13) modified this way seems clearly false.

Let's call the occurrence of a quantifier in an utterance that is such that we can explicitly modified with "which/who exists" without change of truth conditions of that utterance a **Quinean quantifier**. Let's call those occurrences where such a modification is not possible without change of truth conditions a **non-Quinean quantifier**. I'd like to stress

---

[240]One further option is to accept quantification over "non-existent" objects like Santa, but deny that they are properly non-existent. For example, according to van Inwagen quantification over Santa Claus is to be accepted, and in some sense it is true that Santa doesn't exist, but still, Santa isn't a non-existent object. See (van Inwagen 2000). The present considerations are most relevant for this line of reasoning, too, even though the difference between it and Meinongianism isn't discussed in any detail here.

here that the distinction between Quinean and non-Quinean quantifiers is one that applies at the level of individual utterances of quantifiers. It is not a distinction at the level of language. So, even if this distinction is legitimate and not empty, it is a further question whether or not our language has two kinds of quantifiers in it, or whether or not to account for the difference between the two kinds of occurrences of quantifiers in another way.

We can now distinguish two core issues in the debate about non-existent objects:

i) Are there any legitimate uses of non-Quinean quantifiers? Is there a need for us to take recourse to them when we try to make a literally true statement? Is there a need for them outside of metaphysics, in ordinary communication? Should we accept such utterances as true?

ii) If yes, how should we understand the function of the non-Quinean quantifiers in these uses?

12.2.2 Meinongians and non-Quinean quantifiers

Meinongians believe that the question "Are there non-existent objects?", understood as a substantial ontological question, has an affirmative answer. The main, or at least one of the main arguments in favor of this view, is that we do in fact use non-Quinean quantifiers in apparently true sentences. If we look at what we accept to be true we see that it contains statements involving non-Quinean quantifiers. And the way to understand them is, according to Meinongians, as follows:[241]

- An expression like "something" can be used both as a Quinean and as a non-Quinean quantifier, as in

  (15) Something is eating my cheese, probably a mouse.

  and in

  (16) Something is keeping me awake at night, namely the monster I dream about.

- Thus there has to be some difference in the particular occasions of the utterance which makes it that one can be modified with "which exists" without change of truth conditions, whereas the other one can't.

- The way to understand this is simply the following: Quinean quantifiers are a case of a well known way in which the context of utterance of a sentence with a quantifier contributes to the truth conditions, or what is said with the utterance, namely contextual

---

[241]See, for example, (Parsons 1980).

restriction of the quantifier. Quinean quantifiers are implicitly restricted to what exists. Non-Quinean quantifiers don't have this restriction. This phenomenon is just like contextual restrictions of quantifiers in standard examples of utterances like:

(17) Everyone has to die.

(18) Everyone is hungry, let's take a break.

The second occurrence is contextually restricted to the group of people in the room of the utterance (or some group like that), whereas the first one doesn't have such a restriction.

- Since non-Quinean quantifiers don't have such a restriction this shows that the domain of quantification really is what the non-Quinean quantifiers range over. Quinean quantifiers range over a subdomain of this domain, namely over all or some of the things in the domain that exist. Thus the true domain of discourse contains non-existent objects, and thus the substantial picture of reality is justified.

In addition and on top of that, it seems that one can't reasonably draw the line which non-existent objects one takes to be part of reality, if one accepts any at all. It seems that one can't reasonably say that all the non-existent objects there are are the ones that we happen to talk about, like Santa Claus and the like. If non-existent objects are part of reality at all then it seems that there isn't any good reason to assume that just the ones we happen to talk about are part of reality. We might as well have come up with other myths and stories, and everything else would have remained the same. It would be very surprising if we got so lucky that the non-existent things we actually talk about are part of reality, but the ones we might as well have talked about aren't. Thus it seems that if one accepts non-existent objects at all then one has to accept a plenitude of non-existent objects: every conceivable one has to be just as good as any other one. Thus if there are non-existent objects at all then there have to be all conceivable non-existent objects. The only way how it might be otherwise is that what non-existent objects there are somehow *depends* on our talking about them. But this option seems hard to defend. It is already very difficult to make sense of how the existence of something depends on our talking about it. But how can the *non-existence* of something depend on our talking about it?

This reasoning, and the dilemma that arrises from the acceptance of (I), defines much of the debate about non-existent objects. I suspect that it is the apparent implausibility of there being a plenitude of non-existent objects, that reality contains already anything we might conceivably come up with and start to talk about, together with the acceptance of (I), that makes people vehemently deny that there can be any true statements containing non-Quinean quantifiers. On the other hand, there seem to be a number of very plausible cases where we seem to have to accept quantification over non-existent objects. These cases, together with the acceptance of (I), seems to imply such an ontology of non-existent objects.

I think the above reasoning that leads to the acceptance of (I) is mistaken, and in this paper I will try to spell out what the mistake is on which it is based. In particular, I will try to show that the literal truth of statements with non-Quinean quantifiers does not imply the substantial metaphysical pictures. I will defend this by motivating that in ordinary communication quantifiers have more than one function. In the next section we will talk about the functions of quantifiers in ordinary communication. After that we will return to talk about non-existent objects.

12.3 The function of (some) non-Quinean quantifiers

In this section I will argue that quantifiers like "something" really have two different, but related, roles in communication. They have different functions, and they can differ in what contribution they make to the truth-conditions. Once spelled out what these are we will see that this is most relevant to our discussion about non-existent objects.

12.3.1 Subtle contextual contributions to content

The main step in the Meinongian's argument for (I) is to view the contextual difference between Quinean and non-Quinean quantifiers as one of contextual restriction. The Meinongean's motivation that non-Quinean quantifiers are restricted quantifiers is closely related to a certain view about what the role of the context of an utterance is in determining its content. One view is that the context provides

- the values of the indexicals and demonstratives that occur on the sentence uttered, and
- contextually restricts the quantifiers that occur in the sentence uttered.

If this is all the context does, and given that there is a contextual difference between Quinean and non-Quinean quantifiers, then it seems obvious that the difference between these two quantifiers is one of contextual restriction.

Undoubtedly, the context makes at least the above two contributions to the content. The question we have to address here is whether or not this is all that the context does. If the context could contribute in other, maybe more subtle, ways to what the content is then we would have to ask ourselves if the argument that the contextual difference between Quinean and non-Quinean quantifiers indeed is one of restricted quantification. I will now point to several examples that show that there are other, more subtle contributions that context can make. I will go over three cases of this phenomenon, one of them is related to quantifiers. Then we will return to the discussion of non-Quinean quantifiers.

Genitive

Consider a standard use of genitive, like

(19) Joe's car has a flat.

It seems that what the genitive "'s" does in (19) is that it contributes to what is said overall that Joe owns a certain car. It is the car that Joe owns that is said to have a flat. Thus it seems that what the genitive does is contribute the relation of ownership that holds between Joe and a certain car to the content of what is said.

But as it turns out, that is not always so. The genitive can be used in many different ways, and it can contribute many different relations to what is said. In

(20) Joe's book is full of mistakes.

one would usually understand this as saying that the book that Joe wrote is full of mistakes, not the one he owns. But it can also be used to say that the one he owns is full of mistakes. And it can be used to say many different things. Consider, for example, the following situation:

(21) *At the beginning of the academic year the department requires that all graduate students meet in a room and bring the library copy of a book they read in the library last year and liked a lot. In the room the grad students sit around the table with library copies of books in front of them. Noticing the book grad student Joe brought to the meeting, one of the professors says to another one:*

Joe's book is full of mistakes.

In this situation what was said is that the book that Joe picked, or the one that is in front of him, is full of mistakes. It is clear in the context that Joe is neither the author nor the owner of that book. Furthermore, one can construct situations like this for almost any relation you please. An utterance of a certain sentence with a genitive in it will contribute that relation to what is said. Take any relation that can reasonably be said to hold between a person and a book. We can find a situation where it will be clear that an utterance of "Joe's book is F" has the content that a book that has that relation to Joe is F.

Thus the contribution that the meaning of the genitive makes to what is said is not a particular relation. It is rather that there is some relation or other that is said to hold between, say, Joe and a book. What relation this is will be a contribution that the larger context of the utterance makes. This will partly be our knowledge about what kinds of relations usually hold between people and books, or what kinds of relations between people and books have been talked about just a minute ago, or the like.

Plural

Another, very widely discussed, example of a not immediately obvious kind of contextual contribution to content is plural.[242] Consider the following example:

(22) Four philosophers carried three pianos.

The plural phrases "four philosophers" and "three pianos" can each make at least two different contributions to the truth conditions of the utterance. First, they could be read as being about individual philosophers, or individual pianos. Secondly, they could be read as being about a group or collections of philosophers or pianos. Thus an utterance of (22) can have at least the following truth conditions:

(23) a. Four philosophers together carried three pianos each (one after the other).

b. Four philosophers each carried three pianos each (one after the other).

c. Four philosophers together carried three pianos together (all of them at once).

d. Four philosophers each carried three pianos together (all at once).

Now, given what we all know about pianos and the strength of philosophers, the most natural way to understand an utterance of (22) is of course (23a). But an utterance of (22) can have the truth conditions as spelled out in (23d). That it usually doesn't comes from the fact that we talk about pianos, and philosophers, and what we know about them. If we talk about other things then this won't be the default reading, as in

(24) Four philosophers carried three books.

---

[242] A survey of a number of issues related to plural and quantifiers can be found in (Lønning 1997). See also (van der Does 1995) on different attempt to locate the source of the readings.

An utterance of this sentence will usually have the truth conditions that four philosophers each carried three books at once.

This is a general phenomenon about plurals. They at least have a *collective reading*, being about a collection or group of things, and a *distributive reading*, being about the individuals in that group. At the level of language it is not determined which one of these two different contributions to the truth conditions a plural phrase will make in a particular utterance. This is determined by the context of the utterance. We can thus say that plurals are semantically underspecified in a certain respect. The semantics of such phrases, what is determined at the level of language, doesn't specify whether the phrase is about a collection of things, or about the things in that collection. This has to be determined by other features of the utterance. How this determination will work is, of course, very tricky business, and we won't get into the details. What matters here is the general phenomenon of semantic underspecification.

If a sentence contains a semantically underspecified item in it then an utterance of that sentence will have more than one reading. It will be possible to utter it with at least two different truth conditions. This is like ambiguity, but different in certain important respects from (standard cases of) ambiguity. In the case of ambiguity, too, one can utter a phonetically identical sentence with different truth conditions. But in the case of semantic underspecification we are dealing neither with lexical ambiguity, nor with structural ambiguity. It isn't the case that any one of the words in (22) has two different meanings, nor that the sentence can have two different structures. Rather, some of the items in the sentence are not specified completely. The context of the utterance will have to fill in the details that the language left out.

Reciprocals

Another case of this phenomenon is the case of so-called reciprocal expressions, expressions like "each other" or "one another". A sentence involving these expressions will specify some collection of things, and some relation that can hold among the things of that collection, and the reciprocal expression will specify how the things in that collection stand to each other with respect to that relation. A simple case is:

(25) The Smiths like each other.

The collection here consists of certain people, the relation is liking, and what is claimed is that each one of the Smiths likes each other one (except maybe themselves). However, each other does not always contribute the same to the content. For example, consider the following pair of standard utterances of the sentences:

(26) The people in the room were no further than one yard from each other.

(27) The exits on the Santa Monica freeway are no further than one mile from each other.

In the case of (26) can be required for this utterance to be true that everyone in the room could touch everyone else by extending their arm. But in the case of (27) it would still be true even if the first and the last exit are 30 miles apart. All that is required here is that there is another exit every mile.[243]

12.3.2 Back to quantifiers

What these examples show is that the role of context in determining content is much more subtle than simply to contribute the value of indexicals and demonstratives or to contextually restrict quantifiers. Context can make a contribution to content even when there are no overtly context sensitive elements in the sentence uttered. The simplest way to describe this is that certain words and phrases are semantically underspecified: the contribution that the shared language makes to the content of the utterance is only part of the contribution that the utterance of the word or the phrase makes to the content. The rest is supplied by the context. Certain features of the situation of the utterance make it such that one of the other options that the contribution from language allows is picked. To be sure, this is only a rather simplified way of describing a complex phenomenon, but I think it is good enough for now. It allows us to see that the role that context plays in the determination of content is more complex than what the above simple picture seems to suggest. In particular, if the role that context plays in the determination of truth conditions is more complex than to fill in the values of demonstratives and indexicals, and to contextually restrict the domain of quantification, maybe the difference between Quinean and non-Quinean quantifiers, or at least the one's we looked at above, isn't in the ballpark of contextual restriction of quantifiers. In fact, this is exactly what I want to argue for next.

In the remainder of this section I will motivate that quantifiers, too, are semantically underspecified. They do play two different but closely related roles in communication. On different occasions one and the same quantifier can make different contributions to the truth conditions. And only on one of these occasions is quantification closely related to ontology.

I think we can see what the difference between Quinean quantifiers

---

[243] See (Dalryple et al. 1998) for a discussion of such cases.

and (some) non-Quinean quantifiers really is when we look at what use we have for non-Quinean quantifiers in ordinary everyday communication. It is particularly helpful to look at these situations of communication, and not primarily at metaphysical debates and the role of quantifiers there. If we can find a use for non-Quinean quantifiers in ordinary everyday communication, and if we can find out what the function of these quantifiers is in these uses then this should shed light on the use of non-Quinean quantifiers in ontology and metaphysics, too.

In the remainder of this paper I will propose an account of what the function is of some non-Quinean quantifiers (I can't claim to have an account of all uses of quantifiers that are not Quinean quantifiers). According to this account such quantifiers have a real function in ordinary communication. However, if we look at what this function is, and if we have the issues about context from above in mind, we can see that this is more plausibly accounted for in a non-Meinongian framework. This is not to say that I will argue that Meinongeanism is incoherent or absurd. Not at all. But Meinongeanism is motivated in part by a mistaken view about the function of quantifiers. In particular, the motivation for (I) essentially relies on this view about quantification.

12.3.3 Communicative functions of quantifiers

To see whether or not we should accept (I) we have to understand better what we do with quantifiers. What functions do they have in communication? What are we doing when we take recourse to them?

There is one thing we do with them which I take to be quite uncontroversial. In this use we have for quantifiers we make statements whose truth depends on what things there are out there in the world. Among statements of this kind I take to be ordinary utterances of:

(28) Something is eating my cheese, probably a mouse.

(29) Everybody is hungry, let's take a break.

These are the uses of quantifiers where the truth of these statements depends on what things there are in our domain of discourse, or what things make up reality. Statements with quantifiers in these uses in them impose a condition on the domain of discourse for them to be true. These statements are only true if the domain of discourse satisfies that condition (like containing a thing which eats my cheese). Because of that I will call this reading of quantifiers the **domain conditions reading** or also the **external reading**.

There is however also another, different use we have for quantifiers. I think the believers in non-existent objects make the mistake of collapsing this use of quantifiers into the domain conditions use. Let me explain.

A situation where we have to take recourse to strong expressive power that our language offers us is when we communicate information that is lacking in a certain respect. This is well know from the discussion about the function of a truth predicate. Among the needs we have for a truth predicate is the one to communicate information that is "incomplete" in a certain sense.[244] To mention the standard example, suppose I believe everything the Pope said. If I know what the Pope said then I can communicate this without using a truth predicate, as with

(30) The Pope said that p and I believe that p, and the Pope said that q, and I believe that q, etc. (and that's all the Pope said).

But if you do not know what the Pope said you can't put it that way. You will have to say something like

(31) Everything the Pope says is true.

Thus having a truth predicate gives one increased expressive power, and one might think that this is why we have one in the first place.

A similar situation occurs with quantifiers. To do this, lets consider an example where we have "incomplete" information, but we know exactly in which respect the information we have is lacking: the case of forgetting, but remembering that one forgot.

Suppose you have to write a psychological profile of Fred. One day you learn the most valuable information that Fred is a big admirer of Clinton. This is most useful to you since now you know a lot more about what kind of person Fred admires, what character traits he values and so on. You note this to yourself:

(32) Fred admires Clinton very much.

The next day, however, you can't recall who it was that Fred admires so much. You do remember that you knew yesterday, and that it was most useful information to you. But now you just can't recall who that was. But you didn't forget everything you knew yesterday. You still know that whoever that was, he is also admired by many Democrats. This, again, is still very useful information to you, since it allows you to connect Fred in a certain way to Democrats. And you can still express and communicate the information you now have. You can say:

(33) There is someone Fred admires very much, and that person is also admired by many Democrats. I just can't recall any more who that is. . .

---

[244]The information is incomplete in an epistemic sense, a sense where the person who is communicating it finds it lacking in a certain way and would like to be more specific, but for some reason or other isn't able to.

This will communicate the information you still have.

Now, this situation is completely general. Nothing hangs on that who was admired is Clinton. What you might have learned about Fred, and what might have been just as important and useful to you, is that

(34) Fred admires Sherlock Holmes very much.

Again, this allows you to conclude all kinds of things about Fred, about the character traits he values and the like. And again, the next day you might have forgotten who it was that Fred admires so much, but you still remember that whoever it was is also admired by many detectives. This, again, is still useful information, even though not as good as what you knew before. Now it is lacking a certain part, namely who it is that Fred admires so much. However, you can still communicate the "incomplete" information you have by saying something like

(35) There is someone Fred admires very much and who is also admired by many detectives. I just can't remember who that is any more...

We need quantifiers in these situations, when we want to communicate information that is missing certain parts. And in situations like the above, where the speaker doesn't know what the part is that is missing, but only that there is a missing part, one has to use a quantifier to communicate the information one still has.

This situation is one where quantification is necessary to communicate the information we want to communicate, but the only instances of the quantifier might be things that don't exist, like Sherlock, in the above case. In this sense it can be said to be quantification 'over' non-existent objects. This is an example where such quantification is necessary to communicate the information we want to communicate.

One might think that this plays in the hands of the Meinongean, since it only shows that after all we do have to accept quantification over non-existent objects, and therefore the Meinongean ontology. But that would be too fast. Whether or not the truth of such quantified statements brings with it the Meinongean ontology is just what we have to look at here. And to do so we have to see what the communicative function of such quantifiers is. What are they supposed to do on these occasions?

Let's first have a brief look at what we use the quantifier for in the above situation. In the above situation we lost a certain part of the information we had before. The rest that we still remember is most useful and we want to communicate it. But it isn't clear what we can do with the part that was lost. We can't just say

(36) Fred admires ... and ... is also admired by many detectives.

That just isn't grammatical. We have to put something in the place of the forgotten part. And what we have to put in place of the forgotten part has to be neutral with respect to what information the original, forgotten, part contributed. And this is exactly what the quantifier does for us on these occasions. It replaces the forgotten part, and together with the pronoun "who" it makes sure that the truth conditions contain that whoever is admired by Fred is the same as who is admired by many detectives. Whether or not that thing is real isn't what matters here.

If we look at what feature the quantifier must have so that it can do this we can see that it has to have a certain inferential role. The information we originally had, and represented with the use of a singular term, has to imply the representation of the 'incomplete' information that we represent with a quantifier. In other words, $(\ldots t \ldots)$ has to imply $(\ldots \text{something} \ldots)$, and it has to do this whether or not 't' stands for something real. As we saw above this is not what matters in these situations. Whether or not Fred admires someone real or unreal isn't what is of issue here.

When we use quantifiers to communicate incomplete information we use them for their inferential role. Let's call this reading of quantifiers their **internal reading** or **inferential role reading**. How this reading relates to the external reading will be what we will have to look at next.

12.3.4 Inferential role and domain conditions

Whether or not expressions that have as their semantic function to impose conditions on the domain of discourse have a certain inferential role in a certain language depends on a number of factors. In the simplest case, when every object in the domain of discourse is such that some term in the language stands for it, and if in addition every term in the language stands for some object in the domain of discourse then inferential role and domain conditions do coincide. A phrase that has a certain inferential role will make the same contribution to the truth conditions as one that imposes a certain domain condition.[245] If every term in our language stands for some object in the domain of discourse then imposing the domain conditions will still get one the inferential role.

If we grant that we have a need for both inferential role and domain conditions then we have at least two ways of accounting for their relationship. One is to say that in the uses where we use quantifiers for their inferential role they do not make a different contribution to the truth conditions than when we use them for their domain conditions, and the

---

[245]I am assuming for now that inferential role is had because of contributions to the truth conditions.

other option is to say that they do. I will discuss both of these in this order.

Imposing domain conditions would get a phrase a certain inferential role if our language were a certain way. Roughly, if it wouldn't exhibit partiality (and contain intentional verbs, or the like). By partiality I simple mean that some of the terms or names in our language stand for nothing whatsoever. If our language exhibits partiality then inferential role and domain conditions go apart. The inference from $(\dots t \dots)$ to $(\dots \text{something} \dots)$ wouldn't be valid any more if the quantifier were read externally. Thus a quantifier can only do both, impose domain conditions and occupy a certain inferential role, if partiality is not true about our language.

Meinongeanism can be seen as defending the claim that partiality is not true of our language because the domain of quantification is larger than we thought, it is so large that it contains an object for every one of our terms. And the motivation for this, as we saw above, was to first point to uses of quantifiers that apparently range over non-existing objects, and secondly to provide a restricted quantification analysis of the difference between Quinean and non-Quinean quantifiers. We have seen that we need quantifiers to range over non-existent objects in ordinary everyday situations of communication, at least on the sense of ranging over non-existent objects in which the instances of such quantified statements involve terms that do not stand for any existing objects (whether they stand for nothing at all, or non-existing objects). The Meinongean can account for the inferential role by claiming that it is really a case of imposing domain conditions on a larger domain, assuming that partiality isn't true of our language. But this does not seem to be so plausible. It seems that there are several prima facie good reasons for claiming that partiality is true, i.e. that there are names or other terms in our language that stand for nothing whatsoever. The two most prominent are:

- Whatever the mechanism of reference is, however our words manage to stand for objects, they can break down. For one, we are only fallible creatures, and however we manage it that our words stand for things out there in the world, we can fail in cases. So, even in cases where we try to talk about regular existing and concrete things there might be some errors involved that make the referential connection break down, and we end up talking about nothing.

- Sometimes we just make up stories and we do not even try to talk about anything in reality. To be sure, we might do something that we aren't even trying to do, but it sure enough would be a miracle if reality contained all the things already that we might make up, and that we end up talking about real things even when we aren't trying.

To be sure, this is not intended as a refutation of Meinongianism. In this paper I only want to question the motivation for Meinongianism, in particular its reliance on (I), not to refute Meinongianism. The above cases should make it plausible that there are empty names in our language, and thus that partiality is true. In addition, the reliance on empty names is in no way necessary for present purposes. We can give similar examples as the above ones using non-denoting descriptions. If we assume that no single person invented the wheel we can give an example like the above one using:

(37) There is someone Fred admires very much, and who is also admired by many bicyclists, namely the inventor if the wheel.

So, it seems that there is good reason to believe that our language does contain empty names, and that thus domain conditions and inferential role go apart. Imposing a certain domain condition won't get one a certain inferential role. But apparently we need and use quantifiers for both. How can that go together?

12.4 A non-Meinongean proposal

We have seen that we need quantifiers for their inferential role, and for their domain conditions. We have also seen that it is plausible to assume that these two do not coincide with respect to truth conditions in a language like ours, even though they do coincide in simpler languages and are closely related. All this can be accommodated in the following simple theory:

Quantifiers, like many other natural language expressions, are semantically underspecified. They make different contributions to the truth conditions on different occasions, depending how they are used and other contextual features. On one of the ways in which they can contribute to the truth conditions they will have a certain inferential role, on the other they will impose certain domain conditions. This is completely consistent with an endorsement of partiality. The contribution that a quantifier makes in its internal, inferential role reading, does not have to reduce to the contribution is makes in its external reading. These are two different but related semantic functions that quantifiers have. As we have seen, it is a mistake to think that the only contextual difference between two uses of quantifiers is that of contextual restriction. That this is the only difference between them was suggested by the simple picture about the role of context in determining content, but we have seen that this is a mistake. Content plays a much more complex and elusive role, and in particular, there are lots of expressions that are semantically underspecified in the sense that they make different contributions to the truth conditions on different occasions of utterance.

The view that contextual contributions come down to fixing the values of demonstratives and indexicals, and to contextually restricting quantifiers, naturally suggests itself from the background of first order logic. There both of these phenomena are prominent and can be nicely captured within the language and semantics of first order logic. However, the technical tools appropriate for natural languages will go beyond this, and the examples given above, and many others, suggest that taking first order logic as ones ideal is no ideal worth having.[246]

There is, of course, the issue what the truth conditions of the quantifier in its internal role is. In particular, how can the quantifier get the inferential role it is supposed to get by having certain truth conditions. The Meinongeans have an answer to this, but as we saw the answer seems to make an implausible assumption about our language. But the Meinongean's answer isn't the only answer. Quantifiers do not have to impose domain conditions as their contribution to the truth conditions. When they are used for their inferential role it is implausible that they get their inferential role through imposing domain conditions, since this would only work if our language had features it doesn't seem to have. So, what truth conditions would give a quantifier the inferential role we want it for? I won't get into the details of this here,[247] but what we have to find out here is simply what contribution to the truth conditions would give an expression the inferential role for which we want the quantifier. In our case, what contribution to the truth conditions would make the inference from $(\ldots t \ldots)$ to $(\ldots$ something $\ldots)$ valid, whether or not t stands for anything real? There are many different contributions to the truth conditions that the quantifier could make so that it would have this inferential role. The simplest one is for it to make a contribution such that the statement with the quantifier in it is truth conditionally equivalent to the disjunction of all the statements of the form $(\ldots t \ldots)$ that imply it. To be sure, there are infinitely many of such statements, but if the quantifier would make such a contribution to the truth conditions then the statements in which it occurs would have this inferential

---

[246]That first order languages have their limits in capturing natural language quantification, even in cases completely unrelated to our debate here, has been widely discussed. See for example (Barwise and Cooper 1981) or the section on generalized quantifiers in (Gamut 1991) and the references given there.

[247]However, I do get into the details of it in (Hofweber 1999), chapter 2.

role. This is the simplest and most trivial way to get a certain inferential role. To say this is, of course, not to say that the underlying structure of such sentences is in any way infinitary. This relates in certain ways to substitutional quantification. A substitutional interpretation in effect gives the quantifier a certain inferential role. But the present proposal differs from substitutional quantification in a number of ways.[248]

The present proposal can be summed up with the following points:

- Quantifiers like "something" are semantically underspecified and make different contributions to the truth condition of an utterance on different occasions of the utterance. Quantifiers are just one of many items in our language that have this feature.

- The different contributions to the truth conditions that quantifiers can make correspond to different functions they have in communication: occupying a certain inferential role and imposing certain domain conditions.

- In languages like ours inferential role and domain conditions do not coincide with respect to truth conditions.

- It shouldn't be surprising that one and the same item has these different functions on different occasions, since they are closely related and in fact coincide in simpler languages.

12.5 Solving the dilemma

The present proposal nicely resolves the dilemma that we started out with at the beginning of this paper (see page 252). It seemed that one the one hand answering the ontological question about non-existent objects would involve figuring out the truth value of statements whose quantifiers range over non-existent objects, and this seems to be a substantial and difficult task. But on the other hand it seems to follow quite trivially from the fact that Santa doesn't exist that such statements are true. According to the present account both sides have some truth to them.

- On the one hand it is indeed trivial to conclude that there are non-existent objects from nothing more than the premise that Santa doesn't exist. The sense in which this is trivial is that if the quantifier is used in its inferential role reading then it trivially follows from "Santa doesn't exist" that "There is something which doesn't exist, namely Santa." And from "Santa is a non-existent object" it follows trivially that "There are non-existent objects," again assuming that the quantifier is read internally.

---

[248] Again, see (Hofweber 1999) chapter 2 for the details of this.

- On the other hand, it is a substantial metaphysical issue to decide whether or not there are non-existent objects, using the quantifier externally. The speculative ontological issue is not decided by the trivial inferences. Whether or not there are non-existent objects, using the quantifier externally, is left open by the endorsement of the trivial arguments. To answer this question is indeed to engage in speculative ontology.

If what I said so far is right then (I) is wrong, and the Meinongean's motivation for an ontology of non-existent objects is too quick. There are true statements with quantifiers in them such that the only true instances of the quantifiers are with names or terms that do not stand for anything that exists. But even though this is true, it doesn't answer the question whether or not there are non-existent objects in our ontology. This would only be answered if we had a true statement with a quantifier ranging over non-existent objects in it, and that quantifier is used in its external reading. We thus avoid the modus ponens—modus tollens dilemma from page 252 by denying the conditional that gave rise to it.

The Meinongean's view that the difference between Quinean and non-Quinean quantifiers is one of contextual restriction of the quantifier is based on a too simple model of the role of context in determining truth conditions, a view that is based on assuming a too close connection between natural languages and first order languages. The difference between Quinean and some non-Quinean quantifiers is in the ballpark of semantic underspecification and the difference between inferential role and domain conditions. And that inferential role is not had because of imposing certain domain conditions is a plausible fact about our language.

12.6   Objections

Before we conclude I'd like to add a brief discussion of two objections that can be raised against the present proposal. One deals with the fact that I have not said enough about the issue of quantifier scope and how it relates to the use of quantifiers together with intentional verbs. The other deals with the claim that when we use the word 'exists' in conjunction with quantifiers we thereby explicitly restrict the quantifier, thereby giving support to the contextual restriction picture.[249]

12.6.1   Quantification and scope

One might object that I did not pay enough attention to the difference between

---

[249]More details are in (Hofweber 1999) chapter 2.

(38) There is someone whom Fred admires and who is also admired by many detectives.

and

(39) Fred admires someone who is also admired by many detectives.

The latter, the objection continues, is completely compatible with the claim that we never have to quantify over non-existent objects (contrary to what Meinongeans and I claim), because the quantifier is within the scope of the intentional verb. Only in the case of (38) do we quantify over non-existent objects.

To be sure, I have not talked much about this difference, but there is good reason for this. Without a doubt, there is an issue of scope when quantifiers interact with intentional verbs, but I think it is a mistake to closely connect the different scope reading that such quantifiers can have with how these items are arranged in the sentences that get uttered. It seems to me that both sentences, (38) and (39), can have both scope readings, and that using one or the other is rather in the ballpark of topicalization. The difference will be apparent when we notice how we would continue a conversation after (38) or (39). In the first case we would usually continue to talk about the person, whoever it is, who is admired by Fred. In the second case we would normally continue to talk about Fred.

It is a common strategy in philosophy to claim that quantifiers that apparently range over non-existent objects can only occur within the scope of an intentional verb. I think it is a mistake to think that we only have use for quantifiers this way. But I won't be able to defend this here in sufficient detail.[250] This strategy of arguing is, of course, not a defense of Meinongeanism. The option defended in this paper is to accept certain quantified statements as true, but to give a different account of the function of these quantifiers on these occasions than a Meinongean would give.

12.6.2   The role of "exists"

There is a consideration that might be taken to speak in favor of Meinongianism. It is the role of the word "exists". We were able to distinguish Quinean and non-Quinean quantifiers by saying that the Quinean's are the ones that can be explicitly modified with "which exists" without change of truth conditions. The Meinongians can understand this as making a contextual restriction of a quantifier explicit. They can say that this is just like if I would say

---

[250]See, however, (Hofweber 1999) chapter 2.

(40) Everyone (who is in this room) is hungry. Let's take a break.

Here "who is in this room" makes a contextual restriction of the quantifier "everyone" explicit. It is not necessary to make such restrictions explicit. But if a quantifier is contextually restricted then we can make the restriction explicit without change of truth conditions. And this, the Meinongians can say, is what is going on when we make the difference between Quinean and non-Quinean quantifiers explicit.

However, the believer in semantic underspecification has a nice story about this, too. It is based on noticing that there is an interesting parallel between the above situation and other cases of semantic underspecification. Consider plural, again. An utterance of

(41) Four philosophers wrote a book.

can be uttered in such a way that the plural phrase is either used collectively, or distributively. However, one can add more words to this sentence such that it then allows only one of these readings, and it doesn't change the truth conditions of the sentence in that reading. For example, the sentence

(42) Four philosophers together wrote a book.

can only be uttered to have a collective reading of the plural, and the sentence

(43) Four philosophers each wrote a book.

can only be uttered with the plural phrase having a distributive reading. In other words, there are words in our language such that if we expand a semantically underspecified phrase with these words then we force a certain reading of this phrase (or we complete the underspecification). So, with more words we can force a certain reading, or fully specify what was left underspecified. And that this is so should not be surprising. After all, we don't always want to rely on the subtle features of context to determine what was left undetermined. Sometimes we want to determine it without a role for context to play. For example, when we try to make explicit what we or someone else said, in particular how it is supposed to be understood in detail. And the same happens, I think, when we use the word "exists" right after a quantifier. The difference between "something" and "something, which exists" is that the latter forces that the quantifier is used in its external use. It shouldn't be understood as an explicit restriction of the scope of the quantifier, as the Meinongians would want it.

12.7 Quantification and ontology

The present view about contextual differences in different uses of quantifiers has a relevance for ontology beyond the debate about non-existent objects. In fact, if what I said here is right then what is commonly called Quine's criterion for ontological commitment has to be false. We are not committed to all the things our quantifiers range over, even in our best theories. We are only committed to what the quantifiers used externally range over. The more positive alternative view that arises from all this is in certain respects similar to the view Carnap endorsed in his "Empiricism, semantics, and ontology" (Carnap 1956). There will be a difference between internal and external questions about what there is, based on whether or not the quantifier used in asking the question is used internally or externally. And in accordance with Carnap's view, general internal questions (about numbers, properties and the like) will have trivial affirmative answers. The external questions, on the other hand, won't have trivial answers. Contrary to Carnap, however, I do think that these external questions are fully meaningful. This form of neo-Carnapianism about ontology has been developed in (Hofweber 1999).[251]

12.8 Conclusion

We started with a dilemma about whether or not to accept that there are non-existent objects is something trivial, or metaphysically substantial. And we saw that a central claim in the debate about the ontology of non-existent objects is the acceptance of (I). Given (I) there only seem to be two options one has: accept quantification over non-existent objects and an ontology of non-existent objects, or reject both of them. We have seen that a central part of the motivation for (I) is the contextual restriction view of the difference between Quinean and non-Quinean quantifiers. I have argued that once we look at the role of context in general and at what the function of certain non-Quinean quantifiers is in ordinary communication then we can see that these are not our only options. There are uses of quantifiers where they are non-Quinean quantifiers, but they are not restricted external quantifiers. It is a mistake to think that the only contextual difference between different uses of quantifiers is one of contextual restriction. The much more broad thesis of semantic underspecification applies to quantifiers as well as many other expressions, and in particular gives us the distinction between internal and external uses of quantifiers. With this distinction in mind we can see that (I) is mistaken. And we can resolve the dilemma we started out

---

[251](Hofweber a), (Hofweber b), and (Hofweber c) also elaborate on various aspects of it.

with: it is trivial that there are non-existent objects, if the quantifier is understood internally. But it is a substantial metaphysical issue to decide whether or not there are non-existent objects, if the quantifier is understood externally. Whether or not non-existent objects are part of reality is left open by everything I have said here. But if I'm right then it will be harder to argue that there are than Meinongians assume it is.

13

A Paradox of Existence

STEPHEN YABLO

> It seems to me very curious that language should have grown
> up as if it were expressly designed to mislead philosophers;
> and I do not know why it should have.
>
> — G. E. Moore to I.A. Richards

13.1 Introduction

About fifty years ago, Quine convinced almost everyone who cared that
the argument for abstract objects, if there was going to be one, would
have to be *a posteriori* in nature.[252] And it would have to an a posteriori argument of a particular sort: an *indispensability* argument representing numbers, to use that example, as entities that "total science"
cannot do without.[253] This is not to say that a priori arguments are
no longer attempted; they are, for instance by Alvin Plantinga in his
(Plantinga 1965) , and Crispin Wright in his (Wright 1983). But such
arguments carry with them a palpable sense of daring and a distinct feeling of pulling a rabbit out of a hat. Nobody supposes that there are *easy*
proofs, from a priori or empirically obvious premises, of the existence of
abstracta.[254] (The only easy existence proof we know of in philosophy

---

[252] David Hills, Ken Walton, Mark Crimmins, Ralph Wedgwood, Ned Hall, Peter van
Inwagen, Stephen Schiffer, David Chalmers, Kent Bach, Laura Bugge, Sol Feferman,
Thomas Hofweber—thanks! A scattered 15% of the paper is taken from (Yablo 1998).

[253] The classic formulation is Hilary Putnam's: "quantification over mathematical
entities is indispensable for science...; therefore we should accept such quantification; but this commits us to accepting the existence of the mathematical entities in
question," see (Putnam 1971), p. 57.

[254] A possible exception is Arthur Prior in "Entities," who comments: "This is very
elementary stuff—I am almost tempted to apply the mystic word 'tautological'—and
I apologise for so solemnly putting it forward in a learned journal. But I do not think
it can be denied that these things need to be said. For there are people who do not

Empty Names, Fiction, and the Puzzles of Non-Existence.
Anthony Everett and Thomas Hofweber (eds.).
Copyright © 2000, CSLI Publications.

is Descartes's *cogito ergo sum.*)

The paradox is that, if we are to go by what philosophers say in other contexts, such bashfulness is quite unnecessary. Abstract objects are *a priori deducible* from a priori premises and/or obvious, uncontroversial empirical facts.

EXAMPLE 1 As everyone knows, an argument is valid iff every model of its premises is a model of its conclusions; to put it in formal mode, the sentence "A is valid" is true iff A lacks countermodels. I have never seen empirical evidence offered for this equivalence so I assume the knowledge is a priori. On the other hand, it is *also* (often) known a priori that such and such an argument is invalid. From these two pieces of a priori knowledge it follows by modus ponens that there exist certain abstract objects, viz. models.

EXAMPLE 2 That was an example of the first of the two patterns mentioned: a priori deduction of abstract objects from a priori premises. An example of the second is this. It is a priori, I assume, since observational evidence is never given, that there are as many *Fs* as *Gs* iff there is a one to one function from the *Fs* to the *Gs* iff the number of *Fs* = the number of *Gs*. Hence the fact that I have as many left hands as right a priori entails the existence of functions and numbers.

13.2 Platonic objects

The existence of abstract objects exist strikes most of us as an enduringly controversial matter decidable (if at all) only by a complexly holistic a posteriori argument. At the same time, the existence of abstract objects is straightforwardly deducible from premises that few would think to deny, using simple bridge principles widely accepted on the basis of non-empirical evidence.

So far so bad. But the difficulty is actually larger than the last paragraph suggests; because objects that are *not* abstract, or not obviously so, can be similarly "deduced" on the basis of a priori-looking bridge principles. I have in mind principles like "it is possible that B iff there is a B-world," and "Jones buttered the toast F-ly iff there was a buttering of the toast by Jones and it was F," and "Jones is human iff the property of being human is possessed by Jones." That non-abstract objects appear also to admit of "overeasy" proof shows that we have not got an exact bead on the intended paradox.

Second try: There is a widespread practice in philosophy of discovering unexpected objects in truth-conditions, that is, of discerning *X*s in

agree with them...," (Prior 1976), p. 26).

the truth-conditions of statements that are not on the face of it *about* Xs.[255] For instance,

the truth-value of	is held to turn on
"argument *A* is valid"	the existence of *countermodels*
"it is possible that *B*"	the existence of *worlds*
"there are as many *C*s as *D*s"	the existence of 1–1 *functions*
"there are over five *E*s"	the *number* of *E*s' exceeding five
"he did it *F*ly"	the *event* of his doing it being *F*
"there are *G*s which BLAH"	there being a *set* of *G*s which BLAH
"she is *H*"	her relation to the *property H*-ness

Objects with a tendency to turn up unexpected in truth-conditions like this can be called *platonic*. Models, worlds, and properties are platonic, relative to the areas of discourse on the left, because the sentences on the left aren't intuitively *about* models, worlds, and properties. (An example of *non*-platonicness might be *people* considered in relation to population discourse. That the truth about which regions are populated should hinge on where the people are does not make anything platonic, because people are what population-discourse is visibly and unsurprisingly all about.)

Objects are called *platonic* relative to an area of discourse due to the combination of something positive—the discourse depends for its truth-value on how objects like that behave—with something negative—the discourse is not about objects of that type. It appears to be this combination, truth-dependence without aboutness, that makes for the paradoxical result; it appears, in other words, that with *all* platonic objects, abstract or not, there is going to the possibility of an overeasy existence proof. Just as functions can be deduced from the premise that I have as many left hands as right ones, events can be conjured a priori out of the fact that Jones buttered the toast slowly, and worlds out of the fact that she could have done it quickly.

13.3 Quine's way or the highway

The paradox is now shaping up as follows. Let *X* be whatever sort of platonic object you like: numbers, properties, worlds, sets, it doesn't matter. Then on the one hand you've got the Quinean view that

---

[255]To paraphrase Austin, surprising ourselves by what we find in truth-conditions might be considered an occupational hazard of philosophy, if it were not philosophy's occupation.

(Q) to establish the existence of Xs takes a holistic a posteriori indispensability argument;

while on the other hand there is the point just made, that

(R) the existence of Xs follows from "truths of reason"—*a priori* bridge principles—given *a priori* &/or empirical banalities.

The reason this is a paradox and not merely a contradiction is that (Q) is received opinion in philosophy, while (R) is a straightforward (albeit perhaps unintended) consequence of received opinion, viz., the opinion that we are capable of a priori insight into truth-conditions, and that among these insights are the fact that an argument is valid iff it has no countermodels, that it is possible that S iff an S-world exists, and so on.

What is to be done? One option is of course to renounce (Q) and confess that the proof of numbers and models and worlds is trivially simple. I am going to assume without argument that such a course is out of the question. Our feeling of hocus-pocus about the "easy" proof of numbers and the rest, is really very strong and has got to be respected.

If that is right, then our one remaining option is to deny that the bridge principles are a priori. There might be different versions of this. Maybe the principles are not even *true*, as John Etchemendy maintains about the Tarskian validity principle.[256] Or maybe our justification for them is not a priori; the Tarski principle owes its plausibility to the prior hypothesis that there are sets, and the argument for *them* is experiential and holistic. Either way, we resolve the paradox by abandoning the idea that one knows independently of experience that, e.g., the valid arguments are the ones without countermodels.

If only it were that easy! The problem is that our rights of access to the bridge principles do not *seem* to be hostage to empirical fortune in the way suggested; our practice with the principles does not feel like it is "hanging by a thread" until the empirical situation sorts itself out.

This shows up in a couple of ways. It shows up in the "categorical" fact that many or most of us using the Tarski biconditional *have no particular view* about abstract ontology; certainly we are not committed platonists. If the biconditional (as employed by us) truly presupposed such an ontology, then logicians *ought* to feel as though they were walking on very thin ice indeed. I don't know about you but I have never, not once, heard any anxieties expressed on this score.

Also testifying to our (surprising) insouciance about the true ontological situation is the "hypothetical" fact that if someone were to *turn up* with evidence that abstract objects did not exist, our use of models

---

[256] (Etchemendy 1990).

to figure validity would not be altered one iota. Burgess and Rosen begin their book *A Subject with No Objects* with a pertinent fable:

> Finally, after years of waiting, it is your turn to put a question to the Oracle of Philosophy...you humbly approach and ask the question that has been consuming you for as long as you can remember: "Tell me, O Oracle, what there is. What sorts of things exist?" To this the Oracle responds: "What? You want the whole list? ...I will tell you this: everything there is is concrete; nothing there is is abstract...." (Burgess and Rosen 1997), p. 3.

Suppose we continue the fable a little. Impressed with what the Oracle has told you, you return to civilization to spread the concrete gospel. Your first stop is at CSLI where researchers are confidently reckoning validity by way of calculations on models. You demand that the practice be stopped at once. It's true that the Oracle has been known to speak in riddles; but there is now a well-enough justified *worry* about the existence of models that all theoretical reliance on them should cease. They of course tell you to bug off and am-scray. Which come to think of it is exactly what you yourself would do, if the situation were reversed.

13.4 Impatience

Our question really boils down to this: What is the source of the *impatience* we feel with the meddling ontologist—the one who insists that the practice of judging validity by use of Tarski be put on hold until the all-important matter is settled of whether models really exist?

One explanation can be ruled out immediately: we think the principles would still hold (literally) true whether the objects existed or not. Such an explanation might work in certain cases. Should it be discovered, who knows how, that there are no people, we would willingly conclude on the basis of the population principle—"region R is populated iff it contains people"—that strictly speaking, no regions are populated. This is (one of many reasons) why friends of the population principle need not stay up late at night worrying about the existence of people.

Our complacency about the platonic bridge principles does *not* admit of a similar explanation. That would be to think that if, contrary to what many people suppose, there are no models, then every argument is valid. Likewise if the models are found to peter out above a certain finite cardinality—not for deep logical reasons, mind you, but as a matter of brute empirical fact—then a whole bunch of statements we now regard as logically contingent, such as "there are fifty zillion objects," are in fact logically false. It seems as clear as anything that we are not in the market for this sort of result. The moral of the story is that

> *Ontology Matters to Truth*: Our complacency about the bridge principles is *not* due to a belief that they hold literally true regardless of the ontological facts. (It can't be, since we have no such belief.)

Another explanation of our impatience seems equally misguided: we are confident that the negative empirical findings will never be made. It may be that we *are* confident of this. It is not as though any great number of ontological controversies have been resolved by empirical means in the past, and there seems no reason to think that our record of failure is about to change.

Even if it is granted, though, that we do not expect evidence to turn up that casts doubt on the existence of models, why should that prevent us from having a view about what to say if it did? I take it we are also confident that it will never be discovered that there are no people. Nevertheless, it seems clearly true that *if* the right sort of evidence presents itself, we will have to conclude that people don't exist, and hence that no region is populated; and clearly *false* that if the right sort of evidence turns up, this will rationalize disbelief in models leading to the conclusion that all arguments are valid. The moral is that

> *Experience Matters to Ontology*: Our complacency about the bridge principles is not due to a belief that the trouble-making empirical facts will never come to light. That belief may be there, but our complacency runs deeper than it can explain.

If these two morals are correct,then to say that (Q) wins out over (R) does not really solve the paradox. Because now we want to know the following: how is it that the bridge principles are treated, and apparently *rightly* treated, as experience-independent? What accounts for the a priori-like deference we pay to them? How can we feel justified in ignoring evidence that would by our own lights exhibit our belief as false?[257]

Something has got to give, and I think I know what it is. What entitles us to our indifference about evidence that would exhibit the bridge principles as false is that *we were never committed in the first place to their literal truth.*[258] Our attitude towards them is attitude A,

---

[257]The problem stated a little more carefully is how to deal with the following: on the one hand, we feel entitled to the bridge principles regardless of the empirical facts (experience doesn't matter to truth); while on the other hand, we think that the empirical facts are highly relevant to whether the mentioned objects exist (experience does matter to ontology); while on the third hand, we regard the bridge principles as almost certainly false if they do not exist (ontology matters to truth).

[258]To their literal truth, that is; see below.

and attitude A leaves it open whether the alluded-to platonic objects really exist.

13.5 Platonism as the price of access

Attitude A remains of course to be identified. Before embarking on that task, though, we need to consider some reasons for maintaining (against what has just been said) that the bridge principles are in fact true and proper things to believe. It will be easiest to stick with Tarski's validity principle

(V) an argument is valid iff it has no countermodels,

as our example. One obvious reason for thinking that (V) is true is that if it were not, then we could not appeal to it in the ways we routinely do. The point of the "iff" is to give us license to infer back and forth between the left and the right hand sides. Discovering that the right hand side is true, or false, we can conclude that the left hand side is true, or false; and vice versa. If these inferences require us to regard (V) as true, then that is a powerful reason so to regard it.

Humor me for a minute while I state the case a little more guardedly: The back and forth inferences give us reason to regard (V) as true *if* they are inferences that people actually perform.

It may seem that they clearly are. You find a countermodel, you conclude that the argument is invalid. You show that there are no countermodels, you conclude that the argument is valid.

I wonder, though, whether that is a fair description of what really goes on. It takes only a little thought to realize that the activity called "finding a countermodel" *really* just consists in describing to yourself what the countermodel would have to be like if it existed. It consists in laying down a blueprint for a model of the appropriate sort. The issue of whether anything in fact *answers* to the blueprint is not taken up and indeed seems rather beside the point.

As for the other direction, where countermodels cannot be found and we judge the argument to be valid, again, the activity of "finding that there are no countermodels" is misdescribed. The fact one is *really* relying on in judging validity is not that countermodels fail to exist—*that* you could have learned from the oracle, and it would not have altered your validity-judgments one iota—but that there's something in the very notion of a *countermodel to argument A* that prevents there from being such a thing. A consistent blueprint can't be drawn up because the conditions such a model would have to meet are directly at odds with each other. Once again, the issue of whether models do or do not really exist is not broached and seems of no genuine relevance.

Summing up, if you look at the way the Tarski biconditional is actually used, any larger issue of the existence of models "in general" is bracketed. It's almost as though we were understanding (V) as

(V*) an argument A is valid iff, *supposing that models in general exist,* A has no countermodels.[259]

The idea that (V) is in practice understood along the lines of (V*) has the added virtue of explaining our impatience with the ontologist's meddling. If the issue is whether there are countermodels *assuming models in general,* it really doesn't *matter* whether models exist. The truth value of *this* claim:

(a*) supposing that models exist, the argument has a countermodel,

is entirely independent of the truth value of this one:

(b) models exist.

Of course, the question will be raised of why someone would utter (V) when what they really literally meant was (V*). Suffice it to say that linguistic indirection of this sort is not unknown; details will be given below. Right now let's look at some other reasons why a literal interpretation of the bridge principles might seem unavoidable.

13.6 Platonism as the key to clarity

A great, indeed a defining, goal of analytic philosophy is to make our ideas clear. This goal is not often achieved to everyone's satisfaction, but in a few instances there has been undeniable progress. I assume everyone will agree that our notion of cardinality—especially infinite cardinality—was made clearer by Cantor's explanation in terms of 1–1 functions; that the notion of inductive definability was clarified by Tarski's device of quantifying over all sets meeting certain closure conditions; that our notion of validity was clarified by the appeal to models; that our notion of continuity is clearer thanks to the epsilon-delta story; and that various modal notions have been clarified by the appeal to worlds.

The argument for platonic objects is this: if quantifying over functions, worlds, sets, real numbers, etc. enables us to clarify our ideas, and clarification of ideas is a principal goal of analytic philosophy, how can we as analytic philosophers be expected to eschew such quantification and the ontological commitment it encodes?

It helps here to consider a particular example. Think of the controversy sparked early in this century by C.I. Lewis's work in modal

---

[259]Cf. Field in a critical response to Wright: "the conceptual truth is [not 'the number of As = the number of Bs iff there are as many As as Bs' but] rather 'if numbers exist, then...'" (Field 1989a), p. 169.

logic. Lewis distinguished a number of logical systems differing in their attitude towards formulas like

(a) nec(S) → nec(nec(S)),

(b) pos(nec(S)) → S,

(c) pos(S) → nec(pos(S)), ...

Commentators wondered whether their competing intuitions about these systems might not be based in subtly dissimilar ideas of modality. They struggled to articulate these ideas, in the hope that that it would eventually be possible to say that Professor X accepts a principle that Professor Y denies because their concepts of possibility differ in such and such antecedently specifiable ways.

The breakthrough of course came with the advent of possible worlds semantics. It now became possible to link acceptance of (a) with a conception of relative possibility as transitive, acceptance of (b) with a conception of relative possibility as symmetrical, and so on. The benefits were and remain substantial: fewer spurious ("merely conceptual") disagreements, improved self-understanding, fewer fallacies of equivocation, a clearer picture of why modal principles fall into natural packages, and so on. If the clarification that confers these benefits requires us to treat modal operators as (disguised) quantifiers over worlds, then that is how we have to treat them; and that means believing in the worlds.

Isn't there something strange about this line of argument? One normally thinks of clarification as more of a cognitive notion than an ontological one. My goal as a clarifier is to elucidate the content of my idea so that it will be easier to tell apart from other ideas with which it might otherwise get confused. If that is right, then how well I have succeeded in making my ideas clear ought not to depend on ontological matters *except* to the extent that the content of those idea exhibits a similar dependence.

With some ideas, viz. ideas with externalistic identity conditions, this condition might indeed be met. There is no way for me to make my idea of water, or of Hilary Clinton, fully clear without bringing in actual water, or actual Hilary Clinton. (Related to this, unless there is water my idea of water cannot *be* fully clear.) But my ideas of validity and possibility do not appear to be externalistic in this way. That is why it seems so strange to suppose that actual models and worlds would have to be appealed to make them fully clear, and, related to this, strange to suppose that models and worlds would have to exist for them to be fully clear.

The suggestion is that the undoubted clarificatory powers of platonic objects do not depend on their actually existing. I can do just as good a job of elucidating (to myself and others) my modal concepts by saying

> supposing for a moment that necessity is truth at all relatively possible worlds, *my* concept is one that calls for relative possibility to be a transitive (and/or symmetric, and/or...) relation,

as I can by saying:

> according to my concept of necessity, necessity *is* truth at all relatively possible worlds, where relative possibility is a transitive (and/or symmetric, and/or...) relation.

Along one dimension in fact I can do a better job. Suppose I explain my concept of possibility in the second, realistic, way. Then it flows from my concept that if Lewis et al are wrong and there are no counterfactual worlds, then whatever is the case is necessarily the case. This is just false of my concept, and I venture to guess of yours as well. An explication generating false conclusions about a concept's application-conditions is to that extent less accurate and revealing than one that avoids the false conclusions.[260]

13.7 Platonism and proof

A third way in which we appeal to principle (V) is in metalogical proofs. How are we to show, for instance, that validity has the weakening property —that if $P_1 \ldots P_n/C$ is valid, then so is $P_1 \ldots P_n P_{n+1}/C$?[261] The usual argument goes as follows:

(i) An argument is valid iff every model of its premises satisfies its conclusion (this is (V)).

(ii) If every model of $P_1 \ldots P_n$ satisfies C then every model of $P_1 \ldots P_n$, P_{n+1} satisfies C (by logic and definitions).

---

[260] Another example: Suppose I want to distinguish the classical notion of validity from the circumscriptive notion. (The latter allows me to infer "there are exactly two cows" from "Bossie is a big cow and Elsie is a cow that is not big.") An "intrinsic" characterization of the difference might not be easy to devise; some sort of allusion to models seems unavoidable. Why not the following? An argument is classically valid iff, bracketing any worries about the existence of models, it has no countermodels; an argument is circumscriptively valid iff, bracketing any worries about the existence of models, none of its countermodels is a minimal model of its premises. Again, I can explain the notion of a Dedekind-infinite as opposed to numerically-infinite plurality by saying: there are D-infinitely many Fs iff assuming mathematical objects, there is a 1–1 function from all the Fs to only some of the Fs; there are N-infinitely many Fs iff assuming mathematical objects, there is a 1–1 function from the natural numbers into the Fs.

[261] I am grateful here to Peter van Inwagen, and, for the related idea that models are called on to explain validity-facts, to Kent Bach.

(iii) If $P_1 \ldots P_n/C$ is valid, then $P_1 \ldots P_n P_{n+1}/C$ is valid (from (i) and (ii)).

Such an argument depends on taking the validity principle at face value. It has to be said, though, that that the goal of "proving" weakening seems slightly peculiar. That an expanded premise set continues to entail the old conclusions seems intuitively a *more* fundamental fact than the Tarski biconditional that is used in the proof. And other things equal, the more fundamental fact should not be represented as a consequence or offshoot of the less fundamental.

Suppose we rethink the point of the exercise a little. Let the goal be not to establish weakening, but to show that weakening is implicit in our (classical) concept of validity—as opposed to, say, the circumscriptive concept.[262] Then the proof can be rewritten, with (V*) now playing the role formerly played by (V):

(1) An argument is valid (according to my concept) iff, assuming models, models of the premises satisfy the conclusion as well. (this is (V*)).

(2) Assuming models, models of $P_1 \ldots P_n$ satisfy C only if models of $P_1 \ldots P_{n+1}$ satisfy C (whatever holds by logic and definitions is true-assuming-models).

(3) Assuming models, models of $P_1 \ldots P_n$ satisfy C only if assuming models, models of $P_1 \ldots P_{n+1}$ satisfy C (by (2), since logical consequences of truths-assuming-models are themselves true-assuming-models).

(4) $P_1 \ldots P_n/C$ is valid only if $P_1 \ldots P_{n+1}/C$ is valid (from (1) and (3)).

Note that an argument like this is *not* available to someone Jones whose concept of validity was the circumscriptive one. Imagine what her argument would have to look like:

(1) An argument is valid (according to my concept) iff, assuming models, minimal models of the premises satisfy the conclusion as well.

(2) Assuming models, minimal models of $P_1 \ldots P_n$ satisfy C only if minimal models of $P_1 \ldots P_{n+1}$ satisfy C.

The attempt breaks down right here: minimal models of $P_1 \ldots P_n$ may well *not* be minimal models of $P_1 \ldots P_{n+1}$, so (2) is just false.[263] This

---

[262]See an earlier footnote.

[263]E.g., let $P_1 = Fa$, $P_2 = Gb$, and $P_3 = \neg Fb$. Then minimal models of $\{P_1, P_2, P_3\}$ have two elements each, while those of $\{P_1, P_2\}$ have just one.

illustrates how (1)–(4) style "proofs" can be used to draw out consequences of quantificationally-explicated concepts without for a moment supposing that the entities quantified over constitute the real grounds of the concepts' application.

For a second example, consider the set-theoretic proof that multiplication is commutative—e.g., five times three = three times five—from the fact that the Cartesian product of X with Y maps one-one onto the Cartesian product of Y with X. It seems clear that this proof reveals to us neither that commutation holds nor why it does. That said, there might be any number of reasons why conceiving of multiplication in terms of the cardinalities of Cartesian products, doubts-about-sets-bracketed, is a worthwhile cognitive strategy, e.g., one can derive a large body of arithmetical facts from a slender set-theoretic basis.

The proof motive for positing platonic objects is not without merit. When we realize though that the fact proved is not quite what we were led to believe—not that weakening holds, or that multiplication is commutative, but that these results are implicit in concepts disambiguated and/or explicated along such and such lines—then the argument for actually *believing* in the objects falls apart. Once again, we gain as much purchase on the content of the concept by aligning it with a condition on assumed objects as would be gained by treating the objects as real.

13.8   Platonism as a prop for realism

One more try: why would anyone want (V), or any other bridge principle, to be literally true, so that the platonic objects it quantifies over were really there?

One can think of this as a query about the relations between *ontology*, the study of what is, and *alethiology*, the study of what is the case. A lot of people find it highly plausible and desirable that what is the case should be controlled as far as possible by what is, and what it is like—that, in David Lewis's phrase, *truth should supervene on being*. This is a view that Lewis himself accepts, in the following form:

> truth is supervenient on what things there are and which perfectly natural properties they instantiate.[264]

Since the properties things instantiate are themselves in a broad sense "things," the view is really that

> truth is supervenient on what things there are and their interactions, e.g., which instantiate which.

Although Lewis maintains this about truth quite generally, it is more

---

[264](Lewis 1992).

common to find it maintained of truth in a specific area of discourse; the usual claim in other words is that truth supervenes on being not *globally* but only *locally*.

For instance, it is very often said that what is wrong, or at least different, about aesthetic or moral discourse is that there are no moral/aesthetic *properties* out there to settle the truth-value of evaluative utterances. And more generally it is common to hear antirealism about *F*-discourse identified with the thesis that there is no such property as *F*-ness.[265]

But this linking of antirealism about *F*-discourse with the lack of an associated property is only one symptom of a broader tendency of thought. When truth in an area of discourse is controlled by the existence and behavior of objects, that is felt to *boost the discourse's credentials* as fact-stating or objective. The more truth can be pinned to the way a bunch of objects comport themselves, the more *objective* the discourse appears.

"Objective" in what sense? A tradition launched by Dummett says that a discourse is objective if, where S is a statement of the relevant kind, nothing more is needed to settle S's truth value than for its meaning to be made sufficiently clear and precise. IN PARTICULAR: it doesn't matter whether speakers of the language do or would accept that S. Leaving aside the case where the discourse is *about* our opinions, and leaving aside the role our opinions may play in fixing meaning, the line between truth and falsity in the area is entirely independent of what we think.

The pattern here is a familiar one. Talk about possibility feels more objective if its truth-value is controlled by which possible worlds exist. Talk about what happened yesterday, or what will happen tomorrow, feels more objective if its truth-value is controlled by a still somehow lingering past, or a future out there lying in wait for us.[266] And to return to our original example, talk about validity feels more objective if its truth-value is controlled by the existence or not of countermodels.

Why should objects appear to contribute to objectivity in this way? A little more grandiosely, why should *realism*—which holds that a given area of discourse is objective—seem to be bolstered by *platonism*—which points to a special ensemble of objects as determining the distribution of truth values? I am sure I don't entirely know, but here is a sketch of an outline of a hunch.

Realism says that once you get S's meaning sufficiently clear, its truth value is settled. The question is, settled by what? As long as this

---

[265]This is a particular theme of Paul Boghossian's paper "Status of Content," (Boghossian 1990).

[266]Cf. McDowell on yesterday's rainstorm.

question is left hanging, there's room for the anti-realist suspicion that we who employ S are exercising an unwholesome influence.

How is the question to be closed? Well, we've got to point to *another* part of reality that *monopolizes* the influence on truth-value, leaving no way that we by our attitudinalizing about S could be playing a role.

This is where platonism comes in. The existence of objects, especially external objects, is the paradigm of an issue that's *out of our hands*. And much of the character of these objects—certainly the intrinsic character, but also a good deal of the relational character—is out of our hands as well. Either worlds with flying pigs are there, or they're not. Either tomorrow's sea battle awaits us, or it doesn't. Either the countermodels exist, or they don't.

13.9   A dilemma

So—there is this strategy, or tendency of thought, or whatever you want to call it, that links *realism* in an area of discourse to *platonism*: belief in a special range of objects whose existence and behavior settles the question of truth. And this strategy in turn helps to explain why people want to be platonists. For certainly *one* large attraction of platonism—of the idea that truth depends in a certain area of discourse on being—is the way it bolsters or appears to bolster the realistic credentials of that area of discourse.

What are we to make of the platonizing strategy? I guess the main thing I want to say is that I find it highly *suspicious*. The added confidence that the objects are supposed to give us about the objectivity of the discourse strikes me as unearned, or unneeded, or both. Suppose we go back to the example of (V) and (V*). Our claim above was that the right hand side of (V), for instance,

(a) "$\forall x \exists y F x y$, so $\exists x \forall y F x y$" has a countermodel,

is typically used as though it meant:

(a*) *assuming models,* "$\forall x \exists y F x y$, so $\exists x \forall y F x y$" has a countermodel.

Clearly (a)'s truth value so understood is independent of the truth value of (b) *there are models*. But it's just here that the ontologist is going to protest:

> You may be right that the truth value of *particular* claims of form (a) is independent of (b) *there are models*. What you need (b) for is the objectivity of the *form of speech* of which (a) and (a*) are examples. If there really are models, then there's an *objective fact of the matter* about which arguments have countermodels. Take the models away, and all you've

got left is the human practice of developing and swapping around model-descriptions. And this practice, not to say it isn't highly disciplined, doesn't provide as objective a basis for validity-talk as a bona fide mathematical space of models would.

I can't say this is without appeal; the models *do* feel like they provide us with assurances of objectivity. And yet how exactly are the assurances supposed to work? The worry can be put in the form of a dilemma. In logic we speak of "the space of models," the space that allegedly functions via (V) to make discourse about validity especially objective. Do we have a determinate grasp of this space or not? By a determinate grasp, I mean

> a grasp sufficient to determine a definite truth value for each instance of "assuming models, there is a countermodel to argument A."

Does our grasp go fatally blurry, for instance, when it comes to models with very large finite cardinalities? Or is it sufficiently precise as to settle the existence of countermodels in every case?

Suppose the latter; we have a determinate grasp in the specified sense. Almost by definition, that by itself ensures that there's a determinate fact of the matter about which arguments have-countermodels-assuming-the-space-of-models.[267] So the models are unneeded; you've got your determinate truth-values without them.

Suppose next that we *lack* a determinate conception of the space of models; our grasp *fails* to determine an appropriate truth value for each instance of "assuming the space of models, there is a countermodel to argument A." How is it that we nevertheless manage to pick out the right class of mathematical objects as models?

The answer has got to be that the world meets us half way. The intended objects somehow jump out and announce themselves, saying: over here, *we're* the ones you must have had in mind. A particularly attractive form of this is as follows: look, we're the only remotely plausible candidates for the job that even *exist*. This amounts to saying that we understand the space of models as whatever out there best corresponds to our otherwise indeterminate intentions.

But such a response reintroduces the hostage-to-fortune problem. An argument's validity-status would seem to be a conceptually necessary fact about it. Surely we don't want the validity of arguments to

---

[267]Contrast the population principle: region R is populated iff there are people in it. Here a determinate conception of people isn't itself enough to make for an objective fact of the matter about which regions are populated.

be held hostage to a brute logical contingency like what model-like entities happen to exist! (This feeling of not wanting brute ontological facts to influence validity is part of what lies behind John Etchemendy's rejection of Tarski's principle in *The Concept of Logical Consequence* (Etchemendy 1990).)

So Tarski's principle (considered now as objectivity-bolstering) is faced with a dilemma. If we are clear enough about what we *mean* by it, then (V) isn't *needed* for objectivity; you can use (V*). And if we *aren't* clear what we mean, then (V) isn't going to *help*. It isn't even going to be tolerable because an argument's status as valid is going to blow with the ontological winds in a way that no one could possibly want.

13.10 Crime of the century?

It begins to look like the objectivity motive for platonism does not really work. The objects would only be needed if they "stiffened the discourse's spine"—if they had consequences for truth-values over and above anything predictable from our *conception* of the objects. But by that fact alone, we wouldn't trust them to deliver the right results.

The reason this matters is that as far as I can see, the objectivity motive is the *only* one that argues for a truth-link with actual objects. The other principal motives for accepting platonic objects are served just as well by *pretended* or *assumed* ones.

Which suggests a wild idea. Could it be that sets, functions, properties, worlds, and the like, are one and all put-up jobs, meaning, only pretended to exist? Call this the *fabrication hypothesis*, for short the *fab hypothesis*.

How to evaluate it? Bertrand Russell once said that postulation of objects has all the advantages of theft over honest toil. This might seem to apply to the fab hypothesis as well. The suggestion in a way is that an enormous intellectual *crime* has been committed; an entire species of much-beloved and frequently deferred-to objects has been stolen away, leaving behind only persistent appearances.

Suppose we discuss the alleged theft of the platonic objects the way we would any other alleged crime. Means, motive, opportunity—are all these elements present?

The question of means is: how would a job like this be pulled off, where objects appear to be in play but really aren't? The question of motive is: why would anyone *want* to fabricate these objects in the first place? The question of opportunity is: how could a job this big be pulled off without anyone noticing?

13.11 Means

How might it happen that, of the things that regularly crop up in people's *apparently* descriptive utterances, not all really exist, or are even *assumed* by the speaker to exist?

Before we can get anywhere with this question, we have to notice something about the current philosophical climate. A certain effortless indignation about people who "refuse to own up to the commitments of their own speech" has become the rule in philosophy. The attitude goes back at least to *Word & Object*, where Quine misses no opportunity to deplore the "philosophical double talk, which would repudiate an ontology while simultaneously enjoying its benefits" (242).

But rhetoric aside, the phenomenon of people putting statements forward that don't, as literally understood, convey their meaning is extraordinarily familiar and common. The usual word for it is "indirect speech." I utter the words "would you mind getting off my foot?" not to express curiosity about your preferences, but to make a request. I say "this might be a good place to spend the night" not to offer a conjecture but offer a suggestion. I say "that's not such a great idea" not to call your idea less-than-great—leaving it open, as it were, that it might be *very good*—but to call your idea bad.

This last example, of calling an idea not so great meaning that it is quite bad, reminds us that one kind of indirect speech is *figurative* speech. The figure in this case is *understatement*, but the point could equally have been made with, say, *hyperbole* ("they are inseparable"), *metonymy* ("the White House said today that..."), or *metaphor* ("I lost my head"). Not one of the sentences mentioned has a true literal content: the first because it exaggerates, the second because it conflates, the third or reasons still to be explored. But it would be insane to associate the speaker with these failings, because the sentences' literal content (if any) is not what the speaker is putting forward.

The most important example for us is metaphor; but what exactly is that? I am sure I don't know, but the most promising account I have seen is Ken Walton's in terms of prop oriented make-believe:

> Where in Italy is the town of Crotone? I ask. You explain that it is on the arch of the Italian boot. "See that thundercloud over there—the big, angry face near the horizon," you say; "it is headed this way." ... We speak of the saddle of a mountain and the shoulder of a highway....All of these cases are linked to make-believe. We think of Italy and the thundercloud as something like pictures. Italy ... depicts a boot. The cloud is a prop which makes it fictional that there is an angry face...

> The saddle of a mountain is, fictionally, a horse's saddle. But ... it is not for the sake of games of make-believe that we regard these things as props...[The make-believe] is useful for articulating, remembering, and communicating facts about the props—about the geography of Italy, or the identity of the storm cloud...or mountain topography. It is by thinking of Italy or the thundercloud...as potential if not actual props that I understand where Crotone is, which cloud is the one being talked about.[268]

A metaphor on this view is an utterance that represents its objects as being *like so*: the way that they would need to be to make the utterance the right kind of thing to be pretended-true in a game that it itself suggests. Pretendability here is a function of (i) the game's rules and (ii) the way of the world; the point of uttering the metaphor is to say that *the world has held up its end of the bargain.*

Now, normally when people talk about metaphor, the examples that come to mind are of metaphorical *descriptions* of everyday objects; thus a hat is *divine*, or a person is *green with envy*, or *beside herself with excitement*. These standard examples are misleading, or at least limiting, in at least one crucial respect.

Predicative expressions are far from the only ones we use metaphorically. Adverbs, conjunctions, prepositions, and (the case that is most important to us) *referring* expressions—names, definite descriptions, quantifiers—are candidates for this sort of usage too. An appendix to the *Metaphors Dictionary* (Sommer and Weiss 1996) lists 450 examples of what it calls "common metaphors." Approximately *one-half* contain referential elements. Some examples drawn just from the beginning of the list:

> he fell into an *abyss* of despair, *the apple* doesn't fall far from the tree, he is tied to her *apron strings* , she has *an axe* to grind, let's put that on *the back burner,* those figures are in *the ballpark,* you're beating *a dead horse,* he's bit off *more than he can chew,* don't hide *your lamp* under *a bushel* , let's go by *the book,* don't blow *a fuse,* I have *a bone* to pick with you, I've burned *my bridges,* I hate to burst *your bubble,* you hit *the bullseye,* I have *butterflies* in my stomach, I'm going to lay *my cards* on the table, you're building *castles in the air,* we will be under *a cloud* until we settle *this thing,* he claimed his *pound of flesh,* she blew *her cool,* he threw me *a curve,* their work is on *the cutting edge.*

---

[268](Walton 1993), pp. 40–1.

Some additional examples of my own; with some of them you have to rub your eyes and blink twice before its non-literal character comes through:

> they put *a lot of hurdles* in your path, there's *a lot* that could be said about that, there's *no precedent* for that, *something* tells me you're right, *there are some things* better left unsaid, *there is something* I forgot to tell you, viz. how to operate the lock, *nothing* gets my goat as much as chewing gum in class, *a lot* you can do for me, judge then of *my surprise*, let's roll out *the red carpet*, *the last thing I want* is to..., they have been rising in *my esteem*, I took her into *my confidence*, I'll take *my chances*, *a growing number* of these leaks can be traced to your office, they've got *a lot of smarts* , let's pull out *all the stops*; let's proceed along *the lines suggested above.*

Now, the very *last* thing I want to do with these examples is to start a bidding war over who can best accommodate our classificatory intuitions. The one unbreakable rule in the world of metaphor is that there is little to no consensus on how big that world is: on what should be counted a metaphor and what should not. What I do want to suggest is that the same semantical mechanisms that underlie *paradigmatic* metaphors like "your perfume is divine" seem also to be at work with phrases that for whatever reason—too familiar, insufficiently picturesque, too *boring* —strike us as hardly figurative at all. If that is right, then it does little harm I think to *stipulate* that any phrases which turn a shallow and short-lived pretend-commitment to descriptive advantage along the lines suggested above are to be seen as just as much metaphorical as the old campaigners.

This brings me to the main claim of this section. The means by which platonic objects are simulated is *existential metaphor*—that is, metaphor making play with a special sort of object to which the speaker is not committed (not by the metaphorical utterance, anyway) and to which she adverts only for the light it sheds on other matters. Rather as "smarts" are conjured up as a metaphorical carrier of intelligence, "numbers" are conjured up as metaphorical measures of cardinality. More on this below; first there are the questions of motive and opportunity to deal with.

13.12 Motive

What is the *motive* for simulating platonic objects in this way? The motive is that lots of metaphors, and in particular lots of existential metaphors, are *essential.* They have no literal paraphrases; or, perhaps, none with equally happy cognitive and/or motivational effects.

To elaborate a little on the picture so far, a metaphor has in addition to its literal content—given by the conditions under which it is true and to that extent belief-worthy—a metaphorical content given by the conditions under which it is "fictional" or pretense-worthy in the relevant game. If we help ourselves to the (itself maybe metaphorical)[269] device of possible worlds, we can put it like so:

$\underline{S}$'s literal/metaphorical content = the set of worlds that, considered as actual, make $\underline{S}$ true/fictional.

The role of pretend games on this approach is to warp the usual lines of semantic projection, so as to reshape the region a sentence defines in logical space:[270]

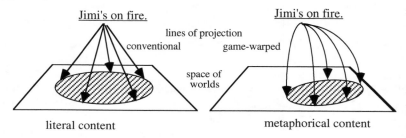

literal content   metaphorical content

The straight lines on the left are projected by the ordinary, conventional meaning of "Jimi's on fire;" they pick out the worlds which make "Jimi's on fire" true. The bent lines on the right show what happens when worlds are selected according to whether they make the very same sentence, meaning the very same thing, fictional or pretense-worthy.

The question of motive can be phrased like this: granted these metaphorical contents—these ensembles of worlds picked out by their shared property of legitimating a certain pretense—what is the reason for accessing them metaphorically?

One obvious reason would be *lack of an alternative*: the language might have no more to offer in the way of a unifying principle for the worlds in a given content than that *they* are the ones making the relevant sentence fictional. It seems at least an open question, for example, whether the clouds we call *angry* are the ones that are literally F, for

---

[269](Yablo 1996).

[270]A lot of metaphors are, literally understood, impossible: "I am a rock." Assuming we want a non-degenerate region on the left, the space of worlds should take in all "ways for things to be," not just the "ways things could have been." The distinction is from (Salmon 1989).

any *F* other than "such that it would be natural and proper to regard them as angry if one were going to attribute emotions to clouds." Nor does a literal criterion immediately suggest itself for the pieces of computer code called *viruses*, the markings on a page called *tangled* or *loopy*, the glances called *piercing*, or the topographical features called *basins*, *funnels*, and *brows*.

The topic being ontology, though, let's try to illustrate with an *existential* metaphor. An example much beloved of philosophers is *the average so-and-so*.[271] When someone says that

(S) The average star has 2.4 planets,

she is not entirely serious; she is pretending to describe an (extraordinary) entity called "the average star" as a way of really talking about what the (ordinary) stars are like on average. True, this *particular* metaphor can be paraphrased away, as follows:

(T) The number of planets divided by the number of stars is 2.4.

But the numbers in T are from an intuitive perspective just as remote from the cosmologist's intended subject matter as the average star in S. And this ought to make us, or the more nominalistic among us, suspicious. Wasn't it Quine who stressed the possibility of unacknowledged myth-making in even the most familiar constructions? The nominalist therefore proposes that *T* is metaphorical too; it provides us with access to a content more literally expressed by

(U) There are 12 planets and 5 stars or 24 planets and 10 stars or...[272]

And now here is the rub. The rules of English do not allow infinitely long sentences; so the most literal route of access *in English* to the desired content is T, and T according to the nominalist is a metaphor. It is only by making *as if* to countenance numbers that one can give expression in English to a fact having nothing to do with numbers, a fact about stars and planets and how they are numerically proportioned.[273]

---

[271]I am indebted to Melia (Melia 1995). Following the example of Quine, I will be using "metaphor" in a very broad sense; the term will cover anything exploiting the same basic semantic mechanisms as standard "Juliet is the sun"-type metaphors, no matter how banal and unpoetic.

[272]Why not a primitive "2.4-times-as-many" predicate? Because 2.4 is not the only ratio in which quantities can stand; "we will never find the time to learn all the infinitely many [q-times-as-many] predicates," with q a schematic letter taking rational substituents, much less the r-times-as-long predicates, with r ranging schematically over the reals ((Melia 1995). p. 228). A fundamental attraction of existential metaphor is its promise of ontology-free semantic productivity. How real the promise is—how much metaphor can do to get us off the ontology/ideology treadmill—strikes me as wide open and very much in need of discussion.

[273]Compare Quine on states of affairs: "the particular range of possible physiological

Whether you buy the example or not, it gives a good indication of what it would be like for a metaphor to be "representationally essential," that is, unparaphrasable at the level of content; we begin to see how the description a speaker wants to offer of his *intended* objects might be inexpressible until *unintended* objects are dragged in as representational aids.

Hooking us up to the right propositional contents, however, is only one of the services that metaphor has to offer. There is also the fact that a metaphor (with any degree of life at all) "makes us see one thing as another;" it "organizes our view" of its subject matter; it lends a special "perspective" and makes for "framing-effects." [274] Here is Dick Moran:

> To call someone a tail-wagging lapdog of privilege is not simply to make an assertion of his enthusiastic submissiveness. Even a pat metaphor deserves better than this, and [the] analysis is not essentially improved by tacking on a...list of further dog-predicates that may possibly be part of the metaphor's meaning...the comprehension of the metaphor involves *seeing* this person as a lapdog, and...experiencing his doggyness.[275]

The point here is not specially about seeing-as, though, and it is not only conventionally "picturesque" metaphors that pack a cognitive punch no literal paraphrase can match. This is clear already from scientific metaphors like *feedback loop, underground economy,* and *unit of selection.* But let me illustrate with a continuation of the example started above.

Suppose that I am wrong and "the average star has 2.4 planets" is representationally accidental; the infinite disjunction "there are five stars and twelve planets etc." turns out to be perfect English. The formulation in terms of the average star is still on the whole hugely to be preferred—

---

states, each of which would count as a case of [the cat] wanting to get on that particular roof, is a gerry-mandered range of states that could surely not be encapsulated in any manageable anatomical description even if we knew all about cats... Relations to states of affairs,...such as wanting and fearing, afford some very special and seemingly indispensable ways of grouping events in the natural world" (Quine 1966), p. 147. Quine sees here an argument for counting states of affairs into his ontology. But the passage reads better as an argument that the metaphor of states of affairs allows us access to theoretically important contents unapproachable in any other way. See also Lewis on counterfactuals: "It's the character of our world that makes the counterfactual true—in which case why bring the other worlds into the story at all? .....it is only by bringing the other worlds into the story that we can say in any concise what character it takes to make the counterfactual true" (Lewis 1986), p. 22.

[274] (Davidson 1984); Max Black in (Ortony 1993); (Moran 1989), p. 108.
[275] (Moran 1989), p. 90.

for its easier visualizability, yes, but also its greater suggestiveness ("that makes me wonder how many moons the average planet has"), the way it lends itself to comparison with other data ("the average planet has six times as many moons as the average star has planets"), and so on.[276]

A second example has to do with the still influential program of "first-orderizing" entailment relations.[277] Davidson in "The Logical Form of Action Sentences" (Davidson 1967) says that a key reason for rendering "S f'd Gly" as "there was a f'd Gly" to "S f'd" now becomes quantificationally valid. Of course, similar claims are often made on behalf of the possible worlds account of modality; unless you want the inference from "possibly S" to "possibly S-or-T" to be primitive and unanalyzable, you'd better understand "possibly S" as "there is a world making S true." Or consider Bealer on propositions; how without quantifying over them can you hope to first-orderize the inference from "I believe whatever the pope believes" and "the pope believes abortion is wrong" to "I believe abortion is wrong"?

The claim these authors make is not that the relevant contents are *inexpressible* without quantifying over events, or worlds, or what have you; that would be untrue, since the contents can clearly be expressed via sentences like "she did it skillfully" and "possibly BLAH." The claim is that the logical *relations* among these contents become much more tractable if we represent them quantificationally. So represented the contents wear their logical potential on their sleeve, at least from the perspective of a first-order-savvy audience like the community of professional philosophers.[278]

Back to the main thread: Along with its representational content, we need to consider a metaphor's "presentational force." Just as it can make all the difference in the world whether I grasp a proposition under the heading "*my* pants are on fire," grasping it as the retroimage of "Crotone is in the arch of the boot" or "the average star has 2.4 planets" or "there is a world with blue swans" can be psychologically important

---

[276] Similarly with Quine's cat example: the gerrymandered anatomical description even if available could never do the cognitive work of "What Tabby wants is that she gets onto the roof."

[277] See (Davidson and Harman 1975). The underlying motivation had to do less with entailment than constructing axiomatic truth theories for natural language.

[278] A question rarely addressed is why this presentational advantage should seem to argue for the truth of the quantificational rendering, as opposed to just its naturalness and helpfulness vis-a-vis audiences like ourselves. Is it that the naturalness and helpfulness would be a miracle if there were nothing out there to answer to the platonic quantifiers? I would like to see an argument for this. I suspect that there are very few putative object-types, however otherwise disreputable, that couldn't be "legitimated" by such a maneuver.

too. To think of Crotone's location as the place it would *need* to be to put it in the arch of Italy imagined as a boot, or of the stars and planets as proportioned the way they would need to be for the average star to come out with 2.4 planets, is to be affected in ways going well beyond the proposition expressed. That some of these ways are cognitively advantageous gives us a further reason for accessing contents metaphorically.

13.13 Opportunity

Now for the question of opportunity. How are these metaphors slipped in without anyone's noticing?

The first thing that has to be said is that figurative elements in our speech are very *often* unconscious, and resistant to being brought to consciousness. To hear "that wasn't very smart" (understatement) or "a fine friend she turned out to be" (irony) or "spring is just around the corner" (metaphor) as meaning what they literally say takes a surprising amount of effort—an effort that bears comparison to trying to make out the the intrinsic color of the paint in some section of an impressionist painting.

As the painting analogy perhaps suggests, a too-vivid appreciation of literal meaning can even *interfere* with the attempted figure. Wittgenstein tells of an art-lover pointing to the bloodshot eyes in a Rembrandt painting and saying *"that's* the color I want for my curtains." Such a person is not—not at that moment, anyway—in tune with the painting's representational ambitions. Just so, overzealous attention to what a "gutsy idea" would be like, or what it would really be to "keep your eyes peeled," or "pour your heart out" to your beloved, prevents any real appreciation of the intended message.

If you're with me this far, consider now statements like "there's something Jones is that Smith isn't: happy" or "another way to get there is via Tegucigalpa?" Taken at face value, these sentences do indeed commit themselves to entities called "happy" and "via Tegucigalpa." But overmuch attention to the fact is likelier to distract from the speaker's intended meaning than to illuminate it; what on earth could *via Tegucigalpa* be? Likewise someone who says that "the number of registered Democrats is on the rise" wants the focus to be on the Democrats, not "their number," whatever that might be. Their number is called in just to provide a measure of the Democrats' changing cardinality; it's expected to perform that service in the most inconspicuous way and then hustle itself off the stage before people start asking the inevitable awkward questions, e.g., which number is it? 50 million? is 50 million really on the rise?

A second reason for the unobtrusiveness of existential metaphors takes longer to explain. Earlier we distinguished two qualities for which a metaphor might be valued: its representational content, and its presentational force. But that can't be the whole story. A metaphor with only its content to recommend it probably deserves to be considered dead; thus perhaps "my watch has a broken hand." A metaphor (like the Crotone example) valued in addition for its presentational force is alive, maybe, but it is not yet all that a metaphor can be. This is because we are still conceiving of the speaker as someone with a definite *message* to get across. And the insistence on a message settled in advance is apt to seem heavy-handed. "The central error about metaphor," says Davidson, is to suppose that

> associated with [each] metaphor is a cognitive content that its author wishes to convey and that the interpreter must grasp if he is to get the message. This theory is false... It should make us suspect the theory that it is so hard to decide, even in the case of the simplest metaphors, exactly what the content is supposed to be.[279]

Whether or not all metaphors are like this, one can certainly agree that a lot are: perhaps because, as Davidson says, their "interpretation reflects as much on the interpreter as on the originator;"[280] perhaps because their interpretation reflects ongoing real-world developments that neither party feels in a position to prejudge. A slight elaboration of the make-believe story brings this third grade of metaphorical involvement under the same conceptual umbrella as the other two:

> Someone who utters S in a metaphorical vein is recommending the project of (i) looking for games in which S is a promising move, and (ii) accepting the propositions that are S's inverse images in those games under the modes of presentation that they provide.

The overriding imperative here is to *make the most of it*;[281] construe a metaphorical utterance in terms of the game or games that retromap it onto the most plausible and instructive contents in the most satisfying ways.

Now, should it happen that the speaker has definite ideas about the best game to be playing with S, I myself see no objection to saying that she intended to convey a certain metaphorical message—the first

---

[279] (Davidson 1984), p. 44.

[280] (Davidson 1984), p. 29. Davidson would have no use for even the unsettled sort of metaphorical content about to be proposed.

[281] David Hills's phrase, and idea.

grade of metaphorical involvement—perhaps under a certain metaphorical mode of presentation—the second grade.[282]

The reason for the third grade of metaphorical involvement is that one can imagine various other cases, in which the speaker's sense of the potential metaphorical *truthfulness* of a form of words outruns her sense of the particular truth(s) being expressed. These include the case of the *pregnant* metaphor, which yields up indefinite numbers of contents on continued interrogation;[283] the *prophetic* metaphor, which expresses a single content whose identity, however, takes time to emerge;[284] and, importantly for us, the *patient* metaphor, which hovers indefinitely above competing interpretations, as though waiting to be told where its advantage really lies.

The interesting thing is that is that it is this third grade of metaphorical involvement, supposedly at the furthest remove from the literal, that can be hardest to tell apart the literal. The reason is that *one* of the contents that my utterance may be up for, when I launch S into the world in the make-the-most-of-it spirit described above, is its literal content. I want to be understood as meaning what I literally say if my statement is literally true—count me a player of the "null game," if you like—and meaning whatever my statement projects onto via the right sort of "non-null" game if my statement is literally false. It is thus indeterminate from my point of view whether I am advancing S's literal content or not. [285]

Isn't this in fact our common condition? When people say that there are more ways of getting to Houston than to Gatlinburg, that the number of As = the number of Bs, that they have tingles in their legs, or that Nixon had a stunted superego, they are far more certain that S is getting

---

[282]This of course marks a difference with Davidson.

[283]Thus, each in its own way, "Juliet is the sun," "Eternity is a spider in a Russian bathhouse," and "The state is an organism."

[284]Examples: An apparition assures Macbeth that "none of woman born" shall harm him; the phrase's meaning hangs in the air until Macduff, explaining that he was "from his mother's womb untimely ripped," plunges in the knife. Martin Luther King Jr. told his followers that "The arc of the moral universe is long, but it bends toward justice"; recent work by Josh Cohen shows how specific a content can be attached to these words, see Cohen (Cohen 1997). A growing technical literature on verisimilitude testifies to the belief that "close to the truth" admits of a best interpretation.

[285]Indeterminacy is also possible about whether I am advancing a content at all, as opposed to articulating the rules of some game relative to which contents are figured, ie., doing some gameskeeping. An example suggested by David Hills is "there are continuum many spatiotemporal positions," uttered by one undecided as between the substantival and relational theories of spacetime. One might speak here of a fifth grade of metaphorical involvement, which—much as the third grade leaves it open what content is being expressed—takes no definite stand on whether the utterance has a content.

at *something* right than that the thing it is getting at is the proposition that *S*, as some literalist might construe it. If numbers exist, then yes, we are content to regard ourselves as having spoken literally. If not, then the claim was that the *A*s and *B*s are equinumerous. [286]

All right, but what does this have to do with the inconspicuousness of platonic metaphors? The fact that I *could* for all anyone knows—for all that I myself know—be speaking literally goes some way towards explaining why these metaphors do not attract attention to themselves. If a literal interpretation is always and forever in the offing, and if no real harm can come of adopting it for argument's sake, then the fact that a metaphorical interpretation is *similarly* always and forever possible is liable to escape our notice. As far as I can see, the main way these metaphors reveal themselves to us is through our—otherwise very peculiar!—insouciance about the existence or not of their apparent objects. The next section offers some additional clues.

13.14 Suggestive similarities

The bulk of this paper has been an argument that it is less absurd than may initially seem that references to platonic objects in everyday speech are not to be taken literally. If someone suspects that the objects are not really there—that, to revert to the crime analogy, they have been "stolen away"—it seems like means, motive, and opportunity for the alleged caper are not all that hard to make out.

Of course, it is one thing to argue that a metaphorical construal is not out of the question, another to provide evidence that such a construal would in fact be correct. That's what I want to do now, by listing a series of *similarities* between platonic objects, on the one hand, and creatures of metaphorical make-believe, on the other, that strike me as being at the very least suggestive. Some of these similarities will just restate in other terms material that was presented earlier, some of them will be new. I want to stress that none of these similarities is anything like decisive, and that not all the features mentioned are common to all POs—platonic objects—or to all MBs—creatures of metaphorical make-believe. But the cumulative effect is I think nothing to sneeze at.

---

[286] "When it was reported that Hemingway's plane had been sighted, wrecked, in Africa, the New York Mirror ran a headline saying, 'Hemingway Lost in Africa,' the word 'lost' being used to suggest he was dead. When it turned out he was alive, the Mirror left the headline to be taken literally" (Davidson 1984). I suspect that something like this happens more often than we suppose, with the difference that there is no conscious equivocation and that it is the metaphorical content that we fall back on.

Paraphrasability

MBs are often paraphrasable away with no felt loss of subject matter, e.g., "that was her first encounter with the green-eyed monster" goes to "that was her first time feeling envious."

POs are often paraphrasable away with no felt loss of subject matter, e.g., "there is a possible world at which S" goes to "it is possible that S."

Impatience

One is unmoved, even impatient, when someone suggests we should get worried about the fact that an MB may not really exist. "I wasn't thinking there was *really* a green-eyed monster."

One is unmoved, even impatient, when someone suggests that a PO or type of PO may not really exist. "So what if the models peter out above such and such a cardinality?"

Translucency

About the best one can do with "What if there is no green-eyed monster?" is to hear it as the (bizarre) suggestion that no one is ever really envious.

About the best one can do with "what if there are no God-worlds?" is to hear it as the suggestion that God is not really possible.

Insubstantiality

Unlike ordinary objects, MBs tend to have not much more to them than what flows from our conception of them. The green-eyed monster has no "hidden substantial nature"; neither do the real-estate bug, the blue meanies, the chip on my shoulder, etc.

Unlike ordinary objects, POs often have not much more to them than what flows from our conception of them. All the really important facts about the numbers follow from (2nd order) Peano's Axioms. Likewise mutatis mutandis for sets, functions, etc.

Indeterminacy

Unlike ordinary objects, MBs can be "indeterminately identical." There is no fact of the matter as to the identity relations between the fuse I blew last week and the one I blew today, or my keister and my wazoo ("I've had it up to the keister/wazoo with this paperwork"). The relevant game(s) leave it undecided what is to count as identical to what.

Unlike ordinary objects, POs can be "indeterminately identical." There is no fact of the matter as to the identity relations between the natural numbers and the Zermelo numbers, or the possible worlds and the maximal consistent sets of propositions, or the events and the property-instantiations. It is left (partly) undecided what is to count as identical to what.

Silliness

MBs invite "silly questions" probing areas the make-believe does not address, e.g., we know how big the average star is, where is it located? you say I have risen in your esteem, by how many inches? do you plan to *drop*-forge the conscience of your race in the smithy of your soul?

POs invite questions that seem similarly silly. [287] What are the intrinsic properties of the empty set? Is the event of the water's boiling itself hot? Are universals wholly present in each of their instances? Do relations lead a divided existence, parcelled out among their relata?

Expressiveness

MBs show a heartening tendency to boost the language's power to express facts about other, more ordinary, entities. "The average taxpayer saves an increasing fraction of his income."

POs show a strong tendency to boost the language's power to express facts about other, more ordinary, entities. "This line here is p times as long as that line there."

Irrelevance

MBs are called on to "explain" phenomena that would not on reflection suffer by their absence. Even if the average taxpayer had not existed, the savings rate would still have increased.

POs are called on to "explain" phenomena that would not on reflection suffer by their absence. If all the one-one functions were killed off today, there would still be as many left shoes in my closet as right.

Disconnectedness

MBs have a tendency not to do much *other* than expressive work. As a result, perhaps, of not really existing, they tend not to push things around.	POs have a tendency not to do much *other* than expressive work; numbers et al. are famous for their causal inertness. [288]

Availability

MBs' lack of naturalistic connections might seem to threaten epistemic access—until we remember that "their properties" are projected rather than detected.	POs' lack of naturalistic connections are widely thought to threaten epistemic access—the threat evaporates if "their properties" are projected, not detected.

Of course we should not forget one final piece of evidence for the make-believe nature of platonic objects. This is the fact that *a metaphorical interpretation of POs solves our original paradox.* (And I'm not aware that it has any serious competition here.) Our reluctance to infer the existence of models from the Tarski biconditionals is just what you'd expect if the inference goes through only on a literal interpretation, and the biconditional is not in the end taken literally.

13.15   Concluding unscientistic postscript

If the a priori approach to ontological questions is undermined by doubts about literality, then Quinean indispensability arguments might seem to be the only game left in town. But it seems to me that Quine's ontological program is in a related sort of trouble.[289]

The Quinean says that we should believe in Xs just to the extent that we find it hard to avoid quantifying over them in our scientific theories. That would be fine if the quantifiers were all to be taken literally. But some quantifiers are metaphorical. That would be fine too if the metaphorical quantifiers could be counted on to disappear as theory progressed. But some metaphors are essential and so presumably permanent.

Not even Quine thinks that figurative quantification is ontologically committal; why should I should take ontological advice from a theory whose literal content I do not even believe? A consistent Quinean should therefore want us to ferret out all traces of non-literality in our theories before we turn to them for ontological guidance. To the extent that

---

[289](Yablo 1998) has details.

there is no sensible project of doing *that*, there is no sensible project of Quinean ontology. All I will say here is that I fear the worst.

Appendix A: Paraphrase

A priori-looking bridge principles of the kind discussed in this paper have frequently appeared in philosophy with their left and right hand sides reversed. That is, instead of

it is possible that B iff there is a B-world,

there are as many Cs as Ds iff the number of Cs = the number of Ds,

x is H iff x has the property of Hness,

we are told that

there is a B-world iff it is possible that B,

the number of Cs = the number of Ds iff there are as many Cs as Ds

x has the property of Hness iff x is H.

Written this second way, the biconditionals present themselves as devices for shrugging off the ontological commitments apparently incurred by their left hand sides.[290] Whenever you are tempted to say that the number of Fs is the number of Gs, you should say instead that the Fs are equinumerous with the Gs. And so on. (Or, treat the rewritten biconditionals' left hand sides as possibly misleading shorthands for what is properly expressed in the less ontologically committal terms indicated on the right.)

Now, it should be clear that any platonic object worth its salt cannot be shrugged off quite so easily; see section XII above and the next Appendix.

But even ignoring that, the "paraphrase" gambit presents a real puzzle—first noted by William Alston in "Ontological Reduction," and much emphasized by Crispin Wright in his book on numbers.[291]

The notion of paraphrase is torn between two incompatible-looking aspirations. On the one hand there's an aspiration to symmetry: paraphrases are supposed to *match* their originals along some important semantic dimension. On the other hand there's an aspiration to asymmetry: paraphrases are supposed to *fix* their originals by shedding unwanted ontological commitments.

---

[290] For a sense of why "P iff Q" should have a different use than "Q iff P," see Jackson on "if" and "only if" in his (Jackson 1979).

[291] (Alston 1958); (Wright 1983), pp. 31ff.

The difficulty of course is to see how can you have the matching and the fixing *together*. It is not easy to think of a dimension or aspect of meaning such that sentences can mean the same along that dimension despite the fact that they assert the existence of different things.

Quine's solution in *Word & Object* is to sacrifice matching to fixing. He says that he expects nothing like synonymy from a paraphrase but just a sentence that "serves any purposes of [the original] that seem worth serving."[292] This is technically unanswerable, but ignores our feeling in many cases that the paraphrase "says the same" as what it paraphrases, or the same as what we were trying to say by its means.

Alston and Wright go the opposite way, sacrificing fixing to matching. Contrary to what we naturally suppose, they say, "there are as many Cs as Ds" carries the same commitment to numbers evident in "the number of Cs = the number of Ds." But then why did the paraphrase seem so ontologically liberating? Was it pure confusion to think that "I have as many left hands as right" was compatible with "there are no abstract objects"?

What we would like, of course, is matching and fixing together. There is a clue as to how this might be arranged in the word "paraphrase" itself. Is it just a coincidence that the word is encountered more often in poetry class than anywhere else? I suggest not, and that the poetry-class notion gives us all we need. The poetry-class notion (crudified, but not in a way that matters) is this:

(#) P_S is a paraphrase of S iff P_S expresses in literal terms what S expresses metaphorically.

With (#) in mind, let S be "the number of Cs is the number of Ds" and P_S be "the Cs are equinumerous with the Ds." Then we get matching in the sense that

the literal content of P_S = the metaphorical content of S,

and fixing in the sense that

the literal content of S requires numbers, that of P_S does not.

This puts aspects of the nominalist/realist debate in a different light. The nominalist who sees in S a misleading way of putting what is better expressed by P_S is quite right: there's a very real danger that S will be taken literally. The realist who sees the reference to numbers in S as more than a notational convenience is right too. Their appearance in S is crucial if we want to preserve inferential links with sentences S' (e.g., "if $m = n$, then $m + n$ is even") that are *not* so easily provided with

---

[292](Quine 1960), p. 214.

numberless paraphrases.

Appendix B: Three Degrees of Platonic Involvement

I have been emphasizing various kinds of expressive advantage afforded by existential metaphor: representational, presentational, procedural, and so on. The most important is probably the first. To put it as dramatically as I know how, if numbers did not exist, we would have to *pretend* they did in order to gain access to desired contents. Add to this that pretend numbers are just as good (representationally speaking) as real ones, and the tempting conclusion is that numbers (and other platonic objects) *don't* exist, and no great loss.

An objection may occur to you at this point. Platonic objects were defined as whatnots that turn up on the right hand sides of a priori-looking bridge biconditionals whose left hand sides made no mention of any such whatnots. The objection is: If the two sides are really equivalent, then how can the access platonic objects buy us to the *right* hand sides possibly boost the language's representational powers? Anything you might try to express with the *right* side—say, with a condition on *models*—is by definition also expressible with *left*-side language. So, how can the models be helping?

The answer to this is that it is quite right as far as it goes; the conditions figuring on the right hand sides of bridge biconditionals do *not* express contents that would be otherwise inaccessible. But that's quite all right, because that's not where the expressive novelty comes in. Once you've got the platonic objects on board, you can use them to formulate *new* conditions. And these new conditions might very well take you into uncharted representational territory.

First example: models are not valued because of the access they buy you to the content of "every model of A's premises is a model of its conclusion." That content was already available courtesy of "A's premises entail its conclusion." But consider the relation, already mentioned, that obtains between A's premises and its conclusion when all *minimal* models of the premises are models of the conclusion. [293] Relations like have been of some importance in work on the frame problem and default reasoning, and it was the the use of model-theoretic methods that made them available.

Second example: A lot of the modal claims we want to make are expressible in ordinary English using modal adverbs like "necessarily" and "possibly," without any explicit mention being made of worlds. But Davies and Humberstone have used the apparatus of possible worlds to

---

[293] A minimal model of P is one with no proper submodels that also models P.

introduce a locution "fixedly" which (one might think) was not expressible in ordinary English.[294]

Why not? Well, the "fixedly" operator falls into the class of what
Kaplan calls "monsters begat by elegance"—it is an operator on character rather than content—and the existence of such an item in English
would violate the principle that, roughly, indexicals always get widest
scope.[295] One can give a *hint* of what "fixedly" means by saying that
it's the modal counterpart to "always" interpreted so that "it's always
now" comes out true, or "wherever" interpreted so that "wherever I go,
here I am." [296] But the indicated variants of "always" and "wherever"
are themselves in violation of Kaplan's principle and so not properly
English if he is right.[297]

The moral is that we need to distinguish different contexts in which
platonic objects can turn up. One place is on the right hand side of biconditionals giving the truth-conditions of "already understood" English
sentences—and we can throw in here contexts where their appearance
is licensed by such a biconditional.

The advantages that platonic objects confer in these—call them
analytic—contexts are presentational rather than representational. A
prominent example is the so-called "first-orderization" of entailment relations already discussed. Against the background of appropriate bridge
principles, that B entails "possibly, B" can be read off the fact "there
is a B-world" follows in first order logic from "the actual world is a B-
world." Similarly, that "there are as many Cs as Ds and as many Ds as
Es" entails "there are as many Cs as Es" emerges from the first-order
truth that if $n = m$ and $m = p$ then $n = p$.[298]

As we have seen, platonic objects can also turn up in contexts where
they are representationally essential: contexts where they facilitate the
expression of contents that are not the literal contents of any English
sentence. Once you've got these contents in hand you can *introduce* sen-

---

[294](Davies and Humberstone 1980).

[295](Kaplan 1989).

[296]"It holds fixedly that S" corresponds more or less to "no matter how matters
actually stand, it's still the case that S." (There are nuances here that I'm ignoring.)
Someone might say: doesn't that paraphrase put the lie to the idea that fixedly is
not expressible in English?

[297]Many apparent counterexamples have been adduced. Kaplan himself cites
Thomason: "never put off till tomorrow what you can do today." And consider this
from a New Yorker cartoon: "of course, that was long ago now; but at the time it
felt like the present."

[298]This phenomenon was brought to prominence recently by Davidson's first-
orderizing of adverb-dropping inferences. He maintains that "she sang K-ly" entails
"she sang" because "there was a singing with her as agent which was K" first-order
entails "there was a singing with her as agent."

tences that will express them literally:

> "A is circumscriptively valid" is literally true iff—using the metaphor of models, now—minimal models of A's premises are models of its conclusion.[299]

> "fixedly B" is literally true iff—using the metaphor of worlds, now—take any world w you like, if w is actual, then B.

> "there are r times as many Cs as Ds" is literally true iff—using the metaphor of numbers—r times the number of Ds = the number of Cs.

Since platonic objects in this sort of use buy us access to new contents—the notions of circumscriptive validity and so on first make their way into the language via a condition on platonic objects—contexts of the second type will be called *creative*.

A third context for platonic objects is in sentences with respect to which they are, well, *not platonic*: Recall that "platonic" is a relational notion: Xs are platonic with respect to a discourse R iff they turn up in truth-conditions of R-sentences that are not intuitively about Xs. But there are plenty of sentences around that *are* intuitively about numbers, sets, models, and the like, e.g., "there are prime numbers over 100," "there are infinitely many sets," and "possible worlds are concrete rather than abstract." Since numbers and the rest do not figure here as part of a representational apparatus directed at other things, contexts of this third type will be called *autonomous*.

Autonomous contexts might be seen as making the strongest case for belief in POs, because here the gap in "we pretend they are there in order to better describe ?????" cannot be filled. I want to make an extremely tentative and undeveloped proposal about how to understand these contexts within the spirit of the make-believe approach.

Often the point of uttering S in a make-believe spirit is to (seriously) advance a game-induced content. At other times, though, the point is to *map out the contours of the inducing game*: e.g., to launch a game, or consolidate it, or make explicit some consequence of its rules, or extend the game by adjoining new rules, or urge the adoption of one proposed new rule rather than another, or articulate a norm implicitly guiding rule choice.[300] Examples of these activities in mathematics and elsewhere:

---

[299]This is as good a place as any to say that a more complicated definition is often given.

[300]I suspect that a "gameskeeping" story will be easier to tell with sets and numbers than events and properties; I hope so, anyway. I look to difficulties with autonomous contexts to provide a natural brake on the creeping metaphoricalism that might otherwise threaten.

Launching: [In tag] "that was no ordinary clap on the back, you're IT!!!" [In math] "why do you say that −1 lacks a square root? aren't you forgetting our old friend i?"

Consolidating: [In tag] "if the IT person tags you *anywhere* on your body, you become IT" [In math] "remember, functions are *arbitrary* assignments."

Explicitating: [In tag] "unless you find someone to tag, you're IT for as long as the game lasts" [In math] "did you realize that .999999.... is no different from 1?"

Extending: [In tag] "if the IT person tags two people at once, they're both IT until one of them tags someone else" [In math] "it's not only intervals that have something worth calling a length, Borel sets have them too."

Urging: [In tag] "there will be fewer interruptions if whoever is IT gets to pick their replacement when they leave" [In math] "let's accept the axiom of determinacy because that way every set of real numbers comes out measurable."

Articulating: [In tag] "the trouble with that rule is, it should always be common knowledge who is IT" [In math] "the trouble with determinacy is, we want to have as many sets as the iterative conception allows"[301]

This last example allows me to illustrate how the "gameskeeping" conception of mathematics might be able to cope with phenomena that a Quinean is bound to find mysterious. Maddy in her recent (Maddy 1997) notes that Quine, in keeping with his picture of mathematics as continuous the rest of "total science," is led to conclusions very at odds with the mathematical scientists he is seeking to emulate. His idea in a nutshell is that in set theory, as elsewhere in science, we should keep our ontology as small as practically possible. As a result he is prepared to

> recognize indenumerable infinites only because they are forced on me by the simplest known systematizations of more welcome matters. Magnitudes in excess of such demands, e.g., $\beth_\omega$ or inaccessible numbers, I look upon only as mathematical recreation and without ontological rights. Sets that are compatible with [Gödel's axiom of constructibility] afford a convenient cut-off...[302]

---

[301] See (Maddy 1997). The tower of sets is made maximally "wide" by replacing ZF's axiom schemata with 2nd order axioms. See (McGee 1997) for an axiom intended to make it maximally "tall."

[302] Quine (Quine 1986).

Such an approach is valued as "inactivat[ing] the more gratuitous flights of higher set theory..." The consensus among set-theorists is of course pretty much the opposite. Cardinals the size of $\beth_\omega$ are not even slightly controversial—they are guaranteed by axioms everyone accepts—and inaccessibles are considered quite innocent except by the lonely few who suspect that ZF is inconsistent; its consistency is deducible in ZF from the existence of an inaccessible. As for Gödel's axiom of constructibility, it has been widely criticized—including by Gödel himself—as much too restrictive. Set-theorists have wanted not only to *avoid* restrictive axioms like constructibility, but to run as far as possible in the other direction, countenancing as fully packed a set-theoretic universe as basic permit.

If Quine's conception of set theory as something like abstract physics cannot make sense of the field's plenitudinarian tendencies, can any other conception do better? Well, clearly one is not going to be worried about multiplying entities if the entities are not assumed to really exist. But we can say more. The likeliest approach if the set-theoretic universe is make-believe would be (A) to articulate the clearest intuitive conception possible and then, (B) subject to that constraint, let all hell break loose.

Regarding (A), some sort of constraint is needed or the clarity of our intuitive vision will suffer. This is the justification usually offered for the axiom of foundation, which serves no real mathematical purpose but forces sets into the familiar and comprehensible tower structure. Without foundation there would be no possibility of "taking in" the universe of sets in one intellectual glance, as it were.

Regarding (B), it helps to remember that sets come in "originally" to improve our descriptions of non-sets, e.g., there are infinitely many Xs iff the set of Xs has a proper subset X' such that the members of X and X' are paired off by some 1–1 function (another set). Given that the notion of "infinitely many" is topic neutral—the Xs do not have to meet some special "niceness" condition for it to make sense to ask whether there are or are not infinitely many of them—it would be counterproductive to have "niceness" constraints on when the Xs are going to count as bundleable together into a set, except to the extent that such constraints are needed to maintain consistency. It would be still more counterproductive to impose "niceness" constraints on the 1–1 functions; when it comes to infinitude, one way of pairing the Xs off 1–1 with just some of the Xs seems as good as another.

So much concerning the "original" applications of sets to talk about non-sets. But it would not be surprising if the anything-goes attitude at work here were to reverberate upward to contexts where the topic is sets. Just as we don't want to tie our hands unnecessarily in applying set-theoretic methods to the matter of whether there are infinitely many stars, we don't want to tie our hands either in considering whether there are infinitely many *sets* of stars. A case can thus be made for (imagining there to be) a plenitude of sets of stars, and a master set gathering all the star-sets together; and a plenitude of 1–1 functions from the master set to its proper subsets to ensure that if the former is infinite, there will be a function on hand to witness the fact. This perhaps gives the flavor of why the preference for a universe as "full" as possible is not terribly surprising on a gameskeeping conception of the theory of sets.

References

Adams, F., and R. Stecker. 1994. Vacuous Singular Terms. *Mind and Language* 9:387–401.

Almog, J. 1986. Naming without Necessity. *Journal of Philosophy* 71:210–42.

Alston, W. 1958. Ontological Commitment. *Philisophical Studies* 9:8–17.

Balaguer, M. 1998. *Platonism and Anti-Platonism in Mathematics*. Oxford: Oxford University Press.

Barth, J. 1967. *The End of the Road*. Doubleday and Company.

Barwise, J., and R. Cooper. 1981. Generalized Quantifiers and Natural Language. *Linguistics and Philosophy* 4:159–219.

Beck, A. 1985. *Anxiety Disorders and Phobias*. New York: Basic Books.

Boghossian, P. 1990. The Status of Content. *The Philosophical Review* 157–184.

Booth, W. 1983. *The Rhetoric of Fiction*. Chicago: Chicago University Press.

Braun, D. 1993. Empty Names. *Nous* 27:449–469.

Burgess, J., and G. Rosen. 1997. *A Subject with no Object*. Oxford: Oxford University Press.

Carnap, R. 1956. Empiricism, Semantics, and Ontology. In *Meaning and Necessity*. Chicago: University of Chicago Press.

Carroll, N. 1990. *The Philosophy of Horror*. London: Routledge.

Cartwright, R. 1954. Ontology and the Theory of Meaning. *Philosophy of Science* 21:316–25. Reprinted in his *Philosophical Essays*. Cambridge: MIT Press, 1987.

Church, A. 1958. Ontological Commitment. *The Journal of Philosopy* 60:1008–1014.

Clark, H., and R. Gerrig. 1984. On the Pretense Theory of Irony. *Journal of Experimental Psychology: General* 113:121–26.

Clark, H., and R. Gerrig. 1990. Quotations as Demonstrations. *Language* 66:764–805.

Cohen, J. 1997. The Arc of the Moral Universe. *Philosophy and Public Affairs* 26:91–134.

Crimmins, M. 1992. *Talk About Beliefs*. Cambridge: MIT Press.

Crimmins, M. 1998. Hesperus and Phosphorus: Sense, Pretense, and Reference. *Philosophical Review* 107:1–48.

Crimmins, M., and J. Perry. 1989. The Prince and the Phone Booth: Reporting Puzzling Beliefs. *Journal of Philosophy* 86:685–711.

Currie, G. 1990. *The Nature of Fiction*. Cambridge: Cambridge University Press.

Dalryple, M., M. Kanazawa, Y. Kim, S. Mchombo, and S. Peters. 1998. Reciprocal Expressions and the Concept of Reciprocity. *Linguistics and Philosophy* 159–210.

Davidson, D. 1967. The Logical Form of Action Sentences. In *The Logic of Decision and Action*, ed. N. Rescher. 81–120. Pittsburgh: University of Pittsburgh Press.

Davidson, D. 1984. What Metaphors Mean. In *Truth and Interprtation*. Chap. 17. Oxford: Oxford University Press.

Davidson, D., and G. Harman. 1975. *The Logic of Grammar*. Encino: Dickerson.

Davies, M. 1983. Idiom and Metaphor. *Proceedings of the Aristotelian Society* 83:67–83.

Davies, M., and L. Humberstone. 1980. Two Notions of Necessity. *Philosophical Studies* 38:1–30.

Denyer, N. 1991. *Language Truth and Falsehood in Ancient Greek Philosophy*. London: Routledge.

Deutsch, H. 1979. The Completeness of S. *Studia Logica* 38:134–47.

Deutsch, H. 1984. Paraconsistent Analytic Implication. *Journal of Philosophical Logic* 12:1–11.

Deutsch, H. 1985. Fiction and Fabrication. *Philosophical Studies* 47:201–11.

Deutsch, H. 1991. The Creation Problem. *Topoi* 10:209–25.

Deutsch, H. 1998. Identity and General Similarity. In *Philosophical Perspectives 12*, ed. James Tomberlin. 177–199. Oxford: Blackwell.

Devitt, M. 1989. Against Direct Reference. In *Midwest Studies in Philosophy, Volume XIV*, ed. P. French, T. Uehling, and H. Wettstein. 206–40. Note Dame: University of Note Dame Press.

Donnellan, K. 1966. Reference and Definite Descriptions. *Philosophical Review* 77:281–304.

Donnellan, K. 1972. Proper Names and Identifying Descriptions. In *Semantics of Natural Language*, ed. D. Davidson and G. Harman. 356–79. Dordrecht: Reidel.

Donnellan, K. 1974. Speaking of Nothing. *Philosophical Review* 83:3–31.

Dummett, M. 1978. Presupposition. In *Truth and Other Enigmas*. Chap. 2. London: Duckworth.

Dummett, M. 1993. Existence. In *The Seas of Language*. Chap. 12. Oxford: OUP.

Etchemendy, J. 1990. *The Concept of Logical Consequence*. Cambridge: Harvard University Press.

Evans, G. 1973. The Causal Theory of Names. *Aristotelian Society Supplementary Volume* 47:187–208.

Evans, G. 1982. *The Varieties of Reference*. Oxford: Oxford University Press.

Faderman, A. 1997. Kripke and the Unicorns. Manuscript.

Field, H. 1980. *Science Without Numbers*. Oxford: Blackwell.

Field, H. 1989a. Platonism for Cheap. In *Realism, Mathematics, and Modality*. Chap. 5. Oxford: Blackwell.

Field, H. 1989b. *Realism, Mathematics, and Modality*. Oxford: Blackwell.

Field, H. 1994. Deflationist Views of Meaning and Content. *Mind* 103:249–85.

Fine, K. 1982. The Problem of Non-existents. *Topoi* 1:97–140.

Fine, K. 1984. Critical Review of Parson's 'Nonexistent Objects'. *Philosophical Studies* 45:95–142.

Fitch, G. 1993. Non Denoting. *Philosophical Perspectives* 7:461–484.

Frege, G. 1979. Pünjer on Existence. In *Frege: Postumous Writings*, ed. H. Hermes, F. Kambartel, and F. Kaulbach. 53–67. Oxford: Blackwell.

Friend, S. 2000. Review of Thomasson. *Mind*.

Gamut, L. T. F. 1991. *Logic, Language, and Meaning*. University of Chicago Press.

Gellner, E. 1979. The Last Pragmatist or the Behaviourist Platonist. In *Spectacles and Predicaments: Essays in Social Theory*. 199–208. Cambridge: Cambridge University Press.

Gombrich, E. 1961. *Art and Illusion*. New York: Pantheon Books.

Goodman, N. 1968. *Languages of Art*. Indianapolis: Bobbs-Merrill.

Goodman, N. 1978. *Ways of Worldmaking*. Indianapolis: Hackett.

Haaparanta, L. 1986. Frege on Existence. In *Frege Synthesized*, ed. L. Haaparanta and J. Hintikka. 155–174. Dordrecht: Reidel.

Hills, D. 1997. Aptness and Truth in Verbal Metaphor. *Philosophical Topics* 25:117–53.

Hofweber, T. n.d.a. Innocent Statements and their Metaphysically Loaded Counterparts. Unpublished manuscript.

Hofweber, T. n.d.b. Number Determiners, Numbers, and Arithmetic. Unpublished manuscript.

Hofweber, T. n.d.c. A Puzzle about Ontology. Unpublished manuscript.

Hofweber, T. 1999. *Ontology and Objectivity*. Doctoral dissertation, Stanford University.

Jackson, F. 1979. On Assertion and Indicative Conditonals. *The Philosophical Review* 88:565–589.

Jackson, F. 1997. Reference and Description Revisited. In *Philosophical Perspectives vol.12*, ed. J. Tomberlin. California: Ridgeview.

Johnston, M. 1988. The End of the Theory of Meaning. *Mind and Language* 3:23–42.

Kaplan, D. 1989. Demonstratives. In *Themes from Kaplan*, ed. J. Almog, H. Wettstein, and J. Perry. 565–614. Oxford: Oxford University Press.

Knights, L. 1947. *Explorations*. New York: George Stewart.

Kripke, S. 1973. John Locke Lectures. Unpublished.

Kripke, S. 1977. Speaker's Reference and Semantic Reference. In *Contemporary Perspectives in the Philosophy of Language*, ed. P. French, T. Uehling, and H. Wettstein. Minneapolis: University of Minnesota Press.

Kripke, S. 1980. *Naming and Necessity*. Cambridge: Harvard University Press.

Kroon, F. n.d. Fictionalism and the Informativeness of Identity. unpublished.

Kroon, F. 1992. Was Meinong Only Pretending. *Philosophy and Phenomenological Research* 52:499–527.

Kroon, F. 1994. A Problem About Make-Believe. *Philosophical Studies* 75:201–29.

Kroon, F. 1996. Characterizing Nonexistents. *Grazer Philosophische Studien* 51:163–93.

Kroon, F. 2000. "Disavowal Through Commitment" Theories of Negative Existentials. In *Empty Names, Fiction, and the Puzzles of Non-Existence*, ed. A. Everett and T. Hofweber. Stanford: CSLI Press.

Lamarque, P., and S. Olsen. 1994. *Truth, Fiction, and Literature: A Philosophical Perspective*. Oxford: Oxford University Press.

Levinson, J. 1980. What a Musical Work is. *Journal of Philosophy* 77:5–28.

Lewis, D. 1970. General Semantics. In *Semantics of Natural Language*, ed. D. Davidson and G. Harman. 169–218. Dordrecht: Dordrecht Reidel.

Lewis, D. 1983. Truth in Fiction. In *Philosophical Papers:1*. Oxford: Blackwell.

Lewis, D. 1986. *On the Plurality of Worlds*. Oxford: Blackwell.

Lewis, D. 1992. Critical Notice of Armstrong. *Australasian Journal of Phlosophy* 70:211–24.

Lewis, D., and S. Lewis. 1970. Holes. *Australasian Journal of Philosophy* 48:206–12. Reprinted in David Lewis's *Philosophical Papers, Vol. I*, New York, Oxford University Press, 1983.

Lønning, J. T. 1997. Plurals and Collectivity. In *Handbook of Logic and Language*, ed. Johan van Benthem and Alice ter Meulen. Elsevier.

M., Hjort, and S. Laver. 1997. *Emotion and the Arts*. Oxford: Oxford University Press.

Maddy, P. 1997. *Naturalism in Mathematics*. Oxford University Press.

Mally, E. 1912. *Gegenstandstheoretische Grundlagen der Logic und Logistik*. Leipzig: Barth.

McGee, V. 1997. Howe to Learn Mathematical Language. *The Philosophical review* 106:35–68.

Meinong, A. 1904. Über Gegenstandstheorie. In *Untersuchungen zur Gegenstandstheorie und Psychologie*. Leipzig: Barth.

Meinong, A. 1960. The Theory of Objects. In *Realism and the Background of Phenomenology*, ed. R. Chisholm. Glencoe: Free Press.

Meinong, A. 1983. *On Assumptions*. Berkeley: University of California Press. James Heanue (ed.), translated from Über Annahmen, 2nd edition, 1910.

Melia, J. 1995. On What There's Not. *Analysis* 55:223–9.

Moran, R. 1989. Seeing and Believing: Metaphor Image and Force. *Critical Inquiry* 12:87–112.

Nakhnikian, G., and W. Salmon. 1957. 'Exists' as a Predicate. *Philosophical Review* 66:535–42.

Neale, S. 1990. *Descriptions*. Cambridge: MIT Press.

Nunberg, G. 1978. *The Pragmatics of Reference*. Bloomington: Indiana University Press.

Nunberg, G., I. Sag, and T. Wasow. 1994. Idioms. *Language* 70:491–538.

Ortony, A. 1993. *Metaphor and Thought*. Cambridge University Press. 2nd edition.

Parsons, T. 1974. A Prolegomenon to Meinongian Semantics. *Journal of Philosophy* 71:561–580.

Parsons, T. 1975. A Meinongian Analysis of Fictional Objects. *Grazer Philosophische Studien* 1:73–86.

Parsons, T. 1980. *Nonexistent Objects*. New Haven: Yale University Press.

Perry, J. 1990. Self-notions. *Logos* XI:17–31.

Perry, J. 1993. *The Problem of the Essential Indexical and Other Essays*. Oxford: Oxford University Press.

Perry, J. 2000. Knowledge, Possibility, and Consciousness. Manuscript.

Plantinga, A. 1965. *The Ontological Argument*. Garden City: Doubleday.

Prior, A. 1976. Entities. In *Papers in Logic and Ethics*. Amherst: University of Massachusetts Press.

Putnam, H. 1971. *Philosophy of Logic*. New York: Harper and Row.

Quine, W. 1940. *Mathematical Logic*. Cambridge: Harvard University Press.

Quine, W. 1960. *Word and Object*. Cambridge: Harvard University Press.

Quine, W. 1966. Propositional Objects. In *Ontological Relativity and Other Essays*. New York: Columbia University Press.

Quine, W. 1980. On What There Is. In *From a Logical Point of View*. Harvard UP.

Quine, W. 1986. Reply to Parsons. In *The Philosophy of W.V. Quine*, ed. L. Hahn and P. Schilpp. La Salle: Open Court.

Recanati, F. 1993. *Direct Reference*. Oxford: Blackwell.

Richards, I. 1969. *Coleridge on Imagination*. Bloomington: Indiana University Press.

Rorty, R. 1970. Realism and Reference. *Monist* 59:321–40.

Rosen, G. 1990. Modal Fictionalism. *Mind* 9:327–54.

Routley, R. 1980. Exploring Meinong's Jungle and Beyond. Department Monography 3. Philosophy Department Australian National University.

Russell, B. 1905. On Denoting. *Mind* 14:479–93.

Russell, B. 1919. *Introduction to Mathematical Philosophy*. London: Allen and Urwin.

Russell, B. 1959a. Mr. Strawson on referring. In *My Philosophical Developement*. George Allen and Unwin.

Russell, B. 1959b. The Philosophy of Logical Atomism. In *Logic and Knowledge*, ed. R. C. Marsh. London: Allen and Urwin. [1918].

Salmon, N. 1981. *Reference and Essence.* Princeton: Princeton University Press.

Salmon, N. 1987. Existence. *Philosophical Perspectives* 7:49–108.

Salmon, N. 1989. The Logic of what might have been. *Philosophical Review* 98:3–37.

Salmon, N. 1999. Nonexistence. *Nous* 32:277–319.

Santayana, G. 1948. A Change of Heart. *Horizon* 18:377–86.

Schiffer, S. 1990. The Mode-of-Presentation Problem. In *Propositional Attitudes: the Role of Content in Logic, Language, and Mind,* ed. C. Anderson and J. Owens. Stanford: CSLI Press. Reprinted in C. Peacocke, ed., Understanding and Sense (Dartmouth Publishing Co., 1993).

Schiffer, S. 1996. Language-Created Language-Independent Entities. *Philosophical Topics* 24:149–167.

Shoemaker, S. 1968. Self-reference and Self-awareness. *Journal of Philosophy* 65:555–67.

Smullyan, R. 1992. *Gödel's Incompleteness Theorems.* Oxford: Oxford University Press.

Sommer, E., and D. Weiss. 1996. *Metaphors Dictionary.* Detroit: Visible Ink Press.

Stevens, W. 1942. *The Necessary Angel.* New York: Random House.

Strawson, P. 1950. On Referring. *Mind* 320–344.

Taylor, K. 1997. Accomodationist Neo-Russelianism. *Nous* 31:538–56.

Taylor, K. 2000. Emptiness without Compromise. In *Empty Names, Fiction, and the Puzzles of Non-Existence,* ed. A. Everett and T. Hofweber. Stanford: CSLI Press.

Thomasson, A. 1996. Fiction and Intentionality. *Philosophy and Phenomenological Research* 56:277–98.

Thomasson, A. 1998a. The Artifactual Theory of Fiction. Presented at the Empty Names Conference at CSLI, Stanford University, March 22, 1998.

Thomasson, A. 1998b. *Fiction and Metaphysics.* Cambridge: Cambridge University Press.

van der Does, J. 1995. Sums and Quantifiers. *Linguistics and Philosophy* 16:509–550.

van Inwagen, P. 1977. Creatures of Fiction. *American Philosophical Quarterly* 14:299–308.

van Inwagen, P. 1981. Why I don't Understand Substitutional Quantification. *Philosophical Studies* 39:281–85.

van Inwagen, P. 1983. Fiction and Metaphysics. *Philosophy and Literature* 7:67–77.

van Inwagen, P. 1985. Pretence and Paraphrase. In *The Reasons of Art/L'Art a Ses Raisons*. Ottowa: University of Ottawa Press.

van Inwagen, Peter. 2000. Quantification and Fictional Discourse. In *Empty Names, Fiction, and the Puzzles of Non-Existence*, ed. A. Everett and T. Hofweber. Stanford: CSLI Press.

Walton, K. 1978. Fearing Fictions. *Journal of Philosophy* 75:5–27.

Walton, K. 1990. *Mimesis as Make Believe*. Cambridge: Harvard University Press.

Walton, K. 1993. Metaphor and Prop Oriented Make-Believe. *The European Journal of Philosophy* 1:39–57.

Walton, K. 1997. Spelunking, Simulation, and Slime: On Being Moved by Fiction. In *Emotion and the Arts*, ed. M. Hjort and S. Laver. Oxford: Oxford University Press.

Walton, K. 2000. Existence as Metaphor? In *Empty Names, Fiction, and the Puzzles of Non-Existence*, ed. A. Everett and T. Hofweber. Stanford: CSLI Press.

Wettstein, H. 1984. Did the Greeks really worship Zeus? *Synthese* 439–450.

Wolterstorff, N. 1980. *Works and Worlds of Art*. Oxford: OUP.

Wright, C. 1983. *Frege's Conception of Numbers as Objects*. Aberdeen: Aberdeen University Press.

Yablo, S. 1996. How in the World? *Philosophical Topics* 24:255–86.

Yablo, S. 1998. Does Ontology Rest on a Mistake? *Proceedings of the Aristotelian Society, Supplimentary Volume* 72:229–62.

Yablo, S. 2000. A Paradox of Existence. In *Empty Names, Fiction, and the Puzzles of Non-Existence*, ed. A. Everett and T. Hofweber. Stanford: CSLI Press.

Zalta, E. 1983. *Abstract Objects*. Dordrecht: Dordrecht Reidel.

Zalta, E. 1987. Erzählung als Taufe des Helden: Wie man auf fiktionale Objekte Bezug nimmt. *Zeitschrift fur Semiotik* 9:85–95. A. Günther (trans.); from "Referring to Fictional Characters: A Reply," URL = http://mally.stanford.edu/publications.html#fictions.

Zalta, E. 1988. *Intensional Logic and the Metaphysics of Intentionality*. Cambridge: MIT Press.

Zalta, E. 1993. Twenty-Five Basic Theorems in Situation and World Theory. *Journal of Philosophical Logic* 22:385–428.

Zalta, E. 1997. A Classically-Based Theory of Impossible Worlds. *Notre Dame Journal of Formal Logic* 38:640–60. Special issue, Graham Priest, guest editor.

Zalta, E. 2000. The Road between Pretense Theory and Abstract Object Theory. In *Empty Names, Fiction, and the Puzzles of Non-Existence*, ed. A. Everett and T. Hofweber. Stanford: CSLI Press. First presented at the Empty Names Conference at CSLI, Stanford University, March 22, 1998.

Index